C#Concisely

We work with leading authors to develop the
strongest educational materials in computing,
bringing cutting-edge thinking and best
learning practice to a global market.

Under a range of well-known imprints, including
Addison-Wesley, we craft high quality print and
electronic publications which help readers to understand
and apply their content, whether studying or at work.

To find out more about the complete range of our
publishing, please visit us on the World Wide Web at:
www.pearsoned.co.uk

C#Concisely

Judith Bishop
University of Pretoria

Nigel Horspool
University of Victoria

PEARSON

Addison
Wesley

Harlow, England • London • New York • Boston • San Francisco • Toronto • Sydney • Singapore • Hong Kong
Tokyo • Seoul • Taipei • New Delhi • Cape Town • Madrid • Mexico City • Amsterdam • Munich • Paris • Milan

Pearson Education Limited
Edinburgh Gate
Harlow
Essex CM20 2JE
England

and Associated Companies throughout the world

Visit us on the World Wide Web at:
www.pearsoned.co.uk

First published 2004

ISBN 0 321 15418 5

British Library Cataloguing-in-Publication Data
A catalogue record for this book is available from the British Library

Library of Congress Cataloging-in-Publication Data
A catalog record for this book is available from the Library of Congress

10 9 8 7 6 5 4 3 2 1
08 07 06 05 04

Printed and bound by Henry Ling Ltd, at the Dorset Press, Dorchester, Dorset, UK

The publisher's policy is to use paper manufactured from sustainable forests.

To William and Michael, as always, and Janet, without whose love and support this book would not have been finished. (JMB)

To Micaela who provided copious support and encouragement during the production of this book; it took longer than either of us ever imagined. (NH)

Contents

Foreword

Many computer books are so heavy that lifting them causes a hernia, yet they have less content than your favorite tabloid. Many academic text books are so boring that they turn your brains to dust, yet they don't teach you anything that is of use in the real world.

Not with this book! This concise book is jam-packed with the insight of many years of accumulated wisdom and experience from the authors. Each chapter comes with ample examples and exercises, but what I like best is the pixie dust of summary 'forms' that is sprinkled throughout the book.

The early introduction and extensive use of the platform-independent Views GUI library makes learning and teaching from this book fun and rewarding. Further evidence of the real-world character is the inclusion of a chapter on debugging. Even in the unlikely event that you never make any coding mistakes, a debugger is a great tool for understanding the dynamic behavior of programs; for the rest of us, it is an additional powerful tool to help us locate errors.

With a copy of *C# Concisely* on your desk, every day is your lucky day.

Erik Meijer
Technical Lead
Microsoft WebData Team

31 July 2003

Preface

C# Concisely has been a year in the making. We'd like to tell you, the reader, instructor or student, why we embarked on this project, and what is in store for you in this book.

C# – where from and where to

C# is a new language designed by Anders Hejlsberg, Scott Wiltamuth and Peter Golde at Microsoft to be the main development medium for the .NET Framework and all future Microsoft products. C# has its origins in other languages, chiefly C++, Java, Delphi, Modula-2 and Smalltalk. Hejlsberg's credentials include being chief architect behind Turbo Pascal and Borland's Delphi, and the depth of experience shows through in a very nicely designed language. More so than the languages mentioned above, C# features deep object-orientation and a new concept – object-simplification – which makes it much easier to enter the world of object-oriented programming, and stay there.

At this stage, C# is manoeuvring its place in the languages chosen for software development and teaching. Since *C# Concisely* is chiefly a textbook, we can say that it is our opinion that C# would be an excellent first teaching language. The main barrier against it reaching that position is inertia: Java is firmly entrenched in most institutions, and a great deal of effort and infrastructure supports its position.

C# is also a good language for later courses. Because it supports more advanced programming features such as delegates and operator overloading, and there is even a proposal out for generics, it could be an excellent vehicle for courses such as Advanced Programming, Data Structures, Net-centric Computing and Distributed Systems, among others. It is also likely that postgraduate courses with an industrial bias, such as many course-based MSc programs, will benefit from C# since it equips their students for the workplace well.

Unlike Java, C# is only free to use in certain circumstances. If an academic institution belongs to the Microsoft Academic Alliance (available at minimal cost), then the software is available for all staff and students. The C# language (but not all of its libraries) has also been ratified as a standard by the European body ECMA (December 2001), and as a result, other compilers for Windows and other platforms are now available, and these are also free. Microsoft itself has produced three of these under the code name Rotor for the Windows, FreeBSD and Macintosh OSX platforms.

A concern with Microsoft products in general is that they tend to be resource hungry, and require computers beyond the means of many student laboratories. The free compilers are therefore an attractive option. However, a notable omission from the ECMA standard was the `Windows.Form` API which is used for programming graphical user interfaces. We have worked with Microsoft since April 2002 to fill this gap, and the result is Views, a small-footprint XML-based GUI system. Versions of Views exist for both the standard Windows system and the other platforms which host Rotor. Together, Views and freely available C# compilers offer a viable, and technologically modern, alternative to a purchased C# and Visual Studio combination from Microsoft, with the added advantage, of course, of being platform independent.

C# definitely has a future in teaching and research, as well as in system development. The objective of this book is to promote that future by spreading the use of the language as widely as possible.

Outline of the book

It has become almost a cliché these days that a programming textbook describes itself as having an 'objects first' approach. When digging deeper into textbooks, and into papers presented at computer science educational conferences, it became clear to us that the meaning of the term 'objects first' was pretty vague. Moreover, it was seldom indicated what came second or third.

Under any definition, *C# Concisely* is an objects-first book, but we believe we have crystallized the meaning of the term with a novel approach. In Chapter 2 we introduce objects first by *using* them rather than defining types for them. We rely on two built-in structured types, `DateTime` (a struct) and `Random` (a class), and develop the concepts related to instantiation, variables, methods and assignment in a much more natural way than would be possible if the types had to be defined first.

Then in Chapter 3, we look at how to define a type, going back and consolidating concepts with which the reader is familiar, and adding more formality to terms like parameters and properties. We have taken the decision to remain firmly in the value-world at this stage, using structs as the means to create objects, and mentioning references only for parameter passing. We believe that covering one concept at a time is good pedagogy, and that the confusion often associated with value *vs.* reference types can be avoided by delaying the detailed treatment of references until Chapter 7. The result of this decision is that classes are not covered until Chapter 8. More so than other current object-oriented languages, C# emphasizes the concept of a type, and it is treated the same whether realized as an int, a struct or a class. We adopt the same view, and therefore delaying classes till later does not cause unnatural programming.

The question of 'if objects are first, what is second?' is answered in Chapter 4: control structures, strings and arrays. These are all essential building blocks for writing programs. Without them, the more powerful features of object-orientation – collections and polymorphism – cannot be exercised properly.

Before we get there, though, we spend two useful chapters on laying a foundation for meaningful programming. Chapter 5 describes the Views system which we have written as an adjunct to any C# program for describing and handling graphical user interfaces. With such a tool, programs that interact with the user can be developed rapidly and in a platform independent manner.

In Chapter 7, we complete the study of input and output by looking at data stored on files and how files are represented as streams in C#. Chapter 6 is almost unique in programming textbooks in that it tackles the issue of errors and debugging. A range of common and novel debugging techniques from print statements to assert calls is described, most of which require no additional software other than a C# compiler. There is a separate section on using a debugger, and more information on Microsoft's Visual Studio debugging capabilities in Appendix G.

At this point, programmers will be able to handle any task that would have been possible in an older language, but in an object-oriented way. Chapters 8 and 9 complete the coverage of objects by dealing with collections (which C# does particularly well) and extensibility and polymorphism. In Chapter 9, we take care to talk about principles, and then show how they can be realized in any of the three techniques provided – inheritance, interfaces and abstract classes.

We have by this stage covered pretty much all of the C# language, but there is of course the wealth of APIs still to consider. Which are essential? Which are for home study? No book would be complete without mention of how to do drawing, or graphics, so we spend some of Chapter 10 on the Systems.Windows.Drawing API, showing it standalone and also integrated into Views. Distributed computing is now so much part of life, that we choose to end with a look at some of the ways in which computers can interact in C#. We show how quite sophisticated programs can be realized quite simply.

Our approach

C# Concisely teaches by means of an even mixture of formality and examples. Each new construct or built-in type (API) is described in a 'form' which gives its syntax and semantics, and then small examples are followed by completely worked out programs. There are over 50 such programs in the book, some of which progress from chapter to chapter, showing how new features can produce more complete solutions to the original problem.

GUIs are important, as is testing. Considerable reliance is placed on the random generator for producing test data where possible, so that programs can be properly exercised and have meaningful amounts of output data.

No language presents a neat sequence of features, each of which can be covered in isolation, and C# is no exception. We have adopted a spiral approach for several features such as output, strings, loops and arrays, introducing them in a simple way early on, and then completing their description later.

A good textbook should be as interactive as possible, and we have provided several learning aids, both in the book itself and on the accompanying website. These include:

♦ extensive appendices listing key APIs and grouping features of the language for easy reference;

♦ multiple choice questions (quizzes) after every chapter;

♦ plenty of exercises of different levels of difficulty after most chapters;

♦ all the examples online at http://www.cs.up.ac.za/csharp or at http://www.booksites.net/bishop;

♦ the complete Views system, with Reference Manual and examples;

♦ a discussion board for questions about C#, the book and Views;

♦ slides and answers for the instructor.

The Views system

The Views system is a special class for creating GUIs in a vendor independent way, using an XML specification. It was developed by the authors as a project under the Rotor initiative started by Microsoft in April 2002. It has been class tested with first and second year students, who were enthusiastic about it as an alternative to programming with the Windows.Forms API or Visual Studio. The latest version of Views can be downloaded from the book's website at http://www.cs.up.ac.za/csharp or at http://www.booksites.net/bishop.

Acknowledgements

We would like to acknowledge the considerable practical input to this book and to Views made by students in the Polelo Group at the University of Pretoria – Basil Worrall, Kathrin Berg, Johnny Lo, David-John Miller, Mandy van Schalkwyk and Sfiso Tshabalala. Many thanks to Edwin Peer who developed and maintained the web-based repository system which supported our book so well. At the University of Victoria, Jonathan Mason helped fix bugs in Views, Rajwinder Panesar-Walawege was responsible for the implementation of a version of Views for Rotor, and Bernhard Scholz (on leave from the Technical University of Vienna) worked on an essential front end to Views, to be released later.

We would like to thank Microsoft for their generous gift which supported this book and Views, and JB is particularly appreciative of the initiative and support given by Leanne Scott-Williams of Microsoft (South Africa). This work was also supported by a matching THRIP grant from the South African National Research Foundation. NH adds thanks to Pamela Lauz of Microsoft Canada for her support.

Working with a 10-hour timezone difference, we could not have survived without the excellent internet support provided by our departments at the Universities of Pretoria and Victoria, and also by Microsoft Research Laboratory, Cambridge, and the Technical University of Vienna, where the book was completed. Most especially, JB thanks Dr. Paul Meyer and the staff of Addenbrooke's Hospital, Cambridge for helping her to C#ly again, while this book was reaching its final stages.

Since much of the work on the book took place at strange hours of the day, NH would like to thank Torrefazione Italia for serving much needed and delicious coffee and KBSG Seattle for supplying the right kind of background music. JB acknowledges gratefully the contribution of the Cape wine industry, and the Late Late Show on Classic FM.

Finally, our thanks go to our families for their forbearance during the long hours spent at home working on this project, and to the stimulating discussions which they, as computer-oriented as we are, enabled us to have. We hope they will be as pleased with the results as we are.

Judith Bishop
Pretoria, South Africa, and Cambridge, England

Nigel Horspool
Victoria, Canada, and Vienna, Austria

August 2003

List of figures

List of examples

CHAPTER 1

Introduction

Learning how to program can be a challenging task. It seems there is so much to understand before even the simplest program can be written and used. In this first chapter, we cover that background. We look at the role of programming languages and how they have evolved over time. The trend has been for them to become less concerned with details and to allow the programmer to focus more on the problem to be solved. There has to be some way to put the programs into the computer and run them, so we look at two different means that are available. Some attention is also paid to software development.

1.1 Preamble

> Any sufficiently advanced technology is indistinguishable from magic.
> Arthur C. Clarke

Anyone who has used a computer is probably in total agreement with that quotation by a famous science fiction writer. (It is also known as Clarke's Third Law.) From the electronic computer's early beginnings in the 1940s, the software used to control a computer has grown ever more sophisticated and more complex. It has now reached a level of complexity where its operation can easily seem like magic. There is simply too much for any one person to comprehend. And no one should try to understand it all.

However, let us consider an analogy. Suppose that we were studying Law. The number of laws and the complexity of the laws that have been adopted by a nation are also far too much for a single person to understand. A law student does not attempt to learn it all. Instead, he or she will learn the basic legal principles, will build up some general knowledge about law in general, will learn to become familiar with the language in which laws are written, will learn to reason about and draw deductions from the legal principles, and will perhaps become intensely familiar with the actual laws for only one legal domain (criminal law, property law, tax law, and so on).

In the study of computer software, we follow a very similar approach. We study some basic principles of computation and how computers work. We learn a language which is used to write software, we learn to reason about the principles, and we probably become truly familiar with only a small fraction of the application areas where software is used.

In this book, we focus on one programming language which is named C# (and spoken out loud as 'C Sharp'). We will learn how to use the C# language to construct simple software applications. Along the way, we will pick up some background knowledge about how computers work.

1.2 The role of programming languages

The computer

The computer is an electronic machine constructed from some basic parts. One component is the memory which holds patterns of ones and zeros. These ones and zeros can be implemented in tiny electronic circuits (current flows forwards for a one, backwards for a zero; or a capacitor is charged for a one and not charged for a zero, or whatever) or by microscopic magnetic fields (the magnetic flux might be clockwise for a one and anticlockwise for a zero) or by the reflective properties of miniscule pits on a metallic layer in a spinning CD, or by different states of any physical property. The possibilities are numerous.

A computer has different kinds of memory that work in different ways. Fortunately the details of how the computer memory works usually do not matter to a programmer. The program manipulates patterns of ones and zeros without regard to how the patterns are physically implemented. The program uses patterns of ones and zeros to represent numbers in binary notation or to represent letters of the alphabet or to represent information according to any representation scheme that we like.

Another standard component of the computer is a *processor* or central processing unit, often abbreviated to CPU. The processor can perform simple changes to the patterns of ones and zeros in the computer memory. For example, it can look into two places in the computer memory and retrieve the patterns for two numbers, add the numbers together and store the result as a new pattern of ones and zeros in another memory location.

The power and the apparent magic of the computer comes from the way that the processor is controlled. It has to be told which memory locations to obtain two numbers from; it has to be told to add these numbers (as opposed to being told to multiply them or subtract them or some other arithmetic operation) and it has to be told where in memory to put the result back. After completing those operations, it has to be told what to do next. The sequence of actions that we want the processor to perform is specified as a long series of ones and zeros in the computer memory.

Figure 1.1 shows the actual pattern of ones and zeros which causes an Intel Pentium computer to take the numbers held in two particular locations of the computer's memory, add them together, and store the resulting number in a third location. It is not very illuminating, but that is what the computer understands. The figure shows the pattern split over three lines because there are three distinct instructions to tell the processor what to do, one after the other.

The spaces between the groups of eight ones and zeros correspond to the way that memory on this computer is organized – on the Intel Pentium (and nearly all computers) it is organized into groups of eight which are called *bytes* or, more rarely, *octets*. The individual ones and zeros are known as *bits*, which is a contraction of the words *binary digits*. The pattern of 16 bytes shown in the figure is, by the way, a small fragment of a much larger computer program. It is very unlikely that we would ever bother writing a program which just performed one addition and then finished.

```
10100001 01101000 10111100 01000001 00000000
00000011 00000101 01101100 10111100 01000001 00000000
10100011 01110000 10111100 01000001 00000000
```

Figure 1.1 A binary program to add two numbers on an Intel Pentium

Data representation

The memory of the computer is organized as groups of bits. On nearly all computers in current use, the groupings consist of 8 bits, 16 bits, 32 bits, often 64 bits and sometimes 128 bits. By using binary notation, a group of bits can be used to represent an integer. For example, the 8-bit group 01101011 represents the integer

$$0{\times}2^7 + 1{\times}2^6 + 1{\times}2^5 + 0{\times}2^4 + 1{\times}2^3 + 0{\times}2^2 + 1{\times}2^1 + 1{\times}2^0$$

which simplifies to 0+64+32+0+8+0+2+1 or 107. The computer's processor can manipulate values in binary notation with ease. However, there is more to the subject than just binary notation because computers have to handle negative integers too. And through a special representation scheme called floating point, computers can work with numbers which have very large magnitudes, such as 6.023×10^{23}. We will cover number representation in much more detail in Chapter 3.

Although the first computers were built purely to perform number crunching, it did not take the early computer programmers long to realize that computers can manipulate text written in a language such as English. All we have to do is associate a number with each symbol in the alphabet and then the computer's memory can be used to hold passages of text. A commonly used scheme for numbering the symbols is ASCII (American Standard Code for Information Interchange). In this scheme, every symbol is given a number between 0 and 127, which conveniently fits into an 8-bit group (a byte), with one bit left unused. In the ASCII coding scheme, the letter 'A' has the number 65, 'B' has 66 and so on. The word 'BANANA' would be represented by the sequence of 6 integers

   66 65 78 65 78 65

which would be stored in 6 consecutive bytes of memory.

It rarely makes sense for the computer to perform arithmetic on the numbers which are being used to represent text (perhaps adding one to get the next letter in the alphabet is a sensible example). However, characters can be moved from one place to another and they can be compared with each other. For example, because the computer can determine that 65<66, it can sort a list of English words correctly putting APPLE before BANANA.

The C# language supports a more extensive coding scheme for symbols called Unicode. In this scheme, each symbol has a 16-bit number. By using more bits than ASCII, symbols from many different alphabets (Greek, Cyrillic, Kanji, ...) have numbers, and accented symbols (â, ä, å, ...) have numbers. The subject of character codes and strings of characters will be covered in more detail in Chapter 4.

Assembly languages

In the early days of computers, programmers really did construct sequences of bits much like the sequence shown in Figure 1.1 and they entered the sequence into the computer's memory by flicking toggle switches up or down on the front of the computer. Needless to say, it was found to be a slow, tedious and highly error-prone activity. It was not long before people realized that the computer could help the programmer. Since the CPU manipulates sequences of ones and zeros in the memory, and the program is just a sequence of bits, why not have the computer help create its own programs? An early step in that direction was the invention of assembly languages. An *assembly language* is a language in which the programmer uses words or mnemonics, rather than patterns of bits, to instruct the computer and tell it what actions to perform. The three assembly language instructions which correspond to the binary patterns shown in Figure 1.1 are as follows.

```
mov    eax,dword ptr ds:[0041BC68h]
add    eax,dword ptr ds:[0041BC6Ch]
mov    dword ptr ds:[0041BC70h],eax
```

Although the notation appears to be just as inscrutable as the binary patterns, there are assembly language programmers who can read and write these instructions with ease. It is simply a matter of practice. The three instructions tell the processor to *move* a number from location 0041BC68 in memory into a *register* named eax (registers are typically used to hold numbers temporarily); to *add* the number from location 0041BC6C in memory to the number in eax and leaving the result in eax; then to *move* the number in eax back to memory at location 0041BC70. Locations in memory are given numbers and it is common in assembly language to write these numbers in base-16 (or *hexadecimal*) notation rather than the conventional base-10 (or *decimal*) notation we use in everyday life. The sequence 0041BC68 is a hexadecimal number. The letter *h* that appears after the sequence of hexadecimal digits is a notation used in the assembly language to differentiate hexadecimal numbers from decimal numbers. We will come across hexadecimal numbers again in this book when we discuss Unicode.

The lines of an assembly language program are read as data by a computer program known as a symbolic assembler (or just *assembler* for short) and converted into the patterns of bits that the processor can understand. The result, a long sequence of bits, is normally saved as a computer file on the hard drive of the computer, ready for later use. When we want to run that program, we use another program usually known as a *loader* which copies the patterns from the computer file into memory and then causes the processor to begin obeying these new instructions.

Onto programming languages

The assembly language example presented above would normally be written by a human programmer as follows:

```
mov    eax,b      // get number from location b, put in the eax register
add    eax,c      // add number from location c to the eax register
mov    a,eax      // store the eax register in location a
```

where three symbolic names (*a*, *b* and *c*) have been used to represent particular locations in memory. Somewhere else in the assembly language program, the programmer would specify which memory locations correspond to the three names and how many bytes to use for each one. For example, the programmer might write these directives which the assembler translator uses to reserve memory locations:

```
a:   .word   0       # reserve one word of memory, initialized with 0
b:   .word   37      # similarly but with initial value 37
c:   .word   15      # similarly but with initial value 15
```

It does not take a big leap forward to imagine a more advanced kind of assembly language where the programmer can write the declarations and the statement

```
int a = 0;     // declare a as a 4 byte number, initially 0
int b = 37;    // similarly for b, initialized to 37
int c = 15;    // similarly for c, initialized to 15

a = b + c;     // add b and c, store result in a
```

instead of the three directives to reserve memory and the three assembly language instructions to perform the addition. These lines are more concise and much more readable by humans. They are representative of a *programming language*. The final line, known as a *statement* in the programming language, uses the symbol + to mean *add*, just as in mathematics. The symbol = does not mean *equals* however in this statement. It means *change a* to make it equal to the value computed from the right-hand side. If we were reading the statement out loud, we would likely say 'assign b plus c to a'. That equals symbol, =, is called the *assignment operator*.

The first programming languages were really just assembly languages in disguise. It was easy for programmers to guess the sequences of assembly language statements which corresponded to each programming language statement. The viewpoint was that a programming language was just a mere convenience for humans. However, over the years, programming languages have become ever more sophisticated. It would now take an expert to deduce what sequence of assembly language instructions corresponds to a typical statement in a programming language. But why should we care what sequence of instructions the computer executes to perform the actions implied by a statement in a program? As long as the effect is what we expect, we should not care. A programmer thinks in terms of the programming language, not in terms of assembly language statements (let alone in terms of the bit patterns that the processor actually executes).

There have been many thousands of different programming languages invented. It is still not at all clear that we are getting close to the goal of having a single programming language which programmers find to be the most productive and the most natural. It seems that different kinds of problem domains require different kinds of programming language. A program used by a bank to manage its financial records is quite different in nature from a program which implements an interactive game, for example. Perhaps the two different problem domains need different programming languages?

The C# language is the latest in a series of programming language designs starting in the 1950s which includes Fortran, Algol60, Simula67, PL/I, C, Pascal, C++ and Java (in that approximate time order). It will most definitely not be the last programming language ever invented. But for writing general-purpose programs today, it is one of the best languages available. It has a design consistency and a completeness which is absent from all its predecessors.

The C++, Java and C# languages all borrow a feature from Simula67 known as the *class*. It is the basic construct of *object-oriented programming*, sometimes abbreviated to *OO* programming or even to *OOP*. The evidence is somewhat equivocal but many people believe that OO programming yields programs which are easier to modify later by adding new features. This property is known as *extensibility*. The OO paradigm also promotes *reuse* of software, making it easier for programmers to develop new software from pieces of other programs.

Syntax and semantics

Programs must conform to the syntactic rules of the programming language. This book gives the syntax rules for C# in tables, each of which looks similar to this example from Chapter 4.

```
WHILE LOOP

while (condition) {
    loop body
}
```

Evaluate *condition*, if it is true then execute the statements in the *loop body*. Next, re-evaluate the *condition* and if it is true, re-execute the *loop body*. Repeat until *condition* evaluates to false.

We call this table a *form* because it gives the form of a construct in the C# language. The name of the construct is given in the title bar, the syntax is given below, and a brief explanation below that. The italicized words in the syntax part represent other C# constructs, whose syntax can be similarly looked up elsewhere. The explanation corresponds to the meaning of the construct – in the study of programming languages, the name *semantics* is often used to refer to the meaning of a language construct. There is a full list of the forms' names in Appendix A.

1.3 About compilation

Compiling a program

A C# program contains statements like the following:

```
int a, b, c;    // declare a, b and c as integer variables
...
b = 23;         // store the number 23 in b
c = 3*4;        // store 12 in c
...
a = b + c;      // add b to c and store result in a
Console.WriteLine("Answer = {0}", a);  // show answer on the screen
...
```

where the dots represent lots of omitted statements. We can create the C# program as a text file on the computer using a text editor program such as Notepad or TextEdit. That text file has to be converted into the bit patterns (the *machine instructions*) that the computer understands. The conversion process is called *compilation* and the program which performs the conversion is called a *compiler*.

Suppose that we have created a C# program and saved it as a file named mypro-gram.cs on our computer. We can, on a computer running Windows, open a command window and run the C# compiler by typing the command

```
csc myprogram.cs
```

If all goes well and the C# compiler program doesn't encounter any problems, a new file named[1] myprogram.exe is created. That new file is called an executable file because it contains machine instructions which the processor understands. We can type the file's name

        myprogram.exe

(the '.exe' suffix is optional when typing the filename as a command) in the command window to cause the file myprogram.exe to be loaded into the computer's memory and then executed by the processor. The command window, showing the commands to compile then run the program and its results will look something like that shown in Figure 1.2.

The command window is itself another program that we run. On a standard Windows system running Windows XP, that program corresponds to the file C:\WINDOWS\system32\cmd.exe. The Command Prompt program is a very special program which, amongst other things, reads commands typed on the keyboard, echoes those commands onto the screen in the command window, causes executable files corresponding to those commands to be read into the computer memory and then executed. The Command Prompt program is complicated but it is just a program.

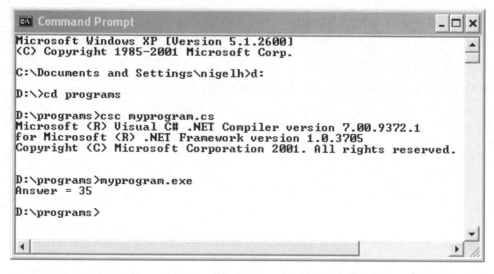

Figure 1.2 Compiling and running a program using a command window

---

1. If the filename extensions are missing when the contents of a folder are displayed on Windows, the 'Hide extensions for known file types' option is enabled. Disabling this particular folder option is strongly recommended for avoiding confusion between two files which appear to have the same name but actually have different extensions. (The different icons for the two files would otherwise be the only clue as to which is which.)

Just-in-time compiling

Although source code programs have to be turned into sequences of machine instructions in memory before the program can be executed, it is not necessary to perform the full translation in advance. The Java language popularized an approach called *interpretation*. The source code for a Java program is converted by the compiler into a format known as *Java bytecode*. When one saves compiled Java source code, one is saving a bytecode file which does not contain the bit patterns for an Intel computer or any other kind of real computer. A bytecode file contains the instructions for an imaginary computer called the Java Virtual Machine, plus it contains additional information which is useful for debugging the program and for linking it with other bytecode files to make a bigger program unit.

When a Java program is to be executed, a program called the Java Virtual Machine simulates the imaginary computer by reading and analyzing the bytecode files. It requires extracting the pattern of bits for one instruction of the imaginary computer, determining what action the imaginary computer is supposed to perform and then doing it. Memory locations in the imaginary computer are represented by variables in the Java Virtual Machine program.

That approach, interpretation, has some important advantages. Whereas Intel instructions can only be executed on Intel computers (and possibly only some models of Intel computers), the bytecode instructions can be executed on any computer for which the Java Virtual Machine program has been provided. A major reason why the Java language became popular was that Java bytecode files could be distributed with web pages (as Java applets) and could be executed on PCs, Macintosh computers, Sun workstations, and other kinds of computer. Bytecode files are more secure too because instructions to perform undesirable actions, such as erasing important files, cannot be hidden in the program. The Java Virtual Machine checks each bytecode file for any security breaches before interpretively executing it.

Interpretation, however, incurs a performance penalty. That analysis of each virtual machine instruction must be performed each time the instruction is reached in the program, and the same instruction can be executed many millions of times during the course of a single program run. Interpretation has now given way to a technique known as *just-in-time* compiling. Java programs are usually executed by just-in-time compilers, sometime abbreviated to JITters for short. C# is *always* executed by just-in-time compiling.

A C# program is converted by the C# compiler into a form called MSIL, which is short for Microsoft Intermediate Language. In the example of Figure 1.2, the file named `myprogram.exe` does not actually contain Intel machine instructions. It contains MSIL instructions. If we are interested, we can see those MSIL instructions using a program provided on Windows which is named `ildasm`.

Typing the command

```
ildasm myprogram.exe
```

brings up a window like that shown in Figure 1.3.

Figure 1.3 Ildasm program window

Selecting parts of the program by clicking on names inside that window causes blocks of MSIL code to be displayed in a human readable form which looks like assembly language. The block of code which adds 25 to 3 times 4 and displays the result is shown in Figure 1.4.

When we type the name of a file, such as `myprogram.exe`, which contains MSIL code, into a command window, the operating system first checks what kind of executable file is to be run. If the file contains MSIL code and if the operating system is Windows, then the operating system starts up a program called the .NET runtime. It is the responsibility of the .NET runtime to make sure that the MSIL program is executed. It does that by invoking the JITter program for the first block of MSIL code which needs to be executed. The JITter translates the MSIL code into an equivalent sequence of machine instructions for our computer – such as Intel instructions. That sequence is held in the computer's memory. The .NET runtime then transfers control to the first instruction in the sequence.

Whenever the translated code needs to transfer control to another part of the program whose MSIL code has not been translated, control is instead transferred to the .NET runtime, which invokes the JITter and then transfers control to the newly created machine instructions. Each block of MSIL code is translated just before it is needed, that is *just in time*. The approach is very efficient because each block is translated only once in the course of executing a program. An interpreter, like the Java Virtual Machine, would instead translate the same blocks of code many times.

```
Try::Go : void()                                                    _ □ X
.method private hidebysig instance void  Go() cil managed
{
    // Code size        27 (0x1b)
    .maxstack  2
    .locals init (int32 V_0,
             int32 V_1,
             int32 V_2)
    IL_0000:  ldc.i4.s   23
    IL_0002:  stloc.1
    IL_0003:  ldc.i4.s   12
    IL_0005:  stloc.2
    IL_0006:  ldloc.1
    IL_0007:  ldloc.2
    IL_0008:  add
    IL_0009:  stloc.0
    IL_000a:  ldstr      "Answer = {0}"
    IL_000f:  ldloc.0
    IL_0010:  box        [mscorlib]System.Int32
    IL_0015:  call       void [mscorlib]System.Console::WriteLine(string,
                                                                  object)

    IL_001a:  ret
} // end of method Try::Go
```

Figure 1.4 MSIL code

Even the simplest computer program contains many details. The programmer must get every one of these details right or else the program will not work. The C# language and the C# compiler have been designed so that the compiler can easily check the program for internal consistency. If an inconsistency is found, an error is reported to the programmer. The early stages of writing a program will often consist of several tries to compile the program, making corrections in response to error messages after each try. Once the program is accepted by the compiler, it would be foolish to assume that the program is correct. It is quite likely to contain errors which cause the program to perform unintended actions. A good programmer would therefore test the program thoroughly, trying it out on a wide variety of inputs.

Software development

The development process for a program may be visualized like that shown in Figure 1.5. The one thing to remember is that time spent initially on understanding the problem before the programming task begins is a good investment. It will more than pay for itself with time saved later in correcting errors.

Even after the program has been finished, fully debugged and distributed to the users, the programming work is usually not over. Users will find additional bugs that were not uncovered during testing, users will request enhancements, and (assuming we are talking about commercial software) the company management will propose adding extra features to make the software more competitive with competing products. All this extra work is classified as *software maintenance*. The amount of software maintenance performed on a

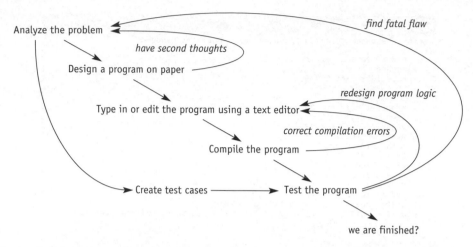

Figure 1.5 The software development process

program can be limitless. The world is still using a considerable amount of financial software that was developed in the Cobol and RPG languages more than 30 years ago, and much of it is subject to frequent revision as taxation laws and other factors change.

1.4 Interactive development environments

Since the early days of computers, programmers have used commands typed on the keyboard to compile programs and execute them. For computers using the Unix operating system,[1] this would very much be the normal way of doing things. However the *interactive development environment*, or IDE, now provides an alternative. On a Microsoft Windows system, the IDE which can be used to help develop C# programs is called Visual Studio .NET. A screen snapshot of Visual Studio as it looks when used to develop a tiny program appears in Figure 1.6.

It is a natural development that programmers should develop software tools to help with the programming task. Although Visual Studio is one such tool, an interactive development environment would typically include:

◆ an interactive text editor, usually incorporating formatting features for rearranging and beautifying the visual layout of a program;

---

1. The name Unix covers all its variants, including Linux, FreeBSD and Solaris.

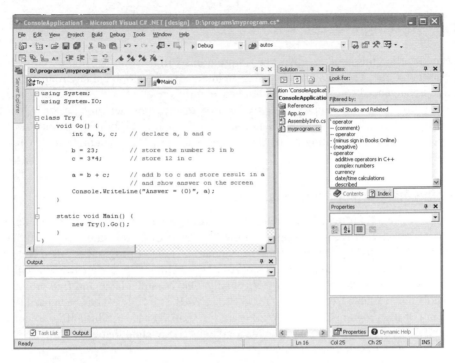

Figure 1.6 The Visual Studio .NET IDE

◆   a help facility to provide information about the programming language and its associated software;

◆   a design tool for creating graphical user interfaces;

◆   a compiler;

◆   debugging tools for running and monitoring the program's execution.

An IDE like Visual Studio .NET is intended for use by professional programmers. Although it provides many facilities which shorten the time needed to develop a program, it is a complicated piece of software to use. It is important that the user has a good under-standing of the basic concepts of a computer and reasonable familiarity with the individual development tools before trying this IDE. In this book, we will be assuming that a simple text editor is used to create the program source code files and that a command window is used to compile and run the programs.

1.5 Getting started with C#

As stated earlier, this book assumes that C# programs will be compiled and executed from the command line. The possibility of using an interactive development environment is left for a more advanced course or for the more adventurous reader.

Everything in this section of the book assumes that a computer running the Windows operating system is used to develop and run the C# programs. ('Windows' refers to several versions of this operating system including Windows ME, Windows NT, Windows 2000 and Windows XP).

Creating and editing source code files

When we write a C# program, we create it as one or more text files. Let's assume the simplest case where we have just a single text file. We can use any text editor program to create that text file. On Windows systems, the standard text editor program is called Notepad. The WordPad program could also be used. A little searching with a web browser will find several alternatives which are more user friendly. One commendable and free program is EditPad Lite, available from `http://www.EditPadLite.com`. It has been used to create many of the programs in this book. Figure 1.7 shows a use of EditPadLite to create a minimal C# source code program. We must give the file a name that ends with the extension '`.cs`', which is short for 'C Sharp'.

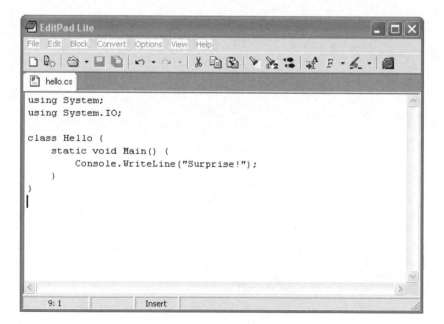

Figure 1.7 EditPadLite used to create a C# program

Compiling the C# program

On a Windows system, the *Command Prompt* program may be used. It can usually be found under `Start/Programs/Accessories` on the taskbar. Starting the program causes a window to be displayed; commands may be typed into this window.

Some commands are:

```
COMMAND PROMPT (SELECTION)

cd               // print the name of current directory
cd path          // change current directory to path
cd ..            // change current directory to parent
d:               // change current directory to d:

dir              // print names of files in current directory

path             // show the setting for the Path variable

help             // list the available commands
help command     // get usage information for a command
```

The Command Prompt window on a Windows system allows the user to enter commands on the keyboard which are similar to Unix commands. Many of the commands are obsolete (dating back to the MS-DOS operating system).

The window has the notion of a current directory or current folder. By default, the name of that current directory is displayed at the start of each new line in the window as a command prompt. For example, the text

```
C:\Documents and Settings\thomas>
```

would indicate that the current directory is the path `C:\Documents and Settings\thomas`. If the C# source code file to be compiled is located in another directory, it is a good idea to change the Command Prompt's directory to be that one using `cd` commands. Note that if the directory you wish to move to is on another filesystem, you should type the name of that filesystem first. For example, to switch to `D:\My Work\Files`, you could use the commands

```
d:
cd "my work"
cd files
```

As this example illustrates, Windows does not differentiate between upper and lowercase letters in filenames. (Unix and MacOS do differentiate however.) The example also illustrates that if the filename contains a space character, we can write the filename inside double quote characters.

Once the current directory is the same as the one where the C# source code file is located, we *should* be able to compile that file with the command:

```
csc /debug:full hello.cs
```

where `hello.cs` is the name of the source code file.

There are a couple of things to explain here. First, what is that `csc` command, and second, what is that `/debug:full` notation?

The csc command. The mnemonic `csc` is not a built-in command known to the Command Prompt program, the way that `cd` is. We really want the Command Prompt program to invoke the C# compiler which is a program named `csc.exe`, and that is what the Command Prompt program will try to do for us. When the name typed is not a built-in command, Command Prompt searches for an executable file whose name, without the suffix, is `csc`. Now where does the Command Prompt program search? It searches only in the current directory and in the directories which are named in the string which is the value of an *environment variable* named `Path`.

If we should see a response from Command Prompt like this

```
'csc' is not recognized as an internal or external
command, operable program or batch file.
```

then it means that the C# compiler, which is a program named `csc.exe`, has not been found in any of the directories listed in the `Path` variable's string value.

If this happens on a computer in a shared environment (e.g. a computer laboratory in a college), it would be advisable to locate a system administrator to have the problem corrected. The correction would involve making sure that the C# compiler was installed correctly and, if it has been, checking the setting of the `Path` variable. The current setting of the `Path` variable can be checked by just typing that word

```
path
```

in the Command Prompt window (capitalization is ignored).

If the problem is just the `Path` variable, it is possible to work around that problem by using the full pathname of the C# compiler. If the path[1] is

```
C:\Program Files\Microsoft.NET\urtinstallpath
```

we can type the command

```
C:\Program Files\Microsoft.NET\urtinstallpath\csc.exe
        /debug:full hello.cs
```

all on one line, and the Command Prompt program will invoke the C# compiler without having to search the directories in the `Path` list.

---

1. This path is not standard – it may be necessary to search for the location of the `csc.exe` file to find where it is on another system.

The /debug option. The second point to be explained about using the C# compiler is that the compilation process can be modified by specifying some options on the command line. The full list of options can be seen by typing this variation of the command

```
csc /help
```

Fortunately, the defaults for all the options are acceptable and we can safely ignore all the possibilities when developing the programs described in this book. The one option where it may be advisable to override the default is the *debug* option. By specifying "full" for the *debug* option, we ask the C# compiler to generate extra information which leads to more detailed error messages when our program goes wrong (which is, unfortunately, a common occurrence). A shorthand which works the same way is to invoke the C# compiler as

```
csc /debug+ hello.cs
```

Bigger programs are usually constructed from several C# source code files. If we have a program composed of files named one.cs, two.cs and three.cs, then we would create the program from them using the command

```
csc /debug:full one.cs two.cs three.cs
```

The resulting executable file will be named one.exe, two.exe or three.exe, depending on which source code file contains the starting point of the program (which is normally a piece of the program named Main – as will be explained in Chapter 2).

Use of the Visual Studio IDE is recommended if many files need to be compiled to create a program. Typing all those filenames can be tedious and subject to error. But for just a few files, the command line approach is adequate.

Running the compiled program

If the C# compiler does not detect any errors in the C# source code file, it will generate an executable file. On Windows systems, the default name for the executable file is the same as the source code file but with the '.cs' suffix replaced by a '.exe' suffix. For example, if the source code file is named hello.cs then the executable file is named hello.exe. We can run the program by simply typing its name in the command prompt window. Typing either the filename without the '.exe' suffix

```
hello
```

or with the suffix, like so,

```
hello.exe
```

should work. If we have compiled several files, then we run the file that contains the Main method in it. Let's now move on to Chapter 2 and find out all about Main methods and other parts of C#.

Concepts in Chapter 1

This introductory chapter looked at some of the history of programming languages, assembly language, programming languages themselves, and the notion of a compiler which translates a program into the binary code executed by a computer. It also covered program development with a text editor and a compiler using a command prompt window.

The concepts covered in the chapter included:

programming	assembly language
binary	hexadecimal
character coding	assignment operator
interactive development environment	running a program

The operators covered were:

=

and the definitions and syntax forms were:

programming languages	definition of a computer
the csc command	command prompt (selection)
software development	

Quiz

The quiz questions in this book are all multiple choice. Here are five quiz questions which test understanding of some of the material covered in this chapter.

Q1.1 How many different combinations of bits are possible in a byte?

    (a)   64   (b)   16

    (c)   8   (d)   256

Q1.2 If the eax register holds the number 7, what do you suppose would be held in that register after executing the following Intel Pentium instruction?

```
add    eax,eax
```

    (a)   impossible to say   (b)   7

    (c)   14   (d)   8

Q1.3 What decimal number does the binary number `00111111` represent?

    (a)   63   (b)   31

    (c)   111111   (d)   6

Q1.4 If 'A' is 65, 'B' is 66, ... in the ASCII coding scheme, what string of text is represented by the following sequence of numbers?
```
72 69 76 76 79
```

    (a)   hello   (b)   GEKKO

    (c)   OLLEH   (d)   HELLO

Q1.5 If our current directory on a Windows system is `C:\a\b\c\d`, where should we be after entering the following commands into a Command Prompt window?
```
cd ..
cd ..
cd c
cd flub
```

    (a)   `C:\a\b\c\d\flub`   (b)   `C:\a\b\c\flub`

    (c)   `C:\a\c\flub`   (d)   `C:\c\flub`

Exercises

Exercises ask you to do something. In subsequent chapters, the exercises will involve writing or changing C# programs. Since we have not yet got that far with programming, these exercises are somewhat simpler.

1.1 For which programming languages do you have compilers on your computer? List as many as you can find.

1.2 Is the Command Prompt program on Windows a compiler? Explain.

1.3 Each character (a letter, digit, punctuation symbol, etc.) requires two bytes of memory using Unicode. Estimate how many bytes would be needed to hold the characters that comprise this entire book.

1.4 Does your text editor recognize the syntax of different languages and colour them accordingly? Can you set it up for C#?

1.5 Find out how much memory your computer has and how much memory is occupied by your C# compiler, editor and/or IDE.

CHAPTER 2

Using objects

We start our journey into programming by looking at an overview of the principles of object-orientation and then go on to realize these concepts in C#. To create objects, we make use of types that already exist in the language, such as those for dates, images, strings, integers and random numbers. Types have data and functions, and we look in particular at four kinds of functions – constructors, properties, operators and methods. Input and output at the line level, and also for images, are covered, and the basic issues of formatting introduced. Through several examples of using objects in the construction of programs, a solid foundation of object-orientation is laid.

2.1 Introduction to objects

What is an object? This is a question frequently asked, and an essential one to answer. Objects are the cornerstone of programs written in a modern computer language like C#.

Such languages are geared for the development of objects which interact in controlled ways. In this section, we take a look at objects in general, together with their associated types, and move on to the C# language itself in the next section.

Informally, an object is a representation of something in the real world, both in terms of what it *is* and what it can *do*. Consider Figure 2.1.

Figure 2.1 Objects

We can identify many real world objects in the picture, for example boats, trees, buildings, and people. The objects themselves obviously cannot exist inside a computer. The function of a computer is to process *information*. Information is an abstract entity, while the objects in the picture are physical real world objects. What a program does is to store and manipulate information about real world objects – and that it can do accurately and very, very fast.

For an object in the picture, such as the boat in the foreground, the computer might record and update details such as the boat's registration number, its passenger carrying capacity and its owner. The information would likely be collected together in the program and that collection of information for a particular boat would be thought of as an object. The boat object in a program is a projection from the real world and it records only a very small fraction of the detail that would normally be associated with a real boat. A manipulation on a boat object in a program could be to change its owner if it is sold, for example.

It is clear that an object in a computer program is not an object in any physical sense. Indeed, some objects in a program may not correspond to any object in the real world at all but to some intangible or abstract concept. We might, for example, have an object which remembers how an individual user likes to have his or her computer screen organized ... should there be icons for a program in a column on the left or along the top of the screen, which icons should be listed and what style of cursor is preferred?

Referring back to Figure 2.1, a representation of the photograph shown there could be held inside the computer as ones and zeros – very many of them. The photograph itself is not held inside the computer, just its representation and some additional information needed to manipulate the image. Such additional information typically includes the width, height and resolution. That collection of information would form an *image* object. A program can manipulate the image by changing its size, rotating or flipping it, and sending it off to be printed.

Objects more formally

So let us look at a more formal definition of objects, as it is used in programming.

OBJECT

An object in a program is a realization of a concept. The object is represented in terms of the *data* associated with the concept, and the *functions* to which it has access in order to set, change or retrieve its own data, as well as data in other objects.

The terms *data* and *function* will be fully expanded in what follows. For our image object above, the data would be the actual pixels of the image, plus its width, height and resolution, and the functions that we could apply would include, resizing, flipping, rotating, and so on.

As another example of an object, consider a date of birth. The data for such an object would be its year, month and day values. The functions associated with a birth object might be:

◆ the ability to subtract it from another date object (from *today*, say) to give a number of years (the age);

◆ a comparison to another data object to see if they are the same (the birthday of a friend, say);

◆ passing it to another object, which has the ability to print values, and thereby have its values displayed on the screen.

In all these three ways, the object can interact with other objects via its functions.

Types

Programs usually have to manipulate many similar objects. For example, we might have a program which manipulates hundreds of different images with different widths and heights. However, all these different images would be similar in that we can rotate, flip, resize or print any of them. They can be used almost interchangeably. It is natural therefore to consider all these image objects as belonging to an image *type*. In programming, each object must belong to a type. A program can have several types and therefore can contain several different kinds of objects.

TYPE

A type provides the definition of *data* and *functions* needed

◆ to describe a certain group of objects, or

◆ to accomplish a specific task.

Types which have both data and functions would describe groups of objects. Examples of such types might be:

◆ a *date* type, whose data keeps the day, month and year of a particular date, and which provides functions to add days, compare dates, and so on;

◆ a *number*, whose data stores the value required, and which provides the usual operations to add, subtract, multiply, compare, etc., numbers.

Some types just provide functions, and then we would not be declaring objects of that type: we would just use its functions. Examples here would be types for

◆ providing *mathematical operations* such as square root, sine and cosine;

◆ enabling *input and output* of data between a program and the outside world.

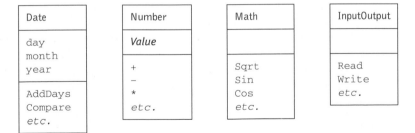

Figure 2.2 Examples of types

Figure 2.2 depicts, in general terms, what these types might look like. Each box shows a type and starts with the *name* of the type, then shows the data, then the functions. In the next section, we shall see how these types are specified and used specifically in C#. We shall also see shortly why the "value" for the Number type is shown in italics.

Now, to complete the picture, consider how created from the first two types might look (Figure 2.3). The objects from the Date type have names – birth and marriage – and the values for each item of data as specified in the type. The functions are not shown in the objects, because these are shared by all the objects of that type, and shown in the type itself. Objects so created are called *instances* of the type. By convention, type names in C# are usually given capital letters, and objects start with small letters.

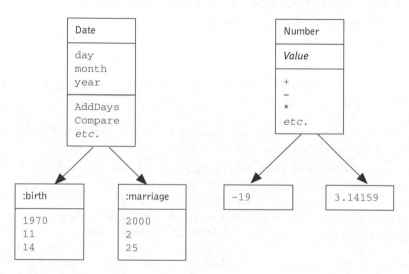

Figure 2.3 Objects created from types

The Number objects look slightly different. They do not have names, and just their values are shown. This is because in most languages (and in C#), special provision is made for types which correspond to the types in the computer, which include the numeric types, such as integers. These are known as *simple types*. So, for example, a type for numbers will allow one data value (such as −19); it would correspond to one of the number types in the computer, and its possible values can be written in the usual decimal integer form. The functions of a simple type are represented by built-in operators such as + − and so on. In Chapter 3, we shall look more carefully at the details of numbers in C#.

SIMPLE TYPE

A simple type usually

◆ represents data for one value;

◆ corresponds directly to a built-in type in the computer;

◆ has a recognized written set of values in the language;

◆ makes use of built-in operators in the language for its functions.

Other simple types that have equivalents in the computer are:

◆ a *boolean* (or logical) type that has values that are either true or false, written as words, not numbers, and has logical operators such as *and* and *or*. Inside the computer, bool values can be represented by one bit;

◆ *characters*, where the values represent the letters, numbers and symbols such as those on the keyboard. Most of these can be written in the program in quotes, as for example 'K' or '8'. Inside the computer, each character is represented as a pattern of bits in a byte, as described in Chapter 1.

Referring to Figure 2.3, we can see that `Date` is clearly not a simple type, since it contains three values, and there is no recognized way for writing a date – in fact there is a whole variety of ways for the same value. For example,

14 November 1970

14/11/70

November 14, 1970

1970.11.14

are all valid ways of representing a date, depending on one's needs and the country one lives in. In contrast, therefore, to the simple types, a date would be called a *structured type*. The simple types are provided by the language because they have their special set of symbols, but C# also provides many structured types as well, such as one for dates.

Another structured type is a *string* of characters enclosed in double quotes, as in "London" or "John Smith". This type falls in the structured group because it is made up of several simple values. However, languages usually provide an operator to join strings, such as + or &. String values can have various representations, but the characters of the string are always stored together.

Programmers have the facility to define new structured types, which do not have a correspondence with computer types, nor to a set of written symbols. However, a structured type could have just one value: the distinction is that a simple type cannot have more than one.

For completeness, here is a definition of a structured type.

STRUCTURED TYPE

A structured type
◆ contains data for one or more values, each of which has its own type;
◆ has user-defined data and functions.

The above description of types is intended to be a little wider than that used in C#, since one always wants to learn *principles* of programming, not just a language.

2.2 Members of objects

As we have seen, types, and hence their objects, have data and functions, the latter sometimes represented by operators. How are these described? In this section we start using
real C# notation and introduce the concept of a form, which shows how constructs in C#
are written, and what their meaning is. How they are written is called the *syntax*, and their
meaning is the *semantics*. A form therefore will look like the following:

FORM FOR A C# CONSTRUCT
The syntax of the construct
The semantics of the construct

The fonts associated with forms are discussed in Chapter 1.

Accessing members

The data and functions of a type are together known as *members*. There is a general notation for accessing the members of types and objects that have *names*. Members that are
depicted by symbols for operators (such as +) are accessed differently, in accordance with
accepted practice for arithmetic.

Members of types that are to be used by all objects of that type (and also other objects)
are known by the general term as *static members*. They are then accessed via a dot notation using the *type name*. Members that are intended to be used for a specific object, which
is an instance of a type, are called *instance members*, and are accessed via the *object name*.
Thus we have the following form:

ACCESSING MEMBERS

`type.member`
`object.member`
 	
`type.method(parameter-list)`
`object.method(parameter-list)`
 	
`object operator object`   `// infix (binary) operator`
`operator object`   `// prefix (unary) operator`

The first two options apply to all data, as well as to most functions. If the member is an instance member, it is applied to the object; if it is a static member, it is applied to the type. Members that are methods (see below) can be passed parameters. The last two options are used when operators (such as + and −) are defined for a type. Further semantics of each access are described below.

For example, based on Figures 2.2 and 2.3, we would identify members as

```
birth.day
marriage.year
birth.AddDays(20)
Math.Sqrt(x)
InputOutput.Read()
6+3
```

So, in front of the dot we give a type or an object, and after we give a member. We now go on to discuss the options for members, both in terms of data and functions.

Data

The data for a type consists of one or more *fields*. Each field is specified with its own type which is known as a *field declaration*. Fields can have several options that govern how they can be used, but for our purposes at the moment, the form for a simple declaration is:

FIELD DECLARATION (SIMPLE)

```
type field;
type field = expression;
type field1, field2, ... ;
```

The first option declares a field of the given type. The second option declares the field and initializes it to an expression which evaluates to a value of the same type. The third option shows that we can declare a list of fields of the same type.

(The term *expression*, used in the above form, will be explained later. Here we can assume that it includes values of the appropriate types.)

What types can we use? In the previous section we mentioned types for numbers, dates, pictures and strings, among others. In C#, these types exist with the equivalent names `int`, `DateTime`, `Image` and `string`. Examples of declarations would therefore be:

```
int temperature;
Image photo1;
DateTime birth, graduation, marriage;
int century = 100;
string taxEnd = "February";
```

By convention, the simple types such as `int` start with a small letter, and structured types such as `Image` with a capital. The predefined type `string` is the exception, and is synonymous with the structured type `String`. C# programmers tend to use `string`.

Structs and classes. C# has two kinds of structured types – `struct` and `class`. `DateTime` is a struct, and `Image` is a class. For the time being, we shall deal mainly with structs. In very many ways, the two constructs are the same, but classes have additional features which make them more powerful. These features include *inheritance* and *polymorphism*. They are not needed for simple programs or for understanding the beginnings of object-orientation, so we shall delay introducing them till later. There is, however, a difference between structs and classes when it comes to initialization.

Initialization. In the above list of data fields, the last two, `century` and `taxEnd`, are given values. What about the others? In C#, all integer fields are initialized to zero when they are declared. When a struct such as `DateTime` is declared, its fields are created, and each is initialized according to *its* type. Thus if `DateTime` has day, month and year fields (as it probably does) and these are all integers (as they are), then they will be initialized to zero.

The fields of `Image`, whatever they may be, can have no significant values until an actual picture is loaded. `Image`, being a class not a struct, has its objects initialized to a single special value called *null*. This will be the value of `photo1` until we do something to change it.

Functions

There are several kinds of functions in C#, but the ones that we shall deal with immediately are known as *constructors*, *methods*, *properties* and *operators*. In keeping with the theme of this chapter, we are looking at how these functions are *used* in a C# program: in Chapter 3, we look at how they can be *defined*.

Constructors. These are a special kind of function used to make (create or instantiate) objects of a given structured type. The constructor is passed some values which are inserted into the fields of the new object. Thus if we want to make some date objects, we would say:

```
DateTime birth = new DateTime(1970, 11, 14);
DateTime marriage = new DateTime(2000, 2, 25);
```

The values in brackets are known as *parameters*, and they must be supplied in the order in which they are expected. In the case of `DateTime`, that order is year, month, day. The form for an object instantiation is:

INSTANTIATING AN OBJECT
type obj = new *type*(*parameter-list*);
An object of the given type is created with the name given by `obj` and its fields are initialized according to the parameter-list.

The use of the equals sign indicates that what is done on the right-hand side is *assigned* to the object name on the left-hand side. Assigning is a very general theme in programming that we shall pick up on in a while.

Objects can also be created via methods, as we shall see for `Image` data below.

Methods. A *method* of a type can be invoked to change values of fields, to perform external actions such as displaying something on the screen, and to compute a result. For example, in the `DateTime` type, there is a method for adding a number of years. As an example of using it, we might say:

```
marriage.AddYears(25);
```

The method here is named `AddYears`. It is being applied to the object `marriage`, and is being passed the value 25 to work with. The number 25 is the parameter to the `AddYears` method. We indicate that the method is being applied to the object by using a *dot operator*. The result of the operation is to alter a field held by `marriage`.

In Section 2.1 and Figure 2.2, mention was made of a type for input and output. In C# this type is a class called `Console`. One of its methods is `WriteLine`, which is used for displaying values on the screen. To display the value of the `birth` object, we can say

```
Console.WriteLine(birth);
```

which activates the `WriteLine` method of the `Console` class with the parameter `birth`.

Another category of method creates an object for a declared field. In this example, `FromFile` also gets a picture into a program from a file.

```
Image photo1 = Image.FromFile("Photo.jpg");
```

The usage is the same as the previous example (`WriteLine`) and uses the type.member access format, as discussed with the form at the start of this section.

Properties. Properties enable us to look up the values of data fields in a controlled way, and perhaps to adjust them. In C#, fields are by default private to an object. We often want to make their values accessible, but to control changes. For example, a day of the month field should not be assigned a value of 32. However, if the field is associated with a property, then the property can constrain what can be done with or to the field. For example, the `DateTime` type does not expose any fields to us, but has many properties which let us access them. Examples of such properties are `Day`, `DayOfWeek`, `Year`, and so on. Properties, like methods, are applied to objects via the dot operator, and start with a capital letter, but they do not have parameters, and hence no parentheses.

Referring to the instantiation above, the `Year` property gives us the value of the `year` field, as in:

```
Console.WriteLine(birth.Year);
```

which would display 1970. Another interesting property of `DateTime` is `Now`, which gives the current date and time. Thus we could also write:

```
Console.WriteLine(DateTime.Now);
```

and have the current date and time displayed, e.g.

```
2002/07/13 08:55:20 PM
```

For images, the dimensions are also properties, so we can write them out, as in:

```
Console.WriteLine(photo1.Width);
Console.WriteLine(photo1.Height);
```

Operators. Operators are represented by symbols, and stand for the calling of a method which performs the operator as indicated between two objects. Each type may have many operators defined, many of them with obvious meanings. For example, we can say

```
temperature + 5
birth.Year - graduation.Year + 1
graduation - birth
photo1.Width < photo1.Height
```

Here we see examples of the operators plus (+), minus (-), less than (<) and dot (.), but used in different contexts. The first two examples deal with integers, and the semantics of integer operators are well known from mathematics and from using calculators. If `temperature` has a value of, say 25, then `temperature+5` is 30, and so on.

The third example uses minus on `graduation` and `birth` which were previously declared as objects of type `DateTime`. What does it mean to subtract one object from the other? If the subtraction operator is defined for `DateTime` objects, then the definition will include a specification of the type of the result. In this case, subtracting two `DateTime` objects creates an object of another type, which gives a value in hours. This may not be very helpful, and we would need to process it further to get years.

The final example will compare two integers (the width and height) and return a true or false value, which can be examined further, as discussed fully in Chapter 4. It also shows the use of the dot operator again.

Namespaces

To round off this section, we look at how types are grouped in C#. A modern language like C# provides a rich selection of predefined types which programmers can use. Some of these are absolutely essential, such as types which enable reading and writing of data, and others which supply components for point and click interfaces that computer users expect. The `Math` type which we mentioned earlier is also in this category. No one would think of having to program the calculation of a square root from scratch: we expect the facility to be provided. Other types such as `DateTime` could be labelled as non-essential, but they are very useful to have, and save the average programmer a lot of work.

There are so many types (thousands of them) that, in order to categorize them, they are divided logically into namespaces. A *namespace* in C# is a collection of associated types. Some namespaces such as `System` are very big with over 100 types of different kinds; some namespaces such as `System.Timers` have only a handful. `DateTime` and `Math` are part of the `System` namespace.

Making use of namespaces (also called packages, libraries or application programming interfaces (APIs)) is the process of *reuse*, and is very much encouraged as a good software engineering principle. If a set of types is supplied with a language, then it makes a great deal of sense to use them. In this chapter, we are going to learn how to program using entirely predefined types. In this way we will be freed from having to know right now how to make our own types: this process follows in Chapter 3.

Terminology summary

Figure 2.4 sums up the terminology for object orientation in C# that we have introduced so far. Words such as 'A program', 'types' and 'data' indicate the concepts we have defined in this section. The lines show how each concept is made up of others, and the italicized words next to the lines give an indication of how that composition is achieved. For example, types have data and functions, and functions can be any of the four concepts listed. When it comes to types, we give examples from actual C#, because we have already mentioned these terms.

Figure 2.4 is merely a beginning: there are many more terms to learn. We shall expand on the information in this figure as we go along. Now let us look at the elements of a program in more detail, with a real C# example.

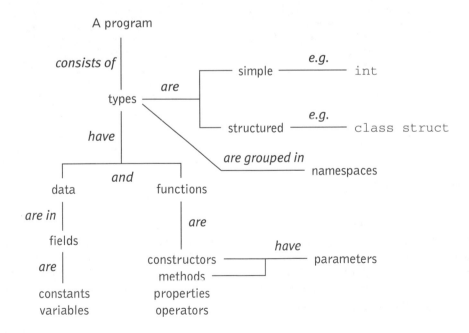

Figure 2.4 Terminology for objects so far

2.3 The structure of a program

Classes

A fundamental term in object-orientation is the class. A *class* is a type that shares many of the attributes of a structured type, as we have been using it up until now. It is the most powerful of the type categories available in C# and needs to be used specifically for certain behaviours. Many of these are only needed later on, but one is important here. A class is the *unit of structure* for a program. Within such a class, we can define data and functions as before, but we also need to define a `Main` method, which is used by the .NET runtime to start the program.

A class used as a program will have the form below. In terms of layout, we use the convention that the brackets associated with classes start on the same line as the class name; the closing bracket is then lined up underneath the first letter of the word `class`. There is another convention where the opening bracket is placed on a separate line and also under the word `class`. You may need to adjust your development environment to assist you with our convention if its editor performs automatic indentation of lines differently.

CLASS FOR A SIMPLE PROGRAM

```
using System;

class classname {
    static void Main() {
        statements
    }
}
```

The program has the name `classname`. Its class is defined between the curly brackets { and }. Its behaviour occurs in the statements of the `Main` method.

Example 2.1 A first program

Consider the first example program which is stored in a file called Welcome.cs. The 'cs' stands for C#, and is recognised by environments and compilers as such. We have given each line a number for ease of discussion. The line numbers are not part of the C# program, though. The result of the program can be guessed from lines 5 and 6. That is, a welcoming message is printed and then on the next line, we get and print the current time. For a real run of the program, the output would be

```
Welcome to C#
It is now 2003/07/13 08:55:20 PM
```

```
File Welcome.cs
    1    using System;
    2
    3    class Welcome {
    4        static void Main() {
    5            Console.WriteLine("Welcome to C#");
    6            Console.WriteLine("It is now " + DateTime.Now);
    7        }
    8    }
```

If we analyze the program, we can identify the following C# concepts:

1. The program starts off by stating that it is going to use the System namespace. The two classes that it makes use of are Console and DateTime, as seen on lines 5 and 6.

2. On line 3, the class Welcome is declared and its contents follows the open bracket The name of the file and the name of the program (the name of the class) do not have to coincide, although they usually are the same or close.

3. Line 4 introduces the Main method which is the entry point of our program. The C# system will come here when we ask it to start running the program.

4. The only real instructions we give are to display some text. We do so through the Console.WriteLine method, using strings and a DateTime property for the current time.

5. In line 6, we use a + operator to indicate that a string and a time should be output on the same line. More on this in the next section.

6. The Welcome class and the Main method both start with curly brackets, so we end them appropriately with the matching closing brackets on lines 7 and 8.

Example 2.2 Introducing the Go method

To make a more interesting program, we could add more statements to the Main method. However, a better structure for our basic program is to keep Main as a very simple method, and to add a second method, which we shall call Go. Go is initiated from Main and will contain the statements we wish to execute. This new structure is shown here. The changes are as follows.

1. The WriteLine statements move into the new Go method (lines 6 and 7 now).

2. The Main method has a statement creating a WelcomeFromGo object and starting up the Go method.

```
File WelcomeFromGo.cs

 1    using System;
 2
 3    class WelcomeFromGo {
 4
 5       void Go() {
 6          Console.WriteLine("Welcome to C# from Go");
 7          Console.WriteLine("It is now " + DateTime.Now);
 8       }
 9
10       static void Main() {
11          new WelcomeFromGo().Go();
12       }
13    }
```

For the rest of the book, we shall use the structure of this program. For completion, we note that the output of the program will be very similar to the previous one:

```
Welcome to C# from Go
It is now 2002/07/13 08:55:20 PM
```

Note that the Go method is a convention, not a C# construct. We use the Main-Go combination because placing field declarations and method calls in the static method Main restricts what can be done with them. The full details are covered in Chapter 8.

Layout

Just as a document in English is constructed from sentences, a C# program is constructed from *statements*. There are different kinds of statements, which will be covered as we work through the language. In C#, statements end with a semicolon, and are usually written on a line all by themselves. Because of the semicolon, it is possible to write more than one statement per line, but this would look quite odd. A more usual occurrence is that a statement does not fit on one line and has to go over to the next one. There will be plenty of examples of this happening soon. The *semicolon* then serves as the end of a multi-line statement.

We can see that all the programs shown thus far are written in an *indented* style. When a language construct such as class or method starts, it acts like a heading and all that follows is indented to the right a few spaces. When the construct ends (usually with a closing bracket), the indentation reverts to its previous level. Many programming environments will assist you in typing programs neatly like this.

Indentation introduces so-called 'white space' into a program, making it easier to read without making it any more complex in actual fact. Another form of white space is a blank line, and these are typically used between methods or to separate important parts of a method. The layout of a program is very important, and good layout is something that one should strive for right from the start.

Keywords and identifiers

A program has several kinds of words in it. There are words which are prescribed by C# to have specific meanings, and which cannot be used again for other meanings. These are known as *keywords*, and examples in our program are:

```
using          class              void
new            static
```

C# has 80 such keywords which serve a variety of functions in the program. They are listed in Appendix B.

Each program defines its own words for the data, methods and properties it needs, and these are known as *identifiers*. Identifiers defined by us in the program are:

```
WelcomeFromGo                    Go
```

and the following ones are defined by C# but used by us:

```
System         Console            WriteLine
DateTime       Now                Main
```

Identifiers have a specific format.They must be whole words, starting with a letter and not clashing with any keyword. By convention, when an identifier has more than one word in it, we capitalize the first letters of the inner words, for ease of reading. There are other capitalization conventions as well. Basically, all identifiers start with capital letters, except those for fields. In the above program, there are no fields, but we did see some previously, such as:

```
birth          graduation         marriage
temperature    century            photo1
```

Notice that it is often the case that a property will have the same name as a field, except with a capital letter. Thus Year is a property for the year field (which we cannot otherwise access).

Operators and symbols

Finally, we note that the program also contains several special characters. Several more operators and symbols will be introduced as we go along. In the program in Example 2.2, we can identify:

- ◆   { } to begin and end a class or a method (three pairs);
- ◆   " " quotes for strings;
- ◆   operator symbols, like + (line 7);
- ◆   semicolon to end a statement;
- ◆   dot to select a member of an object or type;

◆   ( ) around parameters for methods, as in lines 6 and 7 (even if there aren't any parameters, as in lines 5 and 10).

Example 2.3 Days to the year end

We want to calculate the number of days between now and the end of the year. We know that there is a type for dates, so we can create two objects of that type, one for now and one for the end of the year. The date for the end of the year is created by using the year property from today's date, and then 12 for the month and 31 for the day.

A crucial part of the program is the calculation, which is done by subtracting the two DateTimes, and then invoking the Days property on the result.

File TimeDifference.cs

```
using System;

class TimeDifference {

  /// <summary>
  /// The Time Difference Program        Bishop and Horspool June 2002
  /// ============================
  /// Calculates the number of days to the end of the year
  /// Shows printing several lines of strings,
  /// and the use of properties and operators
  /// </summary>

  void Go() {
    Console.WriteLine("The Time Difference Program");
    DateTime now = DateTime.Now;
    DateTime endOfYear = new DateTime(now.Year, 12, 31);
    Console.WriteLine(endOfYear);
    Console.WriteLine(now);
    Console.WriteLine("Days till the end of the year are ");
    Console.WriteLine((endOfYear - now).Days);
  }

  static void Main() {
    new TimeDifference().Go();
  }
}
```

The output from the program could be:

```
The Time Difference Program
2002/12/31 08:55:20 PM
2002/08/04 08:55:20 PM
Days till the end of the year are
149
```

Making this output more explanatory will be taken up in the next section. We have made the assumption – correctly – that we can write out `DateTime` and `int` values. In the next chapter, Section 3.6, we shall see how to control the format of the values, so that they suit our particular country or preference.

Comments

When programs get longer than a few lines, they generally need some accompanying explanation in plain English. Even if the code is quite clear, its purpose and application should be specified up front. C# provides for three different types of comments:

1. XML comments. These start with three slashes and a tag, such as `<summary>` above, continue with lines introduced by `///` and end by using the same tag with a slash, as in `</summary>`. XML is a standard way of annotating almost anything, and we shall see more of it in later chapters. For now, we note that most of our programs and classes will start with such summary tags.

2. Multi-line comments. These start and end with `/*` and `*/`. Anything in between is ignored, no matter how many lines are included.

3. Same line comments. These start with `//` and continue only to the end of the line. They can be used to explain a statement in a few words, for example:

```
DateTime now = DateTime.Today; // Today is a property
```

When commenting a program, we try to achieve a balance in the number and substance of comments, so that the comments are useful and do not just repeat the code. Comments also need to be kept up to date: if the code changes, the comments may need to be changed too.

Example 2.4 Analyzing a program

We have now gone through a considerable number of C# concepts, sufficient to enable us to analyze a program into its constituent parts. The purpose of such an exercise is to check that we do indeed understand the differences between types and objects, data and functions, and so on. So, here is a rather nice program.

File FetchImage.cs

```
using System;
using System.Drawing;
using System.Windows.Forms;

public class FetchImage : Form {
```

```
/// <summary>
/// The Fetch Image program        Bishop and Horspool June 2002
/// ========================
///
/// Displays a picture
/// Illustrates simple drawing of images
/// </summary>

Image pic;

protected override void OnPaint(PaintEventArgs e) {
    this.Width = 500;
    this.Height = 400;
    e.Graphics.DrawImage(pic,30,30);
}

public FetchImage(){
    pic = new Bitmap("photo.jpg");
}

static void Main() {
    Application.Run(new FetchImage());
}

}
```

If a file called 'photo.jpg' exists in the correct place, the program will display the image it contains on the screen. Our task is to take each word and symbol in the program and categorize it according to the terms in this section and the previous one. Not all the identifiers are defined in the program: this is normal in C#. Their meaning has to be deduced from their context.

The output from the program is shown in Figure 2.5 and categories are listed in Table 2.1. How did we know how to analyze a program which dealt with graphics when we have not even got there yet? The point is that the *syntax* tells us what to expect. For example, in the statement

```
e.Graphics.DrawImage(pic,30,30);
```

e and Graphics must be objects or classes, because they have dot operators applied to them. The case of the identifiers provides the clue that e is an object, and Graphics a type. DrawImage has parameters with parentheses, so it must be a method. In a similar way, we can deduce that in

```
Application.Run(new FetchImage());
```

Application is a class, Run is a method and FetchImage is not a method but a constructor, because of the new keyword before it. As an exercise, you might perform the same analysis on Example 2.3.

Figure 2.5 Output from the FetchImage program

Category	As in program
Keywords	using, public, class, protected, override, void, static, new
Namespaces	System, System.Drawing, System.Windows.Forms
Types	FetchImage, Form, Image, PaintEventArgs, Graphics, Bitmap, Application
XML comment	for the summary
Objects	this, pic, e
Method calls	DrawImage()
Methods declared	OnPaint(), Main()
Values	30, 30, "photo.jpg"
Properties	Width, Height
Constructors	FetchImage()
Constructor calls	Bitmap(), FetchImage()

Table 2.1 Terms in the FetchImage progam

2.4 Strings, output and formatting

In this section we focus on the process of getting results out of a program. This process is called *output*, but often the terms writing, printing or displaying are used as well. In Example 2.2, the first output statement is:

```
Console.WriteLine("Welcome to C# from Go");
```

The `Console` class provides various methods for input and output, and `WriteLine` is the main one for output. What we want to output is specified between the parentheses as the parameter. In this case, our parameter is a *string*. When we send a string to a `Write-Line` method, the effect is to write the string on the screen or 'console'. The word *console* is an old fashioned term for a screen, and it has stuck as the name of this class in C#.

Strings

In C# there is a type called `string`. Strings consist of characters enclosed in quotes, which gives them a special representation in a program, like integers, but they are not quite the same because it is possible to access individual characters of a string quite easily. Strings are fully covered in Chapter 4. Here we concentrate on looking at strings from the point of view of output.

Strings cannot continue over more than one line in a program, so if the string gets too long, we have to break it up and make it into two or more strings. These strings can then be joined together again by the plus operator, which is known as a *concatenation operator*. For example, consider the following statement:

```
Console.WriteLine ("Welcome to C# " +
                   "from Go");
```

There are two strings, which would be joined (or *concatenated*) before `WriteLine` is called. The effect of the statement will be exactly as before, i.e.

```
Welcome to C# from Go
```

C# makes provision for special characters that cannot be easily typed from a keyboard to still be output. There are two kinds of such characters: escaped characters and Unicode characters, which are considered in Chapter 4.

Output statements

We have already encountered the `WriteLine` method. Strictly speaking, `WriteLine` is not a statement: it is a *method*, and when we call a method, we are using a *method call statement*. However, often one uses the term 'output statement' to refer to such a call. *Output* is a general word both for what we display on the screen and for the act of doing so.

`Console` has another method, `Write`, which is similar to `WriteLine` but which does not finish the line of output, and is intended to be followed by other `Write` or `Write-Line` calls. An example would be from Example 2.3 where we had these lines

```
Console.WriteLine("Days till the end of the year are ");
Console.WriteLine((endOfYear - now).Days);
```

They would be better written as

```
Console.Write("Days till the end of the year are ");
Console.WriteLine((endOfYear - now).Days);
```

to give the output

```
Days till the end of the year are 149
```

Mostly, though, `Write` is used when there are quite a few output statements and they involve more than strings, i.e. objects.

Outputting objects

Now consider the output of objects. We already assumed in the second program above that we can have statements such as

```
Console.WriteLine(endOfYear);
Console.WriteLine(now);
Console.WriteLine("Days till the end of the year are ");
Console.WriteLine((endOfYear - now).Days);
```

where `endOfYear` and `now` are `DateTime` objects. In C#, every type defines a special method called `ToString`. The `ToString` method will convert the value of the object into a string format in a meaningful way. The method is automatically called when objects appear as parameters in `WriteLine` calls. We could augment the above with some extra strings and a better arrangement as follows:

```
Console.WriteLine("The end of this year is " + endOfYear);
Console.WriteLine("Today's date is " + now);
Console.WriteLine("There are " + (endOfYear - now).Days
        + " days until the end of the year");
```

which would display

```
The end of this year is 2002/12/31 08:55:20 PM
Today's date is 2002/08/04 08:55:20 PM
There are 149 days until the end of the year
```

The `Console` class deals with line by line output. As we have already seen in Example 2.4, we can also output pictures. Here we would use a different class, called `Graphics`, and the method is `DrawImage`. So to get the photo displayed, we used:

```
e.Graphics.DrawImage(pic,30,30);
```

Outputting expressions

In programming, one of the most useful facilities is being able to do calculations easily. Programming languages have the same arithmetical operations as calculators, so plus is +, minus is -, but multiplication is * and division is /. Parentheses can also be used to ensure that the calculation is performed in the correct order. In C#, such calculations are known as *expressions*. Examples of simple expressions are:

`120 * 1.6`	120 miles as kilometres
`74.5 / 80.0 * 100`	a mark out of 80 as a percentage
`(12 + 15 + 17 ) / 3`	average of three numbers
`24 * 60`	minutes in a day
`39.95 * 1.14`	an amount plus 14% tax
`2002 - 1970 + 1`	years between two years

Expressions are discussed in full in the next chapter. Here we note that they can be used in output statements. C# has a facility that will automatically convert numbers to strings so that they can be concatenated together before output. Thus we can use the following statement with its output:

```
Console.WriteLine ("Graduated in " + (2003 + 3));

Graduated in 2006
```

The parentheses around the expression are necessary so that C# can distinguish between the + used for concatenation, and the arithmetic one. Without them, the output would be:

```
Graduated in 20033
```

In other words, each of the numbers 2003 and 3 is appended separately to the string `"Graduated in"`. This is certainly not what we intended, so the parentheses are used to force the arithmetic addition to take place.

2.5 Variables, assignment and input

A deficiency in the calculations above is that they are completely fixed. All the values are specified in the program so that no matter how often the program is run, the same output is obtained. A primary behaviour of most programs that one encounters, even as a layperson, is that they can accept input and thereby vary their output. In other words, in addition to being able to write out values, we want to be able to *read in* values. The question is: read them into where?

Variables

If we are going to read in data, we have to read it into a known place in memory, so we can then refer to it again in expressions and output statements. In programming, memory space is allocated to data fields. The fields may be *variables* or *constants*. The latter are different only in that having been assigned a value, the value may not change. Figure 2.6 shows some variables, as they would be represented in memory. Of course, we have not gone all the way and shown the binary representation of the values. We have shown the integer as a decimal and the string as characters, as is customary. The sizes of the boxes drawn for the variables is not important.

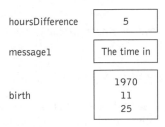

Figure 2.6 Some declared variables

Variables must be declared before they are used. We can initialize variables to some value in the declarations. Examples of declarations with initialization are:

```
int temperature = 30;
int age = 21;
int secondsInHour = 60*60;
string resultText = "";     // initialized to an empty string
string placeOfBirth = "London, UK";
```

Assignment

The equals sign in these initializations is known as the *assignment operator*. It causes the value on the right to be assigned to the variable on the left. It is the nature of variables that their values can be changed during the running of the program.

To change the value of a variable, we assign it a new value. The old value is overwritten and the variable now has the new value. For example,

```
int mass = 63;
Console.WriteLine(mass);
```

```
mass = 65;
Console.WriteLine(mass);
```

will write out

```
63
65
```

More interestingly with numbers, is the case where the right side is an expression, as in:

```
double tempC, tempF;
tempC = 30;
tempF = (tempC*9.0/5.0)+32;
```

which will put 86 in `tempF`. There is more about expressions and some special assignment operators in Chapter 3.

Assigning strings

Assignment also applies to strings, and here we have the + operator to use as well. Thus we could say:

```
string fullName = "James " + "Smith";
```

A rule about assignment is that the left side must match the right-hand side in terms of their types. This means that numbers cannot be assigned to strings and vice versa. Later we shall learn how to perform some conversions, but the fundamental rule still applies.

Assigning objects

Of course, we are most interested in this chapter in developing object-orientation skills. We have already used assignment of objects when we instantiate them, for example, this statement from Example 2.3:

```
DateTime endOfYear = new DateTime(now.Year,12,31);
```

creates a new object on the right-hand side and then associates the object with the field called `endOfYear`. As another example, consider the statement

```
Console.WriteLine((endOfYear - now).Days);
```

It could have been expressed with an extra variable and assignment, thus:

```
int days = (endOfYear - now).Days
Console.WriteLine(days);
```

The second form would be preferable if we were going to reuse the value in the program. These concepts are illustrated in the next example.

Example 2.5 Meeting times

A business has an office in London and in New York. The time difference is five hours in summer, with London being ahead. The London managers like to have a telephone conference starting at 14:00 every Monday. We would like to know the corresponding time in New York and our program will tell us.

As in the previous program in Example 2.3 for days to the end of year, we have two time variables. We also have the name of the city for the branch office (which will be New York) and the offset (which will be −5). To create the meeting date, we use the DateTime property UtcNow, which is the time in London (being on the Greenwich Meridian). For convenience, we first copy the London meeting time into a variable.

The C# program to present the result of these calculations consists of four output statements, plus the outer structure we discussed in Section 2.3.

File TimeMeeting.cs

```
using System;

class TimeMeeting {

   /// <summary>
   /// The Time Meeting program   Bishop and Horspool  April 2002
   /// =========================
   /// Calculates the time in one city
   /// given an offset from another one.
   ///
   /// Shows string and int variables
   /// </summary>

   void Go() {
      string city = "New York";
      int offset = -5; // from London - Utc
      int startTime = 14; // as in 14:00 or 2pm
      Console.WriteLine("The Time Meeting program");
      DateTime now = DateTime.UtcNow;
      DateTime meeting = new DateTime
            (now.Year,now.Month,now.Day,startTime,0,0);
      Console.WriteLine("The meeting in London is "
            + " scheduled for " + meeting);
      Console.WriteLine(city + " is " + offset
            + " hours different");
      DateTime offsetMeeting = meeting.AddHours(offset);
      Console.WriteLine("The meeting in "+city+" will be at "
            + offsetMeeting);
   }
   static void Main() {
      new TimeMeeting().Go();
   }
}
```

If we compile the program and run it, we will get output in the console window as follows:

```
The Time Meeting program
The meeting in London is scheduled for 2002/08/05 14:00:00
New York is -5 hours different
The meeting in New York will be at 2002/08/05 09:00:00
```

The output of the times is not so attractive, and we now look at alternative output methods for types like `DateTime`.

Output formatting

C# has special facilities for formatting numbers and other simple values on output. These are covered in the next chapter. When outputting structured objects, there may be alternative ways of presenting the fields. For example, the arrangement of 2002/12/31 08:55:20 PM for a date and time might not be quite what we want. For this reason, types often provide several different `ToString` methods. `DateTime` has alternatives for long and short dates. It also has extensive facilities for passing a parameter to `ToString` which then controls how the date is formatted. These are illustrated in Example 2.6.

Thus we can see that output of objects can be handled in various ways, but the responsibility for deciding what options to provide rests with the type.

Example 2.6 Dates in different formats

In this example we consider some of the options provided by `DateTime` for alternative formatting of dates and times. The first way of controlling output is to use one of the alternatives to `ToString`. `ToString` is called automatically if an object of `DateTime` is combined with a string and sent to `Write` or `WriteLine`. The following are additional versions, but they have to be called explicitly, using the usual dot notation.

```
ToShortDateString()               // short date and no time
ToLongDateString()                // long date and no time
```

The second way is to use one of the many coded parameters to `ToString`, for example:

```
ToString("f")                     // long date and short time
ToString("g")                     // short date and short time
```

These calls would produce the same output for the date, but the second group will also have the time.

We repeat the `TimeMeeting` program and add extra output statements to show the use of these methods and format parameters. The results are shown in the output below the program.

```
File TimeFormat.cs
```

```csharp
using System;

class TimeFormat {

   /// <summary>
   /// The Time Format Program    Bishop and Horspool   June 2002
   /// =========================
   /// The time printed in different ways
   /// Shows the use of ToString in various forms
   /// </summary>

   void Go() {
     Console.WriteLine("The Time Format Program");
     DateTime now = DateTime.Now;
     DateTime endOfYear = new DateTime(now.Year,12,31);
     Console.WriteLine("Today is " + now);
     Console.WriteLine("End of year is " + endOfYear);
     Console.WriteLine("As a short date " +
             now.ToShortDateString());
     Console.WriteLine("As a long date " +
       now.ToLongDateString());
     Console.WriteLine("As a long date and short time " +
       now.ToString("f"));
     Console.WriteLine("As a short date and short time " +
             now.ToString("g"));
     Console.Write("Days till the end of the year are ");
     Console.WriteLine((endOfYear - now).Days);
   }

   static void Main() {
     new TimeFormat().Go();
   }
}
```

The output from the program looks like this.

```
The Time Format Program
Today is 2002/08/05 13:41:17
End of year is 2002/12/31 00:00:00
As a short date 2002/08/05
As a long date 05 August 2002
As a long date and short time 05 August 2002 01:41 PM
As a short date and short time 2002/08/05 01:41 PM
Days till the end of the year are 147
```

Before we leave any program, even a simple program like this one, we can assess what we have done, and any limitations and extensions we can see. Clearly, this program could be generalized considerably. The London meeting time could change, and the time difference might be different in summer and in winter. Even the names of the cities could vary, if the program was used by another company or other branches. In which case, the time difference will also be different. Fortunately, by using the `DateTime` type, we can handle times that move over day boundaries, though whether this is of practical use in a business context can be argued!

So in general, we could foresee numerous extensions for this small program. To achieve these extensions, though, we another C# construct – input.

Input statements

We now consider how data outside of a program can be read into that program. Communicating with a program is a fundamental activity in computing and so it is right that we should introduce input early. *Input statements* are the counterpart of output statements, but they have a difference: they produce values, which then have to be stored into variables. Thus unlike an output statement, an input statement is phrased as an assignment. The types on the left and right side of an assignment must match, thus strings can only be read into string variables, and integers into integer variables.

The problem is that the `Console` class actually only provides a string reading method, `ReadLine` and any integers have to be converted by means of a special method supplied with the `int` type called `Parse`. This process is summed up in the following form.

SIMPLE INPUT STATEMENTS

```
stringvar = Console.ReadLine();

othervar = type.Parse(Console.ReadLine());
```

In the first option, data is read until the end of a line and copied into var.
The second option is used for other types of variable; data is read up to the
end of the line, but then the `Parse` method of that type is applied to the
string, and it is converted to a value of that type if possible.

Both ways of reading a string use `ReadLine`, which means that the string supplied to the program must be on one line, all by itself. Figure 2.7 shows this process in action for two of the variables in an earlier example.

Figure 2.7 shows how the program drives the reading process. Values are provided, one per line and stored in the specified variables. Thus the first `ReadLine` gets 'London' for the `city` variable. The second `ReadLine` gets the string '5'. This string is then *parsed* or converted into an integer and stored in the `offset` variable. Types other than integer can also be parsed. For example, we can read in and parse a date. A date string must be in one of the standard formats, such as 2002/8/15.

If the data provided for a read is of the incorrect type, then the program will signal an error and stop running. This effect will be most noticeable with numbers, since strings include almost anything and are not subject to restrictions. In Figure 2.7, if the second line of data were typed as the four letters 'five' instead of just the single digit '5', then there would be an error.

In Chapter 6, we shall see how to recover from such errors and enable the user of the program to try again. At the moment, our response to the error will be to restart the pro-

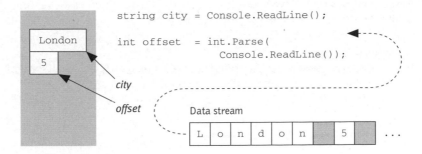

Figure 2.7 The process of reading

gram and type all the data in from the beginning. Data which is read into memory is erased (garbage collected) when a program stops. Those variables are reinitialized to their default values when the program restarts.

Example 2.7 Time with reading

The program in Example 2.5 to set up meeting times in New York and London needs to be updated for other branch offices. At this stage, we are not even sure if meetings are feasible everywhere at the London 14:00 time, but we would like to investigate possibilities for Berlin (one hour ahead), San Francisco (eight hours behind) and Perth (seven hours ahead).

We set up the program so that the city name and offset are read in, and then we rerun the program for each new branch office. Notice that times that are behind can be expressed as negative values.

The program is very similar to before, but shows some of the issues discussed above. The input statements have already been discussed; here they are assimilated into the rest of the program structure and the output. Specifically, we notice that to be user-friendly, input should always be preceded by some request, in the form of a `Write` rather than a `WriteLine` statement. Thus the reply can be typed on the same line.

File TimeReading.cs

```
using System;

class TimeReading {

    /// <summary>
    /// The Time Reading Program   Bishop and Horspool   April 2002
    /// =========================
    /// Still calculates the time in a city given an offset from
    /// another one, but uses reading to enable the second city
```

```
      /// to be set at runtime.
      /// Shows reading string and int values.
      /// </summary>

      void Go() {
        Console.WriteLine("The Time Reading Program");

        string city;
        int offset;
        int startTime = 14;
        DateTime now = DateTime.UtcNow;

        //Read in the second city's details
        Console.Write("City? ");
        city = Console.ReadLine();
        Console.Write("Offset from London? ");
        offset = int.Parse(Console.ReadLine());

        DateTime meeting = new DateTime(now.Year,now.Month,now.Day,
            startTime,0,0);
        Console.WriteLine("The meeting in London is "
            + " scheduled for " + meeting);
        Console.WriteLine(city + " is " + offset
            + " hours different");
        DateTime offsetMeeting = meeting.AddHours(offset);
        Console.WriteLine("The meeting in " + city
            + " will be at "
            + offsetMeeting.ToShortTimeString());
      }

      static void Main() {
        new TimeReading().Go();
      }
    }
```

The results can be shown over several runs of the program. The typed-in parts are shown in plain type.

```
The Time Reading program
City? New York
Offset from London? -5
The meeting in London is scheduled for 2002/08/05 14:00:00
New York is -5 hours different
The meeting in New York will be at 09:00 AM


The Time Reading program
City? Berlin
Offset from London? 1
The meeting in London is scheduled for 2002/08/05 14:00:00
Berlin is 1 hours different
The meeting in Berlin will be at 03:00 PM
```

```
The Time Reading program
City? Perth
Offset from London? 7
The meeting in London is scheduled for 2002/08/05 14:00:00
Perth is 7 hours different
The meeting in Perth will be at 09:00 PM


The Time Reading program
City? San Francisco
Offset from London? -8
The meeting in London is scheduled for 2002/08/05 14:00:00
San Francisco is -8 hours different
The meeting in San Francisco will be at 06:00 AM
```

The output is certainly useful, but it does seem awkward to have to rerun the program for each set of data. What we would like is to be able to have the program itself handle multiple requests. This topic is taken up in the chapters that follow.

2.6 Understanding C#'s APIs

API stands for *application programming interface* and it is a term we use interchangeably with namespace to describe a group of related classes, structs, and so on. The APIs we have encountered in this chapter so far are:

```
System
System.Drawing
System.Windows.Forms
```

The latter two were only used in Example 2.4 for drawing a photo, and we won't consider them further here. But we used some significant classes provided in System, and now we shall specify them, not completely, but at least in enough detail so they can be used as a reference point for the next few chapters.

DateTime

The form for the DateTime struct is shown below. It reveals some more precise information about the data and functions we have used up to now. DaysinMonth and IsLeap-Year could well be useful methods. Then we see that there are two subtraction operators. The second one subtracts two dates and returns a value of type TimeSpan. We have not yet encountered TimeSpan, although we did allude to it when we introduced DateTime.

TimeSpan holds times in days, hours and smaller units. If we wanted an answer in years, we would have to divide by 365 (or 366) ourselves.

```
┌─────────────────────────────────────────────────────────────────┐
│ DATETIME STRUCT (ABBREVIATED)                                     │
├─────────────────────────────────────────────────────────────────┤
│ // ********* Constructors *********                               │
│ DateTime(int year, int month, int day);                          │
│ DateTime(int year, int month, int day,                           │
│          int hour, int min, int sec);                            │
│                                                                   │
│ // ********* Static Properties *********                          │
│ static DateTime Now;     // current date and time                │
│ static DateTime Today;   // current date (time is 00:00:00)      │
│ static DateTime UtcNow;  // current date and time in UTC         │
│                                                                   │
│ // ********* Instance properties *********                        │
│ int Day                                                           │
│ int Month                                                         │
│ int Year                                                          │
│ int Hour                                                          │
│ int Minute                                                        │
│ int Second                                                        │
│ int Millisecond                                                   │
│ int DayOfYear                                                     │
│                                                                   │
│ // ********* Static Methods *********                             │
│ static int Compare(DateTime t1, DateTime t2)                     │
│ static bool Equals(DateTime t1, DateTime t2)                     │
│ static int DaysInMonth(int year, int month)                      │
│ static DateTime Parse(string s)                                  │
│ static bool IsLeapYear(int year)                                 │
│                                                                   │
│ // ********* Operators *********                                  │
│ static DateTime operator -(DateTime d, TimeSpan t)               │
│ static TimeSpan operator -(DateTime d1, DateTime d2)             │
│ static DateTime operator +(DateTime d, TimeSpan t)               │
│ static bool operator ==(DateTime d1, DateTime d2)                │
│                                                                   │
│ // ********* Instance Methods *********                           │
│ int CompareTo(object value)                                       │
│ override bool Equals(object value)                               │
│ string ToString()                                                │
│ string ToString(string format)                                   │
│ string ToShortDateString(                                        │
│ string ToLongDateString();                                       │
├─────────────────────────────────────────────────────────────────┤
│ There are many more offerings in all categories: consult your API help facil-│
│ ity or a comprehensive C# API reference manual.                  │
└─────────────────────────────────────────────────────────────────┘
```

There are four methods listed which relate to equality and comparison. If d1 and d2 are both instances of DateTime type, then these methods can be called as in

```
DateTime.Equals(d1,d2)    // calling the static method
d1.Equals(d2)             // calling the instance method of d1
d2.Equals(d1)             // calling the instance method of d2
```

where all three possibilities yield the same result. However the `DateTime` type also defines operators to perform equality, which just makes a program easier to read. So an equivalent expression to any of the above is simply

```
d1 == d2
```

`DateTime` also supplies all the comparison operators, so we can say, for example:

```
d1 < d2
```

which will return true or false as appropriate, or we can call one of the `Compare` or the `CompareTo` methods, which work slightly differently. They return a negative integer if the first operand is less than the second, 0 if they are equal and a positive integer if the first operand is greater. For example, we can write

```
if (d1.CompareTo(d2) < 0) {
    // d1 is an earlier date than d2
}
```

Clearly it is easier to use the operators if they are provided. Comparison operators are covered properly in Section 3.4 and Section 4.1.

string and int

In the API, `string` does not exist. That is because nearly all types in C# that start with small letters are aliased (or matched to) other types of the same name. The real class for `string` is therefore `String` in the `System` namespace, so it is also called `System.String`. We shall present its form in Chapter 4. If we look up `int` in the APIs we find that unlike `string`, it is aliased to a struct of a different name – `Int32`. Nevertheless, `Int32` (or `int`) provides the fields and methods shown in the following form.

INT OR INT32 STRUCT (ABBREVIATED)	
`// Static fields` `const int MinValue`	`// -2 147 483 648`
`const int MaxValue`	`//  2 147 483 647`
`// Static methods` `static int Parse(string s);`	
`// Instance methods` `string ToString();`	
There are a few more offerings in all categories: consult your API help facility or a comprehensive C# API reference manual. In addition, all the usual operators are available for integers.	

Random

We have introduced types informally, and then in this section started to specify them. Let us now do one more the other way – specify it then use it. The type is a class for random numbers. Its form is shown below. Thus we can imagine using Random to simulate the throwing of a dice as follows:

```
Random throw = new Random();
int dice = throw.Next(1,6);
```

RANDOM CLASS (ABBREVIATED)

```
// Constructors
Random()
Random(int seed);

//Instance Methods
int Next();
int Next(int maxValue);
int Next(int minValue, maxValue);
double NextDouble();
```

The constructors return random objects which will produce sequences of pseudo-random numbers. The Next methods return the next number in a sequence, perhaps between constrained values. NextDouble returns a value in the range 0.0 to 1.0.

The following example uses Random numbers as objects together with all the other API types introduced so far.

Example 2.8 Your lucky day

Suppose we would like to generate a lucky day from a program. To make the day random, we ask the user to enter a lucky number. This starts an individual sequence of numbers. Then we generate a day and a month from that sequence. At first glance, the following would be the statements to get the two numbers:

```
int luckyDay = r.Next(1,31);
int luckyMonth = r.Next(1,12);
```

However, we could end up generating an invalid pair of numbers this way, such as 31 4 (31st April) or even 29 2 (29 February) which might not always be valid. Since this is a 'magic' process, we can avoid problems by starting at March and only going up to day 30. Later on, in Chapter 4, we shall see how to handle the special cases and cover the complete year. The program, Lucky, follows.

File Lucky.cs

```
using System;

class Lucky {

    /// <summary>
    /// The Lucky Day program      Bishop and Horspool  Aug 2002
    /// =====================
    /// Generates a lucky day
    /// Illustrates using Random numbers
    /// </summary>

  void Go () {
    Console.WriteLine("The Lucky Day Program\n");
    Console.Write("What is your lucky number? ");
    int luckyNumber = int.Parse(Console.ReadLine());
    Random r = new Random(luckyNumber);
    int luckyDay = r.Next(1,30);
    int luckyMonth = r.Next(3,12);
    DateTime luckyDate = new DateTime
                (DateTime.Now.Year,luckyMonth,luckyDay);
    Console.WriteLine("Your lucky day will be " +
       luckyDate.DayOfWeek + " " + luckyDate.ToString("M"));
  }

  static void Main() {
    new Lucky().Go();
  }
}
```

Sample output would be:

```
The Lucky Day Program

What is your lucky number? 76
Your lucky day will be Saturday 13 April
```

It is instructive to analyze this program, looking at the types and data. We use five different types: Lucky (the class which forms the program), Console, int, Random and DateTime. There are the two usual methods that we declare – Go and Main – and some common ones that we call from the API, viz. WriteLine, Write, ReadLine, Parse, Next and ToString, The fields are luckyNumber, luckyDay, luckyMonth, luckyDate and r. The fields are declared as needed: see if you can rewrite the program with all the fields declared at the start of the class. There are also some properties and constructors used. Can you find these?

Finally, we note that a program should not be tested with one data item only. Run the program again and check that it does indeed generate different dates – though of course not those in January and February, as we engineered it.

Concepts in Chapter 2

This chapter introduced the following concepts (some of which are covered again):

program	program structure
class	method
parameter	statement
comment	concatenation
input and output	struct
property	simple expression
identifier	type
variable	variable declaration
initializing	operator
assignment	member

with these definitions, syntax forms and APIs:

object	type
simple type	structured type
accessing members	field declaration (simple)
instantiating an object	class for a simple program
simple input statements	DateTime struct (abbreviated)
int or int32 struct (abbreviated)	Random class (abbreviated)

and these operators and punctuation symbols:

{ }	;
( )	" "
.	+ - * /
=	

and made explicit use of the following C# keywords:

```
using                          class
string                         new
int
```

and these two forms of program comment:

```
//                             ///<...>
```

Quiz 57

Quiz

Q2.1 Given the definitions in this chapter, a type

    (a)   defines data and functions   (b)   represents a data value

    (c)   is comprised of objects   (d)   is either a struct or a class

Q2.2 Given the definitions and capitalization conventions in this chapter, the construct Part.Member can only be interpreted as accessing

    (a)   a property of an object   (b)   a method of a class

    (c)   a property of a class   (d)   a field of an object

Q2.3 To join two strings together, we use

    (a)   `concat`   (b)   `+`

    (c)   `&`   (d)   nothing

Q2.4 Reading an integer is done with

    (a)   `Console.ReadLine();`

    (b)   `int.Parse(Console.ReadLine());`

    (c)   `int.Parse.Console.Readline();`

    (d)   `Parse(Console.ReadLine());`

Q2.5 If two strings are to be read, they must be

    (a)   separated by semicolons   (b)   separated by spaces

    (c)   each enclosed in quotes   (d)   on separate lines

Q2.6 In the construct `DateTime.Today`, `Today` is a

    (a)   property   (b)   method

    (c)   constructor   (d)   field

Q2.7 If `endOfYear` and `now` are both `DateTime` variables, what is the type of `endOfYear-now`?

    (a)   `DateTime`   (b)   `int`

    (c)   `TimeSpan`   (d)   cannot tell

Q2.8 If `test` is a `Random` object, then what expression will return a value between 0 and 100?

    (a)   `Next.test(100)`   (b)   `test.Next(100)`

    (c)   `test(0,100)`   (d)   `test(Next(100))`

Q2.9 To get access to the `Console` class, we start a program with which directive?

    (a)   `access Console;`   (b)   `import Console;`

    (c)   `using Console;`   (d)   `using System;`

Q2.10 To create and start an object representing a program called `Test`, as described in this book, we use which statement?

    (a)   `new Test().Go();`   (b)   `new Test();`

    (c)   `Go(new Test());`   (d)   `Go.Test().Main();`

Exercises

Do these examples at the level of Section 2.2, that is, using general object-oriented principles, rather than C# specifically. Present your answers as text or as simple block diagrams.

2.1 **Boat racing game.** UPUV Games Inc. wants to develop a computer game where players are captains of boats, based on what you can see in the picture in Figure 2.1. Write a list of possible types the game will need to define, together with the data and functions for each. For some of the types, show what one or two objects of that type might look like.

2.2 **Dates.** Given that we have one structured type `Date` and two simple types `Integer` and `String`, construct a new structured type for a student enrolled in four courses at university. Be as elaborate as you like with the data, and include at least two functions that would be useful on student objects. Draw the diagram for the type, and then draw two objects of the time, filling in the values.

2.3 **Cameras.** Devise a type for photograph objects, including useful information that might be captured by a modern camera, such as the date and film speed.

2.4 **Kindergarten.** Children in a kindergarten have names, surnames, the group they are in (rabbits, puppies, goldfish or doves) and their date of birth. Create a `Child` type to hold this information about a child and devise some suitable methods that might be required. One of these should be a function which will return the year when the child will leave kindergarten, assuming that this is at age 6. Draw a diagram of the type, and show two objects that could be made from it, with their values.

2.5 **Book chapters.** Over the next few chapters, we are going to develop a program which keeps information about a textbook. Start by defining a `Chapter` type which records a chapter name and number of pages. Include a function that will return the starting page of the chapter. Can you think of any suitable functions at this stage? Using *C# Concisely* as test data, instantiate objects for the first four chapters.

The following exercises involve analyzing or modifying existing programs in the chapter.

2.6 **Analyzing Lucky.** Consider the program in Example 2.8, and analyze it into its constituent parts, as shown in Example 2.4.

2.7 **Correct times.** The program in Example 2.3 displays the year end with a time which is that of the time when the program ran. Fix it so that the `endOfYear` variable is constructed with 23:59 as the time. Hint: you will need the extra constructor shown in the `DateTime` form in Section 2.6.

2.8 **Extending meeting times.** Based on the assessment at the end of Example 2.5 on meeting times, devise some extensions to the programs. Specify them in the comment of the program, and update the program accordingly.

2.9 **Another picture.** Find another picture of your own and run the `FetchImage` program to display it. Does the size of the displayed window adapt to the size of your picture?

Here we have new programs to write from scratch.

2.10 **Library books.** Library books can be borrowed for 14 days. Write a program which reads in the name of a borrower and prints out a short receipt with today's date and the date the book must be returned. Get today's date from a `DateTime` property.

2.11 **Library books testing.** Alter the program in Exercise 2.10 so that it reads in today's date (rather than getting it from a `DateTime` property) and then test your program with various dates to check that it produces the correct answers. Dates to check are those that cross month and even year boundaries.

2.12 **Deadline.** An assignment deadline is given as a date and time. Write a program which reads in the deadline details and prints out how many hours remain till the assignment is due. Your program will need to use the `TimeSpan` class alluded to in the `DateTime` specification in Section 2.6.

2.13 **Boardroom clocks.** A bank has four clocks in its boardroom in London, set to the times at the major stock exchanges, namely London, New York, Tokyo and Hong Kong. Their offsets from UTC (Universal Standard Time) in winter are 0, 5, −9, −8. Write a program which reads in a time in London (in a format that you choose), instantiates objects for each of the four times, then prints them out with the city names. Explain to yourself why you cannot do the steps in this order: instantiate objects, read in time, change times on the objects, print out.

2.14 **Clocks anytime.** Redo Exercise 2.13 so that the time in London is chosen by means of random numbers.

CHAPTER 3

Inside objects

In Chapter 2 we established a foundation by using objects, so now we can see how to define new types of objects. We consider each part of a type in turn starting with fields, constructors and properties and moving on to the statements, expressions and simple types that go into making up methods and operators. The new statement introduced is the simple loop, so that interesting examples with considerable output can be written and discussed.

3.1 The structure of a type

Objects are declared from types. In Chapter 2 we made use of predefined types such as int, and namespace types such as DateTime. In this chapter we shall learn how to create our own structured types. In this way, the programming language becomes infinitely extensible, because in addition to the hundreds of built-in types in the API (like `DateTime`, `Console` and `Random`), we can define as many as we like of our own. We now look at the constituent parts of a type from the point of view of making one.

Data

The data of these new types consist of fields of existing types. These types may be from from the API, such as `int` or `string`, or may be ones we have already declared ourselves. For example, let us propose a type for information about examinations, including their dates. The data part could look like this:

```
struct Exam {
   string   course;
   int      weight; // percentage of the final mark
   string   lecturer;
   DateTime date;
   string   venue;

   static int totalNoOfExams = 0;
}
```

We have shown the data as fields for simplicity: we see below how we make them accessible via properties as well. We can now declare an `Exam` variable with some typical values as follows:

```
Exam COSExam = new Exam(
      "COS110",
      10,
      "Dr Brain",
      new DateTime(2003,4,20),
      "ELB4.2");
```

One of the fields of the `Exam` type is declared as static, which means that it will exist only once for all the `Exam` objects. In `totalNoOfExams`, we record the number of exams in the system across all objects. Moreover, we do not give this field a value in the instantiation, since its value is held and calculated by the type itself.

Functions

The function members of new types are much more interesting as with them we specify the actual behaviour that objects will follow. Behaviour is described in terms of *statements*, and up to now, we have had a very limited exposure to statements. The main ones we have dealt with are

◆   input

◆   output

- ◆ method call

- ◆ assignment.

In this chapter we shall complete the discussion of these four, and learn about a simple loop as well. The remaining statement options are covered in Chapter 4.

   We now go through how functions are defined, and also how to design and group functions to make a coherent and usable set for deployment in a new type. We have already identified four kinds of functions – constructors, properties, methods and operators. Each of these will play a part in what follows.

Constructors

Every type needs a constructor. A constructor is a sequence of statements with the same name as the type which is called when objects of the type are created. For example,

```
DateTime meeting = new DateTime(now.Year, now.Month, now.Day,
    startTime, 0, 0);
```

calls a constructor for `DateTime`. A type can have several constructors, as long as the parameter lists (known as the *signatures*) are different. Another constructor for `DateTime` is used in

```
DateTime endOfYear = new DateTime(now.Year, 12, 31);
```

In order to look at what constructors are like inside, consider a constructor for an `Exam` type, as defined above.

```
Exam(string c, int w, string l, DateTime d, string v) {
   course   = c;
   weight   = w;
   lecturer = l;
   date     = d;
   venue    = v;
   total   += 1;
}
```

Constructors typically copy the values of the parameters supplied into the object's fields, and that's all. Since the parameters and the fields refer to the same things, one convention is to name the parameters with suitable (non-conflicting) initials only.

   Seeing that constructors initialize the fields of an object, how does this match any initializing that might be done when fields are declared? In fact, there are certain rules about structs and initializing fields, as summarized in Table 3.1.

   In other words, the values of the instance fields of a struct must be set inside a constructor, not where fields are declared.

concept	structs
Instance fields	May not be initialized at declaration
Static fields	May be initialized at declaration
If a constructor	All fields must be initialized (not just some)
If no constructor	Values of fields are set to the default for the type, e.g. zero for numbers and null for strings

Table 3.1 Initializing fields of structs

Continuing our example, suppose there are some exams whose venues are not known when the timetable is set up. We could have a second constructor as follows:

```
Exam(string c, int w, string l, DateTime d) {
   course   = c;
   weight   = w;
   lecturer = l;
   date     = d;
   venue    = "To be announced";
   total    +=1;
}
```

There will be no confusion as to which constructor is required, since one needs five parameters and one takes four. Suitable instantiations would be:

```
Exam computers = new Exam("COS110", 50, "Prof Watson",
                          new DateTime(2003,11,13));
Exam maths = new Exam("MATH152", 80, "Dr James",
                          new DateTime(2003,11,18),"Old Hall");
```

C#'s other structured type, the class, provides a default constructor for classes that also leaves all the fields in an initialized state. This again means 0 or 0.0 for numbers, and null for most other objects.

Methods and properties

At the simple method level, we can complete our Exam example with a few well-chosen methods, shown here in one line each, without any statements yet.

```
public TimeSpan DaysToTheExam() { ... }
public override string ToString() { ... }
```

The first method will look at the date field of the object and calculate how many days there are from today's date until then. The second is used to print values. It replaces another method of the same name which is provided in the System class by default, and is called directly from Console.WriteLine statements. It needs the modifier override because it replaces another method. The modifier public is needed for both methods so that they can be seen by, and thus called from, code outside the struct.

Why are there only two methods? Well, it turns out that most of the useful functions in this type – and in many types – are provided by properties. In the first instance, these return the value of fields, but they can also be used to set them. Thus we can postulate the following properties, without yet knowing how we declare a property.

```
public string Course
public int Weight
public string Lecturer
public DateTime Date
public string Venue
public static int Total
```

Accessibility. Notice that we used a modifier, `public`, for both methods and for each of the properties. This modifier is necessary, so that they can be seen outside of the type. By not using `public` on the fields though, they are regarded as private to the type.

The data declared for the struct (`course`, `weight`, and so on) did not have a `public` modifier, and therefore would by default be private. It is normal that data will be private while methods and properties are public.

Type layout

All the ingredients of a type can be present in any order, but there are conventions. Normally, we put data first, then constructors, then methods and operators. With this in mind, consider the form for a struct shown below. The form for the definition of a class is the same, with the keyword `struct` being replaced by `class`.

STRUCT DEFINITION

```
modifiers struct classid {
   field-declarations
   constructors
   property-declarations
   method-declarations
   operator-declarations
   other-declarations
}
```

The elements of a type can appear in any order, though the above order is conventional. The other declarations include events and indexers, which are covered later in the book.

3.2 Fields and properties

A major part of any type is its data, which is represented by the fields that are declared for it. As seen in the general discussion on types in Chapter 2, fields can be variables (most of the time) or constants (rarely). What C# has that most other languages don't, is the concept of a property. A *property* reflects an aspect of the class. Often but not exclusively, it is just the value of a field of an almost identical name. If we made the field itself accessible to all other objects, then they could read it and change it. By specifying a property as well, we can protect the field, and control access to it from within the object's type. This technique is known as *encapsulation*.

The syntax for defining properties is given in the form below.

PROPERTY DEFINITION

```
public type propertyid {
   get {statements including a return name;}
   set {statements including an assignment to name;}
}
```

The body of get defines what happens when the propertyid is used, for example on the right of an assignment, or as a method argument.
The body of set defines what happens when the propertyid is used, for example on the left of an assignment.
Either one or both of the property methods needs to be present.

The keywords get and set signify that assignment is available for that field.

Once the property has been declared, it can be used instead of the field it is protecting. We have seen many examples of this process in Chapter 2 with built-in types. Now let us look at an example assuming we have already defined the Exam type. A property for changing the venue would be defined as:

```
public string Venue {
   get { return venue; }
   set { venue = value; }
}
```

value is a special word in this context that indicates the value of the right-hand side of an assignment to the Venue property. Examples of using this property are:

```
Console.WriteLine("The exam is in " + COSExam.Venue);

// Now change the venue
COSExam.Venue = "HSB3.10";
```

If we define a property without a set part, then changes are not allowed to the underlying variable. For example, suppose we wish to prevent changing the name of the exam. We would write:

```
public string Course {
   get {return course;}
}
```

Now let's put all our new knowledge about data and functions into creating a new type.

Example 3.1 A StarLord type

A central feature of computer games is the setting up of characters that battle each other for supremacy. Supposing we were to write a program for such a game. We would start by setting up a type for such characters. The type is called `StarLord` and it is represented by the following C# struct.

File StarLord.cs

```csharp
using System;

/// <summary>
/// StarLord characters       Bishop and Horspool    May 2002
/// ====================
/// Characters have certain characteristics and the
/// ability to battle against other StarLords
/// </summary>

public struct StarLord {

    string name;
    int strength, points;
    static Random r = new Random();

    public StarLord(string n, int s) {
        name = n;
        strength = s;
        points = s;
    }

    public string Name {
        get {return name;}
    }
    public int Points {
        get {return points;}
        set {points = value;}
    }
    public int Strength {
        get {return strength;}
    }

    public void Attack(StarLord opponent) {
        int damage = r.Next(strength/3,points/2);
        opponent.Points -= damage;
    }

    public override string ToString() {
        return name + " at " + points;
    }
}
```

We have sufficient understanding of types to know that we could declare two `StarLord` objects as follows:

```
StarLord lord1, lord2;
```

and then instantiate them with:

```
lord1 = new StarLord("Darth", 14);
lord2 = new StarLord("Bilbo", 10);
```

Notice that the `points` field is initialized by the constructor, although it does not have a corresponding parameter.

The two objects could then interact through the defined method `Attack` as in:

```
lord1.Attack(lord2);
```

Inside `Attack` the following statements are executed:

```
int damage = r.Next(strength/3+points/2);
opponent.Points -= damage;
```

The amount of damage is calculated based on the current strength of the character and its current points. This amount is then subtracted from the points of the opponent. In this case, the object is `lord1` (with the name of Darth) and the opponent as called in the `Attack` method is `lord2` (with the name of Bilbo).

The `StarLord` class has three properties, `Name`, `Points` and `Strength`. The properties protect the variables so that `name` and `strength` can only be read (`get`), but `points` can be read and changed (`get` and `set`).

Static and instance properties

We have already seen in the API descriptions in Section 2.6 that some properties are declared as static. This means that they apply for all objects of the type. We can also meaningfully define static properties. In the `Exam` type, the `totalNoOfExams` field was static, and would probably have a corresponding static property. In the same way, suppose we wanted to keep track of how many starlords are in existence in the universe. Then we would augment the `StarLord` type as follows:

```
static int count = 0;
public static int Count {
  get {return count;}
}
```

which would be called as

```
Console.WriteLine("There are "+StarLord.Count+" StarLords now");
```

and of course the constructor would need to be suitably updated to increment `count` on each creation.

Example 3.2 A Time type

Even though we used C#'s `DateTime` type extensively in Chapter 2, we can still envisage opportunities when there would be a need for a simple stripped down version, just for times, say. Having learnt about constructors and properties and seen the StarLord example, we are in a good position to define such a type. What this example shows is that there is more than one design, culminating in more than one type, with different ways of accessing the data.

First, we start by defining the data:

```
int hour, min;
```

By default, these fields are private to the type. To make their values accessible, we could say

```
public int hour, min;
```

However, this would allow indiscriminate and possibly conflicting changes to `hour` and `min`. An alternative is to say that a time object is immutable, meaning that once it is created, it cannot be altered. Variations will result in new objects. This leads to the constructor:

```
public Time (int h, int m) {
   hour = h;
   min = m;
}
```

and the two properties

```
public Hour {
   get {return hour;}
}

public Min {
   get {return min}
}
```

which allow 'read-only' access to the corresponding fields.

What else does a type need? It needs its outside structure, and almost always a `ToString` method. Thus we can present the complete version of a simple time type:

File Time.cs

```
struct Time {

   /// <summary>
```

```
/// The little Time class
/// =======================
/// Stores hours and minutes
/// Does not check the times supplied
/// Once created, objects cannot be altered
/// </summary>

int hour, min;

public Time(int h, int m) {
  hour = h;
  min = m;
}

public int Hour {
  get {return hour;}
}

public int Min {
  get {return min;}
}

public override string ToString() {
  return hour + ":" + min;
}
}
```

Suppose we wanted to create a time, change the hour to 12 and print out both times. We cannot say:

```
Time a = new Time(someHour, someMin);
Console.WriteLine(a);
a.Hour = 12;                     // invalid
Console.WriteLine(a);
```

because Hour is a property without a set part. Instead we say:

```
Time a = new Time(someHour, someMin);
Console.WriteLine(a);
a = new Time(12, a.Min);
Console.WriteLine(a);
```

or even better as follows:

```
Time a = new Time(someHour, someMin);
Console.WriteLine(a);
Time b = new Time(12, a.Min);
Console.WriteLine(b);
```

where a and b now exist independently and can be changed and altered at will.

3.3 Numeric types

C# inherits 11 numeric types from the family of C languages. They are grouped as follows:

- ◆ integer, signed (sbyte, short, int, long),

- ◆ integer, unsigned (byte, ushort, uint, ulong),

- ◆ real, floating-point (float, double),

- ◆ real, fixed-point (decimal).

Of these, the ones most frequently used in everyday programming are int and double, as the most convenient representatives of integer and real.

The numeric types have certain characteristics in common:

1. Each of the four groups has a different way of *representing* the numbers in the computer, in terms of the layout of bits. The layout affects the values we can and cannot use and the errors that may occur in precision.

2. Each type has a *size* and uses a certain number of bits from 8 to 96. The size also affects the magnitude of the numbers that can be stored.

3. Each type corresponds directly to a *struct type* in the System namespace, the implications of which are discussed in Chapter 8.

4. Values of one type can generally be *converted* to another, provided that the second type can contain all the values of the first. Thus a short value can be stored in a long variable, but not vice versa without an explicit conversion, and then the conversion might fail. See below for more on conversions.

Table 3.2 gives some details of a selection of five types, with examples. There is a considerable amount of information in this table. Let's go through it carefully.

Integer types

We discuss three integer types – byte, int and long. The byte type is unsigned, and int and long are signed.

A *byte* is a number stored in 8 bits, without a sign, so all the bits are counted for positive values, giving $2^8 = 256$ combinations of zeros and ones. Since one of the combinations is used for 0, the maximum value is 255. Byte values are used when we are writing system programs that manipulate values in the computer at the byte level.

For most of our *integer* value programming, we shall use the int type. The int type gives us 11 digits, which is a pretty big number. Because we are dealing with positive and

Type	Bits	Value range	Approx. digits	Examples
byte	8	0 to 255	3	128 255
int	32	−2147483648 to 21474836487	11	10654 −18765
long	64	$\pm 9 \times 10^{18}$	18	10000000 −1234567890
double	64	$\pm 5.0 \times 10^{-324}$ to $\pm 1.7 \times 10^{308}$	15 to 16	−16.56 8E-06
decimal	96	$\pm 1.0 \times 10^{-28}$ to $\pm 7.9 \times 10^{28}$	28	49.99M −9999.9999M

Table 3.2 Details of selected numeric types

negative values, the actual largest absolute value is 2^{31}, which is in fact the number specified in Table 3.2. There is one fewer positive number than negative, because zero has to be represented as well. If we briefly look at the sbyte type in comparison, we see that it would follow the same pattern. Its 8 bits provide 256 combinations, and are used to represent integers ranging from −127 to 128, including 0 of course.

Long is in the same signed integer group as int but because an 18 digit number is extremely hard to read, we have abbreviated the values to an approximation based on the number of digits that will be represented. 2^{63} (remember half the numbers are negative and the other half are non-negative) is approximately 10^{18}.

Floating point types

We included long in our table because it provides an interesting contrast to double. The two types have the same number of bits, but very different value ranges and number of digits. This is because double values are represented completely differently. The representation is composed of two signed parts, the mantissa and the exponent. The mantissa is the value of the number starting with a digit, then the point, then the rest of the number. The exponent then indicates where the point should actually be among the digits represented. This is known as floating point representation. Although, in the computer, everything is done in binary, we can show the effect of floating point by considering some examples written as ordinary decimal numbers. Consider Table 3.3.

Example (a) is straightforward, but note that if these are to be double values, then they must have a decimal point: values without a point are assumed to be integers. Examples (b)–(g) of the table show the advantage of the floating point representation: zeros at the beginning or end of the number do not appear in the mantissa's representation, but their value is retained in the exponent. Thus the mantissa has more room for more *significant* digits, no matter what the size of the number. This advantage is shown in example (f) which has a number with 19 digits. Table 3.2 reveals that double numbers can have 15–16 digits, but these are only the significant digits. The same number is represented in example

	Number	Mantissa	Exponent
(a)	5.0	0.5	1
(b)	0.005	0.5	-2
(c)	-0.005	-0.5	-2
(d)	5000.0	0.5	4
(e)	500300.0	0.5003	6
(f)	5003000000000000000.0	0.5003	21
(g)	0.00000000000000000005	0.5	-19
(h)	5003000000000.0000077	0.5003	16
(i)	5.0E60	0.5	61
(j)	5.0E-60	0.5	59

Table 3.3 Examples of floating point numbers

(e) as in (f) but with a different exponent. Similarly in example (g), the 5 would not fit in a 16-digit number, but by floating the point it does.

Nevertheless floating point cannot do everything, and sometimes accuracy may be compromised. In example (h), the whole number is significant, all 20 digits, but only the first 15 or 16 can be represented. The last few digits disappear and the number will be returned to the user in a less accurate state than read in.

Examples (i) and (j) illustrate E format (standing for exponential format) whereby we can write a number with an exponent. This format is useful when there are many zeros on one or other side of the point. For example, example (f) could be written in a program as 5.003E20. It could also be written as 50.03E19 if that made more sense to the user. There are some quiz questions on floating point notation at the end of the chapter.

Fixed point types

The last type shown in Table 3.2, `decimal`, is an interesting one. Like the floating point types, it also represents real numbers, but its distinguishing feature is that it represents them precisely, and there is no loss of accuracy. There are always 28 digits. However, the range of values is much more limited.

Decimal numbers in programs must be written with an 'M' after them. They are mostly used in financial matters. For example, we might say:

```
decimal taxRate = 12.50M;
```

Most of the other types shown in Table 3.2 will also have letters to distinguish their values from the more commonly used ones. For example, to write a number that would be of a `float` type rather than a `double`, F must be used instead of E, as in 3.145F0. On the other hand, L, standing for `long`, is optional.

3.4 Expressions

We now come to one of the most important sections of programming: how to write expressions. We mentioned expressions briefly at the end of Section 2.4. Now we shall cover them in detail.

Expressions are the representation in computer language of mathematical formulae, but there are several differences. The rules concerning what kind of values can be combined, and what answers result are tied more to the underlying computer's types than to mathematics, and these rules need to be understood and remembered. Then there are other kinds of expressions in addition to numeric ones – relational, string and bit expressions are some of these. Finally, there are expression statements, of which the assignment is one.

Numerical operators

Operators are used with numbers and fields and functions to build expressions. C# provides operators that correspond to ordinary arithmetic practice, as well as some new ones. The first batch are + − * and /. The * is used for multiplication. Because expressions are always written on one line, the / is used for division. We often need parentheses to ensure that the sense of the expression comes through correctly. Examples of expressions are:

```
cost*exchangeRate
temp*9.0 / 5 - 32
(b * b - 4 * a * c)/(2 * a)
```

Each operator is valid for each of the types. What happens, then, when we mix types in an expression? The simple answer is that the result is *promoted* to the type with the greater range. For the types int, long and double, this implies that

---

TYPE PROMOTION (ABBREVIATED)

◆ if either operand is double, the result is double,

◆ otherwise if either operand is long, the result is long,

◆ otherwise the result is int.

For operations on bytes, the result is always converted to an int. For decimals, the result will be a decimal, except that floating point numbers cannot be mixed with decimals without a conversion (conversions are covered below).[1]

An important spin-off of these rules is that division applied to integers produces an integer result. So for example we have:

---

1. These rules are stated in full in the *ECMA C# Language Specification*, Section 14.2.6.

```
7 / 3            = 2
3 / 4            = 0
```

Thus if we write the fraction one half as `1/2` in a program, it will actually be evaluated as zero.

Finally, the operator, `%`, computes the modulus, or remainder, after division. For example, suppose we have a number of minutes to be converted to hours and minutes, we could do it thus:

```
int totalMins, hours, mins;
totalMins = int.Parse(Console.ReadLine());
hours = totalMins / 60;    // uses integer division
mins = totalMins % 60;     // what is left over
Console.WriteLine(totalMins+" minutes = "+
                  hours+" hours, "+mins+" minutes");
```

Putting the value of 429 in, we would have:

```
429 minutes = 7 hours, 9 minutes
```

and entering −429 would produce the output

```
-429 minutes = -7 hours, -9 minutes
```

Note that 7×60+9 = 429, and −7×60−9 = −429. In general, if x and y are two numbers, then the division and remainder operators satisfy the mathematical identity

$$(x/y) \times y + (x\%y) = x$$

To complete the description of the `%` operator, note that 7%–2 evaluates to 1 and −7%–2 evaluates to −1. That is, the remainder always has the same sign as the left operand. Note that the `%` operator works for all the numeric types, not just the integers.

Example 3.3 The shuttle bus

An airport shuttle bus leaves the airport for downtown on every hour and half hour. Given a time in hours and minutes, we would like to show the time of the next bus. Our sense of time is so well developed, that this is a trivial exercise for us, but for a computer it requires a bit more in the way of computation.

The problem divides up into two parts: representing a time, and doing the computing for 'next bus'. Since we have already started developing a simple time type in Example 3.2, let us start with that. From it, we can create a time object as in

```
Time now = new Time(h, m);
```

where h and m are read in and work with `now.Hour` and `now.Min`.

Moving on, the calculation is quite intricate:

```
int nextBusInMins = (now.TimeInMins+30)/30*30;
```

This takes some explanation. If N is an integer, then $N/30$ is the integer result of dividing by 30. Thus $N/30*30$ is another integer which is a multiple of 30 but is likely to be smaller than N because rounding down usually occurs during the division. The expression will be equal to N only when N is divisible by 30. The formula $(N+30)/30*30$ will give the next higher multiple of 30.

Let us take an example with times. Supposing the time is 9:45. We can get from the object that time measured in minutes (a new property was added to `Time` to perform this operation), i.e. $9\times60+45 = 585$. Adding 30 to the minutes gives 615. Then dividing by 30, using integer division, gives 20. Multiplying that by 30 gives 600 minutes or 10 hours, being the time 10:00. We construct a new `Time` object from this, using a second constructor as follows:

```
public Time(int t) {
   hour = t / 60;
   min = t % 60;
}
```

So the next statement in the main program will be:

```
Time nextBus = new Time(nextBusInMins);
```

One improvement we can make to the program is to generalize it for bus intervals other than 30. Supposing in summer the buses go every 20 minutes. We do not want to dig through the program to find all the places where 30 occurs. So instead we change them at this stage to a field name, and declared the field a constant. This is done in the program that follows.

Now, armed with two time objects, we can proceed to the printing part of the program. Here is the entire file:

File Shuttle.cs

```
using System;

class ShuttleBus {

   /// <summary>
   /// Shuttle Bus Program        Bishop and Horspool August 2002
   /// ====================
   /// Calculates the time of the next bus on the hour or half hour
   ///
   /// Illustrates struct definition, properties and
   /// numeric operators including modulus.
   /// </summary>
```

```
    const int interval = 30;

    void Go() {
      Console.WriteLine("What is the time? ");
      Console.Write("Hour: ");
      int hours = int.Parse(Console.ReadLine());
      Console.Write("Min:  ");
      int mins = int.Parse(Console.ReadLine());

      Time now = new Time(hours,mins);
      int nextBusInMins = (now.TimeInMins+interval)
                          /interval*interval;
      Time nextBus = new Time(nextBusInMins);
      Console.WriteLine("Time is "+now+
                   " and the next bus is at "+nextBus);
    }

    static void Main() {
      new ShuttleBus().Go();
    }
}

struct Time {

  /// <summary>
  /// The little Time class
  /// ======================
  /// Stores hours and minutes; Does not check the times supplied
  /// Once created, objects cannot be altered
  /// </summary>

  int hour, min;
  public Time(int h, int m) {
    hour = h;
    min = m;
  }
  public Time(int t) {
    hour = t / 60;
    min = t % 60;
  }
  public int Hour {
    get {return hour;}
  }
  public int Min {
    get {return min;}
  }
  public int TimeInMins {
    get {return hour * 60 + min;}
  }
  public override string ToString() {
    return hour + ":" + min;
  }
}
```

To test the program, we start by running with one time, say 9:14. The output will be

```
What is the time?
Hour: 9
Min: 14
Time is 9:14 and the next bus is at 9:30
```

To test the program thoroughly, we need to enter a variety of times aimed at checking what are known as the boundary conditions. A suitable set of test data would be:

```
9  14
9  29
9  30
9  45
9  59
10 00
23 35
```

What will happen in the last case? If we read the summary of the `Time` type we see that in fact no checking is done on the values, so this one will go by and the result will be 24:05.

Relational expressions

The next step with numbers is to compare two of them. To this end, most languages provide a variety of relational operators, namely

==	equal to
!=	not equal to
<	less than
>	greater than
<=	less than or equal to
>=	greater than or equal to

The result of comparing two such values is a value of type `bool`, standing for boolean, which can be `true` or `false`. Full details of the `bool` type, which has its own operators, are discussed in Chapter 4. Here we merely note that we can compare numbers. These comparisons will be used to govern loops, which we discuss next.

Each of the operators exists for each of the numeric types. If we mix numeric types in a comparison, then the operator of the 'higher' type is used, as in:

COMPARISON RESULT TYPES

◆ if either operand is `double`, the comparison is done as `double`,

◆ otherwise if either result is `long`, the comparison is done as `long`,

◆ otherwise the comparison is done as `int`.

Because floating point types are not represented precisely for every value, it is best to avoid equality operations on them. Inequality operations will usually suffice.

Examples of relational expressions are:

```
i < 10
t.Year == 2003
DateTime.Now != first
x >= y
```

Increment and decrement operators

Two special operators exist for the numeric types. They are ++ and -- and they can be used to add or subtract one from a variable in an expression. However, most often, they are used standalone instead of inside an expression, so one would see

```
i++;
mass--;
```

The meaning is that one is added to (or subtracted from) the value of the variable. The above statements would be equivalent to

```
i = i+1;
mass = mass-1;
```

There are, in fact, two forms of the ++ and -- operators. It is possible to write either x++ or ++x, and similarly with the -- operator. When used as standalone statements, there is no difference between the prefix and postfix forms of these operators. (Programs in this book always use the operators in standalone statements.) We'll see these operators also being used in loops below.

Assignment operators

Although the primary assignment operator is =, there is a syntax for combining one of the arithmetic operators and creating an assignment operator. For the numbers, these would be

```
+=
-=
*=
/=
%=
```

In all cases, the meaning is to apply the right-hand side of the assignment to the left-hand side's value, then return the result for assigning to the left-hand side again. Thus

```
i += 2;
mass -= 5;
```

add 2 to i and subtract 5 from mass respectively. These operators are essentially short-hands, but save on typing and are popular with C# programmers.

Another extension of assignment is *multiple assignments*. Thus it is valid to say:

```
september = april = june = november = 30;
```

in one line. The assignment operator is, as we shall explain further below, right associative, so the assignments will be done from the right.

Precedence and associativity

Finally, we consider the precedence of all the operators so far. *Precedence* is the concept which governs which operators are executed before others. In normal mathematical formula, multiplication is always done before subtraction, no matter which comes first, so that 10-3*2 gives the answer 4, not 14. Fortunately, in C# the operators work as we would think they would. Table 3.4 lists the operators in the official C# groups. The first group has highest precedence, and so on down.

Group	Operators[1]	Associativity
Primary	`(x)  x.y  f(x)  ++  --  new`	right
Unary	`-`	right
Multiplicative	`*  /  %`	left
Additive	`+  -`	left
Relational	`<  >  <=  >=`	left
Equality	`==  !=`	left
Assignment	`=  *=  /=  %=  +=  -=`	right

[1.] where *x* represents a variable or expression; *y* represents a field or function; and *f* is a function

Table 3.4 Operator precedence and associativity

Associativity dictates how evaluation is performed between operators that are in the same group. All the binary operators are left associative (except for assignment). The unary operators such as dot and new are right associative. So expressions including several plus operators are evaluated from left to right (left associative). The same would apply to minus operators, which is what we want. For example,

```
10 - 4 - 1 + 3
```

should produce 8. We would not expect it to be evaluated as in

```
10 - (4 - (1 + 3))
```

which would give 10.

In practice, the arithmetic operators cause no problems, but one does have to be careful when they interact with the primary and relational groups. Table 3.5 lists some examples which should help clarify the concepts involved.

Expression	Calculated as
`1 + 2/3 + 4`	`1 + (2 / 3) + 4`
`x+y > p+q`	`(x + y) > (p + q)`
`today.Hour + 10`	`(today.Hour) + 10`

Table 3.5 Precedence examples

Conversions

We have alluded to conversions several times. In essence the situation in C# is quite easy to understand. A value can be promoted to the next higher type implicitly. Such an *implicit conversion* might be needed when mixing values in an expression. The rules were spelled out on page 74. In order to convert the other way, i.e. from a larger type to a smaller, we need an *explicit conversion*. The form is

```
EXPLICIT CONVERSION

(typeid) expression
checked ((typeid) expression)
```

> The expression is evaluated and converted to the type specified, with possible loss of information. Real numbers are rounded towards zero to make integral values.
> If the type cannot hold the resulting value and checking is turned on, an error called an `OverflowException` occurs.
> Placing checked in front of the conversion forces the exception to happen, even if the checking option is off in the compiler.

So for example, if we have:

```
int i = 6;
double x = 3.14;
double y = 5.003000000008E+15;
double z;
```

then the following assignments have the effects described in the comments:

```
z = i;        // always valid - value is 6.0
i = x;        // compiler error - must explicitly convert
i = y;        // compiler error - must explicitly convert
i = (int) x;  // valid - value is 3;
i = (int) y;  // execution error if checked is on,
              // unspecified value otherwise
```

The value of i in the last case in an unchecked context would be −1244672188 which bears no relation to y except that some of y's bits were interpreted as an integer. The same kind of behaviour will happen, for example, between integers and bytes, or any two numeric types where explicit conversion is needed.[1]

Clearly, checking number conversions is important, and one should ensure that the checked option is set in the environment in which one is working. Alternatively, the checked context can be used for a particular statement, as shown in the form above.

An explicit conversion and a checked context use parentheses round the expression they are applied to, and they are deemed to be primary operators, as shown in Table 3.4.

3.5 Simple loops

Expressions are a mainstay of any program, but they only become really useful when they are repeated over and over again. Then the true power of a machine like a computer comes into play. Humans are no longer very good or very patient with performing repetitive tasks. We need to let the computer take over. Therefore we introduce here a very simple structure for performing a loop.

This simple loop is governed by a count of how many times we want an operation to be performed. Other loops discussed in the next chapter are more elaborate. The keyword that introduces our loop is for, and therefore these loops are known as for loops. Here is the form:

FOR LOOP (SIMPLE)

```
for (int loopid=start; loopid<=limit; loopid++) {
   body
}
```

The *loopid* acquires the values from start to limit and the statements that form the body are repeated limit-start+1 times.
loopid++ can be replaced by any other expression that updates loopid, such as loopid+=2 or loopid--.

For example, a loop such as

```
for (int i=1; i<=10; i++) {...}
```

will execute 10 times, and i will successively have the values 1 to 10. So, to print a string three times, we can use a loop such as the following.

---

1. The full rules for explicit numeric conversions are in the *C# Language Specifications*, Section 6.2.1.

```
for (int i=1; i<=3; i++) {
   Console.WriteLine("Hip Hip Hooray");
}
```

The loop would give

```
Hip Hip Hooray
Hip Hip Hooray
Hip Hip Hooray
```

The first class of programs that benefit from loops are those that print tables. Let us pick up from an example in Chapter 2.

Example 3.4 Table of meeting times

We would like to review all possible meeting times over the day. Taking Example 2.7, we can adapt it to print a table like this:

```
London      New York
08:00 AM    03:00 AM
09:00 AM    04:00 AM
10:00 AM    05:00 AM
11:00 AM    06:00 AM
12:00 PM    07:00 AM
01:00 PM    08:00 AM
02:00 PM    09:00 AM
03:00 PM    10:00 AM
04:00 PM    11:00 AM
05:00 PM    12:00 PM
06:00 PM    01:00 PM
```

If we recall, in the original program, there were two statements that created two objects, once the details had been read in and before the answers were printed out. These were:

```
DateTime meeting = new DateTime(now.Year,now.Month,
                            now.Day,startTime,0,0);
DateTime offsetMeeting = meeting.AddHours(offset);
```

Pictorially, for an offset of −5, this produce objects as shown in Figure 3.1. Notice that we have shown fields of the objects equivalent to the properties that we have access to, rather than the properties.

Now, in order to produce the table, we need several such pairs of values. But do we need several objects? The answer is no. We can declare the objects outside the loop, and then alter their values each time round. The for loop that matches the table above would be:

```
for (int hour=8; hour<=18; hour++)
```

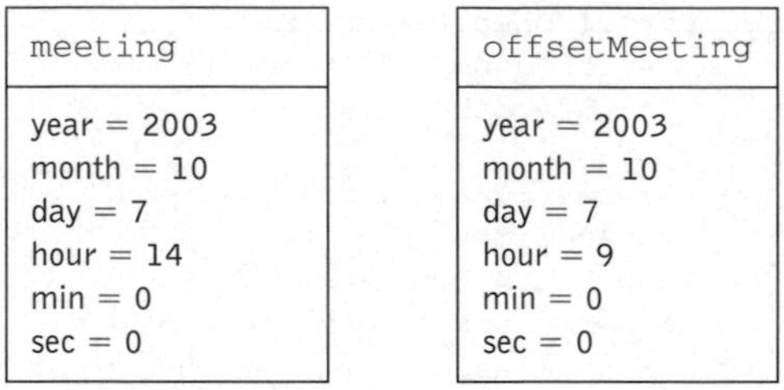

meeting
year = 2003
month = 10
day = 7
hour = 14
min = 0
sec = 0

offsetMeeting
year = 2003
month = 10
day = 7
hour = 9
min = 0
sec = 0

Figure 3.1 DateTime objects

In other words, hour will go from 8 to 18, which is equivalent to 8am to 6pm in the 12 hour clock format. The creation of the meeting object changes as follows:

```
meeting = new DateTime(now.Year, now.Month, now.Day, hour, 0, 0);
```

We can imagine that the values in the fields of the objects shown in Figure 3.1 will change each time round the loop, with a new hour value being inserted. The second column in the table is taken from the object

```
offsetMeeting = meeting.AddHours(offset);
```

which already has the information for the current time, and just has the hours updated.

The full program is as follows.

File TimeLoop.cs

```
using System;

class TimeLoop {

  /// <summary>
  /// Time Looping Program      Bishop and Horspool   August 2002
  /// ====================
  /// Presents a table of times from one city to another
  /// Shows a simple for loop
  /// </summary>

  void Go() {
    string city;
    int offset;
    DateTime now = DateTime.UtcNow;

    //Read in the second city's details
    Console.WriteLine("Table of times in London and ");
    Console.Write("City? ");
    city = Console.ReadLine();
```

```
        Console.Write("Offset from London? ");
        offset = int.Parse(Console.ReadLine());
        Console.WriteLine("London      "+city);
        DateTime meeting, offsetMeeting;

        for (int hour=8; hour<=18; hour++) {
          meeting = new DateTime
            (now.Year,now.Month,now.Day,hour,0,0);
          offsetMeeting = meeting.AddHours(offset);
          Console.WriteLine(meeting.ToShortTimeString()+"     "+
            offsetMeeting.ToShortTimeString());
        }
      }

      static void Main() {
        new TimeLoop().Go();
      }
    }
```

The full output is:

```
Table of times in London and
City? New York
Offset from London? -5
London      New York
08:00 AM    03:00 AM
09:00 AM    04:00 AM
10:00 AM    05:00 AM
11:00 AM    06:00 AM
12:00 PM    07:00 AM
01:00 PM    08:00 AM
02:00 PM    09:00 AM
03:00 PM    10:00 AM
04:00 PM    11:00 AM
05:00 PM    12:00 PM
06:00 PM    01:00 PM
```

Example 3.5 Book chapters

We have been asked to find the total number of pages in a book of four chapters, and to produce a table of contents. We will be given as data the titles of the chapters and the number of pages in each. This example involves a bit more thought in the design and use of a loop. In order to concentrate on the loop, we do not declare a type for the chapters, though we could do so.

Although at the outset, the requirements for printing out a contents seem to bear no relation at all to finding the time of a meeting, let us consider Example 3.4 and use it as a blueprint. Both solutions require the following sections:

- ◆ Setup

- ◆ Loop

- ◆ Body – input, process, output, update

- ◆ Finalize

If we are to calculate page numbers, then we shall have to set a running count of pages to 1 to start with. We also need to initialize the chapter's number to 1. C#'s default of zero would not be helpful here. This would form our Setup section.

Then there will be a loop, over all the chapters. Inside the loop we shall have to read the chapter name and number of pages. That will be the body-input section. In Example 3.4, the input was actually the creation of the next time object value. Clearly there is also a body-output section, because we need to print out the chapter and its starting page. The starting page will already be there for this chapter, but at the end of each time through the loop, we need to calculate the starting page for the next chapter, or the end of the book if this is the last chapter. Finally, we can print out the result of the process, which is the length of the whole book.

Armed with this design, we can now write the program in sections quite easily. Apart from the starting page number that we are quite aware of, we can make provision for a chapter number in the program.

Setup:
```
int chapNumber;
int pages;
int startingPage = 1;
int lastChapter = 4;
```
Loop:
```
for (int i=1; i<=lastChapter; i++) {
```
Input:
```
// For chapNumber, read chapName and pages
```
Output:
```
// Write out the details of the chapter
// and its starting page
```
Update:
```
startingPage += pages;
```
Finalize:
```
Console.WriteLine("Total pages = " + startingPage);
```

We omit from the statements the details of declarations and the class and method structure, so we can concentrate on the logic of the process itself. We also reduce the input and output statements down to comments, because they can get quite messy in reality, and we just capture the sense of those sections.

Is the program correct as it stands? Let us check it out for some preliminary data, such as the following.

```
Introduction              18
Basics                    30
Advanced Concepts         43
Conclusion                5
```

To check a program, we write down the variables we are dealing with, and successively update them, working through the program exactly as if we were the computer.

Variables:

```
startingPage         1 19 49 91 96
chapNumber           1
```

Output:

```
Chapter 1 Introduction         1
Chapter 1 Basics              19
Chapter 1 Advanced Concepts   49
Chapter 1 Conclusion          91
Total pages is 96
```

Clearly, all is not correct. The output lists each chapter as number 1. Where is the error? Well, we set `chapNumber` in the setup section, with the presumption that it would be updated after each chapter, just as `startingPage` would be. However, the appropriate statement does not appear in the update section. If we consider the logic, we see that the chapter number is the same as the loop variable. Thus we can exclude `chapNumber` as a loop variable, and instead make a loop based on `i`.

Loop:

```
for (int i = 1; i<=lastChapter; i++) {
```

with appropriate changes elsewhere. If we now check the program again, all is well, as shown in the output below. We are now ready for the complete program, which is as follows.

File BookChapters.cs

```
using System;

class BookChapters {

    /// <summary>
    /// The Book Chapters     Bishop and Horspool  May 2002
    /// ==================
    /// Calculates a table of contents for a book
    /// and the total number of pages.
```

```
        /// Illustrates loops.
        /// </summary>

        void Go() {
          string chapName;
          int pages;
          int startingPage = 1;
          int lastChapter = 4;
          for(int chapNumber= 1; chapNumber<=lastChapter; chapNumber++) {
            Console.Write("Chapter "+chapNumber+" name: ");
            chapName = Console.ReadLine();
            Console.WriteLine("Chapter "+chapNumber+" pages: ");
            pages = int.Parse(Console.ReadLine());
            Console.WriteLine("\t\t\tChapter "+
              chapNumber+"\t"+chapName+"\t"+startingPage);
            startingPage += pages;
          }
          Console.WriteLine("Total pages = "+startingPage);
        }

        static void Main() {
          new BookChapters().Go();
        }
      }
```

A typical short run for the data mentioned previously

```
    Introduction          18
    Basics                30
    Advanced Concepts     43
    Conclusion            5
```

would be:

```
    Chapter 1 name: Introduction
    Chapter 1 pages: 18
                      Chapter 1 Introduction     1
    Chapter 2 name: Basics
    Chapter 2 pages: 30
                      Chapter 2 Basics   19
    Chapter 3 name: Advanced concepts
    Chapter 3 pages: 43
                      Chapter 3 Advanced concepts            49
    Chapter 4 name: Conclusion
    Chapter 4 pages: 5
                      Chapter 4 Conclusion                   92
    Total pages = 97
```

In the program, we arranged for the output to appear further to the right, so as to separate it from the input, which is happening concurrently. Tabs were used for this purpose. In the next section we shall see how to line up the output better. Later, in Chapter 4, we shall see how the input data could be brought from a file instead, so that the output can be neater and more coherent.

There are many variations on loops, as well as some skills to learn in how best they are used. We shall return to them in the next section, but the main treatment of loops is in Chapter 4. We now have to investigate output formatting for numbers and strings.

3.6 Output formatting

Although the looping structure of the programs in the previous section was fairly easy to obtain, there are definitely problems with the output of the last one. We would really like the numbers to line up properly. There are also situations where we might want to print a `double` value and need to control how many digits are printed after a decimal point.

Fortunately C# provides a simple and powerful way of controlling the output format. Instead of concatenating all the items to be printed on a line into one string, we treat them as separate items, and at the beginning of the `WriteLine` call we include a *format string*. The format string gives all the textual string information, plus a place holder for each of the variable items that follows, and each of these can include a format specification. So as an example, the formatted write we need to get a nicely lined-up table of roots is:

```
Console.WriteLine("{0,4}{1,8:f2}", n, Math.Sqrt(n));
```

which means 'Take the zero[th] item and write it right-justified in four columns followed by the one[th] item written in eight columns using fixed point format with two decimal places'. The result will be a beautifully lined up table as below. We see that the decimal points are now lined up, and each of the roots has exactly two decimal places, even if they are zero.

```
    Table of square roots

      0    0.00
     10    3.16
     20    4.47
     30    5.48
     40    6.32
     50    7.07
     60    7.75
     70    8.37
     80    8.94
     90    9.49
    100   10.00
```

The format parameter

The *format parameter* is therefore the first parameter in a `Write` or `WriteLine` call, which now has the alternative form:

OUTPUT STATEMENT WITH FORMATS

```
Console.WriteLine ("text{fs0}text{fs1}text ...",
                   item0, item1, ... );
```

The items can be any C# variable for which a format specification exists. The format specifications are described below. The text is optional. The format can also be a separate string variable.

This form of the `WriteLine` is distinguished from the previous one in that it has more than one parameter – the format followed by a list of items. The previous form of the `WriteLine` had only one parameter which was a string constructed from concatenating various items together, which were implicitly or explicitly themselves converted to strings.

In order to work properly, a formatted `WriteLine` should contain the same number of *format specifications* as there are parameters following. These specifications are enclosed in curly brackets and numbered from zero. The formats and the items must match up. What if they don't? These are the cases, based on the following example:

```
Console.WriteLine(format,a,b,c,d);
```

1. Everything matches – the four items get printed.
    ```
    string format = "{0} {1} {2} {3}"
    ```

2. The order is different – the format does not have to list the items in a numerical order, and can obtain various effects by not doing so.
    ```
    string format = "{0} {2} {1} {3}"
    ```
    will print a then c then b then d.

3. Too few specifications – only the items with specifications are printed, so c and d won't appear at all.
    ```
    string format = "{0} {1}"
    ```

4. Repeated numbers – if we repeat a number, that item gets printed again.
    ```
    string format = "{0} {1} {1} {3}"
    ```
    will print a, b, b and d but omit c.

5. Too many specifications – will cause an error.
    ```
    string format = "{0} {1} {2} {3} {4}"
    ```
    Since there is no item corresponding to {4}, the format cannot be fulfilled and C# will stop the program.

Format specifications

Each specification, enclosed in curly brackets, can have considerably more information as to how its item should be printed. Specifications have their own syntax which is defined in this form:

FORMAT SPECIFICATION
$\{N, M: s\}$
N is the position of the item in the list of values after the format string passed to the `Write` call; position numbers start from 0. M is the width of the region to contain the formatted value. If M is absent or negative, then the value will be left-justified, otherwise it will be right-justified. s is an optional string of formatting codes which can be used to control formatting of numbers, date-times, currencies, and so on.

The integer N is the position in the list of items to be printed, where 0 refers to the first value in the list, and must always be provided. For printing integers and strings, we are only interested in the width parameter, M. The last part, s, is often absent, but if present, it gives the type of formatting to be applied and a number. Thus in our square roots table we used:

```
{1,8:f2}
```

One of the other formatters is discussed at the end of the section, and the full list is in Appendix C.

Justifying strings and numbers

Using a width M when formatting strings can be useful. Consider how we could fine tune and right-justify the numbers for the chapter table of contents. The statement we used was:

```
Console.WriteLine("\t\t\tChapter "+chapNumber+" "
                   +chapName+"\t"+ startingPage);
```

Rewriting this with a format gives first the `WriteLine`:

```
Console.WriteLine(format,chapNumber,chapName,startingPage);
```

which is fairly neat and helps us understand what is actually going to appear on the line. Then the format is:

```
string format = "\t\t\tChapter {0:2} {1}\t\t{2:3}"
```

which will print out lines such as

```
Chapter 1 Introduction           1
Chapter 2 Basics                19
Chapter 3 Advanced concept      59
Chapter 4 Conclusion            91
```

By using the right-justification feature for the two numeric items, we have been able to line them up, which looks more correct. If the number of pages in the book were to reach a thousand, then we could change the last format specification to {2:4}.

Formatting other types

We saw in Chapter 2 that there were ways of formatting dates via the `DateTime` class. In addition to integers which would use the format {N,M} or real numbers which would use (N,M:Fd}, a useful formatter is that for currencies. To format a currency, we use {N,M:C} and the amount will be printed with two decimal places (automatically) and a currency symbol in front, which defaults to the currency symbol of the country where the computer is located.

For example, if a computer has its settings so that $ is the currency symbol, then we could have:

```
Console.WriteLine("Your new salary is {0:C}",salary*1.04);
```

which for a salary of ten thousand would print

```
Your new salary is $10,400.00
```

If the settings are different, the same statement might print

```
Your new salary is R10 400,00
```

In other words, the currency formatting, like the date formatting, adapts to the locality of the computer, as set in its operating system.

In C# we can override the settings of the computer to ensure that currencies are expressed in a certain way, no matter which computer the program runs on. The way a currency value is displayed is governed by a class called `NumberFormatInfo`. If we create a `NumberFormatInfo` object, we can set properties such as the ones shown in the `NumberFormatInfo` form below.

NUMBERFORMATINFO CLASS (ABBREVIATED)

```
//Constructor
NumberFormatInfo()
//Properties
CurrencyDecimalSeparator
CurrencyGroupSeparator
CurrencySymbol
...
many more properties are omitted
```

A `NumberFormatInfo` object is used with the `String.Format` method to reformat currencies for different countries.

For example,

```
NumberFormatInfo f = new NumberFormatInfo();
f.CurrencyDecimalSeparator = ",";
f.CurrencyGroupSeparator = " ";
f.CurrencySymbol = "R";
```

Then we use the `Format` method of the `String` class to create a string from a format, a format specifier and a value, as in:

```
Console.WriteLine(
    String.Format(f,"Your new salary is {0:C}",salary*1.04));
```

which will print

```
Your new salary is R10 400,00
```

even on a dollar-based computer. `String.Format` is a method in the `string` class which applies a given format (in this case the number format `f`) to a format specification and a list of values.

Assessment of formats

It is a matter of choice whether one uses formats or string concatenation in output statements. Formats are necessary for right-justifying, controlling decimal places, or handling currencies and dates. However, there is another possible use for them. Sometimes, we need to display items in the same way from different places in the program. Then a single format string can be defined, and kept in one place for everyone to use. A change there will have an immediate effect elsewhere. We illustrate this approach in the case study in Section 3.8.

3.7 Methods and parameters

We are building up to the end of our chapter on what is inside an object. If we refer back to the form for a struct on page 65, we see that we still have to complete how to define methods, operators and other functions. In this chapter we shall deal with methods, and leave the other two to Chapter 9.

We have so far made extensive use of methods that have been defined in the types provided by some of C#'s namespaces. These types were `int`, `string`, `Console`, `DateTime`, `Math` and `Random`.

Examples of methods we have used in these contexts are:

```
offsetMeeting = meeting.AddHours(offset);
```

```
totalMins = int.Parse(Console.ReadLine());

int damage = r.Next(strength/3+points/2);

Console.WriteLine(meeting.ToShortTimeString()+"    "+
                  offsetMeeting.ToShortTimeString());

string s = string.Format(f,"{0:C}",amount);
```

In each case, a method call is followed by parentheses, even if there are no parameters, as in the case of `ReadLine()`. In this way we can distinguish method calls from uses of properties.

Declaring a method

We can now consider how to declare our own methods. Consider the general form for a method declaration:

<table>
<tr><td>METHOD DECLARATION (SIMPLE)</td></tr>
<tr><td>

```
access-modifier kind methodid (parameters) {
   statements and variable declarations
   return expression; // if a typed method
}

// parameters
type id, type id, ...
```
</td></tr>
<tr><td>A method is declared with a kind which is typed (given a type name) or untyped (<code>void</code>). As with all members, it can be private or public. Private is the default. Methods can only contain variables, not constants. If the method is typed, it must have at least one <code>return</code> statement with an expression evaluating to the same type as the method. An untyped method may have <code>return</code> statements without expressions.</td></tr>
</table>

For example, the following is a method we included in the `StarLord` type in Example 3.1.

```
public void Attack(StarLord opponent) {
   int damage = r.Next(strength/3+points/2);
   opponent.Points -= damage;
}
```

The method is public and its kind is `void`, i.e. it does not return a value. It has one parameter. Inside, `Attack` declares a variable called `damage`, and executes one assignment statement. Another example of a method in the same type might be one that resets strength and points, as in:

```
public void Renew(int s, int p) {
    strength = s;
    points = p;
}
```

This method is very like a constructor, but it only affects some of the object's fields.

The variables in a method are not initialized and must be explicitly assigned values as computations begin. The variables have *scope* which extends only within the method and every name declared there must have one meaning only.

Typed methods

Typed methods are very common in C# and have the distinguishing feature that they return values. A good example of a typed method would be one to convert temperatures from one scale to another, as in:

```
public double Fahrenheit(double c) {
    return c*9.0/5 + 32;
}
```

It is a rule that any typed method must have a `return` statement, so that it creates a value before it ends. This requirement coincides with how it is called. We now formalize how to call a method.

Calling a method

We are already very familiar with calling methods.[1] The form is:

METHOD CALL (SIMPLE)
methodid(*argumentlist*);
The values of the arguments are passed to the parameters; the method is entered and its statements are executed to the end or to a return statement.

Untyped or void methods are called as statements: they cannot be part of an expression. Typed methods are called as part of an expression, but they can also be called as a statement, in which case their return value is lost.

Examples of calling the methods above would be:

```
lord1.Attack(lord2);
lord2.Renew(10,10);
f = Fahrenheit(tempToday+5);
```

---

1. In C# the official terminology is 'invoking' a method and the action would be a method 'invocation'. Calling and call mean the same as invoking and invoke.

In each case, the parameters are evaluated and the values passed into the parameters of the method. In every way, formal parameters act as variables inside the method. Their values may be changed, as may the values of other variables, but any such changes are not reflected back when the method is ended (except see below for `ref` and `out` parameters).

At this point you might be wondering why `Attack` and `Renew` were used as members of objects, whereas `Fahrenheit` stood on its own. This question is answered next.

Method design

In object-oriented programming, methods are used in several different contexts.

1. **Functions of an object**. Public methods provide visible functionality for an object. They would generally involve calculations based on the parameters and the object's own fields, or on some sort of interaction with the outside world. In C#, types tend to have fewer such methods than in other languages because all the simple functions that merely interrogate or update data are provided by properties. If you look at any C# API listing you will see that the properties for a class often outnumber its methods.

2. **Structuring within an program**. Methods within an program enable the logic to be broken down into smaller more manageable pieces. The division into methods can be a linear one, where a program has a sequence of tasks to perform, and each is encapsulated in its own method, which is only called once by the `Main` or `Go` method. If method names are carefully chosen then the main program is more readable and can also be developed and maintained more easily. A typical such structuring might be:

   ```
   AcquireData();
   Analyze();
   ProduceReport();
   ```

3. **Providing functionality**. Frequently used pieces of code within an object (often calculations like that for Fahrenheit) would be put away in a method so that their inner working can be checked once only and then relied upon to be correct when called.

All of these principles will be illustrated in the examples that follow.

Static methods

Because in this book we have taken the approach to use existing types, we have actually grown quite accustomed to using a variety of method kinds in several contexts. One further distinction between methods is static and instance. Like static fields, *static methods* are declared with the keyword `static` and exist once for the class only. They are called by writing their name after the type name and a dot. Instance methods apply to a particular instance of the class, and are prefixed by an object name and a dot when called.

In the following two statements

```
totalMins = int.Parse(Console.ReadLine());
int damage = r.Next(strength/3+points/2);
```

Parse and ReadLine are both static methods, whereas Next is an instance method. How does one know whether to use static or not? The default in good programming practice is to avoid the use of static. In the examples that follow, instances of when static should and should not be used will be highlighted.

out and ref parameters

In C#, arguments are normally 'passed by value'. This means that the expression represented by the parameter is evaluated and assigned to the parameter. There is no further contact between any variables on the calling list after the method has begun executing. The values of these variables remain untouched. Implicitly, these parameters are known as 'value' parameters.

A second option is a 'ref' parameter, standing for reference, where the argument and parameter refer to the same variable. Thus during the call of the method, any changes it makes to a ref parameter affect the argument – they are the same thing. In order to emphasize the different mechanism being used, the ref keyword must be specified on a method call, as well as on the declaration. Note that each ref argument must have been assigned a value before the method is called.

A third option is provided and is useful when we want to get values out of a method. Typed methods provide a mechanism for getting one value out, but if there are more values to be returned, we can declare some parameters as 'out'. An out parameter is similar to a ref parameter except that the argument need not contain a value before the method is called, and the method *must* assign a value to the out parameter before control returns to the caller. The keyword out must, as with ref, be specified on both the method call and in the declaration of the method's corresponding parameter.

Note that the keyword in is part of the C# language, but it has nothing to do with parameter passing; it cannot be used as an opposite to the out keyword.

The out and ref keywords are not going to be heavily used in programming, but there is one very common example – that of swapping two values. Suppose a wizard declares that two StarLord characters must be interchanged (their names, their points, everything). We could implement this as the method:

```
public void SwapLords(ref StarLord one, ref StarLord two) {
  StarLord temp = one;
  onc = two;
  two = temp;
}
```

which we would call as in

```
StarLord.SwapLords(ref lord1, ref lord2);
```

Comparing objects

Are the relational operators introduced in Section 3.4 available for structured objects too? The answer is – only if we make them available via methods. We have to define what we mean by comparison for these types. The API struct `DateTime`, shown in Section 2.6, bases its comparisons on a real world ordering of dates. But consider the struct for `Exam` discussed at the start of this chapter.

```
struct Exam {
   string   course;
   int      weight;      // percentage of the final mark
   string   lecturer;
   DateTime date;
   string   venue;

   static int totalNoOfExams = 0;
}
```

What would it mean to compare two `Exam` objects, using say the expression e1<e2? If we think about it, we could possibly define an ordering based on the course, and then the date, allowing for more than one exam per course. But there is no way that the C# compiler could work this out for us. Comparison for equality can, by default, be interpreted as meaning all fields have equal values, but even that is subject to alternative meanings.

To provide a meaningful equality operation, we must override a method called `Equals`. For the other forms of comparison, we must override `Compare`, as already explained for `DateTime`. So for `Exam`, we might add:

```
public override bool Equals(object e) {
   return course == ((Exam) e).course && date == ((Exam) e).date;
}
```

This version of `Equals` relies on equality of strings (which is defined) and equality of `DateTime` objects (which we saw in the API specification). It ignores the values of the three other fields provided in the class definition, but we can do this if we want to. Then we can use our `Equals` method as in:

```
e1.Equals(e2)
```

Setting up such a method does not, unfortunately, enable us to say

```
e1 == e2
```

To include this facility, we have to overload the `==` operator, as discussed in Chapter 9. In a similar way, the `CompareTo` method can be declared. Effective use of these methods really requires some additional control structures, so we shall pick up again on the topic in Chapter 4 and its exercises.

3.8 Case study 1 – Phone bill comparison

In our first case study, we are going to consider various designs for types and methods and see how there are several ways of solving a problem

The problem

Different telephone companies offer different costs for their monthly contracts. It is often very difficult to make a sound judgement as to which company will give the cheapest deal. One may have a cheaper basic rate, but charge slightly more per phone call, for example. We would like to simulate a bill for a typical month for a household, and see what the total cost for rival companies will be.

The data

There are two kinds of data needed for the simulation. First, we need to know the different rates for each company. We shall assume we are dealing with companies that have the same cost structure, just different rates. Later on we shall be able to handle more complex contracts. The four rates are:

◆ monthly fee, e.g. 29.95,

◆ basic rate per phone call, e.g. 0.55,

◆ cheap rate reduction, e.g. 0.20,

◆ number of free minutes per month, e.g. 60.

If we imagine a phone company type, then values such as these would be sent to the constructor of each object.

The second aspect of the data is the calls themselves. We need a set of test calls to try out on each company to obtain a valid comparison. The data for each phone call is its duration in minutes (for the moment), and also the rate at which the phone call is being made – normal or cheap rate. At present we do not know enough C# to be able to decide whether we are in cheap rate or not, based on the time of day, so for the simulation, we just generate a 0 or a 1 and use the number to differentiate.

The calculations

While we have the data in mind, let's consider the calculations. The basic calculation is the length of the phone call multiplied by the call rate. Assuming a constant for the max-CallLength, such a calculation is:

```
callLength = r.Next(maxCallLength);
double callCost = callLength*basicRate;
```

where r is a random number generator. By instantiating r with a specific seed, we can ensure that each phone company object will get the same sequence of phone call lengths.

For the reduced call rate, we have set up the figures so that the amount is expressed as a reduction rather than an new rate. Thus the figure of 0.20 above means that the cost for a reduced rate call is 055–0.20 = 0.35. Now, if we generate a 0 or a 1, with 0 regarded as being the normal rate code and 1 the reduced rate, the calculation becomes:

```
callLength = r.Next(maxCallLength);
int callRate = s.Next(2); // 0 for normal, 1 for reduced
double callCost =
    callLength*(basicRate - callRate*cheapRateReduction);
```

For example, Table 3.6 shows some typical values, remembering that 1 indicates cheap rate.

Length	Rate code	Rate	Cost
10	1	35	3.50
1	1	35	0.35
9	1	35	3.15
8	0	55	4.40
8	1	55	2.80

Table 3.6 Sample phone call rates and costs

The next issue is the free minutes. These clock down until used, and then the charges start. A suitable way to handle this is to have two loops: one for the free minutes, followed by one for the rest of the calls.

```
for (int m=freeMinutes; m>0; m -= callLength) {
   ... calculate call cost, but don't add it
}
int restCalls = 8; // or some such number
for (int c=restCalls; c>0; c--) {
   ... calculate call cost, and add to total
}
```

Type design

There will be a driver class for the main program, and then a struct for the phone company. Apart from the rates, we can record the name of the company, and local data will be the random number generators (one for the call lengths and one for the rate category). By having the generators in the struct, they will be duplicated for each object, and therefore produce the same sequence of values, as we require for a simulation.

Output formatting

The output can be presented in the form of a table. Since some of it involves currencies, we can use the C format discussed in Section 3.6 to good advantage. We envisage a table like this:

```
Telco
Monthly R 29.95  Free minutes 60
Basic rate R 0.55    Reduction R 0.20
=======================================
Contract  Mins  Rate    Cost  Charged
    Free    19     1    6.65     0.00
    Free    11     1    3.85     0.00
    Free     1     1    0.35     0.00
    Free    18     0    9.90     0.00
    Free    23     0   12.65     0.00
 Charged     4     1    1.40     1.40
 Charged    12     1    4.20     4.20
 Charged    29     1   10.15    10.15
 Charged     9     1    3.15     3.15
 Charged     8     0    4.40     4.40
 Charged     8     1    2.80     2.80
 Charged     9     1    3.15     3.15
 Charged    20     1    7.00     7.00
                    Total R 66.20
```

The statements to instantiate a phone company object and print the total would be:

```
string format = "{0,23}Total {1:C}";
PhoneCompany pc1 =
    new PhoneCompany("Telco",29.95,0.55,0.20,60);
Console.WriteLine(format,"",pc1.PhoneBill());
```

Within the `PhoneCompany` struct, other formatted output statements are:

```
Console.Write("{0,8}{1,6}{2,6}{3,8:f2}",
    type, callLength, callRate, callCost);
Console.WriteLine("{0,8:f2}",callCharge);
```

In this case, we do not use the C format, since we don't want the currency symbol printed.

Method design

The last matter to discuss is how the methods in the struct are to be set up. We have already intimated, above, that there will be a single method to calculate and print the entire phone bill. But we saw that there were two loops required, where the same calculations would be done. The difference would be whether the word 'Free' or 'Charge' was printed.
    We can postulate a method as follows:

```
double Calculate(string type, out int callLength) {
  callLength = r.Next(maxCallLength);
  int callRate = s.Next(2); // 0 for normal, 1 for reduced
  double callCost = callLength*
    (basicRate - callRate*cheapRateReduction);
  Console.Write("{0,8}{1,6}{2,6}{3,8:f2}",
    type, callLength, callRate, callCost);
  return callCost;
}
```

The method calculates the cost of a call as well as printing out all the details. Thus it is quite self-contained and declares all its own variables. However, if this is a free call, we need to know the call length so it can be deducted from the number of free minutes remaining. We use the out parameter mechanism to return this value as well.

Program

Finally, we can put the complete program together as below.

File PhoneComparison.cs

```
using System;

class PhoneComparison {

  /// <summary>
  /// Phone Comparison        Bishop & Horspool    Dec 2002
  /// ================
  /// Compares the phone bills for two companies
  /// Illustrates type design, method design, parameters
  /// and output formatting
  /// </summary>

  // Simulation parameters
  const int maxCallLength = 30;
  const int maxCallsPerMonth = 10;

  void Go() {
    string format = "{0,23}Total {1:C}";
    PhoneCompany pc1 =
        new PhoneCompany("Telco",29.95,0.55,0.20,60);
    Console.WriteLine(format,"",pc1.PhoneBill());
    Console.ReadLine();
    PhoneCompany pc2 =
        new PhoneCompany("Cellco",17.95,0.45,0.10,30);
    Console.WriteLine(format,"",pc2.PhoneBill());
  }

  static void Main() {
    new PhoneComparison().Go();
  }
```

```
public struct PhoneCompany {
  string name;
  double monthlyFee;
  double basicRate;
  double cheapRateReduction;
  int freeMinutes;
  Random r,s;

  public PhoneCompany(string n, double m,
    double b, double c, int f) {
    name = n;
    monthlyFee = m;
    basicRate = b;
    cheapRateReduction = c;
    freeMinutes = f;
    r = new Random(19);
    s = new Random(13);
  }

  double Calculate(string type, out int callLength) {
    callLength = r.Next(maxCallLength);
    // 0 for normal, 1 for reduced
    int callRate = s.Next(2);
    double callCost = callLength*
      (basicRate - callRate*cheapRateReduction);
    Console.Write("{0,8}{1,6}{2,6}{3,8:f2}",
      type, callLength, callRate, callCost);
    return callCost;
  }

  public double PhoneBill() {
    Console.WriteLine(name);
    Console.WriteLine("Monthly {0:C} "+
      "Free minutes {1}\n"+
      "Basic rate {2:C}    Reduction {3:C}\n"+
      "=====================================",
      monthlyFee, freeMinutes, basicRate, cheapRateReduction);
    Console.WriteLine("Contract    Mins   Rate "+"Cost   Charged");
    Console.WriteLine("Monthly fee{0,-20}{1:f2}","",monthlyFee);
    double cost = monthlyFee;
    int callLength;
    double callCharge;
    for (int m=freeMinutes; m>0;m -= callLength) {
      Calculate("Free", out callLength);
      Console.WriteLine("{0,8:f2}",0);
    }
    int restCalls = 8;  //r.Next(maxCallsPerMonth);
    for (int c=restCalls; c>0; c--) {
      callCharge = Calculate("Charged", out callLength);
      Console.WriteLine("{0,8:f2}",callCharge);
      cost+=callCharge;
    }
    return cost;
  }

 }
}
```

Complete output for the program is as below.

```
Telco
Monthly R 29.95  Free minutes 60
Basic rate R 0.55    Reduction R 0.20
==========================================
Contract   Mins  Rate   Cost  Charged
Monthly fee                    29.95
     Free     19    1    6.65    0.00
     Free     11    1    3.85    0.00
     Free      1    1    0.35    0.00
     Free     18    0    9.90    0.00
     Free     23    0   12.65    0.00
  Charged      4    1    1.40    1.40
  Charged     12    1    4.20    4.20
  Charged     29    1   10.15   10.15
  Charged      9    1    3.15    3.15
  Charged      8    0    4.40    4.40
  Charged      8    1    2.80    2.80
  Charged      9    1    3.15    3.15
  Charged     20    1    7.00    7.00
                      Total R 66.20


Cellco
Monthly R 17.95  Free minutes 30
Basic rate R 0.45    Reduction R 0.10
======================================
Contract   Mins  Rate   Cost  Charged
Monthly fee                    17.95
     Free     19    1    6.65    0.00
     Free     11    1    3.85    0.00
  Charged      1    1    0.35    0.35
  Charged     18    0    8.10    8.10
  Charged     23    0   10.35   10.35
  Charged      4    1    1.40    1.40
  Charged     12    1    4.20    4.20
  Charged     29    1   10.15   10.15
  Charged      9    1    3.15    3.15
  Charged      8    0    3.60    3.60
                      Total R 59.25
```

As expected, the second company is cheaper.

Assessment

There are numerous improvements that we can (and will) make to this program as we go along. However, are there any errors? Well, there is one discrepancy. The idea is that the simulation should present a fair comparison. Therefore each bill would deduct the free minutes, and then charge for a certain number of additional calls. We set the number at eight, just to keep the output short. However, the actual calls for each company, as listed above, vary, because the number of free calls varies. Telco's charged calls have durations

    4   12   29   9   8   8   9   20

whereas Cellco's are

    1   18   23   4   12   29   9   8

What has happened is that the Cellco's first three charged calls were free for Telco. How can we bring the two into line? If we count the calls that the first company gets, then insert a set of dummy calls between the free and charged ones for Cellco, that would work. This optimization is left for the reader.

Concepts in chapter 3

This chapter covered the following concepts:

constructors	instance fields
static fields	accessibility
properties	numeric types
floating point representation	numeric expressions
promotion	modulus
relational expressions	assignment operators
precedence	associativity
conversion	simple loops
output formatting	method declarations
struct declarations	void and typed methods
method calls	static methods
parameter kinds	

Keywords introduced and used in this chapter were:

static	public
int	long
double	float
decimal	for
void	out

```
ref                          value
get                          set
```

Forms were given in this chapter for the following constructs:

struct definition	property definition
type promotion (abbreviated)	comparison result types
explicit conversion	for loop (simple)
output statement with formats	format specification
NumberFormatInfo class (abbreviated)	method declaration (simple)
method call (simple)	

Quiz

Q3.1   A significant difference between a property and a field is

    (a)   capitalization   (b)   parentheses

    (c)   accessibility modifiers   (d)   how they are declared

Q3.2   If a is an object and p is a property and we assign a.p = x, x is represented in p by

    (a)   `value`   (b)   `x`

    (c)   `p.x`   (d)   `P`

Q3.3   A type can have several constructors provided that

    (a)   they all have different names

    (b)   they all have different parameter lists (signatures)

    (c)   at least one is the default constructor

    (d)   one constructor initializes all the locally declared fields

Q3.4   Which statement is true?

    (a)   A property must have the same name as a field in that type, but with a capital letter.

    (b)   A property must always be public.

(c)   A property defines get and set behaviour.

(d)   A property defines get or set behaviour or both.

Q3.5 Adding a `double` and an `int` value will always result in a

(a)   `double` value

(b)   `int` value

(c)   `int` value if the `double` value did not have a fractional part

(d)   `long` value, if the `double` value is more than 2^{31}

Q3.6 The correct expression for the hour of a new `DateTime` object is

(a)   `new DateTime(2003,9,25).Hour`

(b)   `new DateTime(2003,9,25).Hour()`

(c)   `new DateTime(2003,9,25).getHour()`

(d)   `Hour(new DateTime(2003,9,25))`

Q3.7 A loop to print the first 10 odd numbers would be

(a)
```
for (int i=1; i<=10; i+=2)
    Console.WriteLine(i);
```

(b)
```
for (int i=1; i<19; i+=2)
    Console.WriteLine(i);
```

(c)
```
for (int i=0; i<10; i++)
    Console.WriteLine(i*2+1);
```

(d)
```
for (int i=0; i<=10; i++)
    Console.WriteLine(i*2+1);
```

Q3.8 To print an integer, a real number to two decimal places and a currency, all separated by four spaces, and in that order, we would use
```
Console.WriteLine(s,i,r,c):
```
where s is

(a)   `"{0,4}{1,4:f2}{2,4:C}"`

(b)   `"{0}{1,f:4,2}    {2,c:4,2}"`

(c)   `"{0}    {1:f2}    {2:C}"`

(d)   `"{0}\t{1:f2}\t{2:C2}"`

Q3.9 A significant difference between a typed method and a void method is that

    (a)   A void method cannot be called in an expression

    (b)   A typed method cannot be called without an expression or assignment

    (c)   A typed method can only have in parameters

    (d)   A void method must be public

Q3.10 If we have declared a method

```
void Update (x, out y)
```

which of the following is completely correct?

    (a)   `Update(w, z)`   (b)   `Update(w, out z);`

    (c)   `Update(in w, out z);`   (d)   Both (b) and (c)

Exercises

3.1   **Examinations.** Based on the `Exam` type discussed in Section 3.1, develop a program which will read in details of four examinations and print them out with the actual days they will take place. In addition, print out the number of days between each two examinations.

3.2   **Shuttle bus timetable.** Using Example 3.3 as a starting point, write a program to print out a timetable for the shuttle bus starting at 6am and going on till 11.45pm.

3.3   **Reduced timetable.** Between 12 midnight and 5.30, the bus also runs at 30-minute intervals. Include this information in the timetable. The approach used in Case study 1 (Section 3.8) will be helpful.

3.4   **Enhanced Time type.** Starting with the `Time` type of Example 3.2, add methods for adding an hour and comparing two times. Then change Example 3.4 so that the for loop itself runs over `Time` values, not integers.

3.5   **Temperature conversion.** Write a program to print out a table converting Celsius values from 0 to 100 into Fahrenheit. Arrange the output so that there are three values across each line.

3.6   **Currency conversion**. Repeat Exercise 3.5 for converting a suitable range of amounts between the currency on your computer and some other currency. Use the `NumberFormatInfo` class discussed in Section 3.6.

3.7 **Manuscript.** Change the Chapters program in Example 3.5 so that there is a struct which is instantiated for each chapter and records the name and the number of manuscript pages. Add a property which calculates and returns the final number of pages based on an 80% reduction for the typeset version. Check the program, generating 15 chapters with a random number of manuscript pages between 20 and 50.

3.8 **Pizza delivery.** Pizza Delivery 2U is interested in giving more accurate delivery times to its customers when they order pizzas. From the time of the call to the pizza arriving, there are two factors to be taken into account: the length of the queue at the pizza oven (i.e. the number of orders already in the system), and the area in which the customer lives. Customers in areas close by will have faster deliveries than those in areas further away. Pizza 2U makes deliveries in four identifiable areas, and would like to have a quick look-up table next to the phone for times from 9am to 11pm and queue lengths from 0 to 5, in these four areas. Design a system which uses structs and loops to print out the required tables.

CHAPTER 4

Control and arrays

The main focus of this chapter is on studying how programs can repeat and select actions based on tests. Most of the tests involve comparing the values of objects, and comparisons rely on the operators and values of the bool type, which we cover first. Programs that involve repetition will very often need to store multiple results, and the data type that is most often used in this context is the array. In this chapter we consider simple arrays of numbers and objects and some of the classic ways in which loops interact with arrays. The special case of the string, composed of several characters, completes the basic data types of our language.

4.1 Boolean expressions

Several forms of C# statements make use of conditions. These are expressions which evaluate to true or false. For example, the expression 1<2 always evaluates to true, while the opposite expression 1>=2 always evaluates to false. More useful in a program would be an expression like n<10 which evaluates to true only if the variable n holds a value less than 10 and otherwise evaluates to false.

The comparison operators are listed in the form below. They can be used to compare two values of any basic type, which include int, double, char and string. They can also be used with many structured types, including DateTime, provided that the implementation of the type includes methods that support comparisons.

COMPARISON OPERATORS

```
a < b       // test if a is less than b
a <= b      // test if a is less than or equal to b
a >= b      // test if a is greater than or equal to b
a > b       // test if a is greater than b
a == b      // test if a equals a
a != b      // test if a is not equal to b
```

The result of a comparison is a value of the bool type. This type contains just two values, which are written as true and false.

Comparisons may be made between numbers, characters, strings, Booleans and any other types for which comparison operations have been defined.

The name bool is short for *Boolean*. It honours George Boole who invented a branch of mathematics called Boolean algebra. It is closely related to predicate calculus. We can declare variables of type bool in a C# program.

Here are some examples where the result of each comparison is stored in a variable of type bool.

```
bool b1, b2, b3, b4, b5;
int a = 19;
int b = -27;
char c = 'c';
char d = 'd';
string hello = "hello";
string there = "there";
b1 = a < b;           // assigns false
b2 = c != d;          // assigns true
b3 = hello < there;   // assigns true
b4 = there > "the";   // assigns true
b4 = b1 < b2;         // assigns true
```

The assignments to b3 and b4 probably require further explanation. Comparisons of strings use lexicographic ordering based on the Unicode character set. For practical purposes, one need only to know that '0' sorts before '1' which sorts before '2', and so on up to '9'. Similarly, 'a' sorts before 'b' and so on up to 'z', and 'A' sorts before 'B' and so on up to 'Z'. If one string is longer than another but all the characters of the shorter string match, then the shorter string sorts before the longer one – hence the result of the assignment to b4. Appendix D includes a table of some of the common Unicode characters and their ordering.

Finally, it is possible to compare two Boolean values. Although Boolean algebra does not define an ordering for true and false, the C# language implements false with a 0 integer and true with a 1 integer. Thus false sorts before true.

Boolean logical operators

We can combine conditions or Boolean values using the Boolean logical operators.

BOOLEAN LOGICAL OPERATORS	
`test1 & test2`	`// test1 and test2`
`test1	test2`	`// test1 or test2`
`! (test1)`	`// not test1`
test1 & *test2* is true only if both operands are true; otherwise the result is false. *test1* | *test2* is true if either operand is true; otherwise the result is false. ! *test1* is true if the operand is false, and false otherwise.s	

Since there are only two possible values for a Boolean expression, the results of the operations can be easily enumerated and shown in the form of truth tables. Tables 4.1, 4.2 and 4.3 show the &, | and ! operators.

& **operator**		Right operand	
		false	true
Left operand	false	false	false
	true	false	true

Table 4.1 The and operator

	operator		Right operand	
		false	true
Left operand	false	false	false
	true	false	true

Table 4.2 The or operator

! operator	Operand	
	false	true
	true	false

Table 4.3 The not operator

For example, if the variable m holds the value 7, then the Boolean expression

```
m>0 & m<10
```

would evaluate to `true`. We can look that up in the truth table for the & operator by going to the row for true (because `m>0` is true) and the column for true (because `m<10` is also true).

Two of the operators have some very similar cousins, the Boolean conditional operators:

BOOLEAN CONDITIONAL OPERATORS

```
test1 && test2      // test1 conditional and test2
test1 || test2      // test1 conditional or test2
```

The result of *test1* && *test2* is false if *test1* is false; otherwise the result is the value of *test2*. The result of *test1* || *test2* is true if *test1* is true; otherwise the result is the value of *test2*.

Not only do they look very similar but their truth tables are identical. The && operator has the same truth table as &, and the || operator has the same truth table as |. Does this mean that they are identical in meaning? The answer is 'not quite'. However, the conditional operators && and || should be used in preference to & and | respectively, because their use can make the program run faster. Not having to evaluate the right-hand operand means less work to be done.

Boolean expressions

It is possible to combine several tests with Boolean operators. However, it is good style to parenthesize the expressions so that anyone who reads the code later does not become confused about how it is supposed to work. Try reading the following line of code.

```
bool test2 = a > 0 && b < 100 || a <= 0 && b >= 100;
```

Quickly, does `test2` get initialized to true if a is equal to 0 and b equals 99?

The answer is 'no' because the *or* operator has lower precedence than the *and* operator. However, the statement should be parenthesized as follows for better readability.

```
bool test2 = (a > 0 && b < 100) || (a <= 0 && b >= 100);
```

The negation operator, !, has higher precedence than either *and* or *or*. Therefore the expression

```
! (a == 0) || (b == 0)
```

is equivalent in meaning to

```
(a != 0) || (b == 0)
```

The negation operator has, in fact, very high precedence (as do all the unary operators). If we were to write the expression as

```
! a == 0 || b == 0
```

the C# compiler would consider that expression to be equivalent to the following form

```
(!a) == 0 || b == 0
```

and then report an error. Assuming that a has the int type, the error message will say that the ! operator cannot be applied to int values.

4.2 Selection statements

We come to our first statement which uses conditions. The *if statement* has this form.

IF STATEMENT
```if (condition) {` `   statements1;` `} else {` `   statements2;` `}```
If the *condition* evaluates to true then execute *statements1*, otherwise execute *statements2*. The `else` part of the if statement is optional; everything from the keyword `else` to the end may be omitted.

Suppose that we want to write a program that computes the square root of a number. If we want our program to behave nicely, we should make it report an error if the number is negative, since the square root of a negative number is undefined. The relevant part of the program might look like the following.

```
Console.Write("Enter a number: ");
double x = double.Parse(Console.readLine());
```

```
double result;
if (x < 0.0) {
    Console.WriteLine("Error: the number cannot be negative");
    result = 0.0;    // assign a neutral value
} else {
    result = Math.Sqrt(x);
}
```

The if statement is controlled by a condition which produces *true* or *false*. The condition x<0.0 uses the less-than comparison operator. If that condition comes out as true, then the statements between the first pair of curly brackets are executed. If the condition comes out as false, the statements between the pair of curly brackets after the keyword else are executed instead.

The if statement used in this small example is sometimes called the *if-then-else* statement because there are two options. We test a condition, and if it is true (*then*) we perform one action, otherwise (*else*) we perform a different action.

Quite often, we do not want the program to perform any action at all as one of the two possibilities. In that situation, we can omit the *else* part of the statement. Here is a small example where we again compute a square root but we ignore an inconvenient minus sign if it is there.

```
Console.Write("Enter a number: ");
double x = double.Parse(Console.readLine());
if (x < 0.0) {
    x = -x;        // make the number positive
}
double result = Math.Sqrt(x);
```

Example 4.1 Computing a grade from a mark

Suppose that we have a mark for a course and want to convert the mark into a letter grade. Starting off simply, if we know that under 50% produces an F grade, then the statement

```
if (m < 50.0) grade = 'F';
```

would be sufficient. But if m is more than or equal to 50, we would need to differentiate grades further. Suppose we are given that the breakpoints between the letter grades F, D, C, B, and A are respectively 50.0, 65.0, 80.0 and 90.0 then we can employ a sequence of if-then-else statements to gradually establish which grade the mark is in. F is then the final grade if the mark does not exceed any of the other borderlines..

File ComputeGrade.cs

```
using System;

class ComputeGrade {
```

```
/// <summary>
/// The ComputeGrade Program      Bishop & Horspool  2002
/// =========================
/// Converts a mark into a letter grade.
/// Illustrates the use of if-else statements.
/// </summary>

string DetermineGrade(double m) {
   string result = "F";
   if (m >= 90.0) result = "A";
   else if (m >= 80.0) result = "B";
   else if (m >= 65.0) result = "C";
   else if (m >= 50.0) result = "D";
   return result;
}

void Go() {
   Console.Write("Enter the mark: ");
   double mark = double.Parse(Console.ReadLine());
   Console.WriteLine("The grade is " + DetermineGrade(mark));
}

static void Main() {
   new ComputeGrade().Go();
}
}
```

To test the program, we would type in various marks. For example, here is one sample test run:

```
Enter the mark: 77
The grade is C
```

4.3 Repetition statements

Computers are particularly useful for performing repetitive tasks. All programming languages provide some ways to repeat the same statements over and over until the desired result has been achieved. Chapter 3 introduced the for loop, used in that chapter for repeating an action a fixed number of times, so that programs could be more interesting.

The for loop is relatively complicated in its structure. As we shall soon see, Chapter 3 covered only a few of the possibilities. Probably the simplest way to repeat a group of C# statements is with the *while loop*.

The format of the while loop is captured in the following form.

WHILE LOOP
```while (condition) {   loop body }```
Evaluate *condition*, if it is true then execute the statements in the *loop body*. Next, re-evaluate the *condition* and if it is true, re-execute the *loop body*. Repeat until *condition* evaluates to false.

As a small example of the use of a while loop, here is a fragment of program which keeps prompting the user for a number between 1 and 10 until an acceptable number has been provided.

```
int number;
bool ok = false;
while( !ok ) {
    Console.Write("Enter a number from 1 to 10: ");
    number = int.Parse(Console.ReadLine());
    ok = (number >= 1) && (number <= 10);
}
Console.WriteLine("The number is "+number);
```

Next, we shall use while loops in a complete program.

Example 4.2 The unlucky days program

Superstitious people believe that the 13th day of the month is an unlucky day if it falls on a Friday. We want to write a program to create a list of these unlucky days, starting from January in a year provided by the user.

There are several aspects to the solution to this problem:

1. What constitutes a list of days? Well, we just want the list printed out, so what we envisage is a loop which, after each day is found, goes round and finds another. Naturally, this process cannot continue for ever, so we need to stop it. We choose to do so by prompting the user each time with
    Find another? (enter y or n)
    This loop is therefore governed by a Boolean variable which is re-evaluated each time on the basis of the user's response. It looks like this:
    ```
    bool more = true;
    while (more) {
        // .... do something
        Console.Write("      Find another? (enter y or n) ");
        more = Console.ReadLine() == "y";
    }
    ```
    So when the user enters anything other than a y, more is set to false and the loop stops.

2. How do we search for a Friday the 13th? Well, there is only one 13th in each
    month, so what we need is a loop which goes through each month, checking the
    date. The loop itself is once again a while loop. It starts in January of a given year
    (the user can type in the year) and then checks each month until a match is found.
    In outline, the loop is:

    ```
    // construct January 13 in the given year
    DateTime date = new DateTime(year,1,13);
    // advance the month until we hit a Friday
    while (!Fridaythe13th) {
        date = date.AddMonths(1);
    }
    ```

    AddMonths is a method defined in the DateTime class. We did not mention it in
    Section 2.6, but its existence in a well-rounded class is very necessary.

3. How do we check for a Friday the 13th? The condition in the above while loop
    needs to be expanded. We need to know the day of the week that a particular date
    falls upon. As it happens, no method has been provided for the DateTime type to
    return the information directly. However, the ToString method may be given a
    format string to control how a date is converted to a printable representation. As
    well as format strings like "D" which produce a complete date as a string, there are
    also format strings which are building blocks for constructing dates out of smaller
    pieces. One such building block is "d" to generate an abbreviated day (like 'Fri')
    and another is "dddd" which generates the full name for a day (like 'Friday'). We
    use the latter one in the program.

Now we can put all these pieces together for the program. Notice that the second loop is
nested inside the first one. Also, we do not restart the month for the second date in the list,
but carry straight on. Thus the initialization for the second loop is *outside* both the loops.

File Unlucky.cs

```
using System;

class Unlucky {

  /// <summary>
  /// Unlucky Days (version 1) Bishop & Horspool 2002
  /// =======================
  /// Finds unlucky days (Friday 13th).
  /// Illustrates the use of while loops.
  /// </summary>

  void Go() {
    Console.Write("Enter starting year: ");
    int  year = int.Parse(Console.ReadLine());
    bool more = true;

    // construct January 13 in the given year
    DateTime date = new DateTime(year,1,13);
```

```
    while (more) {
      // advance the month until we hit a Friday
      while (date.ToString("dddd") != "Friday") {
        date = date.AddMonths(1);
      }

      // print the full Friday 13th date
      Console.WriteLine("{0:D}", date);
      date = date.AddMonths(1);
      Console.Write("      Find another? (enter y or n) ");
      more = Console.ReadLine() == "y";
    }
  }

  static void Main() {
    new Unlucky().Go();
  }
}
```

If we run the `Unlucky` program, the output should look something like the following:

```
Enter starting year: 2003
13 June 2003
     Find another? (enter y or n) y
13 February 2004
     Find another? (enter y or n) y
13 August 2004
     Find another? (enter y or n) y
13 May 2005
     Find another? (enter y or n) n
```

The structure of the `Unlucky` program can be improved through use of some of the constructs covered later in this chapter. We will therefore revisit parts of the program again later.

The do-while loop

DO-WHILE LOOP
```do {   loop body } while (condition)```
Execute the *loop body*, then evaluate the *condition*. If it is true, re-execute the *loop body*, followed by a re-evaluation of the *condition*, and so on until the *condition* evaluates to false.

With the while loop, it is possible to execute the loop body zero times. However, there are some situations where we need to execute the loop body at least once. It is what we needed to program the earlier example of prompting the user to enter a number between 1 and 10.

Here is another way to write the code using the do-while loop.

```
int num;
do {
   Console.Write("Enter a number in the range 1 to 10: ");
   num = int.Parse(Console.ReadLine());
} while (!(num >= 1 && num <= 10));
```

The new version of the loop is simpler because it does not require a Boolean variable and is a little more efficient. The do-while loop is written with the test at the end to indicate that the loop body is executed and then the test condition is evaluated to see whether the loop body should be executed again. The do-while loop is usually chosen when we are sure that we want to execute the statements at least once, as in this case.

As a second example, here is a revised version of the main part of the Unlucky program given earlier. Since we want to find at least one Friday the 13th, the outer while loop is more naturally expressed in the do-while form.

```
bool more;
do {
  while (date.ToString("dddd") != "Friday") {
     date = date.AddMonths(1);
  }
  Console.WriteLine("{0:D}", date);
  date = date.AddMonths(1);
  Console.Write("      Find another? (enter y or n) ");
  more = Console.ReadLine() == "y";
} while (more);
```

The for loop in detail

Programs frequently need to step through a sequence of values, repeating the same calculations for each one. Although the while and do-while loops may be used for this purpose, the for loop provides a much more succinct way of programming the loop. Here is a while loop and an equivalent for loop for printing the square roots of the integers from 1 to 10.

```
int i = 1;
while (i <= 10) {                      for ( int i=1; i <= 10; i++ ) {
   Console.WriteLine(Math.Sqrt(i));       Console.WriteLine(
   i++;                                       Math.Sqrt(i));
}                                      }
```

The while loop version is programmed with three important components:

1. *Initialization of a control variable* i (the variable that has to step through a sequence), then a while loop controlled by ...

2. *A repetition test* which tests the control variable to decide whether all repetitions have been completed or not, and the loop body ends with ...

3. *A statement that advances the control variable* to the next value in the sequence.

The for loop construct puts all three of those components into the loop header. The first component is for initialization; the second component is for making a test to determine whether one more repetition of the loop is required; the third component is for advancing to the next value in the sequence. As an optional extra feature, the initialization component may declare a variable. That variable would normally be the control variable for the loop. A simple version of the for loop was introduced in Section 3.5: the full syntax of the for loop is summarized in this form.

FOR LOOP

```
for ( initialization; repetition test; advance ) {
    // loop body
}
```

The *initialization* code is executed. Next the *repetition test* is evaluated and if it is true, the loop body is executed. After executing the loop body, the *advance* code is executed and then *test* is re-evaluated to see whether the loop body should be executed again. The loop repeats until *test* evaluates to false.

Note that the initialization part may optionally declare one or more variables for use as the loop control variable.

The for loop is so general that it can be used to produce all sorts of effects. In addition, each of the three parts in the for loop header may be omitted because the different possibilities may not be immediately obvious. Some of these possibilities, and others, are described next.

Forwards loop. This is the conventional use, as in the following code example.

```
for ( int i = 0; i < 10; i++ ) {
    a[i] = 0;
}
```

It initializes an array of 10 elements to all zeros.

Backwards loop. We sometimes have to step through the elements of an array in reverse direction or to have a counter which decreases on each iteration. For example:

```
for ( int i = 10; i >= 0; i-- ) {
    Console.Write("{0} seconds to lift-off ...", i);
}
```

Infinite loop. Sometimes we want to write a loop which appears not to have a termination condition. However, there would usually be some way of leaving the loop somewhere in the loop body – the return statement would be one such possibility. An example occurs in the `ShowBinary` program (Example 4.7 below). As in that program, we could write the loop as follows:

```
while (true) {
    // loop body omitted
}
```

However, many programmers would write the loop like this:

```
for ( ; ; ) {
    // loop body omitted
}
```

The rules are that if the initialization and advance parts of the for loop header are omitted, then no action is performed. And if the test part is omitted, the effect is as if the test is the constant `true`. There is no advantage in using this form of for loop, it is just a common idiom.

Nested loops. Loops within loops are common in programs. If the loops have control variables, they should use different variables or else some confusion may result. The Primes program (Example 4.4) shows nested loops.

Zero-trip loops. With both while loops and for loops, it is possible for the loop body to be completely skipped. For example, a loop that steps through a sequence like this

```
for ( int i = 0; i < n; i++ ) { ... }
```

will not execute the loop body if n has a value of zero.

Double loops. It is easy to have two control variables change in tandem as a loop is repeated. Here is a small example:

```
int i, j;
for ( i=0, j=5;  i<=j;  i++, j-- ) {
   Console.WriteLine("({0},{1})", i, j);
}
```

which prints out the series of pairs `(0,5)` `(1,4)` `(2,3)`. These loops are quite unusual, but can be useful when processing complex data structures.

Multiple-exit loops. If the condition on a loop consists of a Boolean expression with and operators, then the loop could end because one of the conditions in the expression evaluated to false. It will usually be important to know which condition it was, so that immediately after the loop we check the conditions again. For example, suppose we read in 10 numbers, and want to stop when we get a negative number, or when all 10 have been read. The loop would be:

```
int i = 0;
int num;
do {
  num = int.Parse(Console.ReadLine());
  i++;
} while (!(num<0) && i<10);
if (num < 0)
  Console.WriteLine("Number {0} found", num);
else // loop ended on 10 and no negative found
  Console.WriteLine("No negative found");
```

The order in which the conditions are checked after the loop is important: if the tenth and last number is negative, both conditions will turn false at the same time. The intended logic of this loop is that we want to find a negative number, so we would check that first. Multiple-exit loops are used in the Primes program (Example 4.4).

Example 4.3 Unlucky days, version 2

We can change the structure of the Unlucky program again to use a for loop. In this version, everything associated with the iterating through the months is gathered in one place, i.e. in the for loop statement itself, as in:

```
for (DateTime date = new DateTime(year,1,13);
     more;
     date = date.AddMonths(1))
```

The control variable of the loop is now an object – the date variable we are concerned about in the program. The repetition test is the Boolean variable more (as before) and the advance, which was just a statement in the while loop somewhere, is now nicely highlighted. The new program is Unlucky2.cs..

File Unlucky2.cs

```
using System;

class Unlucky2 {

  /// <summary>
  /// The Unlucky program (version 2) Bishop & Horspool 2002
  /// ================================
  /// Finds unlucky days (Friday 13th).
  /// Illustrates the use of for loops to improve program structure.
  /// </summary>

  void Go() {
    Console.Write("Enter starting year: ");
    int year = int.Parse(Console.ReadLine());
    bool more = true;
```

```
      for (DateTime date = new DateTime(year,1,13);
          more; date = date.AddMonths(1)) {
        while (date.ToString("dddd") != "Friday") {
          date = date.AddMonths(1);
        }
        Console.WriteLine("{0:D}", date);
        Console.Write("       Find another? (enter y or n) ");
        more = (Console.ReadLine() == "y");
      }
    }

    static void Main() {
      new Unlucky2().Go();
    }
  }
```

The output of the program is the same as before (see Example 4.2).

Example 4.4 Prime numbers

Here is an example program showing the use of nested and multiple-exit for loops. It computes and prints the prime numbers from 2 to 100, using the simple method of testing whether each number is divisible by a positive integer other than 1 and itself. The algorithm uses two optimizations:

◆ it only checks odd numbers (after 2);

◆ it uses divisors up to (and including) the square root of the number.

(Note: if we need a program which generates a lot of prime numbers, much faster algorithms than this one exist.)

The outer loop causes the variable i to step through the sequence 3, 5, 7 ... 99. It is phrased as:

```
    for (int i = 3; i <= max; i += 2) {
```

The inner loop uses a more complicated test condition to force the loop to terminate as soon as we discover that i is not a prime number or when we have finished trying all the divisors up to the square root of i. It looks like this:

```
    bool prime = true;
    int last = (int) Math.Sqrt(i);
    for (int divisor = 3;  prime && divisor<=last;  divisor += 2)
```

Consequently, when the loop exits, we have to test *why* it stopped – because we found or did not find a prime. The full program is given in file `Primes.cs`.

File Primes.cs

```
using System;

class Primes {

   /// <summary>
   /// The Primes program          Bishop & Horspool   2002
   /// ==================
   /// Prints out all the prime numbers between 1 and 100
   /// Illustrates the use of nested
   /// and multiple-exit for loops.
   /// </summary>

   int max = 100;

   void Go() {
     Console.Write(" 2");  // print the first prime

     for (int i = 3; i <= max; i += 2) {
       // assume the number is prime
       bool prime = true;
       // when to stop checking
       int last = (int) Math.Sqrt(i);
       for (int divisor = 3; prime && divisor <= last; divisor += 2) {
         prime = (i % divisor != 0);
       }
       if (prime) Console.Write("  "+i);
       if (i % 19 == 0)
         Console.WriteLine();
     }
     Console.WriteLine();
   }

   static void Main() {
     new Primes().Go();
   }
}
```

As expected, the output is:

```
 2   3   5   7   11  13  17  19
23  29  31  37  41  43  47  53
59  61  67  71  73  79  83  89
97
```

We added a controlling if statement to print out a certain number (not always the same) of primes per line.

4.4 Simple arrays

An array holds a list of object values which are accessed according to their positions in the list. Each position has an index value. The first position, for the first element in the list, has an index value of 0. The second element has an index of 1, and so on. The declaration of a simple array and its semantics are given in the following form:

ARRAY DECLARATION (SIMPLE)

elementType[] *arrayId* = new *elementType*[*size*]

arrayId is created with *size* objects of type *elementType* which are accessed by indexes numbered 0 to *size*-1.

Examples are:

```
int[]      markCounts   = new int[101];
double[]   rainfall     = new double[13];
string[]   monthName    = new string[13];
DateTime[] myExams       = new DateTime[noOfExams];
People[]    technicians = new People[noOfTechnicians];
```

In all of these examples, the type of the elements is given first, then it is mentioned again when we construct the array with new. Later, when we discuss inheritance, we shall see that the two types need not always be the same. The pair of symbols [ ] is read as 'array' in this context. Finally the size of the array is given. It may be an integer constant, or it could be an expression which yields an integer as its value.

Notice that the size, which is the number of elements in the array, is always one greater than the last valid index. This is a consequence of using zero as the index of the first element in the array. The apparent discrepancy is often the source of errors in programs. It is also why we have declared the rainfall and monthName arrays as having size 13. This would enable us to use the expression monthName[5] to give us the name 'May', and monthName[12] to give us 'December'. Since there is no month numbered 0, we are leaving the 0th element unused in both arrays.

In programs, it is frequently necessary to perform the same calculation on each element of an array. The for loop, discussed previously, provides a convenient control structure for stepping an integer variable through all the index values for an array. We will see several examples of this in the following programs.

Example 4.5 Mark frequencies

Here we want to accumulate how often a certain mark out of 10 occurs in a class of 250 students. For example, we might like to learn that a mark of 0 occurred 13 times amongst all 250 marks. We use an array indexed from 0 to 10 (the range of possible marks) and store in each element the cumulative number of students with that mark. Figure 4.1 shows such an array.

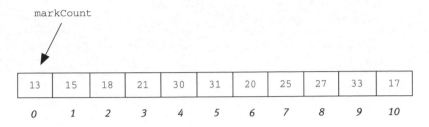

Figure 4.1 An array of mark counts

To keep the program simple, and the output manageable, we shall generate random numbers for the marks, rather than read them in. The program looks like the following.

File Frequencies.cs

```
using System;

class Frequencies {

  /// <summary>
  /// The Frequencies Program        Bishop & Horspool   2002
  /// =======================
  /// Counts the frequencies of marks from 0 to 10.
  /// Tested by generating random numbers.
  /// Illustrates simple array handling.
  /// </summary>

  const int limit = 11;   // to keep the table small
  const int classSize = 250;

  void Go() {
    int[] markCount = new int[limit];
    int score;
    Random r = new Random();

    // generate 250 marks
    for (int i=0; i < classSize; i++) {
      // generates from 0 to limit-1
      score = r.Next(limit);
      markCount[score]++;
    }

    Console.WriteLine("Table of mark counts\n"+
                      "====================\n\n"+
              " Mark  Occurred");
```

```
        int students=0;
        for (int i=0; i < limit; i++) {
          Console.WriteLine(
              " {0,4}{1,6}", i, markCount[i]);
          students += markCount[i];
        }
        Console.WriteLine("Total{0,7}", students);
      }

    static void Main() {
      new Frequencies().Go();
    }
  }
```

Typical output would be:

```
    Table of mark counts
    ====================

      Mark  Occurred
        0     24
        1     26
        2     26
        3     17
        4     21
        5     22
        6     16
        7     24
        8     28
        9     27
       10     19
     Total    250
```

Unlike the figures in Example 4.1, these figures represent an even distribution (rather unrealistic) because the random number generator is geared to do just that.

Working with array indices

Consider the `rainfall` array which we want to fill with the value of the rainfall recorded for each month, in millimetres. It might look like Figure 4.2 and the rainfall for May, 9.8 mm, would be given by

```
        rainfall[5];    // rainfall for May
```

To print the contents of the array, we can use:

```
        Console.WriteLine("   Month    mm");
        for( int month=1; month<=12; month++ ) {
           Console.WriteLine("{0:4} {1:10,1}", month, rainfall[month-1]);
        }
```

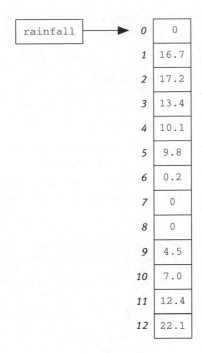

Figure 4.2 An array of rainfall values starting at 1

which would give

```
Month   mm
1       16.7
2       17.2
3       13.4
4       10.1
5        9.8
6        0.2
7        0.0
8        0.0
9        4.5
10       7.0
11      12.4
12      22.1
```

Many programmers would consider it unnecessary, or even wasteful, to create an array which has an extra unused element. It requires very little effort on the part of the programmer to avoid having the extra element. If the unused element at the beginning is omitted, the array will be declared as having size 12, as follows

```
string[] monthName   = new string[12];
```

The diagram of the array would be redrawn as in Figure 4.3. We could print out the rainfall for each month using code like the following, where the array index is adjusted to run from 0 to 11 instead of from 1 to 12.

```
Console.WriteLine("   Month    mm");
for (int month=0; month<12; month++) {
    Console.WriteLine("{0:4} {1:10,1}", month+1, rainfall[month]);
}
```

A professional programmer would almost certainly use the second version of the code and not declare arrays to have an extra element. However, if the program contains only a few arrays, there is usually no great concern about wasting memory. Whichever form seems more natural should be used; program readability is a more important issue.

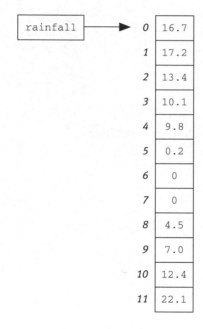

Figure 4.3 An array of rainfall values starting at 0

Size and length of an array

As defined above, arrays once declared always have the same size, and the indices are always integers. These two restrictions can be lifted by using other array-like types in C#, as discussed later in Chapter 8. However, we can customize the size of an array by reading in or calculating a more accurate length than can be guessed at in the program. In Example 4.5, if we wanted to extend the marks considered from 20 up to say 50 or 75 or 100, then the declaration part of the constructor would become:

```
Console.Write("What is the maximum mark? ");
int limit = int.Parse(Console.ReadLine());
int classSize = 250;
int[] markCount = new int[limit];
```

and the rest of the program would remain the same, but it could print out a table of up to however many marks were specified in the data.

Length is a property of an array that would be used inside a method to discover the length of an array passed as a parameter. For example, we could declare a method to print the marks array as follows:

```
void Print(int[] a) {
    for( int i=0; i < a.Length; i++ ) {
        Console.WriteLine("{0}: {1}", i, a[i]);
    }
}
```

The Print method can be passed an array of integers which has any length, and it will print it out. That is why we gave the formal parameter the fairly anonymous name of a.

Example 4.6 Computing a grade from a mark, version 2

As an additional example program, we revisit the program to compute a letter grade from a numerical mark (Example 4.1). This time, we use an array to hold the values at the borderlines between two adjacent grades and another array to hold the names of the grades. We also make use of a method to determine the grade, which leads to a loop with a return in it.

The outer loop, for processing several marks, has an interesting structure. Instead of asking whether there is another mark each time, as we did in the Primes example (Example 4.4), we use an invalid mark (−1) to signal the end of data. The consequence of this approach is that we need to check the mark twice – once before determining the grade (as we cannot grade a negative number) and once to end the loop.

File ComputeGrade2.cs

```
using System;

class ComputeGrade2 {

    /// <summary>
    /// The ComputeGrade Program (version 2)    Bishop & Horspool   2002
    /// ====================================
    /// Converts a mark into a letter grade. Illustrates the
    /// use of arrays and exiting from a loop with return.
    /// </summary>
```

```
double[] boundary = { 90.0, 85.0, 80.0, 75.0, 70.0,
                      65.0, 60.0, 50.0, 40.0 };
string[] grade = { "A+", "A", "A-", "B+", "B", "B-", "C", "D", "E"};

string DetermineGrade(double m) {
  for (int i=0; i < boundary.Length; i++) {
    if (m >= boundary[i]) return grade[i];
  }
  return "F";
}

void Go() {
  double mark;
  Console.WriteLine("Enter -1 to quit");
  Console.WriteLine("Mark     Grade");

  do {
    mark = double.Parse(Console.ReadLine());
    if (mark >= 0)
      Console.WriteLine("            {0}", DetermineGrade(mark));
  } while(mark >= 0);
}

static void Main() {
  new ComputeGrade2().Go();
}
}
```

A typical run of the program would yield

```
Enter -1 to quit
Mark    Grade
77
            B+
65
            B-
64
            C
90
            A+
-1
```

The foreach loop

In addition to the looping constructs discussed in Section 4.3, there is a special one called the foreach loop. The foreach loop is designed especially for *collections*, which are covered in Chapter 8. An array is, however, a simple kind of collection of values and the foreach loop works well with arrays. For example, if we have an array such as one which lists the names of the months, like this

```
string[] MonthNames = { "January", "February", "March",
   "April", "May", "June", "July", "August", "September",
   "October", "November", "December" };
```

then the following loop will print the list of names, in order, and one per line:

```
foreach (string s in MonthNames) {
   Console.WriteLine(s);
}
```

The form for the foreach loop is:

FOREACH LOOP FOR AN ARRAY

```
foreach (type id in arrayid) {
   ... body can refer to id
}
```

The id is assigned successive values from the array. For each value, the body of the loop is repeated.

4.5 Strings and characters

Although this chapter is primarily about control flow, we introduced arrays in order to exercise loops better. Strings share many of the characteristics of arrays, and characters are the elements of strings. We now consider them formally.

The string type

We have used string constants in programs throughout the book. We have also used string concatenation. For example, the statement

```
Console.WriteLine("Result = "+n);
```

works by converting the value n to a string (assuming that its type is not a string already) and concatenating it to the string constant "Result – " to produce a new longer string that is then passed to the WriteLine method of the Console class.

The string type is a structured type which has much in common with other C# types, but also has its own behaviour. Specifically, with strings we can:

♦ assign string values to string variables,

♦ compare two strings,

◆   concatenate two strings,

◆   access properties of string, and

◆   invoke various predefined methods for the string type.

A string is similar to an array the elements of which can be read, but not altered. Suppose we declare and initialize a string as follows.

```
string s = "abcdefghij";
```

We can access and print each character in that string by using the following for loop.

```
for( int i = 0; i < s.Length; i++ ) {
    Console.WriteLine("Element {0} = {1}", i, s[i]);
}
```

which produces 10 lines of output looking like this:

```
Element 0 = a
Element 1 = b
...
Element 9 = j
```

However, strings are not classified as arrays and an assignment such as

```
s[3] = 'x';   // an illegal attempt to replace d with x
```

is illegal because values of the string type are *immutable* – they cannot be changed. To create a new string value, an entire new string must be created.[1]

String operations

Basic string operations are summarized in the following form:

STRING DECLARATION AND USE	
string *svar1*;	// declare a string variable
string *svar2* = "string";	// declare and initialize a string
svar1 = svar2;	// assign a string
svar1 = "string";	// assign a string
svar1 = svar2+"string";	// concatenate two strings
int *len* = *svar1*.Length;	// obtain the length of a string

svar1 is created with the initial value null, while *svar2* is created and initialized with the value "*string*".

---

1. Mutable strings should be implemented as instances of the `StringBuilder` class.

One point that is often confusing is the difference between *null* (or no value) and the *null string* or *empty string*. An example may help.

The following two lines of C# code will cause a runtime error

```
string s1;          // create s with a null value
s1 += "abc";        // wrong, this fails!!
```

because the left operand of the string concatenation operator does not have a value. However, rewriting the code as follows

```
string s2 = "";
s2 += "abc";
```

will succeed and variable s2 will hold the value "abc" afterwards.

String constants start and end with the double quote character, where the constants can have any length from zero up. Something we occasionally need to do is to write a string constant which contains a double quote character. That is accomplished by prefixing the double quote with a backslash character. However, then the backslash character is another special case. How can we write a string constant which contains a backslash character? Same as before – by prefixing the character with a backslash character. Here are a few examples to make things clearer.

```
Console.WriteLine("");          // prints an empty line
Console.WriteLine("\"");        // prints the line: "
Console.WriteLine("\\\\");      // prints the line: \\
Console.WriteLine("\\\"a\\\"");  // prints the line: \"a\"
```

Here is one more example that may help.

```
string s = "\\\"";
Console.WriteLine(s.Length);    // prints 2
```

The important thing to note is that sometimes writing two characters causes only one (special) character to be placed into the string constant. All these special character combinations in C# have backslash as the first character of the pair. Some of the additional special character combinations are listed in the following section dealing with the char type. Any of the combinations allowed for a char constant may be used inside a string constant.

String methods

The string type has many predefined methods. A selection of some useful methods appears in the form for the String class.

Full information may be found in documentation for the System.String class (because string is a synonym for System.String in the C# language).

```
STRING CLASS (ABBREVIATED)

bool s1.StartsWith(string s2)    // true if s1 begins with s2
bool s1.EndsWith(string s2)        // true if s1 ends with s2

int s1.IndexOf(char ch)               // finds ch inside s1
int s1.IndexOf(char ch, int pos) // ditto, but at or after pos
int s1.IndexOf(string s2)             // finds s2 inside s1
int s1.IndexOf(string s2, int pos)  // ditto, but at or after pos

string s1.Substring(int pos)       // extract substring of s1
string s1.Substring(int pos, int len)  // ditto

string s1.ToLower()    // make copy of s1 with letters in lower case
string s1.ToUpper()    // make copy of s1 with letters in upper case

string s1.Trim()      // copy of s1 without leading or trailing spaces
string s1.TrimStart()    // copy of s1 without leading spaces
string s1.TrimEnd()    // copy of s1 without trailing spaces
string[] s1.Split()    // split s1 into words, one per array element

char s1[int pos]   // access character at index position pos
```

StartsWith returns *true* only if the string s1 begins with the string s2; EndsWith performs a similar test at the end of the string.

IndexOf returns the position of the first occurrence, searching from the left in s1, of a character ch or a substring s2. The first position in the string is numbered 0. If the search fails, the result is −1. The two versions with the pos argument start their searches at position pos.

The Substring methods return substrings of s1. The first form returns all the string starting at position pos; the second form returns a substring of length len starting at position pos.

ToUpper and ToLower convert alphabetic characters in s1 to all upper case and to all lower case, respectively.

TrimStart returns a copy of s1 with leading space characters removed; TrimEnd returns it with trailing space characters removed; Trim returns it with both removed.

Split breaks a string into an array of substrings, where each substring appears in s1 delimited by white space characters.

s1 [pos] accesses the character at position pos.

The char type

If string values are similar to arrays, then what type does an element of the array have? The answer is the char type. A variable of type char can hold a value which is a numeric code for one character. Each character, like the letter 'a' or the symbol '&', has a numeric code. It is somewhat arbitrary what these numeric codes are, but all the classes and methods in the C# library which work with strings and characters should use the same coding scheme. The C# library uses a scheme known as *Unicode*. Each Unicode value lies in the range 0 to 65535, meaning that it occupies 16 bits of memory.

In Unicode, the codes for the 26 lowercase letters 'a' through 'z' are numbered consecutively, as are the 26 uppercase letters 'A' through 'Z', and the 10 digit characters '0' through '9'. It is acceptable programming practice to assume that these codes are numbered consecutively. See Appendix D for more on Unicode values.

For example, the following lines of code can be used to see the numeric codes for a range of characters.

```
for (char ch = 'A'; ch <= 'Z'; ch++) {
    Console.WriteLine("Code for {0} is {1}", ch, (int)ch);
}
```

CHARACTER DECLARATION AND USE

```
char ch1;              // declare a character variable
char ch2 = 'X';        // declare and initialize a character
ch1 = ch2;             // assign a character
ch1 = 'Y';             // assign a character
s = s+ch1;             // concatenate a string and a character
s = ch1+s;             // concatenate a string and a character
```

ch1 is created and initialized with the character whose code is 0, while *ch2* is created and initialized with the value 'X'.

A cast from char to int suffices for obtaining the numeric code for a character. The output from the previous loop should be 26 lines looking like the following.

```
Code for A is 65
Code for B is 66
...
Code for Z is 90
```

Assigning a character value to an int variable would also work. The following loop will print the characters at the start of the numeric listing:

```
for(int i=0; i<256; i++)
   Console.Write((char)i+"  ");
```

Roughly, they are:

```
?  ?  ?  ?  ?  ?
   ?  ¤  ?  ?  ?  ?  ¶  §  ?  ?  ?  ?  ?  ?  ?  ?  ?  ?
!  "  #  $  %  &  '  (  )  *  +  ,  -  .  /
0  1  2  3  4  5  6  7  8  9  :  ;  <  =  >  ?  @  A  B
C  D  E  F  G  H  I  J  K  L  M  N  O  P  Q  R  S  T  U  V  W  X  Y
Z  [  \  ]
^  _  `  a  b  c  d  e  f  g  h  i  j  k  l  m  n  o  p  q  r  s  t
u  v  w
x  y  z  {  |  }  ~  |  ?  ?  ?  ?  ?  ?  ?  ?  ?  ?  ?  ?  ?  ?  ?  ?
?  ?  ?  ?
?  ?  ?  ?  ?  ?  ?  ?  ?  ?  ?  ?  ?     ¡  ¢  £  ¤  ¥  |  §  "  c
ª  «  ¬  -  r  _  °  ±  ²  3  '  μ
      ·  ,  1  °  »  ¼  ½  _  ¿  A  A  A  A  Ä  Å  Æ  Ç  E  É  E  E  I  I
   I  I  D  Ñ  O  O  O  O  Ö  x  O  U  U  U  Ü  Y  _  ß  à  á  â
```

```
a  ä  å  æ  ç  è  é  ê  ë  ì  í  î  ï  d  ñ  ò  ó  ô  o  ö  ÷  o  ù
ú  û  ü  y  _  ÿ
```

This output is 'rough' because not all of them can be displayed on the screen.

Escape sequences

A character constant is written like `'X'`, where the single quote character is used as the starting and ending delimiters. Given that there are 65536 different 16-bit codes but a typical computer keyboard has only about 50 keys, and given that some characters display in special ways (such as the tab character), special notations must be used to write most characters as constants of type `char`. All the special notations begin with the backslash character. Some are listed in the form below where they are called *escape sequences*; the backslash is called the *string escape character* (not to be confused with the key labelled *Esc* or *Escape* on a computer keyboard) and is used to escape to an alternative notation.

CHARACTER ESCAPE SEQUENCES (SELECTION)

```
\n       the linefeed character
\t       the (horizontal) tab character
\0       the null character
\'       the single quote character
\"       the double quote character
\\       the backslash character
\uXXXX   the Unicode character with code XXXX (hex)
```

All the combinations may be used inside a string constant or a `char` constant to denote one 16-bit character.

For the `\u` combination, *X* represents any hexadecimal digit (0 to 9 or A to F); thus `\u0041` represents the character whose code is 4×16+1 or 65, and that is the letter 'A'.

A linefeed causes a break to a new line; a tab causes a continuation of output at the next predefined tab column along the current line.

The *null character* is often used to denote no character – it is normally ignored when printed. It can therefore be used as a way of deleting characters from strings. We therefore have the following character and string values with confusingly similar names, but they are all different:

◆   the null character `'\0'`

◆   null

◆   the empty string `""`

◆   the string containing the null character `"\0"`.

They can be created in C# code as follows:

```
char c1 = '\0';
string s1 = null;  // s1 has no value
string s2 = "";    // s2 has a string value; the string length is zero
string s3 = "\0";  // s3 has a string value with length one
```

There is little that a program can do with `char` variables except assign them new values, compare them, and append them to strings. They are, however, extremely useful when reading or outputting text.

Unicode

There are many thousands of characters which are not available on all keyboards. These include those with accents and umlauts, special currency symbols, characters from the alphabets of other languages (Hebrew, Greek) and so on. As we have seen, however, there is an internationally agreed numeric representation for all these characters, called Unicode which you can find out about on the website `http://www.unicode.org`. Some of the more useful codes are shown in Table 4.4.

Character	Unicode
é	00F9
ü	00FC
ø	00F8
¢	00A2
£	00A3
¥	00A5
€	20AC
☺	263A

Table 4.4 Some Unicode characters

To get a Unicode character into a string, we use the escape code \ucccc where cccc is the Unicode. We must write the whole code. So for example, we could write:

```
Console.WriteLine("Dr M\00FCller's salary in Japan will be " +
                "\u00A5200.000");
```

which should print out:

```
Dr Müller's salary in Japan will be ¥200.000
```

If a Unicode character does not print correctly, then you may need to download some fonts to your computer. Instructions to do this are on the Unicode site. Also, the Unicode capabilities of the console window are quite limited, and may not be able to show everything, but it is worth a try.

Char methods

The char type (which is a synonym for System.Char) provides a number of static methods, mostly concerned with classifying a character value into different categories. Some tests for well-known categories are listed below.

```
CHAR TYPE (ABBREVIATED)

bool char.IsDigit(ch)         // true if ch is a digit
bool char.IsLetter(ch)        // true if ch is a letter
bool char.IsLetterOrDigit(ch) // true if letter/digit
bool char.IsLower(ch)         // true if lowercase letter
bool char.IsUpper(ch)         // true if uppercase letter
bool char.IsWhiteSpace(ch)    // true if white space
```
In the above, *ch* represents a char value. The result of each test is false if the test fails.

There are many more categories than letter, digit or white space. Full details may be found with documentation for the System.Globalization.UnicodeCategory type.

The tests are commonly used for searching through input text to pick out the parts that are relevant to the program. For example, if the program needs to find the next identifier in a line of program source code, we could use the following method:

```
string GetNextIdentifier(string line, int pos) {
    int idStart = -1;
    for( int i=pos; i<line.Length; i++ ) {
        char c = line[i];
        if (char.IsLetter(c)) {
            idStart = i;
            break;
        }
    }
    if (idStart < 0) return null;  // no identifier found
    int j;
    for( j = idStart+1; j < line.Length &&
            char.IsLetterOrDigit(line[j]); j++ )
        ;  // do nothing
    return line.Substring(idStart, j-idStart);
}
```

The first parameter is the line of text to search; the second parameter specifies where to begin searching (in case we are searching for a second or subsequent identifier in the line). The second for loop in this example is interesting. It has no statements inside the loop because all we are doing is searching for a position in the string which fails the looping condition.

Note: if the input line is written in a programming language like C#, there would be some special cases to consider. The logic of the method would have to be extended to ignore words inside string constants and comments. Perhaps, also, it would be desirable to ignore the keywords of the C# language.

The next example program illustrates the use of a string variable, a char variable, a while loop and a for loop.

Example 4.7 Visualizing binary numbers

Integer numbers inside the computer are stored in a binary representation. On most current computers, the int type uses 32 binary digits, otherwise known as bits. The software we use will normally disguise that binary representation by converting to and from decimal notation as appropriate.

However, if it is desired to see what the binary representation of an integer is we can use the following process: repeatedly divide the integer by 2 and remember the remainder. For example, the decimal number 13 may be converted to its binary representation of 1101 using these division steps:

- ◆ 13 ÷ 2 = 6 with remainder 1

- ◆ 6 ÷ 2 = 3 with remainder 0

- ◆ 3 ÷ 2 = 1 with remainder 1

- ◆ 1 ÷ 2 = 0 with remainder 1.

We can stop at that last step because the number to divide has become zero. The sequence of remainders, written in the reverse order of their creation, is 1101. Indeed, 1101 is the binary representation of 13 because

$$13 \ = \ 1{\times}2^3 + 1{\times}2^2 + 0{\times}2^1 + 1{\times}2^0$$

The ShowBinary program below repeatedly asks the user to enter a number and then prints that number in binary notation. The program uses two different while loops. One to repeatedly obtain a number from the input and convert it to binary, another to repeatedly divide by 2 and obtain a remainder. We can reverse the sequence of remainders by prefixing each remainder to a string variable.

The first while loop in the ShowBinary program has a test condition k > 0. If that condition is true, the body of the loop (the statements between the curly braces) is executed. Then the test condition is re-evaluated. If it is found to be true again, the body of the loop is executed again, and so on until the test condition evaluates to false. Since the body of the loop divides k by 2 on each iteration, the value of k must keep getting smaller. Eventually, k must equal zero and the loop condition will become false.

The second loop in the program, located inside the Go method, is written as an infinite loop. An infinite loop is usually something to be avoided. In this particular program, the for loop contains a conditional statement which causes the loop to exit in another way, i.e. via a return statement.

File ShowBinary.cs

```
using System;

class ShowBinary {

   /// <summary>
   /// The ShowBinary Program          Bishop & Horspool  2002
   /// =======================
   /// Displays a number in binary notation.
   /// Illustrates the use of while loops.
   /// </summary>

   void PrintBinary(int k) {
     if (k == 0) {
       Console.WriteLine("0");
       return;
     }
     string s = "";
     while (k > 0) {
       if (k%2==0)
         s = '0' + s;
       else
         s = '1' + s;
       k /= 2;
     }
     Console.WriteLine(s);
   }

   void Go() {
     Console.WriteLine("Note: enter -1 to exit the program.");
     for ( ; ; ) {
       Console.Write("Enter number to display in binary: ");
       int num = int.Parse(Console.ReadLine());
       if (num < 0) return;
       PrintBinary(num);
     }
   }

   static void Main() {
     new ShowBinary().Go();
   }
}
```

A typical run of the program would be:

```
Note: enter -1 to exit the program.
```

```
Enter number to display in binary: 13
1101
Enter number to display in binary: 4
100
Enter number to display in binary: 100
1100100
Enter number to display in binary: -1
```

4.6 Additional selection statements

The if statement and the while loop are all that is needed to achieve any desired flow of control from one statement to another in a program. However, programs are more readable and easier to update if some more expressive control constructs are provided. The break and continue statements may be viewed in this way.

The break statement may be used to exit from a loop early, while a continue statement may be used to start the next loop iteration early.

The break statement

Consider the inner loop in the `Primes.cs` program (Example 4.4). As soon as we find a divisor of variable i, we want to make the loop terminate. A different way to program that loop would be as follows.

```
prime = true;
for( int j = 3; j*j <= i;  j += 2 ) {
    if (i % j == 0) {
        prime = false;
        break;
    }
}
```

In one way, the loop is simpler because the for loop header is concerned only with stepping the variable j through a sequence of values. On the other hand, the control flow structure of the program is more complicated because when the break statement is executed, the loop is immediately terminated and execution continues with the next statement after the loop body.

There can be any number of break statements inside the loop body. The break statement can be used inside a while loop, a do-while loop, a for loop, and a switch statement (introduced below) to exit from it.

The continue statement

The continue statement is almost an opposite of the break statement. If executed, it causes an immediate transfer to the head of the loop for the next iteration. When executed inside a while loop, the conditional test expression is evaluated next and, if the result is true, the loop body is executed again; otherwise the loop is terminated. If executed inside a do-while loop, the loop body is executed next. If executed inside a for loop, the code to advance to the next iteration (the third component of the for loop header) is executed next; then the test expression is evaluated and, if it is true, the loop body is executed for the next iteration.

Here is a sample fragment of code which uses both break and continue statements. The for loop reads characters from the input one by one until it hits an empty line or hits the end of input. It then reports how many lines and how many characters were read.

```
int numChars = 0, numLines = 0, lineLen = 0;
for( int k = Console.Read(); k != -1; k = Console.Read() ) {
   char c = (char)k;
   numChars++;
   if (c == ' ' || c == '\t') continue;
   if (c == '\n')
      numLines++;
      if (lineLen == 0) break;
      lineLen = 0;
   } else
      lineLen++;
}
Console.WriteLine("Character count = {0}", numChars);
Console.WriteLine("Line count      = {0}", numLines);
```

The switch statement

The if statement is useful when there are only a few cases with their separate actions to be discriminated between. We can just write a series of if statements in a cascade like the following example.

```
// Test which editing action is to be performed
if (c == 'X')
   DeleteMode();
else if (c == 'I')
   InsertMode();
else if (c == 'R')
   ReplaceMode();
else
   Console.WriteLine("Control code {0} unknown", c);
```

When there are more than a few cases, it becomes tedious to program all those tests. It can also be inefficient, because the program will make test after test before finding the one which works.

The switch statement provides a convenient way to program a collection of tests; it uses a convenient succinct notation and it is executed more efficiently than the equivalent series of if statements.

The previous program fragment can be reprogrammed with the switch statement as follows.

```
// Test which editing action is to be performed
switch(c)
case 'X':
    DeleteMode();
    break;
case 'I':
    InsertMode();
    break;
case 'R':
    ReplaceMode();
    break;
default:
    Console.WriteLine("Control code {0} unknown", c);
    break;
}
```

The format of the switch statement is summarized in the following form.

SWITCH STATEMENT

```
switch(selector) {
case label1:
    action1;
    break;
case label2:
    action2;
    break;
    ...
default:
    default action;
    break;
}
```

If the *selector* expression is equal to *label1* then the statements represented by *action1* are executed; otherwise if the selector expression is equal to *label2* then *action2* is executed, and so on. If the expression matches none of the labels, then the statements after the keyword 'default' are executed.

The rules for use of a switch statement are as follows.

◆ The selecting expression (which appears in parentheses after the keyword switch) must evaluate to an integer, a bool, a char or a string.

◆ Each value used as a case label must be compatible with the type of the selecting expression.

◆ No value may appear as a case label more than once.

◆ The case labels can appear in any order.

- ◆ Several case labels may be attached to the same action.

- ◆ The statements after a case label must always end with a break statement or some other statement (such as a return statement) which causes execution to be transferred elsewhere.

- ◆ A break statement used inside a switch statement causes control to be transferred to the next statement immediately after the end of the switch statement.

- ◆ The default clause (labelled by the keyword `default`) is executed if the selecting expression has a value which does not match any of the case labels.

- ◆ The default clause is optional. If none is provided and the selecting expression does not match any case label, there is no action – execution continues at the next statement after the end of the switch statement.

Example 4.8 Roman numbers conversion

Here is a complete example program which makes full use of the switch statement. It converts from Roman numeral notation to decimal; for example, it should convert XIV to 14. Before we get to that program, here is a brief explanation of the Roman numbers notation.

The Romans probably started their numbering system with unary notation, so that one is written as I, two as II, and three as III. However, the notation soon becomes cumbersome and most people would have trouble distinguishing 12, say, from 13 when written in unary. The Romans therefore expanded the notation to use more letters giving:

I for one

V for five,

X for ten,

L for fifty,

C for one hundred,

D for five hundred, and

M for one thousand.

Numbers in between these main points can be created by combining the letter codes. So, XI is the notation for eleven, XII for twelve, and XIII for thirteen. Similarly, XV is fifteen, XVI is sixteen. When the values of the letters are supposed to be added together, as with XV, the letters must be written in descending order of their values. So VX would be incorrect.

To shorten the lengths of Roman numerals, an inconvenient number like XVIIII (which represents 19) may be written as XIX. The rule is that a single occurrence of a number is to be subtracted from the following number if that following number is larger. And we must apply that subtraction in the last possible position, so XIX is correct while IXX is incorrect. Given these rules, we have

VIII is 8,

XXVI is 26,

XXXIV is 34,

XLI is 41,

MCMLXXXIX is 1989, and

MMIV is 2004.

The Roman2Arabic program repeatedly prompts the user to type a Roman number and then it outputs the equivalent in decimal notation. This program does not report errors if the Roman numerals appear in invalid orders.

File Roman2Arabic.cs

```
using System;

class Roman2Arabic {

/// <summary>
/// Roman2Arabic          Bishop and Horspool      May 2002
/// ============
/// Converts and prints a number in Roman notation
/// that is interactively entered by the user.
/// Minimal validity checking of the number is performed.
/// Illustrates the use of switch statements.
/// </summary>

    int Arabic( string s ) {
        int units, tens, hundreds, thousands;
        units = tens = hundreds = thousands = 0;
        for ( int i=0;  i < s.Length;  i++ ) {
            char c = s[i];
            switch (c) {
            case 'I': case 'i':
                units++;
                break;
            case 'V': case 'v':
                units = 5 - units;
                break;
            case 'X': case 'x':
                tens += 10 - units;
                units = 0;
                break;
            case 'L': case 'l':
                tens = 50 - tens - units;
                units = 0;
                break;
```

```
            case 'C': case 'c':
               hundreds += 100 - tens - units;
               tens = units = 0;
               break;
            case 'D': case 'd':
               hundreds = 500 - hundreds - tens - units;
               tens = units = 0;
               break;
            case 'M': case 'm':
               thousands += 1000 - hundreds - tens - units;
               hundreds = tens = units = 0;
               break;
            default:
               Console.WriteLine(
                  "Error: {0} is not a Roman digit", c);
               break;
            }
         }
         return thousands+hundreds+tens+units;
      }

      void Go() {
         for ( ; ; ) {
            Console.Write(
               "Enter Roman number (or empty line to exit): ");
            string s = Console.ReadLine();
            s = s.Trim();
            if (s.Length == 0) break;
            Console.WriteLine(
               "{0} is the Roman notation for {1}",s,Arabic(s));
         }
      }

       static void Main() {
          new Roman2Arabic().Go();
       }
   }
```

Note how the label values in the cases of the switch statement are used in pairs, such as 'X' with 'x', and so on. That is an easy way to make the code work regardless of whether the Roman numerals are entered in upper or lower case.

When the program is run, the results look like the following.

```
Enter Roman number (or empty line to exit): XIX
XIX is the Roman notation for 19
Enter Roman number (or empty line to exit): MCM
MCM is the Roman notation for 1900
Enter Roman number (or empty line to exit): MCMXIX
MCMXIX is the Roman notation for 1919
Enter Roman number (or empty line to exit): MCMLXXVII
MCMLXXVII is the Roman notation for 1977
Enter Roman number (or empty line to exit):
```

4.7 Case study 2 – The Rock-Paper-Scissors game

Introduction to the game

The game of Rock-Paper-Scissors is normally played by two people, and there are many rounds. For each round, both players put one hand behind their backs. Then, on the count of three, both players bring out their hands very quickly. If a hand is brought out as a closed fist, that represents 'Rock'. If it is brought out with an open palm and all fingers together, that represents 'Paper'. Finally, if it is brought out with forefinger and index finger making a V-shape, then that represents 'Scissors'. If the two players bring out their hands making the same shape, the round is drawn. Otherwise, scissors beats paper (because a pair of scissors can cut paper), paper beats rock (because a sheet of paper can be wrapped around a rock), and rock beats scissors (because hitting the scissors with a rock would damage the scissors).

Typing the words 'rock paper scissors' into a web search engine will find many thousands of websites about the game.[1] (Even if you do not take the game seriously, there are many people who do.)

Table 4.5 shows an outcome matrix for the game, where +1 represents a win for player A, −1 a win for player B, and 0 represents a draw.

		Player B move		
		Rock	Paper	Scissors
Player A move	Rock	0	−1	1
	Paper	1	0	−1
	Scissors	−1	1	0

Table 4.5 Outcomes for Rock-Paper-Scissors

Played between two humans, the game is one of psychology – each player tries to guess what the other one will do. Played by a human against the computer, the strategy is definitely not based on psychology, especially if the human knows the source code of the program. Our program uses random numbers to make its moves hard to predict.

Structure of the program

The program has been divided into two classes which are stored in two different files. One class, `DriveRPSGameConsole`, is responsible for all interaction with the user. It also keeps track of how many rounds have been won, lost or drawn by the human player. The other class, `RPSGame`, actually plays the game – it selects the computer's play and, when told what the human's play is, reports who has won the round.

---

1. The website `http://www.worldrps.com` is highly recommended.

The source code is shown below. Its control structure of `DriveRPSGameConsole` uses an outer loop which, on each iteration, asks the user to select a play and then responds to that play. For convenience to the user, the input is just a single letter: 'r' for rock, 'p' for paper and 's' for scissors. When the user wishes to end the game, he or she can enter 'q' which is short for *Quit*.

Dividing the program into two classes has required us to add the keyword `public` to the constructor and two methods of the `RPSGame` class. The first class, `DriveRPSGame-Console`, needs to call the constructor and the two methods, `ComputersChoice` and `ComparePlays`, of the `RPSGame` class. Without the keyword `public`, the constructor and those two methods are, by default, *private*. That is, they are hidden from and cannot be called from code located in the other class, `DriveRPSGameConsole`. In contrast, the method named `Result` is called only from code inside the class and therefore does not need to be declared as `public`. There is a full discussion of all C#'s accessibility modifiers in Chapter 9.

File DriveRPSGameConsole.cs

```
using System;

class DriveRPSGameConsole {

    /// <summary>
    /// RSPGame        Bishop and Horspool      August 2002
    /// =======
    /// Plays the Rock-Paper-Scissors game with the user,
    /// using the Console for input-output
    /// </summary>

    void Go() {

        /// <summary>
        /// Drives the Rock-Paper-Scissors game.
        /// </summary>

        RPSGame game = new RPSGame();
        int noOfWins, noOfDraws, noOfLosses, round;
        noOfWins = noOfDraws = noOfLosses = round = 0;
        string computersChoice;
        string result;

        for( ; ; ) {
            computersChoice = game.ComputersChoice;
            string playersChoice = null;
            do {
                Console.Write(
                    "Enter R (Rock), P (Paper), "+
                    "S (Scissors), or Q (Quit): ");
                string b = Console.ReadLine().ToLower();
```

```
          switch(b[0]) {
            case 'r':
              playersChoice = "Rock";   break;
            case 'p':
              playersChoice = "Paper";   break;
            case 's':
              playersChoice = "Scissors";   break;
            case 'q':
              playersChoice = "Quit";   break;
          }
        } while(playersChoice == null);

        if (playersChoice == "Quit") break;
        result = game.ComparePlays(playersChoice);
        round++;
        Console.WriteLine("Round "+round);
        Console.WriteLine("The computer's choice = "+computersChoice);
        Console.WriteLine("The player's choice = "+playersChoice);

        switch (result) {
          case "draw":
            Console.WriteLine("  This round is drawn");
            noOfDraws++;
            break;
          case "lose":
            Console.WriteLine("  Sorry, you lose this round");
            noOfLosses++;
            break;
          case "win":
            Console.WriteLine("  Well done, you win this round");
            noOfWins++;
            break;
        }
        Console.WriteLine("Status: {0} wins, {1} draws,"+
                  "{2} losses", noOfWins,
          noOfDraws, noOfLosses);
      }
    }

    static void Main() {
      new DriveRPSGameConsole().Go();
    }
  }
```

The second file is named RPSGame.cs and contains the code for the RPSGame class. It
defines a property which provide access to the next choice of play by the computer. The
ComparePlay method calculates and reports who has won the round.

File RPSGame.cs

```
using System;

class RPSGame {
```

```
/// <summary>
/// Keeps track of state of the Rock-Paper-Scissors game.
/// </summary>

string[] MoveNames = {"Rock", "Paper", "Scissors"};
string computersChoice;
Random r;

public RPSGame() {
  r = new Random();
}

public string ComputersChoice {
  get {
    // generate a random 0, 1 or 2 and convert it to a string
    // and save it for the compare phase
    computersChoice = MoveNames[r.Next(3)];
    return computersChoice; }
}

public string ComparePlays(string playersChoice) {
  /// <summary>
  /// Determines whether the player beats the computer.
  /// Calls constructMessage where the parameters are
  /// - the player's choice
  /// - the choice the player could beat
  /// - the choice that could beat the player.
  /// </summary>
  switch (playersChoice) {
    case "Rock" :
      //            Player P win     P lose
      return Result("Rock","Scissors","Paper");
    case "Paper" :
      //            Player   P win   P lose
      return Result("Paper", "Rock", "Scissors");
    case "Scissors" :
      //            Player      P win    P lose
      return Result("Scissors", "Paper", "Rock");
    default:
      return null;
  }
}

string Result(string player, string Pwin, string Plose) {
  if (computersChoice==Pwin)
    return "win";
  else if (computersChoice==Plose)
    return "lose";
  else
    return "draw";
}
}
```

When the program is executed, the output might look like the following.

```
Enter R (Rock), P (Paper), S (Scissors), or Q (Quit): R
Round 1
The computer's choice = Scissors
The player's choice = Rock
  Well done, you win this round
Status: 1 wins, 0 draws, 0 losses
Enter R (Rock), P (Paper), S (Scissors), or Q (Quit): R
Round 2
The computer's choice = Rock
The player's choice = Rock
  This round is drawn
Status: 1 wins, 1 draws, 0 losses
Enter R (Rock), P (Paper), S (Scissors), or Q (Quit): R
Round 3
The computer's choice = Paper
The player's choice = Rock
  Sorry, you lose this round
Status: 1 wins, 1 draws, 1 losses
Enter R (Rock), P (Paper), S (Scissors), or Q (Quit): Q
```

Since the computer is selecting its plays using a random number generator, the proportions of wins, losses and draws should approach 33% each in the long run.

While the input interface is easy to use (it cannot be much simpler than having the player type a single letter for each round), the output is somewhat lacking in visual appeal. A version of Rock-Paper-Scissors that uses a GUI will be presented in Chapter 5.

Concepts in chapter 4

This chapter covered the following concepts:

arrays	array indexing
different styles of loops	Boolean expressions
break statement	continue statement
if statement	switch statement
while loop	do-while loop
bool type	string type
char type	escape and Unicode characters

and these operators:

```
&                              |
&&                             ||
!
```

It covered these C# keywords:

```
for                            while
do                             if
else                           break
continue                       switch
case                           default
foreach                        char
string                         bool
```

and defined the following forms:

comparison operators	Boolean logical operators
Boolean conditional operators	if statement
while loop	do-while loop
for loop	array declaration (simple)
foreach loop for an array	string declaration and use
string class (abbreviated)	character declaration and use
character escape sequences (selection)	char type (abbreviated)
switch statement	

Quiz

Q4.1 If we want to set a Boolean variable `freePass` for children under 15 or for students under 25, which would be correct?

(a) `freePass = age < 15 || age < 25 || student;`

(b) `freePass = age < 25 && student;`

(c) `freePass = age < 15 || (age <25 && student);`

(d) `freePass = student || age < 15;`

Q4.2 What is the correct framework for a while loop which is intended to repeat until the user types 'q' for Quit?

(a)
```
bool more = false;
while (!more) {
   ... statements
   more = Console.ReadLine() != "q";
}
```

(b)
```
bool quit = true;
while (!quit) {
   ... statements
   quit = Console.ReadLine() != "q";
}
```

(c)
```
bool quit = true;
while (!quit) {
   ... statements
   more = Console.ReadLine() == "q";
}
```

(d)
```
bool more = true;
while (more) {
   ... statements
   more = Console.ReadLine() != "q";
}
```

Q4.3 What sequence of values does the follow code fragment print out?
```
int i = 17;
while(i != 1) {
    Console.Write("{0}", i);
    i = 3*i + 1;
    while(i%2 == 0)
        i /= 2;
}
Console.WriteLine();
```

(a) 17 13 5 1   (b) 17 15 13 11 9 7 5 3 1

(c) 17 13 5   (d) 17 13 5 4 1

Q4.4 What is important to include with a multiple-exit loop?

(a) a break statement   (b) an if statement afterwards

(c) a continue statement   (d) a return statement

Q4.5 What do the following statements print?
```
string s = "\"hello!\"\n";
Console.WriteLine("{0}",s.Length);
```

(a) 9   (b) 8

(c) 6   (d) 12

Q4.6 If an array is declared as follows:

```
DateTime[] myExamDays = {new DateTime(2003,11,4),
                         new DateTime(2003,11,7),
                         new DateTime(2003,11,12),
                         new DateTime(2003,11,19)};
```

then the day of my second exam is given by

(a)	`myExamDays[2]`	(b)	`myExamDays[1].Day`
(c)	`myExamDays.Day[1]`	(d)	`myExamDays[2].Day`

Q4.7 If a switch statement does not include a default clause, the effect is

(a)   a compilation error

(b)   that if the value of the selector expression does not match any of the labels, then the case with a label closest to the selector value is chosen

(c)   that if the value of the selector expression does not match any of the labels, then execution continues at the statement after the switch

(d)   an execution error

Q4.8 A valid switch statement for setting the days in a month (ignoring leap years) would be:

(a)
```
int DaysIn(int month) {
  switch (month) {
    case 9: case 4: case 6: case 11: return 30;
      break;
    case 2 : return 28;
      break;
    else return 31;
      break;
  }
  else return 31;
}
```

(b)
```
int DaysIn(int month) {
  switch (month) {
    case 9, 4, 6, 11: return 30;
      break;
    case 2 : return 28;
      break;
    default: return 31;
      break;
  }
}
```

```
(c)   int DaysIn(int month) {
         switch (month) {
            case 9: case 4: case 6: case 11: return 30;
            case 2 : return 28;
            default: return 31;
         }
      }

(d)   int DaysIn(int month) {
         int days;
         switch (month) {
            case 9: case 4: case 6: case 11: days = 30;
              break;
            case 2 : days = 28;
              break;
            default: days = 31;
              break;
         }
      }
```

Q4.9 In the ComputeGrade2 program (Example 4.6) how best would the two arrays be printed out ? The output required is:

```
90.0          A+
85.0          A
```

etc.

```
(a)   foreach (double mark in boundary)
         Console.WriteLine(mark+"   "+grade[mark]);

(b)   for (int i=0; i<boundary.Length; i++)
         Console.WriteLine(boundary[i]+"   "+grade[i]);

(c)   foreach (double mark in boundary)
         Console.WriteLine(mark+"   "+grade[boundary[mark]]);

(d)   foreach (double mark in boundary, string symbol in grade)
         Console.WriteLine(mark+"   "+symbol);
```

Q4.10 If we had the string s=" by A A Milne " and want to return just the name "A A Milne", which of the following would do it?

```
(a)   s.TrimStart().Substring(s.IndexOf('A')).TrimEnd();

(b)   s.Substring(s.IndexOf('A')).Trim();

(c)   s.Substring(s.IndexOf('A'));

(d)   s.TrimStart().Substring(s.IndexOf('A'),s.Length).TrimEnd();
```

Exercises

4.1   **Loop variety.** It is relatively easily to convert a for loop into an equivalent while loop, and *vice versa*. The following code extract is meant to read in strings into an array, and then print them out.

```
string s;
int lineNum = 0;
string[] line = new string[10];
for (s=Console.ReadLine(); s!=null; s=Console.ReadLine()) {
  line[lineNum] = s;
  lineNum++;
}
for (int i = 0; i < lineNum; i++) {
    Console.WriteLine("{0,4}: {1}", i+1, lineNum);
}
```

Incorporate the extract into a complete program and test that it works. Then rewrite the for loops as while loops and test that the program still gives the correct results. Rewrite it again with do-while loops.

4.2   **Any cities.** Adapt Example 2.7 (Time with reading) so that data can be read in until the user signals enough. Decide how the signal is to be formulated.

4.3   **Histograms.** If we have an array of values, such as that created in the mark frequencies program (Example 4.5) or the rainfall array (Figure 4.2), we can obtain a more interesting output by representing the value as a list of stars across the page. Thus one might have the following for the first few lines of output:

```
Mark   occurred
   0     24      *************************
   1     26      **************************
```

Design a method which, when given a value as a parameter, displays that number of stars. Incorporate the method in the Frequencies program.

4.4   **Rainfall histogram.** Referring to Exercise 4.3, sometimes the number of stars will need to be scaled in order to make the histogram meaningful. For example, the values in Figure 4.2 could be doubled before being passed to the Histogram method. Devise a means of finding out whether and how scaling should occur and incorporate your technique in a program to print out rainfall histograms.

4.5   **Base numbers.** Adapt the ShowBinary program (Example 4.7) so that it will print a number in any base up to 10, where the base is read in.

4.6   **Hexadecimal numbers.** Hexadecimal is an accepted number form, using base 16. The 16 digits to be used are 0–9 and the letters A–F. Thus 15 is written as F and 16 as 10. Adapt the ShowBinary program to print numbers in hexadecimal. Hint: a switch statement can be used to select the higher digits, or a conversion from `char` to `int` and back to `char` will work. Try both approaches.

4.7   **Arabic to Roman.** A much more challenging program, but similar in some ways, is to convert Arabic (i.e. base 10) numbers to Roman numerals. Use Example 4.7 and Example 4.8 for guidance.

4.8   **Text typing.** Text (or SMS) messages are often typed in lowercase, but many cell phones have the intelligence to switch to uppercase for the first letter after a punctuation symbol such as a full stop or question mark. Write a program to read in a message as a string (on one line) and process it to produce a new string with capital letters in appropriate places.

4.9   **Currency symbols.** A company handles its employees' expenses in dollars. When they return from a trip, they can submit their expenses in any one of the following currencies:

- sterling, e.g. £2050
- euro, e.g. € 5196
- Canadian dollars, e.g. C$4987
- US dollars, e.g. $5000
- Yen, e.g. ¥200000
- Swedish kroner, e.g. 7000kr

Write a program to read in one of these expense amounts and translate it to US dollars. Some current exchange rates can be stored directly in your program. Get them from a website such as `www.xe.net`. Watch out for the currencies whose symbol comes *after* the number.

4.10   **Marathon runners.** There are five main contenders for a marathon race. They come from England, Germany, Italy, Spain and Norway. The organizers of the race receive the following information about each runner: name, country, age, best marathon time so far (in hours and minutes).

- Create a class which will represent a marathon runner. You could use the Time class for the best time. Usually marathon times are around two hours.
- Write a short program to test that you can create five runners of the class successfully.
- Now write a Race program which will create the runners, then generate randomly a final time for the race for each, then print out the list of runners, indicating all their details, plus this time, plus their new best time.
- Determine the winner.

4.11   **Weight watchers.** Two friends have been trying to lose weight over several weeks. The first started off weighing 100 kg and with a 98 cm waist, the second weighing 85 kg and having a 95 cm waist. Each week they record their new weight and waist measurements and work out who lost more in each category.

- Design and program a class for recording progress in terms of current weight and waist measurements.
- Test the class out by creating objects for up to six people.
- Now write a program to run for four weeks, where each week new weight and waist measurements are generated randomly but which are roughly similar to those currently held (for example, current weight ± up to 1.5 kg and current waist ± up to 2 cm). Print out the new measurements and store them back in the objects, and also print out who lost more in each case.
- Keep a running total of losses and, at the end, print out the total loss for each person.
- Determine the Thinner of the Month, i.e. the person who lost the most weight.

4.12   **Voting.** A board of directors consists of three members, each of which has a two-way switch marked yes/no. When votes are taken, a lamp comes on if the yes votes are in the majority. The circuit that implements the turning on of the lamp is represented by the Boolean function

```
L = a & (b | c) | b & c
```

Write a program which writes a table of the alternative yes/no values for a, b and c, and the value of L. Implement L using a Boolean method.

4.13   **Birthdays.** The probability of two people in a group of n having the same birthday is

$$p(n) = 1 - \frac{365}{365} \times \frac{364}{365} \times \frac{363}{365} \times \ldots \times \frac{364 - n + 1}{365}$$

Write a program to evaluate and print this probability for groups of 2 to 60 people. Draw a table of n and $p(n)$ for values of n from 10 to 50. If you completed Exercise 4.3, plot the values for 10, 20 ... 50 on a histogram.

4.14   **The Fibonacci series** consists of a series of numbers in which each number is the sum of the two preceding ones, i.e.

```
1    1    2    3    5    8    13    21    34    55 ...
```

Write a program to display the first 50 terms of the series. Using a nested for loop, adapt the program so that it displays only every third number. What do you notice about the numbers?

4.15   **Phone companies.** Extend the case study in Chapter 3 to include in the data the times during which cheap rate operates, and for each call its starting time. (You can use the `Time` struct from Example 3.2 to represent times.) Replace the random number generated for indicating whether we are in cheap rate or not by a check against the times. Complete the program by printing a message to say which company, on that simulation, would be cheaper.

CHAPTER 5

Graphical user interfaces with Views

The programming examples up to this point have used text input and output. In this chapter we learn how to create Windows forms on the screen through which we can interact with the program. The interaction uses a variety of standard controls such as buttons and text boxes, and includes facilities for handling images. The interaction is provided through a customized namespace, Views, written in C# and available with the book. Views uses XML, a notation similar to HTML, to define the layout of the Windows form. Interaction with the form at runtime employs many of the control structures, such as loops and switch statements, that were covered in Chapter 4.

5.1 Graphical user interfaces

Programs up to this point in the book have been controlled by text input, read from the keyboard or from a text file, and they write their results as text – either to a file or to a console window on the screen. Although this form of input–output is quite sufficient for harnessing the power of the computer, the output is visually unappealing to the average computer user. And we should not think this is just a matter of aesthetics. There are many kinds of input where selection of input choices using the mouse would be far more convenient to the user than alternatives based on typing text with the keyboard.

So, we would like our programs to create windows on the screen for interacting with the user, and we want the programs to look as interesting to use as commercially available software. The good news is that it is possible in C# to have a program create a window on the screen which displays different messages, has buttons which can be clicked by the user, has input fields into which text can be typed, and so on. This kind of window, which uses non-textual elements for presentation of choices and other information and which relies on a cursor or pointer moved by the mouse, is known as a *graphical user interface* or GUI (pronounced like *gooey*) for short.

A C# program running on the Windows computer platform can use classes in the `System.Windows.Forms` namespace to display a GUI on the computer screen and to handle associated input from the mouse and keyboard. Figure 5.1 shows a simple GUI created in this way.

Figure 5.1 A simple GUI from Windows forms

The intention of the example is clear: a picture is displayed and the two buttons can be pushed to hide it or show it again. This example was developed using a Windows tool called Visual Studio, and the resulting program is 124 lines long, with 15 lines written by the programmer, and the rest generated by the tool. There is a steep learning curve associated with the classes and the tools used to develop programs in using Windows forms, because there are many classes, each with many methods and properties, and they interact in complicated ways.

In this book, we are trying to focus on the C# language and to keep the example programs and the C# namespaces that are covered as independent of Windows (the operating system) as reasonably possible. In so doing, we can concentrate some of our time also on *GUI design* – how best to lay out the GUI. For example, in Figure 5.1, the buttons are positioned from the left, but the overall result would look nicer if they were centred over the picture.

In order to stay platform independent, and to provide an easy way of experimenting with GUI design, we shall initially develop programs that create GUIs for their input–output using a namespace called `Views` which has been specially created for this book. The `Views` namespace can be downloaded in both source code and compiled form for use with the Windows operating system. The files are available from the website which is provided to support this book. A reference manual for Views is provided as an appendix.

Views is related to Windows forms in that the terms and concepts it uses match those in the `System.Windows.Forms` class exactly. As a subset, though, it is a more palatable way of working with GUIs. Thus what we learn in Views can be carried over to Windows forms very easily.

5.2 Elements of a GUI

Let us first look at GUIs in general. We shall introduce the following terms:

◆ control

◆ form (i.e. Windows form)

◆ menu bar

◆ layout

◆ interaction.

A GUI is a window on the screen which contains a number of different *components* or *controls*. Controls can be labels, buttons or text boxes, for example. In programming terms, the GUI is implemented as a *Windows form*. The GUI very likely has a *menu bar* across the top which contains the name of the program or window and some buttons.

There will normally be three such buttons for hiding (the minus sign), resizing (the two boxes) and destroying (the cross) the GUI display. The positioning of these buttons is dependent on the platform, for example in Figure 5.1, which was created on Windows, they are on the right of the menu bar.

What appears below the menu bar is very much determined by the program which created the window. The controls are said to have a certain *layout* relative to each other and their position on the screen. Both the choice of the controls and their layout are the concern of the programmer. When we have looked at an example and become familiar with some components, we shall come back to the issue of layout.

Once the controls are on the screen, we interact with some of them via the mouse and keyboard. Moving the mouse over a control, and then clicking can make things happen (as with a button). At other times, we can be in a control that allows us to type from the keyboard. These controls essentially reflect text input. Other controls define areas for outputting data, both text and images, as we have already seen.

Introduction to simple controls

Writing and using games on a computer is fun and we are nearing the point where we can make the games look good on a screen. Figure 5.2 shows the GUI created by a sample program which plays the Rock-Paper-Scissors game described in the case study of Chapter 4. The rules of the game were explained then: here we are going to see how to make a GUI for it. First, let us examine Figure 5.2 in detail.

The screen area under the menu bar contains a variety of different controls, and we can group them as follows.

Buttons. At the bottom, there are three *Button* controls, and the one labelled 'Scissors' is indicated. The user can move the mouse cursor onto the button and click the mouse button. That causes an input into the operating system, which in turn signals an *event* to the program. There are two other button controls, named 'Paper' and 'Scissors', which similarly send events to the program.

Labels. Several other controls are simply text strings; for example, one in the GUI reads 'Choose your selection ...'. These controls are called *Labels* and they are inactive – nothing happens if the user moves the mouse over those strings and clicks the mouse or types on the keyboard.

ListBox. There is a large white rectangle on the right which is used by the program to display a record of the selections made by the user and what happened. This box contains a vertical list of strings and is therefore called a *ListBox* control.[1]

---

1. In what follows, we use the plain English terms for controls where possible, that is 'text box' rather than TextBox. Only when a specific C# instance is referred to, will we use the programming term `TextBox`.

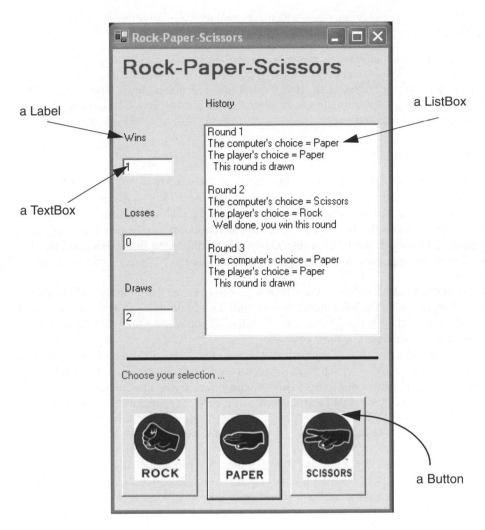

a Label

a TextBox

a ListBox

a Button

Figure 5.2 GUI for the Rock-Paper-Scissors game

TextBoxes. There are three rectangular white boxes which contain numbers; these are *TextBox* controls. In the Rock-Paper-Scissors game, they are used to display some results produced by the program. They show the number of rounds which the user has won, lost or drawn. It would be possible to write our program to accept input typed by the user in these windows, but that possibility has not been used in this particular program.

The program which creates the GUI has to specify which controls are needed, how large they should be and exactly where inside the window they should be located. Such details are a necessary part of the GUI design, and they can be very tedious to program explicitly.

If `rockButton` is a class instance which creates and draws a button in the GUI, we do not really want to write a statement like

```
rockButton.Location = new System.Drawing.Point(55, 275);
```

to set its position as 55 pixels in from the left and 275 pixels down from the top. It is almost always time consuming to get the placement of controls in a GUI to look just right, involving a lot of trial and error.

Layout in a GUI

When designing a GUI, we can just add controls to the window as we think of them, but that would not usually make a very pleasing arrangement. A key feature of GUIs is to group controls that are similar together. Thus we would put all the buttons at the top, or at the bottom. We can split the screen in half, and have input boxes on one side, and output on another, and so on. All these arrangements will be illustrated in the examples that follow. The question is, how do we manipulate controls like this? There are three options:

Drag and drop.   One is to use a tool which allows us to create the code for a GUI by dragging a control from a list showing all the possibilities and dropping it onto the spot which looks right visually. We can change the placement of controls by dragging them with the mouse, and change their sizes just as easily.

Such tools are actually very sophisticated pieces of software and take a lot of room on a computer. An example is Visual Studio which is built specifically for C# and other languages on the Windows platform. Visual Studio offers many options and is a difficult environment to use if one is still learning how to program. It generates C# code which uses advanced features. However, there are other more lightweight tools, which have the advantage of being cross-platform. One is available for Views as well, as discussed later.

Absolute positioning.   Without using drag and drop, we can write calls to Windows form methods which precisely position a control down to the last pixel. On a typical display screen, pixels are numbered across a screen from 0 up to at least 800 on the x-axis, and from 0 to at least 600 on the y-axis, with the axes being drawn as in Figure 5.3. In this figure, the button would have been placed at position $x=300$, $y=150$, i.e. slightly less than halfway along each axis.

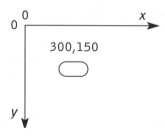

Figure 5.3 The axes on a computer screen

The code to place a button at position *x*=300, *y*=150 would be something like the following:

```
button = new Button();
button.Location = new Point(300, 150);
```

which in itself is not difficult to write or understand, but working with controls in absolute coordinates brings with it many extra small things to specify, and can become very long-winded. Another problem is that some screens these days are bigger than 600×800, in which case absolute positioning has to be done most carefully to obtain results which look good across a variety of computers.

Relative positioning. There is much less to specify, and less to worry about, if we allow the system to position controls for us, within certain basic guidelines. This approach usually relies on creating vertical and horizontal lists, nested within one another as much as one likes. So for example, Figure 5.1 is laid out as shown in the diagram in Figure 5.4.

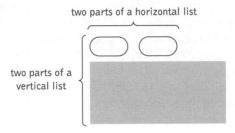

Figure 5.4 Relative layout of controls

The specification of such a layout would (never mind the notation) be as follows:

```
vertical
  horizontal
    button
    button
  end horizontal
  image
end vertical
```

In other words, we start with a vertical list. The first element is a horizontal list, which consists of two buttons. That element ends, and the next element is an image.

The Views namespace used in this book uses relative placement, yet also has some absolute placement features for finer positioning. It provides a much simpler alternative to creating a GUI with Visual Studio, yet it still gives a great degree of control over the way that the GUI looks.

5.3 Introduction to Views

Programming a GUI in Views consists of the following steps:

1. Specifying the layout of controls.
2. Creating a GUI object.
3. Reacting to the controls.
4. Interacting with the controls.

In the context of GUIs, reacting means a response to user events like clicking on a button. Interacting is broader, and specifically means that we can put things into a control, such as write into a text box.

Specifying the layout

In Views, the specification is done in XML. The term XML is short for eXtensible Mark-up Language and its syntax is related to the HTML (HyperText Markup Language) used for specifying the appearance and content of web pages. However, XML is more regular in its structure and is designed to be extensible, which makes it suitable for a great variety of tasks.

The XML notation consists of tags and attributes. Each *tag* has a name and is enclosed in angle brackets or matched by a corresponding close tag. Close tags are preceded by a slash character. *Attributes* are identifiers with assigned values.

For each domain in which XML is applied, certain tags and attributes are defined. Thus for Views, we will be defining a set of some 15 tags, each with up to five or six optional attributes.

The elements of the XML notation used by Views are shown in the form below.

VIEWS XML NOTATION

```
<tag attributes>
   other tags
</tag>

or

<tag attributes />

where attributes is a list of attribute definitions written
as
id=value
```

Tags and ids are written as letters only; values of attributes can have a variety of forms (number, string, etc.) as required by the attribute). If the specified tag identifies a control which can be displayed via Views and is used interactively then a `Name` attribute is required.

Consider some of the tags in the Views XML that would be used for the Show-Hide program referred to in Figure 5.1 and Figure 5.4.

```
<horizontal>
  <Button Name=Show/>
  <Button Name=Hide/>
</horizontal>
```

In this example, `<horizontal>` is a tag without any attributes which contains other tags, so its closing tag stands by itself with the tag name repeated. The tags for the buttons are simple, but since they identify an interactive control on the GUI Windows form, they must specify a `Name` attribute. To clarify the two tag forms, the specification

```
<Button Name=Show/>
```

is equivalent to

```
<Button Name=Show> </Button>
```

Notice that open and close tags are properly nested in the example. Views will report an error if they do not match.

Another example from the same GUI would be

```
<PictureBox Name=pic Image='Jacarandas.jpg' Height=4cm/>
```

Here there are more attributes, for the name of the file holding the picture, and for a defined height. If we specify either the height or width that we want the picture to be displayed in, the other dimension is scaled by Views accordingly, which is very convenient. There is more about measurements in Views attributes in Section 5.5.

Creating a GUI object

The XML for a Views GUI does not mean anything in itself to C#. It only means something to the `Views.Form` class that we have defined. To create a GUI, therefore, we need to create a `Views.Form` object and pass it the XML as an initializing parameter. The following form sums up this process.

VIEWS.FORM OBJECT CREATION
```Views.Form GUIname = new Views.Form(@"   Views XML specification ");```
At runtime, an object called GUIname is created. The @ character introduces a multi-line string, consisting of the Views XML specification.

In any one program, we can have several GUIs running, either one after each other, or at the same time. For example, we could have one GUI where the user logs on, and then another which handles the main interaction. The Views form specification string does not have to be listed directly as a parameter to the `Views.Form` constructor, but can be initialized or read in elsewhere in the program. For example, a valid GUI creation would be:

```
string spec = @"<Form>
    ... Views XML specification
    </Form>";
Views.Form f = new Views.Form(spec);
```

We can also store the specification in a separate file altogether. The name of the file would then be provided as the argument to the constructor. (Although the argument is a string in both cases, the constructor can easily distinguish a XML specification from a filename.)

Views capitalization and quotes

The `Views.Form` class does not care how the word 'Button' is capitalized; it could equally well be written as 'bUtToN', but that would be a bad idea. The text 'Show' would, however, appear as the button's label in the GUI with the same capitalization as given in the specification.

Although Views ignores how the control names are capitalized, we have been careful in this chapter to capitalize tags associated with controls in the exact same way as the corresponding class names in the `System.Windows.Forms` namespace. Similarly, the attribute names are capitalized in the same way as properties of those classes. Uncapitalized tags in our examples (such as `<vertical>`) do not correspond to Windows class names, and similarly for uncapitalized attribute names which we shall encounter later.

Note that the quotes around the label for each button can be omitted if the label does not contain a space or a special character. This is a special convenience provided by `Views.Form`. With standard XML, double quote characters are necessary around the label or around any other text value; putting double quote characters inside C# strings is less convenient than putting single quote characters inside (and definitely less convenient than none at all).

Reacting to the controls

Creating an instance of the `Views.Form` class causes the GUI to be displayed on the computer's screen. The program can then wait for the user to do something, such as to click a button or type some text. These stimuli are detected by the operating system and passed to the part of the program which has elected to receive them, which in this case is the `Views.Form` object we created.

The part of the program which receives such a prompt is known by the general term of an event handler. *Event handlers* are typically methods which can be passed as a parameter the name of the particular control that was activated. Then the handler can decide what to do about it. Active controls such as buttons should definitely have handlers, whereas potentially passive ones such as labels and images need not.

In Views, we wait for events to happen in an event loop, based on a special method called `GetControl`. `GetControl` will supply the program with the name of the control that was activated, and from there we can go onto a handler. The style of programming is shown in the next form.

VIEWS CONTROLS INTERACTION

```
void Go() {
    SetUp(); // create and initialize the GUI
    for ( ; ; ) {
        string cname = f.GetControl();
        if (cname == null) break;
        ActionPerformed(c);
    }
    f.CloseGUI();
}

void ActionPerformed(string cname) {
    switch (cname) {
    case "control1":
        statements;    break;
    case "control2":
        statements;    break;
    etc.
    default:
        break;
    }
}
```

`f.GetControl` returns the name of the control which was activated. Clicking the close box in the top right corner of the GUI causes *null* to be returned so that the loop can end and close the GUI. The `ActionPerformed` method uses a `switch` statement to test which control has been used, and executes the corresponding statements.

Interacting with controls

Once in a handler, we can interact with a control in two ways. The first and preferred way is to call one of the Views methods which are specifically designed for the purpose. There is a full discussion of these methods in Section 5.6, but we mention two here because they will be used in the next examples. These are GetText and PutText which enable values to be read from and written into text boxes and list boxes. The methods to do so are summed up in the form:

VIEWS TEXT BOXES AND LIST BOXES INTERACTION

```
str = GetText(controlid);
PutText(controlid, str);
```

For a given control with the name stored as a string in `controlid`, GetText will return the string currently displayed in the control. PutText will insert the given string. In the case of a `TextBox`, `PutText` overwrites the current value; in the case of `ListBox`, it adds the string on the next line.

For example, in the Rock-Paper-Scissors Game illustrated earlier in Figure 5.2, we write a message into the list box named `"results"` at the end of each round. One such message would be:

```
form.PutText("results", "This round is drawn");
```

We also write a number into the text boxes on the left and a statement to do so is:

```
form.PutText("draws", noOfDraws.ToString());
```

As we shall see, the text box's name is `"draws"` and there is also an integer variable `noOfDraws` keeping track of the number of draws. Because `PutText` only accepts strings, we first convert the integer by using `ToString`.

Since the Views controls are actually real controls supported by the part of the operating system which is drawing them on the screen and watching out for signals like mouse clicks, a second way of interacting with the controls is to directly set any of their attributes. To do so requires knowing what the attributes are, and as we stated at the beginning of the chapter, acquiring all this knowledge is time consuming and error-prone. It is therefore more desirable to stay within the Views world if possible. Nevertheless, it is technically possible to access the rich array of classes provided by `Windows.Forms` or other systems that Views runs on (which will be very similar), and how to do so is covered in Section 5.7.

Example 5.1 Rock-Paper-Scissors game with a GUI

The Rock-Paper-Scissors game of Chapter 4 provides an ideal opportunity to investigate GUI programming. Games cry out for GUI interfaces. We have already shown the GUI we are after, in Figure 5.2. How did we arrive at such an interface? We followed the same steps mentioned above. That is:

Establish the controls. For the three choices in the game, we need three buttons. Figure 5.2 shows them as pictures, and we shall see how to do this below. However, they could also have been just plain buttons. For the results, we decide on recorded wins, losses and draws, hence there are three text boxes. And to report what is going on, we use a list box, with a label above it.

Group the controls sensibly. The grouping is fairly obvious. We should keep the buttons together and the text boxes together. Otherwise, the layout is up to us.

Sketch an outline of the GUI. There are many ways that we could lay out the GUI. Figure 5.5 shows two options other than the one we chose, shown in Figure 5.2.

Translate the GUI to Views notation. Whichever format we choose, we note that the concept of vertical and horizontal lists prevails. In Figure 5.5(a) the appropriate Views specification would be:

```
<vertical>
   <horizontal>
      three buttons
   </horizontal>
   listbox
   <horizontal>
      three text boxes
   </horizontal>
</vertical>
```

Interpreting from the top, it means that the GUI consists of a vertical list, with three elements – a horizontal list, a list box and another horizontal list. Each of the two horizontal lists has three elements in it. An alternative arrangement as shown in Figure 5.5(b) would be specified by

```
<horizontal>
   <vertical>
      three buttons
   </vertical>
   listbox
   <vertical>
      three text boxes
   </vertical>
</horizontal>
```

This represents a single horizontal row, with three vertical elements. They are a vertical list, a list box and another vertical list. As it is, the arrangement chosen for Figure 5.2 (omitting the labels) would be expressed as follows.

```
<vertical>
   <horizontal>
      <vertical>
         three text boxes
      </vertical>
      listbox
      <horizontal>
         three buttons
      </horizontal>
   </horizontal>
</vertical>
```

The above three specifications illustrate the versatility of the Views approach, in that layout is very easily kept distinct from the controls.

Positioning is only one aspect of layout, though. We also need to consider spacing. Views will space the controls in some sensible way, but if we want more control, we can use two adjustments. Firstly, every control can have a `Width` and `Height` attribute. The

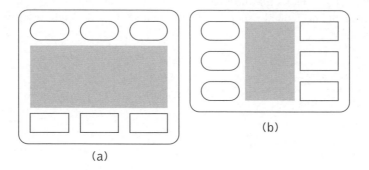

(b)

(a)

Figure 5.5 Options for a Rock-Paper-Scissors GUI

measurements can be given in centimetre units, among others, and so a typical Views tag might be:

```
<TextBox Name=winBox Width=2cm/>
```

which will make the box larger than the default which Views would supply.

Another way of changing the spacing is to use the `<space>` tag which simply allows the `Height` and `Width` attributes to be set on a (usually empty) rectangle, as in:

```
<space Height=1cm/>
```

If we set the height quite small and set the colour to black, we can even draw a line, as in:

```
<space Width=10cm Height=0.1cm
    BackColor=Black halign=center/>
```

Add the handlers for the active controls. The three controls which the user can activate are the buttons. So the `ActionPerformed` method must provide a handler for each of these. In fact, the action required is the same in each case – record the name of the button pushed. Thereafter, the program proceeds to output values into the text boxes, as explained earlier. The calls to `PutText` fall under the heading of interaction with the GUI.

The program is written as a class, `DriveRPSGameGUI`, which replaces `DriveRPSG-ameConsole.cs`. It must be compiled together with the existing `RPSGame.cs` class from Chapter 4. In addition, we have to indicate that we are using the Views namespace, and we do so at the start of the program, along with the usual `using System` statement.

File DriveRPSGameGUI.cs

```
using Views;
using System;

class DriveRPSGameGUI {
```

```
/// <summary>
/// RSPGame with GUI      Bishop and Horspool      May 2002
/// ================
/// Plays the Rock-Paper-Scissors game with the user.
/// Illustrates GUI interaction, and switch on string.
/// Uses the class RPSGame from Chapter 4.
/// </summary>

string fspec =
  @"<form Text='Rock-Paper-Scissors'>
    <vertical>
      <Label Text='Rock-Paper-Scissors' ForeColor=Red Font=Bold18/>
      <horizontal>
        <vertical>
          <space Height=1cm/>
          <Label Text=Wins/>
          <TextBox Name=winBox Width=2cm/>
          <space Height=0.5cm/>
          <Label Text=Losses/>
          <TextBox Name=lossBox Width=2cm/>
          <space Height=0.5cm/>
          <Label Text=Draws/>
          <TextBox Name=drawBox Width=2cm/>
        </vertical>
        <vertical>
          <Label Text=History/>
          <ListBox Name=history Width=7cm/>
        </vertical>
      </horizontal>
      <space Width=10cm Height=0.1cm BackColor=Black
             halign=center/>
      <Label Text='Choose your selection ...' ForeColor=Red/>
      <horizontal>
        <Button Name=Rock Image='Rock.gif' Width=3cm/>
        <Button Name=Paper Image='Paper.gif' Width=3cm/>
        <Button Name=Scissors Image='Scissors.gif' Width=3cm/>
      </horizontal>
    </vertical>
  </Form>";

string playersChoice;

void Go() {
  /// <summary>
  /// Drives the Rock-Paper-Scissors game.
  /// </summary>

  RPSGame game = new RPSGame();
  int noOfWins, noOfDraws, noOfLosses, round;

  Views.Form form = new Views.Form(fspec);
  noOfWins = noOfDraws = noOfLosses = 0;
  round = 0;
```

```
        form.PutText("drawBox", "0");
        form.PutText("winBox", "0");
        form.PutText("lossBox", "0");

        string computersChoice, c, result;

        for ( ; ; ) {
          computersChoice = game.ComputersChoice;
          c = form.GetControl();
          if (c == null) break;
          ActionPerformed(c);  // sets playersChoice
          result = game.ComparePlays(playersChoice);

          round++;
          form.PutText("history", "Round "+round);
          form.PutText("history",
                  "The computer's choice = "+computersChoice);
          form.PutText("history",
                  "The player's choice = "+playersChoice);

          switch (result) {
            case "draw":
              form.PutText("history", "  This round is drawn");
              noOfDraws++;
              form.PutText("drawBox", noOfDraws.ToString());
              break;
            case "lose":
              form.PutText("history", "  Sorry, you lose this round");
              noOfLosses++;
              form.PutText("lossBox", noOfLosses.ToString());
              break;
            case "win":
              form.PutText("history", "  Well done, you win this round");
              noOfWins++;
              form.PutText("winBox", noOfWins.ToString());
              break;
          }
          form.PutText("history", "");
        }
        form.CloseGUI();
      }

      void ActionPerformed(string c) {
        switch (c) {
          case "Rock":
          case "Paper":
          case "Scissors": playersChoice = c;
            break;
          default:
            throw new Exception("Unhandled control "+c);
        }
      }
    }
```

```
   static void Main() {
      new DriveRPSGameGUI().Go();
   }
}
```

Before running this program, we first need to compile it with both the `RPSGame.cs` file which was given earlier and with the `Views` classes. Running the executable file causes a window to appear on the computer screen. It should look similar to the GUI shown in Figure 5.2.

Comparing the source code of `DriveRPSGameGUI.cs` with Figure 5.2, we see that the string constant used to initialize `fspec` provides a specification for which controls should appear in the GUI. The constructor for the `Views.Form` class, which is invoked early in the `Go` method, takes the `fspec` string as its argument and uses it to determine which controls are wanted and where they should be placed.

The Rock-Paper-Scissors example contains several examples of nesting vertical and horizontal pairs. A row of buttons, such as those showing the pictures of the three hands, is created by enclosing them inside a `<horizontal>` ... `</horizontal>` pair, but that group is itself an element of a vertical list. And there are a few other nested groups in the GUI layout.

After creating the `Views.Form` object, the `Go` method enters a loop and calls the `Get-Control` method to wait for the user to click a button. Our program displays its results by writing text into one of the `TextBox` controls and into the `ListBox` control, as explained earlier. In Chapter 7, we shall look at extensions to this program, to make it more intelligent.

5.4 Views layout

We spend this section going through Views layout in more detail. Notice that these tags do not correspond to `Windows.Form` controls and are therefore written with small letters by convention.

The GUI form

The specification for the whole GUI form must begin with the `<Form>` tag and end with the matching close tag `</Form>`. These two tags should enclose a group of controls, as explained below. The `<Form>` tag can have a `Text` attribute, which will set the name of the window on the menu bar. If the text is other than a single word, it must be enclosed in single quotes. For example:

```
<Form Text='RPS Game'> ... </Form>
```

Groups of controls

There are three ways to specify the layout of groups of controls with Views – a vertical list, a horizontal list, or absolute placement at specified coordinate positions.

Vertical lists. A vertical list of controls uses the `<vertical>` ... `</vertical>` pair of tags to enclose the controls. As a simple example, suppose that we wish to display three buttons of different sizes. We might use the following specification.

```
@"<Form>
    <vertical>
        <Button Name=one Width=2.5cm Height=1cm/>
        <Button Name=two Width=4cm Height=2cm/>
        <Button Name=three Width=3cm Height=1.5cm/>
    </vertical>
</Form>"
```

It creates a GUI form like that shown in Figure 5.6(a).

Horizontal lists. A horizontal list is similar but uses the `<horizontal>` ... `</horizontal>` pair of tags to enclose the controls. A horizontal list is shown in Figure 5.6(b).

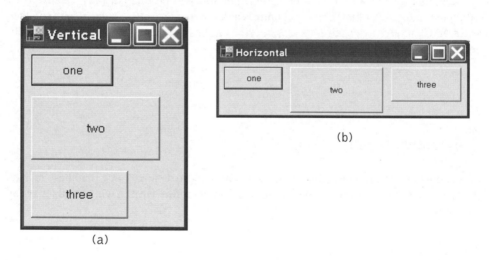

(b)

(a)

Figure 5.6 Vertical and horizontal lists of controls

Note that by default the controls in a vertical list are aligned on their left sides, and controls in a horizontal list are aligned along their tops. The `halign` attribute may be used to select the horizontal alignment for the items in a vertical list, one of `left`, `right` or `centre` (or `center` for those who use American spelling), while the `valign` attribute may be used to select the vertical alignment of items in a horizontal list, it must be set to one of `top`, `bottom` or `middle`.

Spacing. The `<space>` tag is useful for creating space between tags, as well as for drawing lines. The size of the space is determined by setting the `Height` and `Width` attributes. In the latter case, the `BackColor` attribute should be set to the desired colour of the line.

Absolute placement. It is implemented via panels, which are discussed at the end of the chapter.

Fonts

Apart from where to put controls, Views allows the changing of the lettering on the GUI form to achieve a much more pleasing effect. The way letters appear is known as their *font*. Fonts can have different families, styles and sizes. By default, Views outputs all text in a sans serif font (e.g. Helvetica), in an upright or plain style, in size 10. Sizes are given in points: 8 would be about the smallest one should go, and 24 would be a large size which would be used for a heading, say.

Controls that have text, such as labels and buttons, can specify a `Font` attribute with a value which consists of various font descriptors concatenating together. Each descriptor, other than the font size, is a word or a short abbreviation. Some of these words are listed in Table 5.1 and the full list is given in Appendix F.

	Default	**Alternatives**	
Family	SansSerif	Serif	Monospace
Weight	medium	bold	
Style	upright	italic	
Size	10 pt		

Table 5.1 Font options

The name *Serif* refers to a generic serif font, usually Times Roman; *SansSerif* usually refers to Arial or Helvetica; *Monospace* refers to a generic monospaced font such as *Courier*. The size of the font may be obtained by writing the size in points as a decimal number; that number may optionally contain a fractional part.

The descriptors may be combined in any order. Some examples are shown in Table 5.2.

Font Description	**Sample**
`Font=Bold14`	**Hello there**
`Font=ItalicSansSerif18`	*Hello there*
`Font=Courier`	`Hello there`

Table 5.2 Examples of fonts

5.5 Views controls

Views supports many of the controls available in `Windows.Forms`. An alphabetical list of the controls is displayed in Table 5.3.

Views.Form control	Brief description
`<Button/>`	A push button
`<CheckBox/>`	A box which can be checked or unchecked

`<CheckedListBox>`
`...`
`</CheckedListBox>`
	A pull-down list of check boxes

`<DomainUpDown>`
`...`
`</DomainUpDown>`
	A pull-down list from which a single item in the list can be selected as the current value

`<GroupBox>`
`...`
`</GroupBox>`
	A rectangular region holding a group of radio buttons

`<Label/>`	Displays a string of text on the GUI
`<ListBox/>`	A rectangular area which can be used for input or output of many lines of text
`<OpenFileDialog/>`	A button which causes a new window to open where an existing file can be selected by navigating through the file system

`<Panel>`
`...`
`</Panel>`
	A rectangular region in which controls may be placed at specific locations

`<PictureBox/>`	Displays a graphics image
`<ProgressBar/>`	A horizontal bar where the shaded part on the left is used to indicate how much of a task has been completed
`<RadioButton/>`	A round button which becomes checked when clicked. A list of radio buttons is enclosed by `GroupBox` tags
`<SaveFileDialog/>`	A button which causes a new window to open where either an existing file to be overwritten can be selected by navigating the file system or a new filename can be entered
`<TextBox/>`	A rectangular area which can be used for input or output of a short text item
`<TrackBar/>`	A slider control used for input of an integer; dragging a marker backwards or forwards with the mouse changes that integer

Table 5.3 Views.Form controls

More detail on these controls is given in Appendix F. In this section, we introduce each control by means of examples, and look at how to put them together in a few well-chosen ways. When specifying controls using the XML notation supported by the `Views.Form` class, all attributes except the `Name` attribute may be left undefined. Views will provide default values, although these defaults will not always be appropriate to your program's needs.

The classes for the controls provided in the `System.Windows.Forms` namespace have many more attributes and support much more functionality than is provided through the `Views.Form` class. A full discussion is, however, beyond the scope of this book. For more detailed information, please refer to documentation for programming the Windows system or run the help facility of the Visual Studio development tool.

Measurement units

The `Width` and `Height` attributes represent desired sizes for the displayed control on the screen. If we define one of these as a simple number, e.g.

```
Width=100
```

then the units are assumed to be pixels. The actual size on the screen would depend on the computer screen's resolution. A typical resolution might be 72 pixels per inch, and is the resolution often assumed by web pages, but your screen's resolution may be set differently. There is also a choice of measurement units understood by Views, as shown in Table 5.4. For example,

```
Width=1.5cm
```

in the XML specification, will display a control with a width of approximately 1.5 centimetres. Other measurements are millimetres, picas and points. Of these, points are often used for font sizes, as described in Section 5.4.

Units name	Meaning
in	Inches
cm	Centimetres
mm	Millimetres
pc	Picas (one pica is 1/6 of an inch)
pt	Points (one point is 1/72 of an inch)

Table 5.4 Views measurement units

Attributes

Each Views tag can have certain attributes. Table 5.5 shows all the attributes available. The precise association of attributes to tags is given in Appendix F. The attributes in the left column are available for almost every control; those in the right column are more specialized.

Name=S	Image=F
Text=S	Value=D
Width=M	Minimum=D
Height=M	Maximum=D
ForeColor=C	Checked=D
BackColor=C	Font=S

Table 5.5 Attributes available in Views XML

The Label control

A `Label` control is used to display a text string on the GUI. For example, the following Views specification could be used to display information to the user of a program:

```
Views.Form f = new Views.Form(
  @"<Form Text='Label Test'>
      <Label Text='Version 3.12beta' Width=200 Height=50
             Font=SansSerif18/>
  </Form>");
```

and the result would look like Figure 5.7(a).

(a) Label control

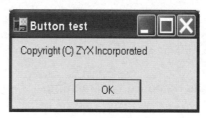

(b) Button and Label controls

Figure 5.7 Examples of controls

The Button control

A `Button` control allows the user to send a signal to the program which displayed the GUI. We can associate any actions we like with that signal – performing a computation and displaying the result or simply making the GUI close. To keep the example simple, that is the action we program in the following code fragment:

```
Views.Form f = new Views.Form(
  @"<Form Text='Button test'>
    <vertical>
      <Label Text='Copyright (C) ZYX Incorporated'
                      Width=200 Height=25 halign=centre/>
      <Button Name=OK halign=centre/>
    </vertical>
  </Form>");
f.GetControl();      // wait for user to click close button
f.CloseGUI();        // close the form
```

The displayed result looks like that in Figure 5.7(b).

More interesting forms can be created if pictures instead of words appear on the buttons. If we have an image file stored in some standard format, for example a GIF file or a JPEG file, it can be displayed on the button using notation like the following:

```
<Button Name=Tulip Image='tulip.jpg'/>
```

If the width and height are omitted, the size of the button will be whatever size is needed to display the image at its normal resolution. It is often more convenient to arrange the controls on the GUI in a tidy arrangement by imposing a particular size on the button. An example of a program which uses buttons labelled with images was the Rock-Paper-Scissors game (Figure 5.2).

The TextBox control

A `TextBox` control may be used for both input and output of short text items. The data that is typed into a text box can be strings or numbers, but there is only a Views method to read a string. Thus, any anticipated numbers have to be converted from strings by using `Parse` as in:

```
string aText = form.GetText("A");
int aVal = int.Parse(aText);
```

Data which is written into a text box will be left justified. Writing can be done by setting the `Text` attribute initially in the Views specification, such as

```
<TextBox Name=A Text = 0/>
```

or by using `PutText`, as in

```
form.PutText("A", "0");
```

Both of these will initialize the text box with a value of 0.

The CheckBox control

A `CheckBox` control has various options, several of which can be selected at once. An option can selected by clicking in the appropriate box. The resulting tick mark is removed by clicking in the box again. The check box provides an easy way to input true or false values with a GUI.

An example GUI that uses check boxes to set up various font options is displayed in Figure 5.8, and the corresponding Views specification is as follows.

```
Views.Form f = new Views.Form(@"<Form Text='Check boxes'>
  <vertical>
    <CheckBox Name=Case Text='Upper Case' Width=100/>
    <CheckBox Name=Style Text='Bold' Width=100/>
    <CheckBox Name=Font Text='Italics' Width=100/>
    <Button Name=Proceed/>
  </vertical>
</Form>");
while (f.GetControl()!="Proceed");
f.CloseGUI();
```

Figure 5.8 CheckBox control example

The code to access the first of the check box values is as in the following statement:

```
bool caseFlag = f.GetValue("Case") != 0;
```

The result from GetValue is 0 if the check box is unchecked, and 1 if it is checked.

The PictureBox control

A PictureBox control, as its name suggests, is used to display a picture inside a box. The picture is normally read from a disk file and may be in any of the common formats. These formats include the Windows bitmap format (and whose filenames have the '.bmp' extension), JPEG format (the '.jpg' extension), and GIF format (the '.gif' extension). The Views implementation of a picture box allows specification of either or both of the width and height of the image which is to be displayed; the image will be scaled to fit the specified dimensions. If neither the width nor the height is specified, the image is displayed using dimensions which are taken from the image file.

A simple example of a GUI which shows the same image in four different sizes is shown in Figure 5.9; its XML specification is as follows.

```
@"<Form >
  <vertical>
    <PictureBox Image='CSharp.gif'/>
    <PictureBox Image='CSharp.gif' Height=100/>
    <PictureBox Image='CSharp.gif'
            Width=100 Height=100 halign=right/>
    <PictureBox Image='CSharp.gif' Width=50 halign=right/>
  </vertical>
</Form>"
```

Figure 5.9 PictureBox control example

The TrackBar control

A track bar is used for input of an integer value into a program by dragging a marker left or right along a line. The attributes `Minimum` and `Maximum` are used to specify the range of integers represented by the track bar; if omitted, their default values are 1 and 100. The attribute `Value` may be used to specify the initial setting of the track bar; if omitted, its default value is the same as `Minimum`.

Each time the slider on the track bar is moved, the `GetControl` method returns with the name of the `TrackBar` control. Calling `GetValue` returns the integer value represented by the track bar. A track bar is illustrated in Example 5.3.

The ProgressBar control

A progress bar is similar in concept to a track bar but is conventionally used to display the amount of progress made by a program. Making regular updates to a progress bar is one of the ways in which a long-running program can give reassurance to the user that the program is still working and has not become stuck.

The GroupBox control

A group box is a rectangle displayed on the GUI enclosing a collection of two or more radio buttons. The name 'radio button' refers to an old-fashioned mechanical push button on a radio, typically used to select the waveband. There might be a row of buttons labelled SW, MW, LW and FM on the radio (for choosing between reception on the short wave, medium wave, long wave or frequency modulation bands); only one button may be down at a time; pushing a new button down causes a previously selected button to pop up. The GroupBox and RadioButton controls simulate the same effect.

A <GroupBox> ... </GroupBox> pair of tags may be used in the Views specification to enclose a list of radio button specifications.

The RadioButton control

A radio button is similar to a check box except that only one of the options may be checked at any one time. Each radio button has a name, which is displayed alongside the button on the GUI. An optional attribute is checked, which may be used to determine which button is initially displayed in the selected state. Radio buttons are grouped with the GroupBox control. An example of a GroupBox and its RadioButton controls appears in Figure 5.10.

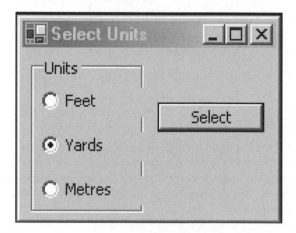

Figure 5.10 GroupBox and RadioButton controls example

The specification of this Views form is as follows:

```
string fspec = @"<Form text='Select Units'>
    <horizontal>
      <GroupBox Name='Units'>
        <RadioButton Name='Feet' Checked=1/>
        <RadioButton Name='Yards'/>
        <RadioButton Name='Metres'/>
      </GroupBox>
      <Button Name='Select' valign=middle/>
    </horizontal>
  </Form>";
```

The program which displays the GUI may retrieve the current selection of the radio buttons using a method call similar to the following.

```
string units = f.GetText("Units");
```

Other controls

The two controls relating to files (`OpenFileDialog` and `SaveFileDialog`) are covered in Chapter 7. Programming the `DomainUpDown` control is covered in Appendix F.

5.6 Views methods

The example programs in this chapter should show how to use most of these methods. A list of the methods appears in Table 5.6.

Class constructor

There are two constructors for the Views.Form class:

```
Views.Form(string formSpecification)
Views.Form(string formSpecification, string parameters)
```

The main constructor argument is a string. This string either contains the XML specification for the Views form to be displayed or else it is the name of a file which contains the XML specification.

As a convenience, attribute values may be provided as separate arguments by using the {0}, {1} notation. For example, another way of showing a picture from a read in filename is to read in the name before the GUI is constructed, as below:

```
Console.Write("Show what picture? ");
string fileName = System.Console.ReadLine();
```

Views.Form method	Description
`Form(string spec, ...)`	The constructor
`void CloseGUI()`	Closes the GUI and releases its resources
`string GetControl()`	Waits for the user to perform an action on the GUI and returns the name of the control that was clicked or changed
`string GetText(string name)`	Returns a text value associated with the named control
`int GetValue(string name)`	Returns an integer value associated with the named control
`int GetValue(string name, int index)`	For a `CheckedListBox` control, the result is the status of the check box at position *index* in the list
`void PutText(string name, string cval )`	Sets the `Text` attribute of the named control
`void PutValue(string name, int v )`	Sets an integer value associated with the named control
`void PutImage(string name, string filename)`	Sets an image value from the given filename in the named PictureBox control
(instance of Views.Form) [string name]	This is an indexer operation which returns the named control in the GUI

Table 5.6 Views.Form methods

```
string xmlSpec =@"<Form>
    <vertical>
      <PictureBox Width=3cm Height=3cm Image={0}/>
    </vertical>
  </Form>";

Views.Form form = new Views.Form(xmlSpec, fileName);
```

The {0}, {1} ... notation provides substitution of text (any value which can be converted to text may be supplied as an argument), but only for attribute values.

Associated with the constructor is the `CloseGui` method. This method should be called when the program has finished using the GUI. It causes the GUI to no longer be displayed and all resources associated with the GUI to be deallocated.

The GetControl method

Calling `GetControl` causes the program to wait for the user to interact with a control that responds to mouse clicks or movements, e.g. click on a button. When the user has performed one of these actions, a string result comes back from the `GetControl` call. The result is the value of the name attribute of the control which was specified in the GUI specification. For example, if the control was specified as

```
<Button Name='Start processing'/>
```

and the user selects a file using that control, then the string returned by GetControl would be "Start processing".

As a special case, if the user clicks on the quit button (the button in the top right corner of the Windows form), the result returned by GetControl is null.

The Get and Put methods

Views has a small selection of methods which enable one to get and put data from suitable controls such as text boxes, track bars, and so on.

GetText(string name). The argument passed to this method is the name of a control as defined by the name attribute in the Views form's XML specification.

♦   If the control is a TextBox or ListBox, the result is the text which is currently displayed in that control. Thus, the program can read text entered by the user.

♦   If the control is OpenFileDialog or SaveFileDialog, the result is the full name of the file chosen by the user. If no file has been selected (perhaps because the user clicked the Cancel button in the file selection dialogue) the result is null.

♦   If the control is a GroupBox, the result is the name of the RadioButton in the group which is currently selected.

GetValue(string name). This method is similar to GetText but is used when the value to be obtained from a control is an integer.

♦   For a CheckBox control, the result would be 0 or 1 to indicate whether the box is checked.

♦   For a RadioButton, the result of 0 or 1 indicates whether the button is selected.

♦   For a TrackBar control, the result would be an integer in the range from the minimum to the maximum values defined for the control in the XML specification.

GetValue(string name, int index). This variation of the GetValue method is useful when the control named is a CheckBox.

PutText(string name, string value). This method displays a string, the second argument, in the control named by the first argument. The PutText method is used to display messages or other strings in a TextBox or ListBox control.

PutValue(string name, int value). This method saves an integer value associated with a control. It is used for a ProgressBar control to adjust the progress indicator between the minimum and maximum values defined in the XML specification.

PutImage(string name, string file). This method finds the image stored at the filename and displays it in the `PictureBox` control indicated. The current dimensions of the control are used to adjust the size of the image.

Example 5.2 A simple calculator with a GUI

To illustrate how these methods are used, consider an example of a simple calculator. Actually, programs which mimic the working of a calculator can be quite difficult, so in this example, we shall just have two operands, and the usual four operators. We shall not have memories or any other facilities, nor allow a succession of operands.

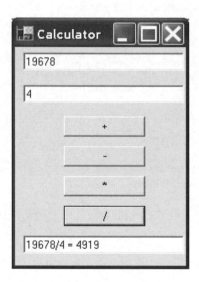

Figure 5.11 A simple calculator

The output we are aiming for is shown in Figure 5.11. It provides two text boxes where the user can enter numbers, a series of four buttons with which the user selects one of the four arithmetic operations (plus, minus, times or divide) and a text box to show the result. The Views specification is rather simple, relying entirely on Views to lay out the controls, with an attribute setting `halign=center`.

The `ActionPerformed` method has far more to it than the Rock-Paper-Scissors game's one. Here we have to get two values from the text boxes, convert them to integers, then depending on the button value, we perform a calculation. The result is entered into the final text box. Notice that entering values into the text boxes does not trigger `ActionPerformed` – only pressing the buttons does.

File SimpleCalculator.cs

```csharp
using Views;
using System;

class SimpleCalculator {

  /// <summary>
  /// SimpleCalculator    Bishop and Horspool    Sept 2002
  /// ================
  /// Adds/Subtracts/Multiplies/Divides two numbers.
  /// Illustrates reading and writing into a control
  /// </summary>

  Views.Form form;
  string formSpec = @"<Form Text=Calculator>
      <vertical>
          <TextBox Name=A halign=center Text = 0/>
          <TextBox Name=B halign=center Text = 0/>
          <Button Name='+' halign=center/>
          <Button Name='-' halign=center/>
          <Button Name='*' halign=center/>
          <Button Name='/' halign=center/>
          <TextBox Name=Result halign=center Text = 0/>
      </vertical>
    </form>";

  void ActionPerformed( string c ) {
    string aText, bText;
    int aVal, bVal;
    string[] operators = {"+", "-", "*", "/"};
    int result = 0;
    aText = form.GetText("A");
    bText = form.GetText("B");
    aVal = int.Parse(aText);
    bVal = int.Parse(bText);
    switch(c) {
      case "+":
        result = aVal+bVal;  break;
      case "-":
        result = aVal-bVal;  break;
      case "*":
        result = aVal*bVal;  break;
      case "/":
        result = aVal/bVal;  break;
      default:
        return;
    }
    form.PutText("Result", aText + c + bText +
        " = " + result);
  }

  void Go() {
      form = new Views.Form(formSpec);
```

```
        for( ; ; ) {
          string c = form.GetControl();
          if (c==null) break;
          ActionPerformed(c);
        }
        form.CloseGUI();
    }

    static void Main() {
      new SimpleCalculator().Go();
    }
}
```

5.7 Advanced uses of Views

Absolute positioning of controls

Views already provides several ways for positioning controls so that quite sophisticated arrangements of the controls can be achieved. These are:

◆ nesting lists inside lists;

◆ specifying the dimensions of the controls by using the `Width` and `Height` attributes;

◆ using the `<space>` tag.

However, if more precise direction over the placement of the controls is needed, there is one more grouping construct available. It is intended more for expert users and should be used with caution because it can cause controls to be placed on top of each other. This extra grouping tag is `<Panel>`.

A *panel* is a rectangular area within which each control may be explicitly placed at specified *x* and *y* coordinates. These coordinates are given relative to the top-left corner of the rectangle. The width and height of the rectangle must be specified. There is no checking as to whether the controls are being placed at sensible positions inside the rectangle. If your controls are placed at coordinates where they do not fit inside the panel, the panel will have a scroll bar along the bottom or down the right-hand side, as needed.

In fact, Views allows every control on the GUI to be placed at explicit coordinates. So, for example, referring back to Figure 5.6, we could reposition the buttons precisely as follows, which would give Figure 5.12.

```
@"<Panel Name=p Width=150 Height=150>
   <position x=10 y=10>
      <Button Name=one Width=50 Height=20/>
   </position>
   <position x=50 y=40>
      <Button Name=two Width=80 Height=40/>
   </position>
   <position x=30 y=100>
      <Button Name=three Width=60 Height=30/>
   </position>
</Panel>"
```

Notice that we have switched from centimetres to pixels in this example. Pixels are mostly used for positioning, and one needs to get used to what they mean.

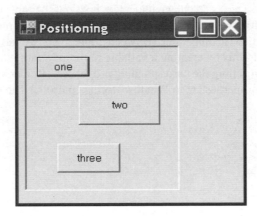

Figure 5.12 Positioning controls

However, as explained earlier, it is very time consuming to get the coordinates of each control exactly right. If the exact layout of the GUI is important and the simple horizontal and vertical lists provided in Views are inadequate, one should definitely use a visual design tool.

Direct access to controls

Table 5.6 included a reference to being able to index into a Views form to get hold of a control. The purpose of this facility is to allow attributes to be accessed and even changed while the program is running. In contrast, the setting of attributes in a Views specification is a static operation, performed once when the GUI object is constructed. The Views attributes that are accessible were listed in Table 5.5. The next example illustrates the direct access facility.

Example 5.3 An image scaler

We would like to have an image on the screen and then resize it dynamically. An image is drawn in a `PictureBox` control, and two of the attributes of a such a control are `Width` and `Height`. What we are after is to be able to change these attributes while the program is running, and have the effect of the change shown on the screen. Thus we want to

◆ input new dimensions;

◆ redraw the picture with them.

There are various ways to input new dimensions. We first decide that we shall do the scaling as a percentage of the original size, so that we do not have to be bothered with absolute values. We could type a new percentage into a text box, but the most convenient control is a track bar, which enables us to set a new value just by moving the mouse.

Once we have the new scaling value (between 1 and 100), we have to alter the picture box's attributes. We do this by creating a variable in the program which directly refers to the control, and then resetting the corresponding properties. (Remember that attributes are to Views XML what properties are to Windows forms controls.) The code to do so is:

```
// Get original size
PictureBox pb;
pb = form["image"];
originalWidth = pb.Width;
originalHeight = pb.Height;

// Reset size
pb.Width = originalWidth*factor/100;
pb.Height = originalHeight*factor/100;
```

Because we are referring to the `PictureBox` class in the program (as opposed to the `<PictureBox>` tag in Views XML) we need to import the `Systems.Windows.Forms` namespace. For other operating systems, other import directives would be needed.

The program follows, and the GUI displayed by the program appears in Figure 5.13.

File ImageScaling.cs

```
using System;
using Views;
using System.Windows.Forms;

class ImageScaling {

   /// <summary>
   /// Image Scaling          Bishop and Horspool       Oct 2002
   /// =============
```

```
/// Displays an image at sizes varying at runtime.
/// Illustrates a TrackBar as well as direct access to
/// control attributes.
/// </summary>

Views.Form form;
PictureBox pb;
int originalWidth, originalHeight;

string formSpec =
  @"<Form Text='Image Scaler'>
  <vertical>
    <vertical>
      <horizontal>
        <Label Text='Set Scale' Width=2cm valign=middle/>
        <TrackBar Name=scale Width=6cm Height=0.5cm Value=100/>
        <TextBox Name=percent Width=1cm Text='100%'/>
      </horizontal>
      <space Height=0.3cm/>
      <horizontal>
        <space Width=2cm/>
        <Label Text='1%'/>
        <space Width=1.8cm/>
        <Label Text='100%'/>
        <space Width=1cm/>
      </horizontal>
    </vertical>
    <Panel Width=12cm Height=9cm>
      <position x=0 y=0>
        <PictureBox Name=image Image={0} Width=11cm Height=8cm/>
      </position>
    </Panel>
  </vertical>
</Form>";

void ActionPerformed( string c ) {
  switch(c) {
    case "scale":
      int factor = form.GetValue("scale");
      form.PutText("percent", factor+"%");
      pb.Width = originalWidth*factor/100;
      pb.Height = originalHeight*factor/100;
      break;
    default:
      break;
  }
}

public void Go() {
  form = new Views.Form(formSpec, "Bridge.jpg");
  pb = form["image"];
  originalWidth = pb.Width;
  originalHeight = pb.Height;
  string c;
```

```
      for ( ; ; ) {
        c = form.GetControl();
        if (c==null) break;
        ActionPerformed(c);
      }
      form.CloseGUI();
    }
    static void Main() {
      new ImageScaling().Go();
    }
  }
}
```

Parameters to a Views.Form

As mentioned earlier in Section 5.6, the Views constructor can take a second argument which gives some additional runtime control over the GUI that will be drawn. In Example 5.3, this feature was used to supply a filename to a Views form. The filename could also have been read in, or supplied as an argument when running the program, for greater flexibility.

Further extensibility of Views

It is also possible to access, via the same approach, any property or method defined with a control – provided we know its name. The next example illustrates calling some methods.

Figure 5.13 TrackBar control example

Example 5.4 Show-Hide

The Show-Hide program has already been alluded to earlier in the chapter, and its output shown in Figure 5.1. Setting up the GUI is simple enough, as sketched with Figure 5.4. What about the handlers? Presumably, we want to make the picture disappear and reappear. A `PictureBox` control has methods defined for this purpose, called, conveniently, `Show` and `Hide`. So using direct access to controls, we can say:

```
PictureBox pb = f["pic"];  // access the control
pb.Hide();  // use the Hide method of PictureBox
```

where f is the Views form, `"pic"` identifies the control we want to affect and `Hide` is a method of the `PictureBox` control.

Putting the GUI translation and the handlers together, we then have the program.

File ShowHide.cs

```
using System;
using System.Windows.Forms;

class ShowHidePic {
  Views.Form f;

  void SetUp() {f = new Views.Form(
    @"<Form Text='Queens Bridge'>
      <vertical>
        <horizontal>
          <Button Name=Show/>
          <Button Name=Hide/>
        </horizontal>
        <Picturebox Name=pic Image='QueensBridge.jpg' Height=200/>
      </vertical>
    </Form>" );
  }

  void Go() {
    SetUp();
    string c;
    for (;;) {
      c = f.GetControl();
      if (c == null) break;
      ActionPerformed(c);
    }
    f.CloseGUI();
  }

  void ActionPerformed(string c) {
    PictureBox pb = f["pic"];
    switch (c) {
```

```
      case "Show" :
        pb.Show();
        break;
      case "Hide" :
        pb.Hide();
        break;
    default :
        break;
    }
  }

  static void Main() {
    new ShowHidePic().Go();
  }
}
```

If we run this program, it will print the now familiar GUI. Pressing each of the buttons shows and hides the image. Pressing the close box in the menu bar (usually top right) returns a null from GetControl, which causes the program to end, as explained earlier.

5.8 Case study 3 – The supermarket till

We want to implement a program representing a supermarket till for fruit and vegetables. The till has keys labelled with the product being sold, and some control keys. For this particular application, the products are all kinds of fruits. The cashier can weigh the products, select the kind of fruit, and then print a price tag.

Layout and controls

The kind of interface we envisage is sketched in Figure 5.14.

If a customer brings some oranges, say, to the checkout counter, the cashier would weigh the oranges, type in the mass, click a Weigh button, then click on a button labelled with the picture of an orange. Finally, clicking a button labelled Print will cause the price of the weighed quantity of fruit to be displayed in a Receipt window. Thus the controls to be inserted into the GUI are:

◆   labels – the heading,

◆   buttons – weigh, print and product buttons,

◆   text boxes– mass (for input) and receipt (for output).

An actual realization of a suitable GUI is shown in Figure 5.15. It shows the result of buying 5 kg of oranges. (The price is shown in South African rands.)

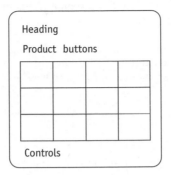

Figure 5.14 Sketch of a supermarket till

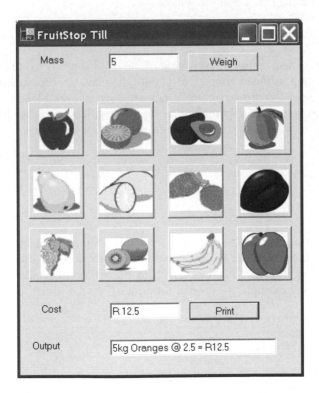

Figure 5.15 The Till program GUI

The Views specification for the GUI is straightforward, except that it does make use of the constructor parameter to enter the names of the products from the program. This parameter is an array which has twice the length of the number of products, with each second element being the name of the .gif file which holds the button's picture. The array parameter is set up as follows:

```
for (int count=0; count < maxProducts; count++) {
  formParameters[2*count] = item[count];
  formParameters[2*count+1] = item[count] + ".gif";
}
```

and used as in:

```
<Button Name={0} Image={1} Width=60 Height=60/>
<Button Name={2} Image={3} Width=60 Height=60/>
```

In this GUI we have again made a transition to making measurements in pixels. There are roughly 20 pixels to a centimetre. Pixels are used by most programmers in other GUI systems, so we are getting practice in using them too.

Event handling

A feature of this system is that the activation of the input controls has to happen in a certain order. It is not possible to print a receipt until the mass has been entered and product chosen. How does one arrange to force a certain sequence of events? We use Boolean variables (sometimes known in programming as *flags*) to indicate what has happened so far, and check them when we get to the next step. The sequence we want is:

1. Weigh.
2. Choose.
3. Print.

Therefore we set up two flags, both initially set to false. The first, `weighed`, will be set to true once a mass is entered. The second, called `chosen`, will be set after any product button is clicked. Then the event handlers can check these flags to decide whether or not to react to an event. For example, the handler for printing has the structure:

```
void printCost() {
  if (chosen) {
    // print the receipt
    ...
    // reset the variables
  } else
    form.PutText("message", "First choose an item!");
}
```

The program

The source code is shown below as file `Till.cs`..

File Till.cs

```
using System;
using System.Collections;
using Views;

class Till {

  /// <summary>
  /// The Till program       Bishop and Horspool      2002
  /// ================
  ///                        C# and Views version May 2002
  ///                        Picture buttons N Ros March 2001
  ///                        updated August 2000
  ///                        original in Java Oct 1996
  ///                        Java 1.1 Abbott and Bishop Oct 1997
  ///
  /// Simulates a supermarket till; Illustrates advanced features
  /// of Views as well as managing linked events.
  /// </summary>

    Views.Form form;

    // tally variables
    double total, kg;
    int select = 1;
    const int maxProducts = 12;

    // managing variables
    bool chosen = false;
    bool weighed = false;

    // arrays
    double[] unitCost =  {2,3,5,2.5,3,7,10,6,2,4,4,4};
    string[] item = {"Apples", "Pears", "Grapes", "Oranges",
                "Lemons", "Kiwis", "Avocados", "Strawberries",
                "Bananas", "Peaches", "Plums", "Apricots"};
    string[] formParameters = new string[maxProducts*2];

    string tillGUISpec = @"<Form Text='FruitStop Till'>
      <vertical>
        <horizontal>
          <Label Text='    Mass ' Width=80/>
          <TextBox Name=weight Width=75/>
          <Button Name=Weigh/>
        </horizontal>
        <horizontal height=5/>
        <horizontal>
          <vertical>
            <Button Name={0} Image={1} Width=60 Height=60/>
            <Button Name={2} Image={3} Width=60 Height=60/>
            <Button Name={4} Image={5} Width=60 Height=60/>
          </vertical>
```

```
        <vertical>
          <Button name={6} Image={7} Width=60 Height=60/>
          <Button name={8} Image={9} Width=60 Height=60/>
          <Button name={10} Image={11} Width=60 Height=60/>
        </vertical>
        <vertical>
          <Button name={12} Image={13} Width=60 Height=60/>
          <Button name={14} Image={15} Width=60 Height=60/>
          <Button name={16} Image={17} Width=60 Height=60/>
        </vertical>
        <vertical>
         <Button name={18} Image={19} Width=60 Height=60/>
         <Button name={20} Image={21} Width=60 Height=60/>
         <Button name={22} Image={23} Width=60 Height=60/>
        </vertical>
      </horizontal>
      <horizontal height=5/>
      <horizontal>
       <Label Text='     Cost' Width=80/>
       <TextBox Name=cost Width=75/>
       <Button Name=Print/>
      </horizontal>
      <horizontal>
        <vertical width=75>
          <horizontal>
            <Label Text='Output' />
            <TextBox Name=message Width=180/>
          </horizontal>
        </vertical>
      </horizontal>
    </vertical>
  </Form>";

void Go() {
  // Set up the Views parameter
  for (int count=0; count < maxProducts; count++) {
    formParameters[2*count] = item[count];
    formParameters[2*count+1] = item[count] + ".gif";
  }

  form = new Views.Form(tillGUISpec, formParameters);
  form.PutText("message", "The till is open");

  for ( ; ; ) {
    string c = form.GetControl();
    if (c == null) break;
    ActionPerformed(c);
  }
  form.CloseGUI();
}

  void ActionPerformed( string c ) {
      switch(c) {
```

```
          case "Weigh":
            weighItem();
            break;
          case "Print":
            printCost();
            break;
          default :
            chooseItem(c);
            break;
      }
   }

   void weighItem() {
     kg = double.Parse(form.GetText("weight"));
     weighed = true;
   }

   void chooseItem( string c ) {
     form.PutText("message", c+" was selected.");
     if (weighed) {
       select = Array.IndexOf(item,c); // see Chap 8 for this one
       chosen = true;
     } else
       form.PutText("message", "First weigh the items");
   }

   void printCost() {
     if (chosen) {
       total = kg*unitCost[select];
       form.PutText("cost", "R "+total);
       form.PutText("message", kg+"kg "+
         item[select]+" @ "+unitCost[select]+
         " = R"+total);
       //resetting the variables
       kg       = 0;
       weighed = false;
       chosen  = false;
       total   = 0;
     } else
       form.PutText("message", "First choose an item!");
   }

   static void Main() {
     new Till().Go();
   }
}
```

Updating prices

The actual fruits on sale and their prices should not, of course, be built into the program, since the system then becomes very inflexible. We would like to keep the prices some-where else as data. Because we need to know about files, this facility is picked up again as an extension in Chapter 7.

Concepts in Chapter 5

This chapter covered the following concepts:

graphical user interfaces (GUIs)	XML notation
GUI layout	GUI controls
Views layout	Views controls
Views methods	event handling
drag and drop	absolute positioning
relative positioning	tags
attributes	measurements in GUIs
Button	TextBox
ListBox	PictureBox
Form (a GUI form)	menu bar
GUI interaction	Label
Font	

The forms defined in this chapter were:

Views XML notation	Views.Form object creation
Views controls interaction	Views text boxes and list boxes interaction

Quiz

Q5.1 The closest alternative word for a GUI window is a

(a) component   (b) form

(c) control   (d) menu

Q5.2 The @ symbol at the beginning of a Views specification string indicates that what follows is

(a) in XML notation   (b) in Views XML notation

(c) a multi-line string   (d) not strictly capitalized

Q5.3 The Views method `GetControl` returns a value of type

  (a) `string`   (b) `Views.Form`

  (c) `Button`   (d) `Control`

Q5.4 Which method call would we use to write text into a `ListBox` control which was set up with the following Views tag?
```
<ListBox Name=history Text=Results/>
```

  (a) `PutText(Results, "Answer is ");` (b) `PutText("Results", "Answer is ");`

  (c) `PutText(history, "Answer is ");` (d) `PutText("history", "Answer is ");`

Q5.5 To read an integer from a TextBox "T", we would use

  (a) `string s = f.GetText("T"); int n = int.Parse(s);` (b) `string s=f.GetValue("T"); int n = int.Parse(s);`

  (c) `int n = f.GetValue("T");` (d) `int n = f.GetNumber(s);`

Q5.6 If we were showing the number of seconds elapsed in a computation scheduled to last about two minutes, what would be the best control to use?

  (a) A `TextBox`   (b) A `TrackBar`

  (c) A `ProgressBar` (d) A `ListBox`

Q5.7 The `ActionPerformed` method is called from

  (a) the `Go` method   (b) the `GetControl` method

  (c) the operating system (d) anywhere the programmer chooses

Q5.8 The attribute `Text={0}` in a Views specification `spec` instantiated with
```
Views.form f = new Views.Form(spec,p);
```
means that `Text` will have the value

  (a) `0`   (b) `null`

  (c) `""`   (d) `p[0]`

Q5.9 `halign` and `valign` are usually written without capital letters in Views XML, because they are

  (a) associated with alignment rather than values (b) not directly associated with Windows forms properties

  (c) attributes (d) unnested tags

Q5.10 If a Views specification gives

```
<PictureBox Name=image Image=daughter.jpg/>
```

how would we access the image directly to change its height to `newValue`?

(a)   `PictureBox p = form["Image"];`
       `p.Height = newValue;`

(b)   `PictureBox p = form["image"];`
       `p.Height = newValue;`

(c)   `PictureBox p = form["Image"];`
       `p.Image.Height = newValue;`

(d)   `PictureBox p = form["daughter.jpg"];`
       `p.Height = newValue;`

Exercises

5.1   **RPS different view.** Alter the Views specification for the Rock-Paper-Scissors program so that the GUI reflects one of the designs shown in Figure 5.5.

5.2   **Calculator clear.** Add a C button to the simple calculator (Example 5.2) which will clear all the TextBoxes. Alter the program so that it can continue running until the window is closed.

5.3   **Length converter.** Complete the program begun around Figure 5.10 so that it can represent a given value in any one of the three length units (feet, yards, metres). The value is assumed to be entered in the units which are reflected by the `RadioButton` currently active (depressed).

5.4   **Any image.** We would like to display any image in the Show-Hide program (Example 5.4). Add a TextBox where the user can type in the name of a file where an image is stored and use `PutImage` to display the image at runtime.

5.5   **Meeting times.** Take Example 2.7 and design a GUI for it which will enable the city and time difference to be entered and the same output shown in a ListBox, say. Experiment with a TrackBar for the time (sliding in units of one hour between 0 and 23).

5.6   **Boardroom clocks again.** Adapt Exercise 2.13 so that the clocks and cities are shown on a GUI. The clocks should resemble digital clocks, and there is no need (yet) to show them actually running. Integrate this GUI with Exercise 5.5 so that the user can just click on a clock–city pair to get the meeting time.

5.7   **Digital watch.** Design the display and knobs of a digital watch. Make the watch work by changing the time at regular intervals in a loop.

5.8   **Working boardroom.** Encapsulate your solution to Exercise 5.7 and use it to extend the answer to Exercise 5.6 so that the clocks actually tick.

5.9   **Door locks.** There is a brand of door lock which consists of a panel of the ten digits 0–9, plus a C button for clearing the lock and a P button to open the door once a code has been entered. A code consists of C followed by four digits. If a correct code is entered, the P button glows green, otherwise it changes to red. Pressing C will clear it back to a neutral colour. Design a GUI for such a lock, and give the corresponding Views specification for it. Write a program to interact with the GUI, simulating the operation of the lock.

5.10   **Bilingual tills.** The FruitStop store is exporting its software to a country with another language (e.g. French, German, Spanish, etc.). Choose a language you know and translate the fruit names into it (or find a set of names on our website). Include in the program a second array for the alternative fruit names. Then add to the GUI a pair of RadioButtons for switching between languages. The effect should be that the buttons and messages are displayed in the alternative language. (Hint: this solution will need direct access to Views attributes, and some changes to the Till program.)

5.11   **Currency converter.** Design a GUI using two sets of RadioButtons that will enable a given amount in dollars, euros or sterling to be converted into one of the others. Write the program to interact with such a GUI. Later on we shall see how to generalize this program to all currencies.

CHAPTER 6

Exceptions and debugging

A computer program can go wrong in many different ways. To limit the effects of errors, many operations performed by the program are checked. If, for example, an index for an array is out of range then a description of the error is created as a value of a special type called IndexOutOfRangeException. That value can be used to create an error message or the program can intercept the error itself using the try-catch statement and provide special handling. In this chapter, we cover Exception values and how to handle them.

We usually want to eliminate all errors from our programs and that is a process known as debugging. There are some tools and techniques which help locate errors, and we also look at those in this chapter.

6.1 Errors

Unfortunately, it is extremely easy to make mistakes when writing a computer program, either by not remembering exactly how a construct is put together, or mistyping or just plain wrong thinking. Mistakes in any kind of scientific endeavour are strictly speaking *errors.* Most of our programming errors are caught by the C# compiler. However, others are not discovered until the program is run and it exits with an error message or it does something unexpected.

Different kinds of errors

We can classify programming errors into three broad categories:

◆   lexical and syntactic errors,

◆   compile-time semantic errors,

◆   run-time semantic errors.

Lexical and syntactic errors. The following line of C# code contains an example of a syntax error which is caught by the C# compiler:

```
if (a > 0( x = 99;   // wrong!
```

The error appears to be that the wrong kind of parenthesis has been accidentally typed after the test expression. The compiler tries to match that statement against the pattern for an if statement and is unable to do so. The compiler therefore generates an error message, and that message looks similar to the following.

```
MyProgram.cs(38,20): error CS1026: ) expected
```

The message begins with the position in the source code where the error has been detected (the filename, the line number in the file, and the column number in that line). Then comes an error number which can be used as a reference for looking up further information about the C# language rule which has been broken. Finally there is a succinct description of what the C# compiler thinks the error is.

A lexical error is reported when the program contains a malformed language element. An example would be a double constant mistyped as follows: `1.234e-s`. The compiler happily reads the constant up to the negative sign for the exponent part, but that negative sign must be followed by a decimal integer not by a letter.

Compile-time semantic errors. A compile-time semantic error occurs when the program obeys all the syntactic rules (parentheses are paired correctly, keywords are used correctly, etc.) but a C# rule regarding how language constructs interact has been violated. Those of the rules that can easily be checked by the compiler fall into this category. Examples of such semantic errors would be:

◆   misspelling a method name (and in so doing, attempting to invoke a method which does not exist); or

◆   using operands of inappropriate data types in an expression (e.g. multiplying strings).

Here is a fragment of code which causes a semantic error to be detected by the compiler:

```
int x;
...              // some lines of code omitted
x = "123";
```

The C# compiler will produce an error message similar to the following when it checks the assignment statement:

```
MyProgram.cs(42,7): error CS0029: Cannot implicitly convert type
'string' to 'int'
```

That message is reasonably informative about the C# rule which is being broken. (The C# language only allows assignment of a value of one datatype to a variable of another datatype for combinations of datatypes where implicit conversion rules have been provided. Evidently, conversion from a string to an integer is not automatic in C#.)

Run-time semantic errors. Finally, we come to run-time errors. There are so many different things which can go wrong, or which can otherwise prevent a program completing its execution in the desired way, that it is difficult to do more than provide a few examples. Table 6.1 shows three different code fragments which will cause a C# program to end abnormally if they are executed.

```
//********** Sample 1 **********
int[] arr = new int[20];
for (int i=1; i<=20; i++)
   arr[i] = i;  // this will fail

//********** Sample 2 **********
string s = "abc";
int n = int.Parse(s);  // this will fail

//********** Sample 3 **********
string s = null;
Console.WriteLine("First char = "+s[0]);  // this will fail
```

Table 6.1 Some run-time errors

As an exercise, try to figure out what is wrong with each code fragment before reading the explanations below.

1. The error in code sample 1 is that the loop variable i ranges through the values 1 to 20 inclusive. The array, though, has elements only in positions 0 through 19. Therefore on the 20th iteration of the loop, the loop body attempts to access a non-existent element of the array.

    The C# run-time system will halt the program on that 20th iteration and produce an error message which looks similar to the following.

```
Unhandled Exception: System.IndexOutOfRangeException: index
       was outside the bounds of the array.
   at Fudge.Go(String x)
   at Fudge.Main(String[] args)
```

The message begins with a description of the problem that was detected, and then reports where the error occurred in the program. If the program had been compiled with the /debug:full option, there would have been line numbers as well as the names of the methods which had been called and were still active (i.e control had not yet returned from them).

2. The error in code sample 2 is that the string does not contain a sequence of characters that form a valid decimal number.

    The Parse method of the int type generates an error message similar to the following.

```
Unhandled Exception: System.FormatException: Input string was not
       in a correct format.
   at System.Number.ParseInt32(String s, NumberStyles style,
          NumberFormatInfo info)
   at Fudge.Go(String x)
   at Fudge.Main(String[] args)
```

3. The problem with code sample 3 is that *null* is not a string value; null is synonymous with 'no value'. Thus trying to access the first character of the string held in the variable s cannot succeed.

    The C# run-time system detects the error, halts execution and generates the following error message.

```
Unhandled Exception: System.NullReferenceException: Object
       reference not set to an instance of an object.
   at Fudge.Go(String x)
   at Fudge.Main(String[] args)
```

6.2 Exception handling

In each of the explanations relating to Table 6.1, the error message contains the name of a class in the System namespace. When the system software detects the error, or in general some difficulty that prevents the program from continuing in the manner intended, an instance of a class that describes the difficulty is created. The name of the class includes the word Exception and will give a clue as to the kind of error (for example, NullReferenceException). An *exception* is another word for an instance of an error; it is the term used in the C# language to refer to errors that occur at runtime.

One or more fields of the class will contain some further information about the error (for example, the `Message` property is set to 'Object reference not set to an instance of an object' in the last example, above). Finally, the class contains a field named `StackTrace` which, when printed, shows where in the program the problem was encountered. In the final example, above, that string is as follows:

```
"    at Fudge.Go(String x)\n    at Fudge.Main(String[] args)"
```

The method `Go` in class `Fudge` was apparently the section of the program where the error occurred, and `Go` was called from the `Main` method in the same class. (If the program is compiled with the `/Debug:full` option in effect, the `StackTrace` message will be more detailed because line numbers will be included.)

Once the exception object has been created, the system software looks for some code that will deal with it. Such code is often called an *exception handler*. The system software provides its own handler which will be used if the program does not provide one. That default handler writes the name of the class, the `Message` property, and the `StackTrace` property, exactly as in the three examples above, to the Console window. Finally, execution of the program is terminated.

Providing an exception handler to catch, and perhaps recover from, errors in a program is remarkable easy. All it takes is the `try-catch` statement.

The try-catch statement

The way to imagine the use of the try-catch statement is that the program will *try* executing some code and, if something goes wrong so that an exception is generated, it will *catch* the exception. An example fragment of code that uses `try-catch` is as follows:

```
int[] A = new int[20];
int i, k;
i=21; k=3;
try {
   int temp = A[i]/k;
   A[i+1] = int.Parse("10"+temp);
} catch(System.IndexOutOfRangeException e) {
   Console.WriteLine("Error: {0}; carrying on", e.ToString());
}
```

The code fragment will generate this output when executed:

```
Error: System.IndexOutOfRangeException: Index was outside the bounds
of the array.
   at Test_ArrayList.Main() in C:\home\my work\csharpbook\programre-
pository\tester\class1.cs:line 11; carrying on
```

However, look carefully at the *catch* part of that `try-catch` statement. It asks to catch only one kind of error – an `IndexOutOfRangeException` error. If variable k happens to be zero, there could be a `DivideByZeroException` error instead, or if the string concatenation produces a string that does not form a valid decimal number, there could be a FormatException error.

If desired, each kind of error can be intercepted separately. An example is as follows.

```
try {
   int temp = A[i]/k;
   A[i+1] = int.Parse("10"+temp);
} catch(System.IndexOutOfRangeException) {
   Console.WriteLine("Indexing error");
} catch(System.DivideByZeroException) {
   Console.WriteLine("Divide by zero error");
} catch(System.FormatException) {
   Console.WriteLine("Parse integer string error");
}
```

Note that if the catch parameter (usually called e) is not going to be used in the statements that follow, it should be omitted.

Finally, we can write a catch clause which intercepts as many errors as possible. For that, our catch clause must name the System.Exception type, as follows:

```
try {
   int temp = A[i]/k;
   A[i+1] = int.Parse("10"+temp);
} catch(System.Exception e) {
   Console.WriteLine("Something went wrong: {0}",
      e.ToString());
}
```

Here, the WriteLine no longer gives a specific error message but relies on the value stored in the object variable e, as presented through ToString. Unfortunately, there is no guarantee that all errors will be intercepted. Running out of memory might, for example, make it impossible for the C# run-time system to continue execution and the program will simply terminate.

The format of the try-catch statement is summarized below.

TRY-CATCH STATEMENT

```
try {
    statements;
} catch(ExceptionType1 e) {
    statements1;
}
```

The *statements* in the try clause are executed. If an error of type *ExceptionType1* is raised while those statements or methods they invoke are running, then control is transferred to *statements1* in the catch handler. There can be any number of catch clauses; the first one which is applicable to the error is executed.

If e is not used in the subsequent statements, it must be omitted.

The throw statement

A program can raise an exception explicitly. For example, if we are writing a method which converts information from one format to another, a statement similar to the following may be useful.

```
throw new System.FormatException("Invalid string");
```

In practice, the string argument should be more specific than this in providing an appropriate description of what the format error was.

Control never passes to the statement following the `throw` statement. Control continues at a `catch` clause which handles this kind of exception, if there is one. Otherwise the program is halted with an appropriate error message.

6.3 Debugging

Unfortunately, almost every piece of software contains deficiencies and outright errors. Given the complexity of software and the intricate relationships between the parts of a program, it seems almost inevitable that programmers will overlook something. The C# programming language and its compiler have been designed so that most errors will be detected when the program is compiled. However, some errors always seem to slip through and only surface when the program is executed. Thorough testing of the program is essential. Almost certainly, bugs (the popular name for programming errors) will be found. If the bugs are not found by the tests, they will eventually be found later by users – and users tend to be quite unhappy when they find bugs. The process of identifying bugs in the program and correcting them is known as *debugging*. In this section, we will look at some techniques that should help with debugging.

Writing robust code

Before we even get to debugging, we should design the program so that fewer bugs survive the testing process. It should not require much effort and it saves time in the long run. Some simple rules to follow are shown in the box below.

TIPS FOR ROBUST CODE
◆ Use simple logic. ◆ Perform validity checks on input data and input parameters. ◆ Include tracing statements in the program.

Simple logic. [1] It seems obvious that the complexity of the program logic (whether expressed as the number of methods, the depth of nesting of loops and if statements, the number of operators in an expression, or the number of statements in a method) should be kept under control. However, it is very easy to delude oneself that the program should be contorted to minimize the number of executed statements in the belief that it will make the program better and faster. It is unlikely that the time saved when the program is executed will ever make up for all the extra thought that was needed to make the program work correctly. Keep the program simple and there will be fewer bugs.

Validity checks using if statements. The next piece of advice is to assume that some bugs will creep into the program, and therefore to program defensively. Our goal is to detect the symptoms of a bug in the program soon after the bug has occurred, and to halt the program or to report the error. A standard technique is to insert checking statements at the beginning of every method and after every method call that reads data from a file. For example, if we are programming a method to add two vectors of numbers, we might check that the two vectors have the same length, as follows:

```
// Add two vectors of numbers yielding a vector result
double[] Add(double[] a, double[] b) {
  int len = a.Length;
  if (len != b.Length)
    throw new Exception("Error: mismatched vector sizes");
  double[] result = new double[len];
  for (int i = 0; i < len; i++)
    result[i] = a[i]+b[i];
  return result;
}
```

Note that throwing an exception is the normal action to take when an error has been found. The stack trace that can be obtained from the exception object will allow the person debugging the program to discover where the method was called from.

If we invoke the Add method from somewhere else with invalid arguments (two vectors with different lengths), the exception is thrown and, assuming that there is no try-catch clause in the program which catches it, program execution is halted and a message box is displayed. It should look similar to the one shown in Figure 6.1. That message box gives the name of the exception type but provides no additional information that would be useful.

To obtain information about the location of the exception in the program, we need to click on 'Yes' as our response to the question 'Do you want to debug using the selected debugger?' If Visual Studio is installed on the Windows system, the CLR Debugger program (rather than the other option) is invoked by default. The debugger brings up a message box which includes the message string passed as the argument to the constructor of the Exception class. An example message box is shown in Figure 6.2.

---

1. Otherwise known as the KISS *(keep it simple, stupid)* principle.

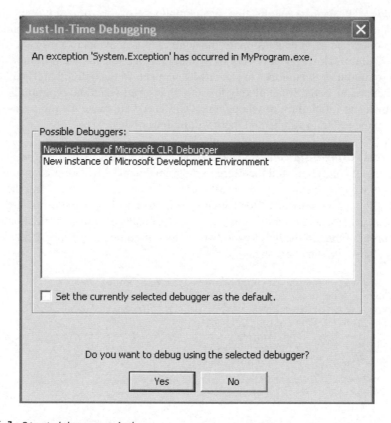

Figure 6.1 Start debugger window

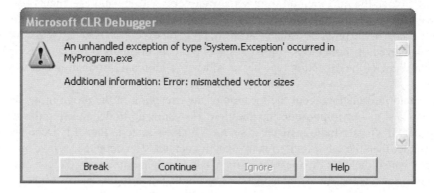

Figure 6.2 Initial debugger window

Additionally, if the C# program was compiled with the /debug:full option in effect, the debugger displays a second window indicating where in the program the problem was encountered. A portion of that second debugger window is shown in Figure 6.3.

```
double[] Add( double[] a, double[] b ) {
int len = a.Length;
if (len != b.Length)
    throw new Exception("Error: mismatched vector sizes");
double[] result = new double[len];
for( int i = 0; i < len; i++ )
    result[i] = a[i]+b[i];
return result;
}
```

Figure 6.3 The error location displayed by the CLR Debugger

The debugger has actually highlighted the line following the statement that threw the exception. This is because the debugger always shows the statement that is about to be executed or has been partially executed (which happens when the statement contains method calls which have not all yet been completed).

The debugger allows the stack trace to be displayed, the values of variables to be inspected, and much more. More information about the CLR Debugger is provided in Section 6.4.

We have concentrated on verifying that parameter values passed into a method are valid. Note, however, that it is even more important to validate data read from a file or from the keyboard. It is not unknown for data files to be accidentally corrupted by other programs on the computer or for a human to mistype information on the keyboard. If we have statements like these in our program

```
Console.Write("Enter your weight in kg ==> ");
int w = int.Parse(Console.ReadLine());
```

then it should become second nature either to check the data value using statements similar to these

```
if (w < MinWeight || w > MaxWeight)
  throw new Exception("Unreasonable weight entered: "+w);
```

or to program additional logic that forces the user either to confirm the validity of the data or to re-enter a valid number. It is good practice to include input like this in a loop that repeatedly asks for input, perhaps up to three times before an exception is thrown. The above example becomes:

```
for (int tries = 1; tries<=3; tries++) {
  Console.Write("Enter your weight in kg ==> ");
  int w = int.Parse(Console.ReadLine());
  if (w < MinWeight || w > MaxWeight) {
    if (tries == 3)
      throw new Exception("Unreasonable weight entered: "+w);
    else
      Console.WriteLine("Unreasonable weight. Try again.");
  }
}
Console.WriteLine(w+" is an acceptable weight");
```

Sample output for such interaction would be:

```
Enter your weight in kg ==> 600
Unreasonable weight. Try again.
Enter your weight in kg ==> 60
60 is an acceptable weight
```

Allowing an unvalidated number to get into a program and control its actions is asking for trouble.

If the data is read from a file that has been generated by another program, an erroneous value in the file would normally indicate that something has gone badly wrong. Throwing an exception to force the program to be halted with an error message would be a normal way of handling such an eventuality.

Validity checks using the Assert method. The .NET Framework on the Windows platform provides a `Debug` class in the `System.Diagnostics` namespace. It implements a method named `Assert` which is intended for validity checking.

DEBUG.ASSERT METHOD

`using System.Diagnostics;`
 	
`Debug.Assert(`*test*`, `*message*`);`

If the Boolean expression *test* evaluates to false, a message box reporting the error and including the additional text of *message* pops up on the screen. The compiler option `/define:DEBUG` must be in effect, for example   `csc /define:DEBUG myprogram.cs` otherwise the calls to `Debug.Assert` are ignored.

We could use the `Assert` method instead of the `if` statement in the `Add` method example, as follows.

```
double[] Add(double[] a, double[] b) {
  int len = a.Length;
  Debug.Assert(len==b.Length, "mismatched vector sizes");
  ... // as before
}
```

If the test fails, a window pops up on the screen. That window should look similar to the one shown in Figure 6.4.

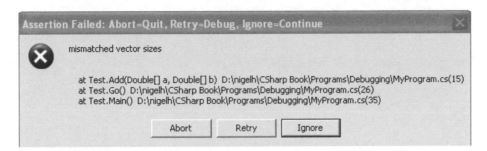

Figure 6.4 Assertion failure message window

Of the three buttons at the bottom of the window, only the 'Abort' button is likely to be useful. It causes the program to be terminated. The 'Retry' button would cause the Boolean expression to be re-evaluated. Unless the expression involves a data value that might be different (e.g. a number read from the keyboard), there is no point in re-evaluating it because the result will be the same and the message window is redisplayed. The 'Ignore' button would cause the program to resume execution at the next statement, but the likely result will be another error later on.

When the program has been debugged and is thought to be correct, the program can be compiled without the `/define:DEBUG` flag. That will cause the compiler to ignore all the statements which invoke `Debug.Assert`.

Tracing statements. Validity checking statements help when the first obvious symptom of a bug is a data value being out of range. Sometimes, though, the symptom appears as control having followed an unexpected path through the program. Although throwing an exception and then looking at the stack trace can provide some information about how control reached the point where the error was observed, it may be insufficient information. The stack trace only shows which method calls are active, it doesn't show exactly how control reached the method calls at each level. Knowledge of which `if` statements were executed, how many times loops were repeated, and so on, is sometimes invaluable.

A general solution is provided by a debugger program (see Section 6.4), but it can be a difficult tool to master. A much simpler approach is to insert trace output statements into the program. Many programmers make a practice of doing this, whether they believe the program to contain bugs or not.

Suppose that we have a method in our program with the following header:

```
int Calculate(int n, double tolerance)
```

and that ends with the line:

```
return result;
```

We could insert two lines at the beginning of the method and an extra line at the end of the method, so that it has the following structure:

```
int Calculate(int n, double tolerance) {
  if (Tracing.IsEnabled) Console.WriteLine(
    "* Entering Calculate(n={0}, tolerance={1})",
    n, tolerance);
...
... // body of the Calculate method
...
  if (Tracing.IsEnabled) Console.WriteLine(
    "* Exiting Calculate, result={0}", result);
  return result;
}
```

Similar modifications are made to all methods in the program. Finally, an extra class is defined somewhere in the program as follows:

```
class Tracing {
  public static bool IsEnabled = true;
}
```

This extra class definition could be inserted at the top of the program just after all the using declarations (and after a namespace declaration if there is one).

When the program is run, all the tracing messages appear in the console window. We might see a series of messages looking something like those shown in Figure 6.5.

```
* Entering Main
* Entering Go
* Entering RepeatCalculations(tries=3)
* Entering Calculate(n=1, tolerance=0.1)
* Exiting Calculate, result=37
* Entering Calculate(n=2, tolerance=0.01)
* Exiting Calculate, result=36
* Entering Calculate(n=3, tolerance=0.001)
* Exiting Calculate, result=35
* Exiting RepeatCalculations, result = 35
* Exiting Go
* Exiting Main
```

Figure 6.5 Sample trace output

Examination of the trace output may provide enough information to deduce where a program computes an unexpected answer or otherwise went wrong. If it is not enough information, we can insert more output statements at strategic points inside the method bodies. For example, we might generate a trace output message at the top of a loop body.

When the bug has been corrected, the tracing output is easily disabled. All we have to do is replace this line in the `Tracing` class

```
public static bool IsEnabled = true;
```

with

```
public static bool IsEnabled = false;
```

and no more tracing messages will be generated.

It would worry some programmers that all the extra `if` statements and calls to `Console.WriteLine` make the program bigger and slower. The concern should not be a big one because most programs run fast enough, even with a few extra statements, and the small amount of extra memory needed will have little effect. However, if space and time should turn out to be important, it would be a mistake to delete the tracing statements. Few programs are ever completely free of bugs and those tracing statements may be needed again. Here are two better solutions. They have the effect of causing the tracing statements to be completely ignored in the final version of the program.

The first solution uses conditional compilation and is described as follows.

TRACING STATEMENTS – CONDITIONAL COMPILATION

```
#if TRACE
Console.WriteLine("... trace output message ...");
#endif
```

The tracing output statement can print whatever message will help follow the flow of control and help track the values of variables.

If the program is compiled with the option `/define:TRACE`, for example:
```
csc /define:TRACE file1.cs file2.cs
```
then all the statements between the `#if TRACE ... #endif` pairs of lines are included in the program; otherwise they are ignored.

The second solution uses methods provided by the `Debug` class in the `System.Diagnostics` namespace.

The `Debug.WriteLine` method generates a line of trace output. However, the output disapppears without a trace[1] unless a listener for the output has been provided. The method call `Debug.Listeners.Clear()` first removes any existing listeners (the call should be unnecessary but it does not hurt to call the method anyway). Then the method call `Debug.Listeners.Add` adds a new listener, which is created as an instance of the `TextWriterTraceListener` class. The argument of that class's constructor would normally be the name of a file, to which the trace output will be written.

However, it is also possible to send the trace output to the console window by making this call:

```
Debug.Listeners.Add(new TextWriterTraceListener(Console.Out));
```

---

1. An irresistible pun. Sorry.

DEBUG CLASS – USE FOR TRACE OUTPUT

```
// This using declaration should be provided
using System.Diagnostics;

// These three statements should be executed when
// the program is started
Debug.Listeners.Clear();
Debug.Listeners.Add(
    new TextWriterTraceListener("trace.txt"));
Debug.AutoFlush = true;

// This statement is used to generate trace output
Debug.WriteLine("... trace output message ...");

Debug.Indent(); // indents subsequent trace messages
Debug.Unindent(); // undoes the call to Indent()
```

If trace output is desired, the `/define:DEBUG` flag must be supplied when compiling the program; otherwise all the calls to the `Debug` methods will be ignored.
The trace output is written to the file named in the call to the `TextWriter-TraceListener` class constructor.

That call could be used instead of, or in addition to, a call that provides a listener.
   Making the following assignment before any calls to `Debug.WriteLine`

```
Debug.AutoFlush = true;
```

is desirable because it causes each line to be written to the trace output file immediately. Otherwise, several lines may be accumulated in a buffer and written only when the buffer is full. Sometimes that buffering may cause the last few lines of output to be lost when the program halts with an error.

Example 6.1 Using Debug methods

Consider a program to print out Fibonacci numbers (described in Exercise 4.14). A short program that uses the Debug methods appears below.

File FibExample.cs

```
using System;
using System.IO;
using System.Diagnostics;
```

```
class FibExample {

  int fibonacci(int n) {
    Debug.WriteLine("Entering fibonacci, n="+n);
    Debug.Indent();
    Debug.Assert(n>=0,
      "argument for fibonacci cannot be negative");
    int result;
    if (n < 2)
      result = 1;
    else
      result = fibonacci(n-1) + fibonacci(n-2);
    Debug.Unindent();
    Debug.WriteLine("Exiting fibonacci, result="+result);
    return result;
  }

  void Go() {
    Debug.WriteLine("Entering Go");
    Console.WriteLine("Fibonacci(4) = {0}", fibonacci(4));
    Console.WriteLine("Fibonacci(-1) = {0}", fibonacci(-1));
    Debug.WriteLine("Exiting Go");
  }

  static void Main() {
    Debug.Listeners.Clear();
    Debug.Listeners.Add(
        new TextWriterTraceListener("trace.txt"));
    Debug.AutoFlush = true;
    new FibExample().Go();
  }
}
```

The trace output that gets written to the file `trace.txt` when the program is run appears below.

```
Entering Go
    Entering fibonacci, n=4
        Entering fibonacci, n=3
            Entering fibonacci, n=2
                Entering fibonacci, n=1
                Exiting fibonacci, result=1
                Entering fibonacci, n=0
                Exiting fibonacci, result=1
            Exiting fibonacci, result=2
            Entering fibonacci, n=1
            Exiting fibonacci, result=1
        Exiting fibonacci, result=3
        Entering fibonacci, n=2
            Entering fibonacci, n=1
            Exiting fibonacci, result=1
            Entering fibonacci, n=0
            Exiting fibonacci, result=1
```

```
        Exiting fibonacci, result=2
      Exiting fibonacci, result=5
      Entering fibonacci, n=-1
      Fail: argument for fibonacci cannot be negative
      Exiting fibonacci, result=1
  Exiting Go
```

Indentation of the messages has been used to show nested calls to methods. When the program contains recursive methods, as this one does, the trace output can be very difficult to read unless some visual clues are provided to show which messages come from which method calls. It is easy to make the indentations work correctly: as soon as a method is entered, we call Debug.Indent() and just before exiting the method we call Debug.Unindent().

Note in the output that when the Boolean expression used in the call to Debug.Assert evaluated to false, the error message was written to the trace output file and execution continued.

Designing test cases

When a program or even a small piece of a program has been newly written, we should test the code by making test calls to the methods in the program and verifying that the results are as expected. It is usually impossible to test all combinations. However, a little thought can usually create test cases that exercise all or most paths through the program code.

As a general principle, when a program accepts values in some range, it is a good idea to create test cases which use values at the extreme ends of the range as well as a few values in the middle. For example, if a numeric input to a program must be in the range 0 to 100, then both of the values 0 and 100 should be explicitly tested. Programmers frequently make mistakes with end conditions, perhaps making an array have one element too few or iterating over a loop one too many times.

6.4 Using a debugger program

A typical installation of the .NET Framework and Visual Studio on a Windows system provides three different debugger programs. Unix systems provide other debugger programs, these include dbx, dbxtool and gdb.

Debugger programs have two distinct purposes:

1. When a program has gone wrong, we can use a debugger to discover exactly where in the program the error was detected and to examine the values of all the variables at the time of the error.

2. We can use a debugger to watch a program being executed. The debugger allows us to follow the execution path, seeing which statements are executed, and to examine the values of variables.

It is possible to have separate debugger programs for the two different purposes, however the normal practice is to have one debugger program which is used for both purposes.

Many features of the debugger programs require advanced knowledge of how software is executed on a computer system. The information provided in this book is necessarily limited to the simpler features.

Analyzing a program crash with the CLR Debugger program

Figure 6.1 showed the message window which pops up when a C# program running under Windows throws an exception and that exception is not caught by a `try-catch` statement. Clicking on 'Yes' to select a new instance of the Microsoft CLR Debugger to be executed allows us to obtain information about the program.

Microsoft calls this 'just in time' debugging, because the debugger program is activated at the last possible moment, only when it is needed.

Clicking on 'Yes' in the message box window of Figure 6.1 causes the computer screen to be filled with a GUI for the CLR Debugger program, with a message box window like that shown in Figure 6.2 overlaid on top. Clicking on the 'Break' button of that message box causes control to be given to the debugger. With the debugger, it is possible to see where in the program the error was discovered and to inspect the values of variables. (It would also be possible to allow the program to continue execution, tracking control flow and the values of variables along the way.)

Example 6.2 Using the CLR Debugger

Let's follow an example from the beginning. A program with a bug in it, File `buggy.cs`, appears below. The program is supposed to tell a cashier how to give change for a purchase. The `Go` method asks the user to enter the cost of the item being purchased and then to enter the amount of money handed over to pay for the item. For example, if the item costs $2.75 and $10 is handed over, the program should respond with output similar to the following.

```
The change will be ...
  1   5 dollar note
  2   1 dollar notes
  1   25 cent coin
```

Unfortunately, when the program was typed into the computer, an error was made when listing the values of the notes and coins which can be used to make change. Somehow, the value 100 was typed as '10,0'. There is no syntax error when the program is compiled.

File buggy.cs

```csharp
// There is a bug in this program!!
using System;

class Buggy {
  int[] unitValues = { 10000, 5000, 2000, 1000,
                       500, 10,0, 25, 10, 5, 1 };

  string unitName(int value) {
    if (value >= 100)
      return value/100 + " dollar note";
    return value + " cent coin";
  }

  void MakeChange(int Cost, int AmountOffered) {
    int change = AmountOffered - Cost;
    if (change == 0) {
      Console.WriteLine("No change required");
      return;
    }
    Console.WriteLine("The change will be ...");
    for (int i=0; i < unitValues.Length; i++) {
      int unit = unitValues[i];
      int num = change/unit;
      string plural;
      if (num != 0) {
        if (num > 1)
          plural = "s";
        else
          plural = "";
        change -= num*unit;
        Console.WriteLine("  {0}  {1}{2}",
          num, unitName(unit), plural);
      }
    }
  }

  void Go() {
    for (; ;) {
      Console.Write("Enter cost of item   ==> ");
      double c = double.Parse(Console.ReadLine());
      Console.Write("Enter amount offered ==> ");
      double a = double.Parse(Console.ReadLine());
      MakeChange((int)(c*100), (int)(a*100));
    }
  }

  static void Main() {
    new Buggy().Go();
  }
}
```

When the program is executed, we first observe that for the input of $2.75 for the item's cost and $10 for the money offered, the output is

```
Enter cost of item    ==> 2.75
Enter amount offered ==> 10
The change will be ...
   1   5 dollar note
  22  10 cent coins
```

which is very strange, and then we see a message window pop up similar to the one shown in Figure 6.1, but this one says the exception type is `System.DivideByZeroException`. Clicking on the 'Yes' button to start the CLR Debugger causes the Debugger GUI to appear along with a second message box window like the one in Figure 6.6. Clicking on 'Break' causes the message box to go away, leaving us with just the GUI for the CLR Debugger as shown in Figure 6.7.

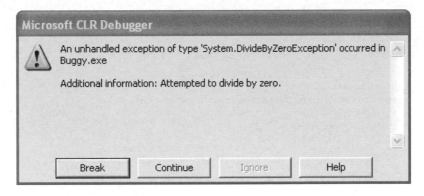

Figure 6.6 DivideByZeroException message box

By default, the GUI displays four separate windows (or panels). The largest panel displays source code. It starts by showing the region of the program where the error was encountered, just as shown in Figure 6.7. The line of code where execution was interrupted is shaded in yellow and marked with the horizontal arrow.

If the cursor is placed on top of a variable's name in the source code panel, a small box appears alongside saying what the current value of the variable is. For example, if we put the cursor on top of the identifier `change` in the line which caused the error, a box appears which says

```
change=5
```

```
Buggy.cs                                                              ◁ ▷ ×

    void MakeChange( int Cost, int AmountOffered ) {
      int change = AmountOffered - Cost;
      if (change == 0) {
        Console.WriteLine("No change required");
        return;
      }
      Console.WriteLine("The change will be ...");
      for( int i=0; i < unitValues.Length; i++ ) {
        int unit = unitValues[i];
⇨       int num = change/unit;
        string plural;
        if (num != 0) {
          if (num > 1)
            plural = "s";
          else
            plural = "";
          change -= num*unit;
          Console.WriteLine("  {0}  {1}{2}", num, unitName(unit), plural);
        }
      }
    }
```

Figure 6.7 Source code panel in debugger

and if we pass the cursor over the identifier unit, the box says

> unit=0

and that is apparently the immediate cause of the error.

We might wonder now how the variable named `unit` got to hold the value zero. Looking up to the previous line in the program, we can inspect variable i by putting the cursor on top and see that it holds the value 6. That now causes us to ask what is in position 6 of the array named `unitValues`. If we pass the cursor over that identifier, the debugger tells us only

> unitValues={Length=11}

If we want to see the contents of the array, we first need to double-click on the identifier `unitValues` (so that the name becomes highlighted), then we pull down the `Debug` menu on the toolbar across the top of the debugger and select `QuickWatch`. That creates a scrollable window which shows the values of all the elements in the array, as reproduced in Figure 6.8.

How do we find out where the current method was called from, and how do we see the values of variables in that method? The toolbar across the top of the debugger's GUI has a box labelled 'Stack Frame'. On the right-hand side of the box (it looks like it is part of the box), there is a downward pointing arrow. Clicking on that arrow brings up a list of locations in the program. There is one line in the list for each active method – a method which has been entered but has not yet returned. The top line in the list corresponds to the location of the error, the line below corresponds to the line which called the current method, and so on. Selecting a line in the list causes the source code panel to change its contents. For example, selecting the second line changes the window to display the lines shown in Figure 6.9. Running the cursor over variable names in the window shows their current values.

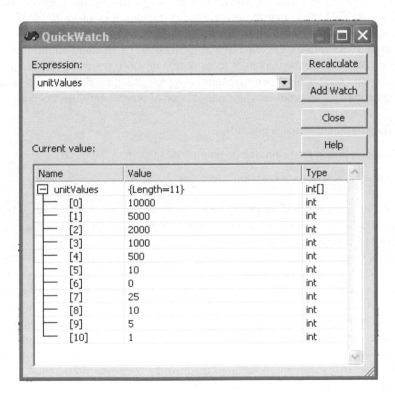

Figure 6.8 QuickWatch display of an array's contents

```
double c = double.Parse(Console.ReadLine());
Console.Write("Enter amount offered ==> ");
double a = double.Parse(Console.ReadLine());
MakeChange((int)(c*100), (int)(a*100));
}
```

Figure 6.9 Source code of calling method

Tracing program control with a debugger

Although the ability to follow a program's execution may seem like a panacea, enabling any error to be diagnosed, life is not quite that easy.

The basic principle of the debugger is that it allows us to execute one statement at a time. By clicking the mouse or by hitting keys on the keyboard, we can make the program advance one statement. This is called *single-step execution*. After executing one statement, we can then, if we wish, inspect the values of variables before using the mouse or the keyboard to advance one more statement. By watching the execution path and by inspecting the values of variables, the cause of any bug will eventually be revealed.

An obvious difficulty is that the program may execute tens of millions of statements before getting to the interesting part where the symptoms of a bug manifest themselves. Debuggers provide various solutions to that difficulty. The standard solution is by use of *breakpoints*. We can ask the debugger to mark one or more statements in the program as being breakpoint statements. Then we run the program at full speed (i.e. we do not use single-step execution). The program will run until one of these conditions occurs:

1.   The program terminates normally.

2.   An exception is thrown in the program (i.e. an error occurs). Or

3.   Execution reaches a breakpoint statement.

In cases 2 and 3, we can use the debugger to examine the values of variables and we can then ask the debugger to resume execution (though this may not make sense if execution was stopped by an exception being thrown).

Appendix G provides some basic information about using the debuggers provided on Microsoft Windows systems to trace execution. However, use of a debugger in this way should be considered to be the tool of last resort, and that is why we will not examine it in detail here. It is usually a much more productive use of one's time to sit down and read the source code of the erroneous program, thinking through all the assumptions that went into writing the code. A highly recommended technique is to ask a friend to sit down next to you while you explain to your friend, statement by statement, how the program is supposed to work. It is surprising how often the mistake becomes obvious just by having a passive listener, someone who just listens and does not ask any questions.

Concepts in Chapter 6

This chapter introduced the `try-catch` statement, the `throw` statement, and several C# classes dealing with exceptions in the `System` namespace:

```
Exception                           IndexOutOfRangeException
```

```
DivideByZeroException          FormatException
IOException
```

Forms for the following constructs were provided.

try-catch statement   Debug.Assert method

tracing statements – conditional com-   Debug class – use for trace output
pilation

Quiz

Q6.1 If the following is written in a program, what will happen?

```
1    double[] a = new double[10];
2    for (int i=1; i<=10; i++)
3      a[i] = i;
4    Console.WriteLine("Completed");
```

    (a)   `Completed` will be printed

    (b)   `IndexOutOfRangeException` will be raised

    (c)   Compilation error at line 3 because a is a double array

    (d)   Compilation error because a[0] does not have a value

Q6.2 An exception is implemented in C# as

    (a)   an object   (b)   a string

    (c)   an array   (d)   an integer variable

Q6.3 If all tests get past the `Debug.Assert` method, it is most likely that:

    (a)   The program is perfectly correct

    (b)   The tests in `Debug.Assert` used or's instead of and's

    (c)   The `/define:DEBUG` option was not set

    (d)   The `/define:DEBUG` option was set

Q6.4 A programmer puts `Debug.WriteLine` statements in a program, but there is no output. The likely cause is:

    (a)   The `/define:DEBUG` option was not set

    (b)   No listener was provided for the output

    (c)   Debug.AutoFlush was not called

    (d)   Any of the above

Q6.5 If the following is written in a program, what will happen?

```
1    int i = 3;   int j = 0;
2    try {
3      Console.WriteLine("Answer = "+(i/j));
4    } catch(DivideByZeroException) {
5     Console.Writeln("Zero");
6    } catch(Exception) {
7     Console.WriteLine("Exception");
8    }
```

    (a)   Answer = 0 will be printed

    (b)   Exception will be printed

    (c)   Zero will be printed

    (d)   Nothing will be printed

CHAPTER 7

Files and streams

Computer programs must communicate to receive input and to transmit output. Such communication is not necessarily with the user directly, it may be with other computer programs or it may involve saving information on a disk drive and reading it back again later. In this chapter, we look at how to perform these methods of communication.

7.1 Files and streams

Some of the power of a program comes from its ability to remember information from one run to the next. Or, perhaps, we want to remember the results of one program and then have another program process those results soon afterwards.

The computer has one or more disks, or hard drives, used for storing data over long periods of time. Unlike the main memory (the RAM), the data on a hard drive is retained even when the power to the computer is turned off.

Information recorded on the hard drive is organized into files. Each file is just a sequence of bytes. A file has a name and various other properties which the computer operating system will keep track of. These properties normally include information about when the file was created, when it was last modified, when it was last accessed, and which users of the computer can read or write to the file. However, until our programs become fairly advanced, we need not be concerned with properties other than the file name.

Types of files

Some files contain only text, where each character is represented using a standard coding scheme such as Unicode or 8-bit UTF-8 codes. On Windows systems, text files normally have the suffix '.txt' at the ends of their names. The contents of such a file can be viewed or edited with an editor program like the Windows Notepad program. Other files contain data in other formats. If we try to view such a file with Notepad, we see gibberish with, perhaps, the occasional recognizable word embedded somewhere.

C# programs can read and write text files using the `ReadLine` and `WriteLine` methods. These methods were used in Chapter 2 for reading from the keyboard and writing text to display on the computer screen. It takes only a few more lines of programming to read from a file or to write to a file. The class libraries provided with C# allow programs to create files, write data to files and to read data back from files. The classes belong to the `System.IO` namespace. There are many different ways to use files. The full repertoire of classes and methods in those classes for creating, deleting and accessing files is somewhat overwhelming. In this chapter, we will cover only text files and we will look at only the simplest ways to work with files.

Streams

Writing programs is made simpler when there are fewer special situations to worry about. Although the keyboard and a file on disk are two quite different concepts, we use the same C# methods for reading text from them. Similarly, we use the same methods for writing to a text file or for displaying text on the computer screen. The generalization that covers reading from many different sources is an *input stream*. For writing, the generalized concept is the *output stream*. As far as the program is concerned, it reads from input streams and writes to output streams. The name 'stream' is meant to denote a flow of data (like a river or a stream). At either end of a stream is a device which generates input, like a keyboard, or a device which accepts output, like a printer, or a disk file, or a program. The two endpoints may be on the same computer, or they may be on two different computers which are connected via a network.

Namespaces for streams

The types needed for implementing streams in C#, and hence all the methods we will be calling frequently, are contained in two namespaces:

- ◆ `System` contains the `Console` class for screen and keyboard interaction; and
- ◆ `System.IO` contains the classes for file interaction, including `StreamReader` and `StreamWriter`.

7.2 Streams for output

If we want our program to write text to a disk file, it must either create a new file or it must write to an existing file. Let us suppose it is the former case. We start with the `Stream-Writer` class in the `System.IO` namespace, and *should*, if the file does not already exist, be able to create a new text file named `mydata.txt` through simple object instantiation.

```
using System.IO;
...
StreamWriter outStream = new StreamWriter("mydata.txt");
```

If the statement succeeds, the file will be created in the current directory, and the variable `outStream` created as a `StreamWriter` object which may be used for writing data to the file in subsequent statements in this program.

If the file `mydata.txt` already exists when the program invokes the `StreamWriter` constructor, then the file should be wiped clean and our program can proceed to write to the file, replacing its previous contents.

Output stream errors on opening

Unfortunately, there are several reasons why the statement to create the output stream may not succeed. Perhaps our computer account does not have the privileges needed to create a file in the current directory, or perhaps there is no room on the disk to create a new file, or perhaps the file exists but the file is tagged as read-only, and so on. Whatever the reason, we should not be overly surprised if the statement fails to work. Our C# program will stop and report back with an error message if the desired output stream cannot be created.

If we prefer to have our program produce its own error messages or if there is some action other than halting the program that we want to perform (e.g. asking the user to provide a different filename), then we should open the file inside the scope of a `try-catch` statement. For example, we can write the code to open the file as follows.

```
using System.IO;
...
StreamWriter outStream = null;
string outFileName = "mydata.txt";
try {
    outStream = new StreamWriter(outFileName);
} catch (Exception e) {
    Console.WriteLine("Unable to create file {0}", outFileName);
    Console.WriteLine("Reason: {0}", e.ToString());
    // and now perform some corrective actions?
}
```

The `catch` clause attempts to intercept all possible problems when opening the file. There are several more precise exception types which would be applicable when opening the file, namely

```
IOException
DirectoryNotFoundException
FileLoadException
FileNotFoundException
PathTooLongException
```

However, there would be no advantage in providing separate `catch` clauses for any of these, since the above code will output the reason anyway.

Specifying filenames

The string that provides the filename may specify a location other than the current directory. For example, if we will be running our C# program on a Windows system, we can create the `mydata.txt` file in the usual directory for temporary files using statements like the following.

```
string fname = "C:\\WINDOWS\\Temp\\mydata.txt"; // Windows
StreamWriter outStream = new StreamWriter(fname);
```

The notation used to specify the path to a directory on a Windows system begins with the disk drive letter (`C:`) and then uses a backslash character to separate directory names along the path to the desired file location. The backslash character is the escape character so, it needs to be escaped with another backslash character and that is why the C# string is shown with pairs of backslashes. The actual path is `C:\WINDOWS\Temp\mydata.txt`. Today's Windows systems will accept forward slashes as well, and they do not need to be escaped.

If we specify the file simply as `"mydata.txt"`, then it will be created in the directory in which the program is running. This is often the most convenient method.

If we are running C# on a Unix system, the notation used to identify paths to directories is different. To create the file in the usual location for temporary files on a Unix system, we would write the following statements.

```
string fname = "/tmp/mydata.txt"; // Unix temporary file
StreamWriter outStream = new StreamWriter(fname);
```

Writing to a stream

If the program has successfully invoked the `StreamWriter` constructor, it may proceed to write text to the file. The `StreamWriter` class has the two methods with the same names as the ones which we previously used in our C# programs to write messages on the computer's screen. They are `Write` and `WriteLine`. Thus the program can proceed to execute statements similar to the following. These statements assume that `outStream` has been successfully opened, as described above.

```
outStream.WriteLine("** The first line of output");
outStream.Write("i = " + i + ", ");
outStream.WriteLine("j = {0}, f*2 = {1}", j, f*2.0);
```

Closing a stream

When the program has finished writing to a stream, it should *close* the stream. The action of closing tells the computer operating system that any pending, incomplete, writes should be completed and that any temporary memory used for accessing the file or the computer screen can now be reused for other purposes. If our program terminates without closing its input and output streams, the computer operating system will close them anyway. It is, however, considered to be good programming style to close each stream explicitly as soon as the program has finished with it. Some programs use many streams in the course of one run and then it is important to close them as soon as possible, otherwise there is a risk that a system limit on the number of active streams may be reached.

The following statement will close the stream outStream.

```
outStream.Close();
```

7.3 Streams for input

If a text file already exists and our program needs to read data from it, we should create an instance of the StreamReader class, which is also in the System.IO namespace. The following statement will attempt to open a text file named mydata.txt in the current directory and use it as the source for an input stream.

```
StreamReader inStream = new StreamReader("mydata.txt");
```

The statement may fail and produce an error message if the file does not exist or if our computer account lacks the privileges needed to read that file. Therefore it is advisable to enclose the operation of opening a file inside a try-catch statement, as follows:

```
using System.IO;

StreamReader inStream;
string inFileName = "mydata.txt";

try {
   inStream = new StreamReader(inFileName);
} catch( Exception e ) {
   Console.WriteLine("Unable to open file {0}\n{1}",
      inFileName, e.ToString());
   return;  // or do something to stop the program
            // from using inStream.
}
```

Assuming the operation of opening the file succeeds, the inStream variable may subsequently be used for reading text from the input stream.

Reading from a stream

Our program can read an entire line from an input stream using the `ReadLine` method, as follows.

```
string s = inStream.ReadLine();
```

If the input stream has been exhausted, i.e. there is no more data in the file left to be read, the `ReadLine` method returns `null`.

It is also possible to read one character at a time from the text stream using the `Read` method. Here is a sample loop which will read everything from an input stream, one character at a time.

```
int k;
while((k = inStream.Read()) != -1) {
    char c = (char)k;
    // process the next character c
    ...
}
```

The usage details are made complicated by the `Read` method returning a 32-bit integer instead of a `char` value. That design choice was made in C# so that there is a simple way to test whether a character was actually read or whether no more characters remained in the file to be read. As the test condition on the `while` loop example shows, the special value of −1 is expected to be returned if the file has been exhausted.

Finally, it is possible to read an entire file into the program as a single string. The `StreamReader` method is `ReadToEnd`. The logic of our program may be considerably simplified if we have all the file copied into memory. However, we should use this method only if we know (or if the program has verified) that the size of the file is reasonable. That is because it is possible for a file to be many gigabytes in size and to exceed the amount of memory available to the program. Attempting to read a large file may cause the `Out-OfMemoryException` exception to be thrown.

Example 7.1 Expanding tabs to spaces

The following program makes a copy of a text file, but modified by replacing tab characters with space characters. Many text editing programs and word processing programs accept tab characters in the input. They are typically used to cause text to line up in columns. The effect of a tab is supposed to cause one or more columns to be left blank, so that the following character on the line appears in a column which has an associated tab stop. Old-fashioned electric typewriters allowed tab stop positions to be set by the user. Computer software usually imposes some predefined tab stop positions.

When the font has characters of equal width (i.e. it is a monospaced font like Courier), the tab stop positions always occur at particular columns in a line of text. We assume the font to be monospaced. Unfortunately, there is no agreed convention for which columns have associated tab stops. It is a default rule for Unix that tab stops are placed at every eighth column. That is, in columns 1, 9, 17, ..., etc. However, it is a rule that does not exist for other computer systems and it is an easily overridden default for Unix in any case.

If tab characters are replaced by spaces, the indentation of lines of code in a program become independent of vaguely defined tab stop positions, and that is where our program might be useful.

Specifications. By default, the program assumes that a tab stop is placed at every eighth column. That default is easily changed by providing a different value for the constant `inputTabSize`. The user is prompted to enter the name of the text file to read. The program writes its result to a new file whose name is the same as the input file but with the characters 'CopyOf' placed at the front. For example, if the input file is named `MyData.txt` then the output file will be called `CopyOfMyData.txt`.

Approach. The program reads one line at a time. Each line is passed to a method named `expandTabs` which returns a copy of the line with the tabs replaced by spaces. That method looks at each character in the line from left to right, figuring out which column the character would print in. If the character is a tab, the method calculates the position of the next tab stop and then stores the appropriate number of spaces in the output line to get to that column.

The output line is built up, character by character, by appending one character or one string at a time. It is possible to use the string datatype, as in the following code fragment.

```
string result = "";
int count = 0;
...
result += ' '; // append a space to result
result += "; count = "; // append a string to result
result += count; // append a number to result
```

However that is quite inefficient in C#, especially if we repeatedly append characters inside a loop, because a new instance of the string type is created each time something is appended.

The C# class library provides a type, `StringBuilder`, which is more appropriate when the string is frequently changed. Our program uses this type for efficiency. A summary of a few of the methods provided by `StringBuilder` is given in the form below. `StringBuilder` is in the `System.Text` namespace, so we specify that we are using it.

```
File ExpandTabs.cs
```

```
using System;
using System.Text;
using System.IO;
```

```
class ExpandTabs {
  ///<summary>
  /// ExpandTabs program          Horspool and Bishop     Dec 2002
  /// ==================
  /// Replaces tab characters with equivalent numbers of spaces
  /// Illustrates file and string handling
  ///</summary>

  const int inputTabSize = 8;

  string expandTabs(string s) {
    StringBuilder result = new StringBuilder(s.Length+20);
    int col = 0;
    foreach (char c in s) {
      if (c == '\t') {
        do {
          result.Append(' ');
          col++;
        } while(col%inputTabSize != 0);
      } else {
        result.Append(c);
        col++;
      }
    }
    return result.ToString();
  }

  void ProcessFile(string inFileName, string outFileName) {
    StreamReader inStream = new StreamReader(inFileName);
    StreamWriter outStream = new StreamWriter(outFileName);
    for ( ; ; ) {
      string s = inStream.ReadLine();
      if (s == null) break;
      outStream.WriteLine(expandTabs(s.TrimEnd()));
    }
    outStream.Close();
    inStream.Close();
  }

  void Go() {
    Console.Write("Enter the file name: ");
    string inFileName = Console.ReadLine();
    inFileName = inFileName.TrimEnd();
    try {
      StreamReader inStream = new StreamReader(inFileName);
    } catch(Exception e) {
      Console.WriteLine("Unable to open {0}\n{1}",
            inFileName, e.ToString());
      return;
    }
    string outFileName = "CopyOf"+inFileName;
    ProcessFile(inFileName,outFileName);
  }
```

```
static void Main() {
  new ExpandTabs().Go();
}
}
```

The `ExpandTabs.cs` program should probably be improved so that it verifies that the output file does not already exist before proceeding to overwrite it, or at least asks the user to confirm that the file can be overwritten.

Here is the form for the `StringBuilder` class showing some of the methods used in the program.

STRINGBUILDER CLASS (ABBREVIATED)

```
StringBuilder()                      // constructor
StringBuilder(int capacity)          // constructor

s.Length            // get current length of s
s[int ix]              // access character at position ix in s

s.Append(char c)              // append character c to s
s.Append(string s1)           // append string s1 to s
s.Insert(int ix, char c)      // insert c after position ix
s.Insert(int ix, string s)1   // insert s1 after pos'n ix
s.Remove(int ix, int len)     // delete len chars
s.ToString()                  // convert to an ordinary string
```

A `StringBuilder` value holds a string which can be changed.
If the constructor is given an integer argument, that value is used as an initial estimate of how large the string can grow to. However, the string can become longer if necessary.

7.4 File processing as a design pattern

It is a common programming task to read lines from the input and perform some processing task on each line. A few of the tasks which fit the pattern are:

◆   searching a file for occurrences of a particular word or identifier;

◆   reformatting a program source code file to have proper indentation;

◆   checking a text file for spelling errors;

◆   reformatting a text file so that no line is longer than, say, 72 characters;

◆   reading lines from a table and updating information in the table;

◆   extracting text from a web page in HTML;

◆   searching a web page in HTML for e-mail addresses.

Most of these tasks are difficult to program using the C# constructs and class libraries covered so far in this book. However, the first example in the list is a reasonably simple task. That is our next example program.

Example 7.2 Searching a file

Let us assume that we want our program to ask the user for the name of the file and the word to search for. Then our program will read the lines of the file, one by one, and check if the desired word occurs in each line. If it does, the program will report the line and its number, then continue searching.

To achieve that effect, we can replace the `ProcessLine` method in the `ModifyTextFile.cs` file with C# code to:

1. Increment the line number.

2. Search the line for the word. And

3. Print the line number and the line if the search succeeds.

Our revised program, where we remove the statements to create an output file and add statements to prompt the user for the search word would then be as shown below as file `SearchTextFile.cs`.

The program prompts the user for the name of a file. Then after the file has been successfully opened for input, the program prompts the user for a word to search for. The program then reads the file and every time it finds a line containing the desired word, it prints the line prefixed with its line number.

Our approach is to read the file one line at a time, and pass the line to a method named `ProcessLine`. That method keeps track of the line number and it searches the line for the desired word. If found, it prints the line number and the line itself. The `IndexOf` method provided in the `string` class is used for searching the line.

File SearchTextFile.cs

```
using System;
using System.IO;

class SearchTextFile {
```

```
///<summary>
/// SearchTextFile program     Horspool and Bishop Dec 2002
/// =======================
/// Searches a text file for occurrences of a string
///</summary>

  int lineNum = 0;
  string word;

  public void ProcessLine( String s ) {
     lineNum++;
     if (s.IndexOf(word) >= 0)
        Console.WriteLine("{0,4}: {1}", lineNum, s);
  }

  public void Go() {
     Console.Write("Enter the file name: ");
     string inFileName = Console.ReadLine();
     StreamReader inStream;
     try {
        inStream = new StreamReader(inFileName);
     } catch(System.Exception e) {
        Console.WriteLine("Unable to read file {0}\n{1}",
           inFileName, e.ToString());
        return;
     }
     Console.Write("Enter word to search for: ");
     word = Console.ReadLine();
     string s;
     while((s = inStream.ReadLine()) != null) {
        ProcessLine(s);
     }
     inStream.Close();
  }

  static void Main() {
     new SearchTextFile().Go();
  }
}
```

The s.IndexOf(word) method call returns the position of the leftmost occurrence of *word* inside the string *s*; the result is −1 if there is no match. We use a non-negative result as our indication that *word* occurs somewhere.

If we run the program using its own source code as the input file, the results could be.

```
Enter the file name: SearchTextFile.cs
Enter the word to search for: word
   6:    string word;
  10:           if (s.IndexOf(word) >= 0)
  18:           Console.Write("Enter word to search for: ");
  19:           word = Console.ReadLine();
```

Summary of text file classes and methods

Some of the useful classes and methods for working with text files are listed below.

STREAMREADER AND STREAMWRITER (ABBREVIATED)

```
StreamReader instr = new StreamReader(filename);
StreamWriter outstr = new StreamWriter(filename);

string s = instr.ReadLine();    // returns null at end
int k = instr.Read();           // returns -1 at end of file

string s = instr.ReadToEnd();   // reads the whole file

outstr.Write(string1);
outstr.WriteLine(string2);

instr.Close();
outstr.Close();
```

The StreamReader class is used to read from text files, the StreamWriter class to write to them.

The Read and ReadLine methods read, respectively, a single character or an entire line from a text file. The ReadToEnd method reads the whole file as a single string which may contain newline characters.

The Write and WriteLine methods write, respectively, strings and lines to a text file. The argument to Write and WriteLine may contain {0}, {1} ... notation, possibly extended with format codes and field widths, to cause additional arguments to be fetched and inserted into the output.

The Close method terminates access to the text file and frees resources used by the operating system.

Here are a few more file methods which may be useful. These work for all kinds of files, not just text files.

FILE OPERATIONS (GENERAL)

```
bool File.Exists(filename);
File.Copy(srcFileName, dstFileName, overwrite);
File.Delete(filename);
```

The Exists method returns true if the file exists and the program has sufficient privileges to read from it.

The Copy method duplicates a file. If the *overwrite* flag is true and the destination file already exists, it will be overwitten; otherwise the copy operation is not performed.

The Delete method deletes the file if the program has sufficient privileges to do so.

7.5 Files in Views

In Chapter 5, we mentioned that there were various Views tags which related to files. We now look at how these work, and extend some of the programs to use files.

Image files

Starting with files that contain images, we note that there are several ways in which we can get a picture displayed on a form.

1. Set an image filename in a `Button` control, e.g.

    ```
    <Button Name=Rock Image='rock.gif'/>
    ```

2. Set an image filename in a `PictureBox` control, e.g.

    ```
    <PictureBox Name=pic Image='Jacarandas.jpg'/>
    ```

3. Set the filename through the form constructor parameter, e.g.

    ```
    string spec = @" ....
              <PictureBox Name=pic Image={0}/>
         ... ";

    Views.Form f = new Views.Form(spec, filename);
    ```

    The filename can be constructed or input in any way, but it has to be finalized before the form is constructed. The filename cannot, therefore, be read using the same `Views.Form` instance. (However, it would be possible to use one form to select a file which is later used to construct another form.)

All three of the above methods display the image as soon as the form appears. However, Views has a facility for displaying an image after the form has been set up. To do so, we use the `PutImage` method listed in Table 5.6.

Example 7.3 Photo album

Digital cameras can create photographic images as JPEG image files for uploading to a computer. Alternatively with cameras that use photographic film, the developing shop will often offer a facility to convert the pictures to JPEG files. Suppose we have some image files in JPEG format and would like to show them in a window.

We can set up a simple Views form with a picture box and a *next* button. When *next* is clicked, the file number is increased and `PutImage` called with the new name.

The only complexity in the program is creating successive filenames, which is handled proficiently by the `String.Format` method for decimals, which retains leading zeros.

File PhotoAlbum.cs

```
using System;
using Views;
using System.IO;

class PhotoAlbum {

    /// <summary>
    /// Photo Album program      Bishop and Horspool    Jan 2003
    /// ===================
    /// Displays jpg images from a disk
    /// Image names have the form A:\001.jpg
    /// Illustrates PutImage()
    /// </summary>

    string spec = @"<Form Text='Photo Album'>
      <vertical>
        <PictureBox Name=photo Height=400 Width=600/>
        <Button Name=next/>
      </vertical>
    </form>";

    void Go() {
      Views.Form f = new Views.Form(spec);
      for ( int n = 1; ; n++ ) {
        string photo = String.Format("{0:D3}",n);
        string filename = "A:\\"+photo+".jpg";
        f.GetControl();
        if (!File.Exists(filename)) break;
        f.PutImage("photo",filename);
      }
      f.CloseGUI();
    }

    static void Main() {
      new PhotoAlbum().Go();
    }
  }
}
```

Typical output during the run of the program is shown in Figure 7.1.

File dialogues

Filenames cannot usually be created by a formula as in the previous example. More normally, the user will expect to browse and select a filename. For this purpose, Views provides two dialogue controls, OpenFileDialog and SaveFileDialog. Each of these is actually a button control which displays the name or text given in the tag. When the button is pressed, the file dialogue boxes of the operating system are activated. They return a string, and it is this string which is then available as the filename through GetText. The use of the dialogues is illustrated in an extension to the previous example.

Figure 7.1 The Photo Album display

Example 7.4 Selecting and renaming photos

Once we can flip though photos, we might also want to be able to go directly to a photo, and then to save it under a more descriptive name. The photo album program can be expanded to have three buttons, and a proper event handling loop as follows:

Filename PhotoAlbum2.cs

```
using System;
using Views;
```

```
using System.IO;

class PhotoAlbum {

   /// <summary>
   /// Photo Album program            Bishop and Horspool    Jan 2003
   /// ====================
   /// Displays jpg images from a disk
   /// Image names have form A:\001.jpg
   /// or they can be read off file dialogues.
   /// Illustrates dialogue and PutImage()
   /// </summary>

   string spec = @"<Form Text='Photo Album'>
     <vertical>
       <PictureBox Name=photo Height=600 Width=400/>
       <horizontal>
           <Button Name=next/>
           <OpenFileDialog Name='Select a photo'/>
           <SaveFileDialog Name='Save as'/>
       </horizontal>
     </vertical>
   </form>";

   void Go() {
      Views.Form f = new Views.Form(spec);
      int n = 1;
      string filename = null;
      for (;;) {
         string c = f.GetControl();
         if (c == null) break;
         switch (c) {
           case "next" :
              string photo = String.Format("{0:D3}",n);
              filename = "A:\\"+photo+".jpg";
              if (!File.Exists(filename)) break;
              f.PutImage("photo",filename);
              n++;
              break;
           case "Select a photo" :
              filename = f.GetText("Select a photo");
              f.PutImage("photo",filename);
              break;
           case "Save as":
              string savename = f.GetText("Save as");
              OpenAndSave(filename,savename);
              break;
         }
      }
      f.CloseGUI();
   }

   void OpenAndSave(string source, string target) {
      File.Copy(source,target,true);
   }
```

```
        static void Main() {
          new PhotoAlbum().Go();
        }
    }
```


Example 7.5 Cashier's window for the supermarket till

The Till program introduced in Chapter 5 has a major drawback in that the types of fruits
and their prices are actually stored in the program itself. We definitely want to make the
program more flexible, and be able to update the data, especially the prices, on a regular
basis.

In order to keep the till flexible and able to adapt to changes in prices, this data is stored
and updated in a data file. It is our job to get the data into the program before the main
GUI is activated. To do this, we use an introductory GUI. It has space for the cashier's
name and the data file. On activating, the data is read into the arrays which were previously set in the program. When the setup is completed, this GUI can be closed, and the
main one activated. The setup form used by the cashier is shown in Figure 7.2.

The Views specification for this window is:

```
    string setupForm = @"<Form Text='FruitStop Till Setup'>
        <vertical>
          <Label Text='Daily set up of the Cash Register Till' />
          <Label Text=' '/>
          <TextBox Name=Name Width=180 Text={0}/>
          <OpenFileDialog Name=DataFile
                  Text='Select Price Data File' Width=200/>
          <ListBox Name=Message Width=200 Height=80/>
          <ListBox Name=prices Width=200 Height = 100/>
          <Button Name=Continue/>
        </vertical>
      </Form>";
```

The setup is handled by a method called `SetUpTill`, which has a Views handler in it.
When the button labelled 'Select Price Data File' is pressed, the open file dialogue window appears and the user can select a file. The handler looks like this:

```
    bool ReadDataFile(string filename) {
      StreamReader inStream;
      try {
         inStream = new StreamReader(filename);
      } catch(FileNotFoundException) {
        return false;
      }
      ... read lines from the file
      return true;
    }
```

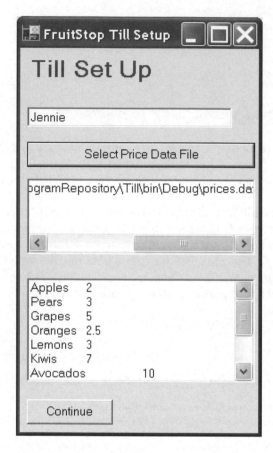

Figure 7.2 Setup form displayed by Till program

The file we are interested in is called `prices.dat`, and reads as follows:

```
File Prices.dat
```

```
Apples        2
Pears         3
Grapes        5
Oranges       2.5
Lemons        3
Kiwis         7
Avocados      10
Strawberries     6
Bananas       2
Peaches       4
```

```
Plums      4
Apricots   4
```

This name is returned to Views and can be read by `GetText`. The file is opened in the usual way and then we have to process the data, which requires some string processing, but not much. The opening, reading and processing is done in a method called `Read-DataFile`.

```
void SetUpTheTill() {
  string cashierName = null;
  string initialName = "** Cashier name goes here **";
  string fileName;

  form = new Views.Form(setupForm, initialName);
  bool gotFile = false;
  do {
    string c = form.GetControl();

    switch (c) {
      case "Name":
      case "DataFile":
        cashierName = form.GetText("Name");
        if (cashierName == initialName) {
          form.PutText("Message", "First enter your name");
        } else {
          fileName = form.GetText("DataFile");
          form.PutText("Message", fileName);
          gotFile = ReadDataFile(fileName);
        }
        break;
      case null:
        form.CloseGUI();
        return;
      default:
        break;
    }
  } while (!gotFile);
  form.GetControl(); // Continue
  return;
}

bool ReadDataFile(string filename) {
  StreamReader inStream;
  try {
    inStream = new StreamReader(filename);
  } catch(FileNotFoundException) {
    return false;
  }
  int count;
  char[] whiteSpaceChars = {' ', '\t', '\r'};
  string s, product, price;
```

```
for (count=0; count < maxNumProducts; count++) {
  s = inStream.ReadLine();
  if (s == null) break;
  s = s.Trim();
  int nameEnd = s.IndexOfAny(whiteSpaceChars);
  product = s.Substring(0,nameEnd);
  price   = s.Substring(nameEnd+1);
  item[count] = product;
  formParameters[2*count] = product;
  formParameters[2*count+1] = product + ".gif";
  unitCost[count] = Convert.ToDouble(price);

  form.PutText("prices",product+"\t"+unitCost[count]);
}
inStream.Close();
return true;
}
```

The complete revised program can be found on the web. None of the other parts of it changes. More extensions are suggested in the exercises. To test the program, we need a data file. Then we must make sure the picture files are available. When the program is activated we get the first GUI, as in Figure 7.2. We select the filename, `prices.dat`, and the GUI closes, with the main one appearing. We can then run the program as described in the previous chapter.

Views specifications on file

We alluded in Chapter 5 to the possibility of having a Views specification stored in a file. This has considerable merit because once a program is running, we can change the layout and design, the colours and the fonts, just by changing the data file. The program does not need to be recompiled. Any of the Views examples so far could be reprogrammed to have their specifications read into a string. Because the string extends over many lines of the file we would normally use the `ReadToEnd` method to read it in.

Example 7.6 Rock-Paper-Scissors with files

The computer's strategy when it plays the Rock-Paper-Scissors game is not very sophisticated. It simply makes a random choice of move each time, picking each of the three choices with equal probability. A human player would soon get bored with the game. A better strategy would be to learn the patterns of moves made by the human player and to choose accordingly. For example, if the human player has played 10 rounds and in those 10 rounds, he chose Rock eight times while picking Paper and Scissors only once each, then our program might reasonably skew its next response to counter a play by the human of Rock. To keep the human guessing, our program should pick the response of Paper with probability 80% and the other two plays with 10% probability each.

However, the human player might base his next move on what happened in the previous round (and this would be the way two human players behave when playing each other). If, after the computer plays Rock, the human makes a next move of Scissors 70% of the time, Paper 20% of the time and Rock 10% of the time, then the program can predict such behaviour will continue and make countermoves of Rock with probability 70%, Scissors with probability 20% and Paper with probability 10%. The pattern of probabilities may be quite different for the human's move after a computer's move of Scissors, and so on. Our program can keep count of how often each move by the human occurs after each kind of move by the computer. These counts are known as *order-one statistics*, because *one* previous move is used as the context for keeping track of the counts.

We can use order-two statistics if we decide that the human's previous move and the computer's response both affect the choice of next move by the human, and that is what has been implemented in our improved version of the Rock-Paper-Scissors game.

The interesting feature of the program is that it learns the patterns of plays by the human and saves the information in a file. Each time the program is invoked, it checks to see if the file exists and, if so, reads that file. Just before the program finishes, it writes updated information back to the file.

Some C# features have been used for the first time in this program:

◆ The `NextDouble` method of the `Random` class returns a random `double` value which is greater than or equal to 0.0 and less than 1.0.

◆ The `Split` method of the `string` class splits a string into an array of strings, where the original string is split wherever a whitespace character occurs. For example, if a string s has the value " abc def gh", then `s.Split` returns a five element array where these elements are {"", "abc", "def", "", "gh"}. The empty string appears as an array element whenever a whitespace character appears at the beginning or end of the original string, or whenever two whitespace characters appear consecutively.

◆ The program has to go to extra effort to ignore the empty strings that are produced.

File RPSGameFile.cs

```
using System;
using System.IO;

public class RPSGame {

    /// <summary>
    /// RPSGame (File version)    Horspool and Bishop    December 2002
    /// Keeps track of state of the Rock-Paper-Scissors game.
    /// </summary>

    public const int Rock = 0;
    public const int Paper = 1;
```

```
    public const int Scissors = 2;
    string[] MoveNames = {"Rock", "Scissors", "Paper"};
    const string hFileName = "C:\\WINDOWS\\Temp\\rpsdata.txt";
    Random r;
    int computerChoice, userChoice;
    int numWins, numLosses, numDraws;
    int[,] WinMatrix = { {0,-1,1}, {1,0,-1}, {-1,1,0} };
    int[,,] Context2 = new int[3,3,3];

    public string ComputersChoice {
      get { MakeRandomChoice(); return MoveNames[computerChoice];} }

    public int    Wins    { get { return numWins; } }
    public int    Losses  { get { return numLosses; } }
    public int    Draws   { get { return numDraws; } }

    public RPSGame() {
      r = new Random();
      LoadHistoryFile();
    }

    public void EndRPSGame() {
      SaveHistoryFile();
    }

    void LoadHistoryFile() {
      try {
        StreamReader hfile = new StreamReader(hFileName);
        // read in the entire history file as one string
        string contents = hfile.ReadToEnd();
        hfile.Close();
        // split it into separate strings
        string[] nums = contents.Split();
        int ix = 0;
        for( int i=0; i<3; i++ ) {
          for( int j=0; j<3; j++ ) {
            for( int k=0; k<3; k++ ) {
              while(nums[ix] == "") ix++;
                Context2[i,j,k] = int.Parse(nums[ix++]);
            }
          }
        }
        while(nums[ix] == "") ix++;
        computerChoice = int.Parse(nums[ix++]);
        while(nums[ix] == "") ix++;
        userChoice = int.Parse(nums[ix++]);
      } catch(Exception) {
        // the history file did not exist or did not
        // contain data in the expected format
        for( int i=0; i<3; i++ )
          for( int j=0; j<3; j++ )
            for( int k=0; k<3; k++ )
              Context2[i,j,k] = 1;
      }
```

```
        computerChoice = r.Next(3);
        userChoice     = r.Next(3);
}

void SaveHistoryFile() {
    try {
        StreamWriter hfile = new StreamWriter(hFileName);
        for( int i=0; i<3; i++ ) {
            for( int j=0; j<3; j++ ) {
                for( int k=0; k<3; k++ )
                    hfile.Write("{0} ", Context2[i,j,k]);
            }
            hfile.WriteLine();
        }
        hfile.WriteLine("{0} {1}", computerChoice, userChoice);
        hfile.Close();
    } catch(Exception) {
        Console.WriteLine("Unable to write to {0}", hFileName);
    }
}

public void MakeRandomChoice() {
    int rcount = Context2[userChoice,computerChoice,Rock];
    int pcount = Context2[userChoice,computerChoice,Paper];
    int scount = Context2[userChoice,computerChoice,Scissors];
    double total = rcount+pcount+scount;
    double d = r.NextDouble();
    if (d < rcount/total) {
        computerChoice = Paper;
    } else if (d < (rcount+pcount)/total) {
        computerChoice = Scissors;
    } else {
        computerChoice = Rock;
    }
}

public string ComparePlays(string userPlay) {
    ///<summary>
    /// Determines whether the userPlay beats the computer.
    /// The result is a string "win", "lose" or "draw"
    ///</summary>
    int prevUserChoice = userChoice;
    userChoice = MoveToInt(userPlay);
    Context2[prevUserChoice,computerChoice,userChoice]++;
    int result = WinMatrix[userChoice, computerChoice];
    switch (result) {
    case -1:  numLosses++;  return "lose";
    case 1:   numWins++;    return "win";
    default:  numDraws++;   return "draw";
    }
}
```

```
int MoveToInt ( string move ) {
  switch(move.ToLower()) {
  case "rock":   return Rock;
  case "paper": return Paper;
  case "scissors": return Scissors;
  default:
    throw new Exception("Unrecognized move: "+move);
  }
  }
}
```

The new version of the game, RPSGameFile.cs, can be compiled with either the command-line or GUI driver programs. Assuming that the GUI version is preferred, the appropriate command to create the executable program would be:

```
csc /r:Views.dll DriveRPSGame.cs RPSGameFile.cs
```

(The /r:Views option may not be required; it depends on how Views has been installed.) As can be deduced from reading the source code, when the program is first executed, it tries to create a file named C:\WINDOWS\Temp\rpsdata.txt. This filename may need to be adjusted, depending on which computer system is being used.

Concepts in Chapter 7

We used streams, methods for opening text files for input and output, reading from text files, and writing to text files. The following C# classes and methods from the System.IO namespace were discussed:

StreamReader.ReadLine	StreamReader.Read
StreamReader.ReadToEnd	StreamReader.Close
StreamWriter.WriteLine	StreamWriter.Write
StreamWriter.Close	File.Copy
File.Delete	File.Exists

The forms provided in this chapter covered the following topics:

StringBuilder class (abbreviated)	StreamReader and StreamWriter (abbreviated)
file operations (general)	

Quiz

Q7.1 The difference in response to an error in interactive input and file input should be:

    (a)   nothing

    (b)   interactive input should raise an exception, file input should continue

    (c)   file input should raise an exception, interactive input should continue

    (d)   file input should raise an exception, interactive input should try to continue

Q7.2 If a file called `guidance.dat` does not exist, and we attempt to create a stream object with the following statement

```
StreamReader input = new StreamReader("guidance.dat");
```

what happens?

    (a)   An empty file called `guidance.dat` is created and opened for reading

    (b)   A window pops up and the user is asked to browse for the location of the file and press OK

    (c)   A `FileNotFoundException` is raised

    (d)   A `FileLoadException` is raised

Q7.3 If a file called `secret.dat` exists, and we attempt to create a stream object with the following statement

```
StreamWriter out = new StreamWriter("secret.dat");
```

what happens?

    (a)   The contents of `secret.dat` are cleared and the stream readied for new output

    (b)   Any new output is added (appended) onto the end of the existing data in the file

    (c)   A `FileLoadException` is raised

    (d)   A file called `secret1.dat` is opened instead

Q7.4 To read one character at a time from a file, we use the `Read` method. This method returns

    (a)   the next character, and the null character if there are no more

    (b)   a string, from which characters can be split off, and null if there is no more data

    (c)   an integer representing the next character and 0 if there are no more

    (d)   an integer representing the next character and −1 if there are no more

Q7.5 If the following is written in a program and executed, what will be printed?

```
1    StringBuilder b = new StringBuilder();
2    b.Append("abcdefgh");
3    b.Remove(3,2);
4    b.Append("xyz");
5    b.Insert(4,'*');
6    Console.WriteLine(b.ToString());
```

    (a)   `abe*fghxyz`   (b)   `abcfg*hxyz`

    (c)   `abcf*ghxyz`   (d)   `abc*fghxyz`

Exercises

7.1   **Price changes.** Extend the setup GUI of Example 7.5 so that the manager can select a given fruit and enter a new price for it.

7.2   **Book chapters on file.** Extend Example 3.5 so that the data about the book chapters comes from a file, and the resulting contents page is written to a file.

7.3   **E-mailed phone bills.** Some phone companies send their phone bills by e-mail as an attached text file. The layout of the file is always the same for a given company. Building on Case study 1 in Chapter 3, write a program to generate such bills with all the required information. It is your task to decide on the data format as well as write the program. Then adapt the program in the case study to read in the bills you have created in order to perform the comparison. Note that the case study was also extended in Exercise 4.15, and you may wish to use your solution to that program as a starting point.

7.4   **Multilingual tills.** Exercise 5.10 proposed having two alternative languages for the display of the supermarket till. Generalize this idea to several languages, with the choice being made on the SetUp window discussed in Example 7.5. Store the names of the fruits in different files, one for each language. By selecting a language on the Views SetUp GUI, the appropriate file can be opened and read in for the produce names.

7.5   **File check.** Make the suggested improvement to Example 7.1 so that the user is asked whether an existing output file can be overwritten.

7.6 **Indenting.** There are two styles of handling curly brackets in a program:

- opening bracket after a construct, closing bracket under the construct;
- opening and closing brackets under the construct.

This book uses the first style. Write a program which will take a program in a file and, on instruction from the user, transform it from one style to the other. You can make various assumptions about there being no brackets in strings and comments.

7.7 **Weighted averages again.** A computer science course has three parts to it: a test, an assignment and an examination, which are weighted at 20%, 30% and 50% respectively. Write a program to read in a set of 30 or so marks from a file, together with student numbers, and print each student's average as well as the overall average. You can either create the data file yourself, or have a separate program to generate it using random numbers.

7.8 **CD length.** Assume that CDs have up to 22 tracks. Using a Views GUI to input the time for each track in hours and minutes, calculate the total length of a CD. Use a button to signal the end of the data. When the data for one CD has been read, write it out to a file. Include the name of the CD. Investigate whether C# has an Append method for output files. If not, create one, so that the existing data can be read in and the average length of all CDs so far reported on.

7.9 **Room bookings.** We want to have a system that will allocate the most appropriate room for a class of a given size. We are going to do this problem using only files and a GUI, although in the next chapter we will see other ways of handling it.

- Set up a file with names of rooms and the number of people they can hold (between about 50 and 500). Work with about 10 rooms.
- Design a program with Views GUI that asks for a number of people and the booker's name.
- Read through the file, finding the first room, if any, that is no more than 10% larger than the size required.
- Report on the booking, if successful.
- If not, and if the program detected that a larger room was available, run through the file again, getting any room available that will take the number required, even if too large.

7.10 **Room reservations.** We augment Exercise 7.9 as follows:

- Now we can make a booking by writing out to a second file the data as read, but with a marker next to the booked room and the name of the booker. This file becomes the one read next time, and that room cannot be booked again.
- However, the program can report that a particular room would be ideal, and is currently booked by the person listed.

7.11 **Experiments.** A laboratory takes pairs of readings and the results required are the first reading divided by the second. The readings are stored on a file. Write a program which processes the file, but catches an exception when a division by zero is encountered. In this case, the program should ask, via a Views GUI, for a pair of replacement values for the particular reading number, and continue processing until the end of the file.

CHAPTER 8

Collections

In this chapter we take a major step forward in programming by looking at collections of objects. We examine how collections can be accessed by number or by name, both very common operations in the real world. Accessing by number, as with arrays, is a fundamental programming technique, while accessing by name is a more recent addition to programming languages and has simplified the programmer's task considerably.

8.1 More about classes

In Chapters 2 and 3, we concentrated on structured types composed as structs. We mentioned that classes were largely analogous to structs, and that we would deal with them when the time comes. That time is now.

A *class* is the main structured type in any object-oriented language. In C#, classes contain all the same elements of a struct – and more. While a struct is meant for simple datatypes, such as those defined in earlier chapters, a class can be used to create complex objects in a variety of patterns. These patterns stem from being able to:

◆   *link* together such objects in classic or novel ways;

◆   *group* objects in collections of various kinds; and

◆   *create hierarchies* where each new object retains some features of the objects in
     other classes.

Linked and grouped object structures are made possible through *references*, and hierarchies through *inheritance*. This chapter looks in details at linked structures, with inheritance being covered in Chapter 9.

Examples of complex objects

Let us first consider a few examples of the patterns mentioned above. A classic linked
structure is a known as a *tree*. In a tree, each object can link to other objects, where the
links have specific meanings. For example, we can represent in the computer a family tree,
which shows information about each person in the family, including their relationships to
each other. A typical family tree might be drawn on paper as in Figure 8.1, using just minimal information, namely the name and date of birth.

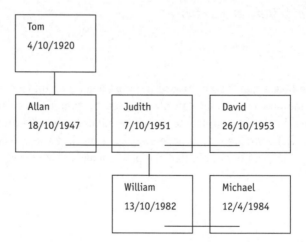

Figure 8.1 A family tree

When transferring the tree to a computer, each person is represented by an object but the
lines reveal considerably more information. In the accepted way of depicting family trees,
siblings are linked horizontally, and children (or more specifically, the firstborn) are linked
vertically.

Thus starting at Tom, we can go down through Allan to Judith, and then to William,
being Tom's grandchild. Thus accessing an object somewhere in the tree will entail fol-

lowing links from the top in a given manner. In further courses in computer science, you will learn how to traverse and manipulate such trees.

Looking at groups of objects, we can consider, for example, the results of a query to an airline's web page for flights to a certain destination on a given day. The data might look like that in Figure 8.2.

Berlin-Schonefeld – London Stansted
Click on the Flight Number to view valid operating dates.

FR 8543	0940	1030	Mon	Tue	Wed	Thu	Fri	Sat	-
FR 8545	1740	1830	Mon	Tue	Wed	Thu	Fri	Sat	Sun
FR 8547	2210	2255	Mon	Tue	Wed	Thu	Fri	-	Sun

London Stansted – Berlin-Schonefeld
Click on the Flight Number to view valid operating dates.

FR 8542	0625	0915	Mon	Tue	Wed	Thu	Fri	Sat	-
FR 8544	1425	1715	Mon	Tue	Wed	Thu	Fri	Sat	Sun
FR 8546	1855	2145	Mon	Tue	Wed	Thu	Fri	-	Sun

Figure 8.2 Results of an airline query

The data for each line of the results would be the flight number, the two times, and then the days on which the flight operates. This information would all be encapsulated in an object. The relevance of the collection pattern, though, is that similar objects can be grouped, and there is some ordering associated with them. In this case, the data has been ordered by departure time, which also happens to coincide with the flight number ordering.

In these collections, the links are not obvious, but there is some association between one object and the next. To access a flight, we would start at the first and then step through, or there could be more direct ways of going to a flight at a specific time of day, and so on. Note that in Figure 8.2 there are actually two groups of objects – the one for flights from Berlin to London and the other for flights from London to Berlin. These two groups could be related, but we would not normally put their details in the same group.

Finally, we look at an example of a hierarchy. The key point here is that an object can retain features and behaviour of a previously defined object – or it can redefine them. Classic examples relate to people, nature, entertainment events, books, music, and so on, where classification is already well established and understood. The idea is that having established a hierarchy, we can view the data at different levels, appropriate to what we want to do. Consider a simple example of entertainment events depicted in Figure 8.3.

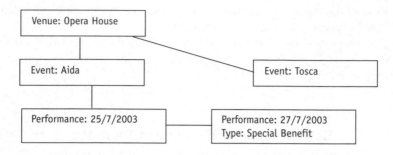

Figure 8.3 Entertainment events

In this hierarchy, if we work on a performance object, for example, it includes the event name and the venue name which were defined in the objects it inherits from. More interestingly, the operations which we can perform on each of the objects may well have the same name, but different implementations.

For example, deleting a performance (because the main singer is sick, say) will be different from deleting a venue (because it may have burnt down). But the operation is still 'delete'. This distinction may be clearer if we note that the second performance of Aida is a different type of object from the first, in that it has two fields. It may be that if an ordinary performance is deleted, patrons are refunded their money, but not so for special performances.

References

Now we can look at how these concepts of links, groups and hierarchies are realized in C#. So far, we have dealt with what C# calls *value types*. These are the simple types (numeric, boolean, character), enums[1] and structs. Variables of value types directly contain their data. C# also has *reference types* where the variables hold references to their data. Chief among the reference types is the *class*; other reference types are arrays, strings, interfaces and delegates. Both structs (which come from the value types) and classes (which come from the reference types) are structured types, as we defined them back in Chapter 2. So what is the difference?

Figure 8.4 shows the conceptual difference between objects created from a struct and a class, for two of C#'s built-in types that we have already encountered. The `DateTime` variable d is shown as directly containing its data, whereas the `Random` variable r refers to a different place where the value is kept. Every time we declare a struct, it has a name, the name of the variable. Because value types directly contain their values, one thing we cannot do is define a field of the same type as the struct inside a struct. In other words, we cannot do the following:

---

1. Enums are discussed in the case study in Section 8.5.

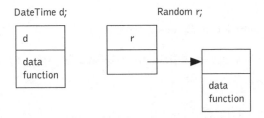

Figure 8.4 Struct and class objects

```
struct MyType {
   int i;
   double d;
   MyType t;
   string s;
}
```

The compiler will complain with the error message

> **Struct member 'MyType t' of type 'MyType' causes a cycle in the structure layout**

One can see that the compiler is correct: inside an object of type MyType, there will be field t, which will have a field t, which will have a field t, and so on forever. To be able to have an object in objects of the same type, we need references together with class objects. Therefore, to fix the above problem, we would rewrite the type as a class, as in:

```
class MyType {
   int i;
   double d;
   MyType t;
   string s;
}
```

This will now compile. If we declare two MyType objects, as in:

```
MyType a, b;
```

and (assuming an appropriate constructor), we construct them with appropriate information, such as:

```
a = new MyType(6, 3.5, null, "object-a");
b = new MyType(9, 4.0, null, "object-b");
```

then we can access the fields of a and b as in

```
Console.WriteLine(a.s+"  "+a.i+"  "+b.s+" as seen from b"+b.i);
```

which would display:

```
object-a  6  object-b as seen from b  9
```

However, suppose we now use the t field to establish a link from a to b. We do this as in:

```
a.t = b;
```

Then we can also access b from a, with appropriate output:

```
Console.WriteLine(a.s+" "+a.i+" "+a.t.s+" as seen from a  "+a.t.i);
```

```
object-a  6  object-b as seen from a  9
```

What is more usual is that the second object is not declared with a name, but gets its name from the reference in the first. Thus the declarations will be:

```
a = new MyType(6, 3.5, null, "object-a");
a.t = new MyType(9, 4.0, null, "object-b");
```

The structure we have now created is shown in Figure 8.5. *Null* is shown in italics because it is not a data value like the others, but represents a special reference value, which does not link to anything. The next example takes the idea of using references as links further.

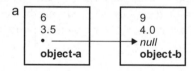

Figure 8.5 Two linked objects

Example 8.1 Listing pets

As a simple illustration of classes and references, let us consider the problem of reading in a list of pets and printing them out again. We don't want to use an array, as we want to illustrate a solution to the problem raised above. We start with a simple class for the pets:

```
public class Pet {
    string name;
    string type;
    int age;
    Pet previous;
```

```
public Pet Previous {
  get {return previous;}
  set {previous = value;}
}

public void GetData() {
  name = Console.ReadLine();
  type = Console.ReadLine();
  age = int.Parse(Console.ReadLine());
}

public override string ToString() {
  return name+"  "+type+"  "+age;
}
}
```

The class does not have an initializing constructor, nor are any of the fields initialized. Instead, `Pet` objects are created using a default empty constructor, which initializes all the fields of the object to their own default values. As a separate step, we get values into the object via a call to the `GetData` method.

So, for example, when a `Pet` object is created, as in

```
Pet p = new Pet();
```

p is a reference to the new `Pet` object, name and type are set to the empty string, and `previous` is set to the special reference value `null`. Generally, the next statement would be:

```
p.GetData();
```

The part of the program that is going to read in the pets and create the list goes like this:

```
Pet list = null;
Pet p
for (int i=1; i<=5; i++) {
  p = new Pet();
  p.GetData();
  p.Previous = list;
  list = p;
}
```

We have a `Pet` object, `list`, defined which starts off with a null reference. We then make a new `Pet` object, p, and read in its data. The last two lines in the loop are the important ones. The previous field of p is assigned to what the list was, and then the list is moved on to be p. Immediately afterwards, we go round and repeat the same process. Figure 8.6 shows the state of the variable: (a) at the start; (b) after one pet; (c) after two pets; and (d) after all the pets have been read in.

Each time round the loop, `list` moves on to the new pet, which is linked back to the previous one. This does mean that the list of pets ends up being in reverse order of appearance. To set up the links the other way is more difficult, and left till later.

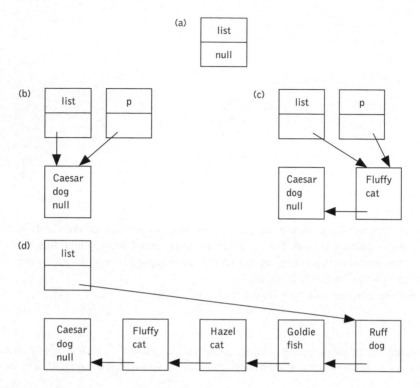

Figure 8.6 Creating a linked list of pets

Using the same linking mechanism, though, we can go through the list and print it out as follows:

```
p = list;
while (p != null) {
  Console.WriteLine(p);
  p = p.Previous;
}
```

or more concisely as

```
for (p = list; p != null; p = p.Previous ) {
  Console.WriteLine(p);
}
```

When we put the example together, we need to assign appropriate accessibility options to members of the `Pet` class. `GetData` is called directly and therefore will be public; `previous` is a field and should not be accessed directly, but via a property, so we create a public property to shield it. Here is the program.

```csharp
using System;

class ListPets {

  /// <summary>
  /// The List Pets Program      Bishop & Horspool     September 2002
  /// =====================
  ///
  /// Reads in five pets and lists them again.
  /// Illustrates classes and references
  /// for building a simple linked list
  /// </summary>

  void Go() {
    Console.WriteLine("Type five pets with "+
      "name, kind and age on separate lines");
    Pet list = null;
    Pet p;
    for (int i=1; i<=5; i++) {
      p = new Pet();
      p.GetData();
      p.Previous = list;
      list = p;
    }
    Console.WriteLine("Your list of pets from the most recent is:");
    p = list;
    while (p != null) {
      Console.WriteLine(p);
      p = p.Previous;
    }
  }

  static void Main() {
    new ListPets().Go();
  }

  public class Pet {
    string name;
    string type;
    int age;
    Pet previous;

    public Pet Previous {
      get {return previous;}
      set {previous = value;}
    }

    public void GetData() {
      name = Console.ReadLine();
      type = Console.ReadLine();
      age = int.Parse(Console.ReadLine());
    }
```

```
    public override string ToString() {
      return name+"  "+type+"  "+age;
    }
  }
}
```

A run of the program looks like this:

```
Type five pets with name, kind and age on separate lines
Caesar
dog
3
Fluffy
cat
9
Hazel
cat
7
Goldie
fish
1
Ruff
dog
2
Your list of pets from the most recent is:
Ruff dog 2
Goldie fish 1
Hazel cat 7
Fluffy cat 9
Caesar dog 3
```

Of course, classes are not the only types that have references. Arrays and strings are also reference types, as are interfaces and delegates (see Chapters 9 and 10 respectively). For arrays and strings, the differences only emerge in semantics, as outlined later in this chapter.

Comparison with references

We saw in Chapter 3 that in order to compare objects instantiated from structs, we had to supply Equals and CompareTo methods. The same is true of references – if we want to achieve the same effect, that is, to compare the values inside the objects. Referring to the previous example, we can add the standard Equals method, as in:

```
public override bool Equals(object d) {
    Pet p = (Pet) d;
    return name==p.name && type==p.type && age==p.age;
}
```

Then we could add functionality to the loop that reads and constructs the list so that any repeated data could be excluded. (To keep things simple, we shall look only at immediately repeated data.) The new loop would be:

```
int i=1;
while (i<=5) {
  p = new Pet ();
  p.GetData();
  if (i>1 && p.Equals(list)) {
    Console.WriteLine("Oops - repeated data. Ignored.");
  } else {
    p.Previous = list;
    list = p;
    i++;
  }
}
```

The expression p.Equals(list) will compare the values of the new pet just read into object p with the top of the list just read before that. As you can see, we were careful to protect the access to list, since it would be null if this is the first pet, and then the function call to Equals would fail.

One problem with reference equality is that C# does not force us to insert the Equals method. If we forgot, and wrote p==list instead, it would compile. But the meaning would be to compare the two *references*, which would never be equal for two different instances, even if the values inside the instances were.

8.2 Collections

In this section, we introduce a concept in C# which uses classes to extend the idea of arrays considerably. The classes we consider are special ones called *collections*, because they are intended to hold or manage many objects.

Accessing by number

Where an object is replicated many times, it is normal practice in real life to number the objects. For example, consider the following:

◆ days in a month are numbered 1 to 31 (or less);

◆ houses in a street can be numbered from one up to the thousands;

◆ floors in a building can be numbered to a hundred and something (although the bottom floors may have a variety of names: below 1 there may 0, -1, -2 or G, P1, P2, P3);

◆ contestants in a marathon race may be numbered from 1 to hundreds of thousands;

◆ the counts of the numbers of students in a class who earned each mark between 0 and 100.

Translating these examples into collections and objects, we can identify the different schemes shown in Table 8.1.

Collection	Object	Numbers
Month	Day	1 to 31
Street	House	1 to 5000
Building	Floor	−5 to 200
Race	Contestant	1 to 1 000 000
Class	Mark count	0 to 100

Table 8.1 Examples of collections accessed by number

We can see from these examples that the kind of object we are collecting can be a single item such as an integer representing a count, or an object with several fields, as yet unspecified. For example, a contestant in a race will have name, address, previous best time, and so on. Once we have a collection, we refer to contestant number 304 or floor 5 or the count for mark 50. In other words, the natural way of accessing collections is via the object name, and a number.

This concept of collections accessed by number translates into the *array* feature in a programming language. As was introduced in Chapter 4, we can declare an array as follows:

```
int[] markCount = new int[101];
```

and then be able to refer to `markCount[50]`, which holds the count of the number of students who received a mark of 50. Suppose this count is 27, then

```
markCount[50]++;
```

increases the number of students found with a mark of 50% by one to 28. The use of square brackets is crucial and is discussed again below in Section 8.3.

Part	Example
The array	`markCount`
The type of the array	`int[]` (read as 'int array')
An index	`50`
An element	`markCount[50]`
The type of an element	`int`
A value of an element	`27`
The range of indices	0 to 100
The range of element values	anything in `int`

Table 8.2 Example of the parts of an array

In programming, `markCount` is now the array. It consists of a defined number of *elements*, in this case 101. The admissible numbers (known as the *range*) are from 0 through to 100. The number by which we access a particular element of the array is called an *index*. Another name for an *array element* is an *indexed variable*.

To emphasize the terminology again, we examine `markCount` in detail in Table 8.2, showing also the difference between the types of the array itself and its elements.

As an exercise, take one of the other examples in Table 8.1 and create a table similar to Table 8.2 for it.

Accessing by name

The above examples were chosen so that the array indices we would need would be integers, as required by C# and most current languages. The exception is the floors of the building, where we might need to handle some awkward cases. Ways of dealing with these are discussed later.

More generally, though, there are many cases where a contiguous sequence of integers is not appropriate for accessing a collection. Consider these examples:

◆ teams of the countries in the Olympic games,

◆ lecture times on a timetable,

◆ dates of public holidays,

◆ registered cars in a province or country,

◆ frequency of marks within a given percentage range.

If we place these in the context of Table 8.1 again, we get Table 8.3. Now we see that a collection can validly be accessed by a set of values, which is defined by real world circumstances, and may not always have a simple correspondence with integers. Even if there does exist such a correspondence (as in the case of days of the year, which can go from 1 to 365[1]), it is often much better practice to keep to the original format of the data. Otherwise information tends to get lost. For example, it is not a well-known fact that the 14th of February is the 45th day of the year, but in many cultures it is well known as Valentine's Day. In the case of the country names and the licensed cars, there may be no possible numeric equivalent.

C# therefore provides an alternative way (in fact several ways) of storing objects as a collection of key-and-value pairs. In Table 8.3, the keys would be in the 'Accessed by' column and the values would be whatever was stored for that key. A key is the equivalent of an index in an array. The two kinds of collections are *sorted lists* and *hash tables*, and they are discussed in detail in Section 8.4. Because they have much the same mechanisms, we can just take a brief look at sorted lists now, for the purpose of illustration.

---

1. Or to 366 in a leap year.

Collection	Object	Accessed by	Example
Games	Team	Country name	Great Britain
Timetable	Lecture	Time	11:30
Calendar	Public holidays	Date	14 February
Licensed cars	Car	Licence plate	567 DKY
Class	Mark count	Range of marks	50 .. 59

Table 8.3 Examples of collections accessed by name

A *sorted list* is a collection of pairs, each consisting of a *key* and a *value*. Both the key and the value are C# objects, that is, they can be anything. A simple example of a non-numeric key is a string. If we declare

```
SortedList holidayTable = new SortedList();
```

and if d is a Date object with fields day=14 and month="February" then we can put into the holidayTable the information for Valentine's Day as follows:

```
holidayTable["Valentine's Day"] = d;
```

Then if we access the table using d again with

```
Console.WriteLine("Valentine's Day is " +
        holidayTable["Valentine's Day"]);
```

it should print (depending on how the ToString method for Date is set up of course):

Valentine's Day is 14 February

Consider a second example, comparing it to the markCounts array earlier. Suppose we declare

```
SortedList markRangeTable = new SortedList();
```

and Range is a class with two integer fields, for example with values 50 and 59. We can first get the current value in the list for that range by saying:

```
Range r = new Range(50,59);
int count = (int) markRangeTable[r];
```

Then we add one to this range count as in

```
count++;
```

and store the new value back in the list for (50..59):

```
markRangeTable[r] = count;
```

In summary, we can treat lists almost like arrays, but they are much more powerful in their accessing capabilities. We now go on to look at the syntax of both types of collections, and include as well the extended form of arrays called *multi-dimensional arrays*, and the generalized concept of indexing.

8.3 Arrays as collections

Frequently, we find that arrays are used to hold collections of objects, such as the ones mentioned in Table 8.3. Suppose we do not know how many contestants there will be in a race, and it could be a very small race of 100 up to a huge marathon of nearly a million. `Contestants` is a class that we have defined earlier with the necessary fields and methods. We can then declare an array as follows:

```
Contestants[] contestant;
```

As part of the data or the instructions to the program, we can give a likely limit on the number of contestants, always overestimating slightly of course. Suppose this number is read into n. Then we could instantiate the array as follows:

```
contestant = new Contestants[n];
```

Each time we get a new contestant signing up for the race, we will instantiate that element of the array and increase a counter as follows:

```
contestant[k] = new Contestants(name,number,bestTime);
k++;
```

Now the picture of how the array looks is somewhat different from those shown in Chapter 4 when integer arrays were introduced, and is shown in Figure 8.7.

For such an array, we could have statements such as

```
if (contestant[i].time.LessThan(contestant[j].time))
   Console.WriteLine("Contestant " + i +
     " wins with time " + contestant[i].time);
```

So `contestant` is the array, `contestant[i]` is a `Contestant` object, and `contestant[i].time` is a field of that object.

What will happen if we do have more contestants than expected? Because arrays have a fixed size, the instantiation statement above will actually fail, and an `IndexOutOfRangeException` will be thrown. This illustrates a danger of simple arrays, one that can be overcome with the `ArrayList` class.

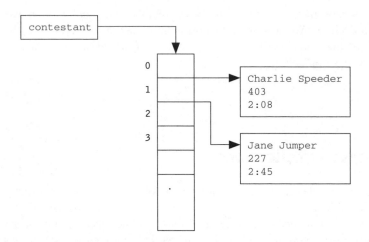

Figure 8.7 An array of objects

The Array class

In order to provide additional functionality for arrays, C# has defined an `Array` class. All arrays that we construct fall into this class. The `Array` class provides the methods listed in the form below. Note that this is not an exhaustive list, and that more than one version of some methods are provided by the C# API.

ARRAY CLASS (ABBREVIATED)

```
// static methods
int BinarySearch(a, v)
Clear(a, first, num)
Copy(src, dest, len)
int IndexOf(a, v)
int LastIndexOf(a, v)
Sort(a)
```

`IndexOf`, `LastIndexOf` and `BinarySearch(a,v)` all search the simple array `a` for a value `v`. `IndexOf` finds the first occurrence of `v`, `LastIndexOf` finds the last occurrence of `v`, and `BinarySearch` finds any occurrence of `v` in a very fast way but requires the elements to be in sorted order (duplicates allowed). If the value is found, the index of `v` in the array is returned; otherwise the result is a negative number.

`Array.Clear(a,first,num)` sets the elements `a[first]`, `a[first+1]` ... `a[first+num]` to be zero, null or *false*, depending on the element type of the array. `first` and `num` can be omitted.

`Array.Copy(src,dest,len)` copies one array to another, copying `len` elements from array `src` to array `dest`; `src` and `dest` can be omitted.

`Array.Sort(a)` sorts the array `a` so that the elements are in ascending order.

Example 8.2 Testing the Array methods

The following program illustrates the above methods in action. In addition, it shows the
difference between `Array.Copy` and a straight assignment of arrays.

File ArrayTest.cs

```
using System;
using System.Collections;

class ArrayTest {
  void Go() {
    int[] a = {31,28,31,30,31,30,31,31,30,31,30,31};
    int[] b = new int[12];
    Console.WriteLine(p(a)+"\n"+p(b));
    Console.WriteLine("\nCopy");
    Array.Copy(a,b,12);
    Console.WriteLine(p(a)+"\n"+p(b));
    Console.WriteLine("\nChange b[1]");
    b[1] = 29;
    Console.WriteLine(p(a)+"\n"+p(b));
    Console.WriteLine("\nAssign and change b[1]");
    a = b;
    Console.WriteLine(p(a)+"\n"+p(b));
    int index;
    Console.WriteLine("\nIndexOf");
    index = Array.IndexOf(a,30);
    Console.WriteLine("Value {0} Index is {1}",30,index);
    Console.WriteLine("\nLastIndexOf");
    index = Array.LastIndexOf(a,30);
    Console.WriteLine("Value {0} Index is {1}",30,index);
    Console.WriteLine("\nBinarySearch");
    index = Array.BinarySearch(a,30);
    Console.WriteLine("Value {0} Index is {1}",30,index);
    Console.WriteLine("\nSort");
    Array.Sort(a);
    Console.WriteLine(p(a));
  }

  string p(int[] a) {
    string s = "";
    for (int i=0; i<a.Length; i++) {
      s += a[i]+"  ";
    }
    return s;
  }

  static void Main() {
    new ArrayTest().Go();
  }
}
```

If we consider the output, we see that `Array.Copy` takes each value and copies it into an array of the same size. If an element of b is changed, it has no effect on a. However, if we assign b to a, we assign the references, and there is in fact only one array. Thus changing b[i] means that a[i] will also have the changed value.

```
31  28  31  30  31  30  31  31  30  31  30  31
0   0   0   0   0   0   0   0   0   0   0   0

Copy
31  28  31  30  31  30  31  31  30  31  30  31
31  28  31  30  31  30  31  31  30  31  30  31

Change b[1]
31  28  31  30  31  30  31  31  30  31  30  31
31  29  31  30  31  30  31  31  30  31  30  31

Assign and change b[1]
31  29  31  30  31  30  31  31  30  31  30  31
31  29  31  30  31  30  31  31  30  31  30  31

IndexOf
Value 30 Index is 3

LastIndexOf
Value 30 Index is 10

BinarySearch
Value 30 Index is 5

Sort
29  30  30  30  30  31  31  31  31  31  31  31
```

The searches are also interesting. `Array.IndexOf` performs a linear search from the beginning of the array. Hence searching for 30 yields index 3. A `BinarySearch`, which is a faster method useful for very large arrays, could return any valid index, in this case 5. The `Sort` operates as expected.

The ArrayList collection

The worrying idea that an array might be created with too small a size can, in C#, be overcome quite easily. There is a built-in class in the `System.Collections` namespace called `ArrayList`. If we declare an object of this class, we essentially get an array which operates in most respects as an ordinary simple array, but it will grow if its initial or current size is going to be exceeded. So we could declare

```
using System.Collections;
...
ArrayList contestant = new Contestants(100);
```

and it will no longer matter if we exceed 100 objects. The array will be expanded by the system as and when necessary. How this actually happens need not concern us at all. The number supplied in the statement which creates the initial array list is nothing more than an estimate of how large we expect the array to be.

Because C# has made the [] symbols available to collections in general, not just arrays (a process called overloading operators), we can still refer to

```
contestant[i]
```

and so on, once the elements have been set up. The difference with an array list is that elements must initially be put into it using the Add method. Thereafter, indexing is possible. In other languages such as Java, for example, indexing is not available, and using a class instead of an array means that one must use methods to access elements.

As an example, consider the following code which sets up an array list and prints its values.

```
ArrayList a = new ArrayList(100);
Random r = new Random();
for ( int i=0; i<10; i++)
  a.Add(r.Next(20));
for ( int i=0; i<a.Count; i++)
  Console.WriteLine(a[i]);
```

The fourth line cannot be written as

```
// wrong!
  a[i] = r.Next(20);
```

Notice that Count is the equivalent of Length for an ordinary array. The following form lists some of the useful members of ArrayList, several of which are similar to those in the Array class.

Notice, however, that the Array class has only static members, and therefore the object being worked on is a parameter. With array lists, the object is the collection. Thus one can contrast these two method calls:

```
Array.Sort(declaredAsAnArray);
declaredAsAnArrayList.Sort();
```

Collections of objects

The Array and ArrayList methods such as BinarySearch and Sort rely on being able to compare the elements of the collection. The examples we used involved simple types, and comparisons are built in for them. The same applies for some system structs such as DateTime or strings.

However, suppose we had a collection of the Pet type defined in Example 8.1. We could apply a BinarySearch because we have defined an Equals method. However, we would first have to define a CompareTo method before we could Sort the collection. This topic is explored in the exercises.

ARRAYLIST CLASS (ABBREVIATED)

```
// properties
int Count
// methods
int BinarySearch(v)
bool Contains(v)
void Clear(first, num)
int IndexOf(v)
int LastIndexOf(v)
void RemoveAt(i)
void Sort()
void Array ToArray(Type)
```

`Count` returns the number of occupied elements in the list. `IndexOf`, `LastIndexOf`, `BinarySearch` and `Contains` all search the array list for a value v. `IndexOf` finds the first occurrence, `LastIndexOf` finds the last occurrence, and `BinarySearch` and `Contains` find any occurrence. `BinarySearch` requires that the elements are in sorted order. If the value is found, the index of v in the array list is returned; otherwise the result is a negative number, except for `Contains` which only returns *true* or *false*.

`Clear` removes all the elements; `RemoveAt` removes the element at index i.

`Array.Sort(a)` sorts the array a so that the elements are in ascending order.

`ToArray` copies the elements to an array of the given type.

Rectangular and jagged arrays

Arrays can have more than one dimension, and there are two choices for such multi-dimensional arrays – rectangular and jagged. The choices are shown in the form. To make it clearer, we use only two dimensions, but there can be as many as we like.

ARRAY DECLARATIONS – RECTANGULAR AND JAGGED

```
type [ , ] rectangulararray;
rectangulararray = new type [dim1, dim2];

type [] [] jaggedarray;
jaggedarray = new type [dim1][];
for (int i=0; i<jaggedarray.Length; i++)
  jaggedarray[i] = new type [somenum];
```

The rectangular array is set up with the two dimensions so that it forms a rectangle. The jagged array has one fixed dimension (the number of rows) and then for each row, the number of elements can be different.

So for example, supposing we wish to record the rainfall on every day of a year, but wish to structure it according to a 52-week cycle. The declaration would be a rectangular array expressed as:

```
double[,] rainfallByWeek = new double[52, 7];
```

and we could refer to

```
rainfallByWeek[9,0]
```

which would give the rainfall for Sunday (day 0) of the 10th week (week 9, starting from 0).

On the other hand, if we want to store the rainfall according to months, and want to be particular about each month having exactly the right number of days, we'd use a jagged array and have:

```
double[][] rainfallByMonth = new double[12][];
for (int i=0; i<rainfallByMonth.Length; i++) {
  int d = DateTime.DaysinMonth(2003,i);
  rainfallByMonth[i] = new double[d];
}
```

The rainfall for the first day of May would then be:

```
rainfallByMonth[4][0]
```

The difference between these two approaches is illustrated in Figure 8.8. In addition to being used for rows of varying length, multi-dimensional arrays that are declared with the [] [] syntax also have the property that rows can stand by themselves as arrays, which is not the case with arrays declared as [,]. As such, the rows can be sent to methods as parameters. The next example exploits this property.

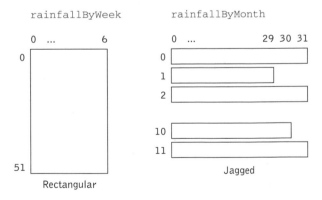

Figure 8.8 Multi-dimensional arrays

Example 8.3 Rainfall statistics

We have statistics collected of rainfall per month for several years. We would like to calculate and print the average (i.e. mean) and standard deviation of the rainfall for each
month over the period given.

Solving this problem falls into the following steps:

1. Designing the format of the input data and reading it in.

2. Designing the multi-dimensional array to hold the data.

3. Calculating the required figures.

4. Printing them out.

The pivot is really step 3. If we are to have functions to perform the calculations, then they
will be passed arrays as parameters, as in:

```
public static double mean(double[] a) {
```

which we would intend calling with something like:

```
averagetable[m] = Stats.mean(rainTable[m]);
```

where mean is assumed to be in a class called Stats. In other words, for each month, we
pass an array of all the values for each year that we have records. Such a structure ties in
nicely then with step 1, where one year's data will look like this:

```
2002    17    17    17    15    0    0    0    0    6    17    8    20
```

In order to send a row of data to methods, we need to use a jagged array. The array's first
dimension will be 12 or 13 (this issue was discussed already in Chapter 4). We shall
choose 13 and let the zero[th] element be empty. The declaration for such an array is always
in two stages – first the rows, then instantiations for all the columns. The code to do so is:

```
double[][] rainTable  = new double[13][];
for (int m=1; m<=12; m++)
  rainTable[m] = new double[nYears];
```

Note that C# does not allow one to say:

```
// WRONG!
double[][] rainTable = new double[13][nYears];
```

We have to go through the instantiation process.

It turns out that reading in the data is a little tricky. In previous examples, we have
arranged the data so that there is one space between elements, and have made use of
string.Split to get individual strings and numbers off one line, as in:

```
string line = fin.ReadLine();
if (line==null) throw new EndOfStreamException();
string[] elements = line.Split(' ');
```

The data we have to deal with here was set up independently and has more than one space between elements. The result for a split will then be many more elements than we expected, with some of them just empty strings. To process the elements array correctly, we need to ignore any empty strings. The code to do so is:

```
while (elements[i].CompareTo("")==0)
   i++;
```

The calculations for mean and standard deviation follow well-known formulae. Since it is possible that the functions may be needed again, we put them both in a separate class. The complete program is as follows:

File WeatherStats.cs

```
using System;
using System.IO;

class WeatherStats {

  ///<summary>
  /// The Weather program        Bishop & Horspool    2003
  /// ===================        Java by J M Bishop    Jan 1997
  ///                            updated June 2000
  ///
  /// Calculates mean and standard deviation of rainfall
  /// for each month over the number of years provided.
  /// Illustrates handling of matrices and passing columns
  /// as parameters.
  ///
  /// The data must be in a file in the form:
  /// year followed by the 12 rainfall figures for
  /// the months of that year.
  /// </summary>

  int startYear, endYear; // range from 1950 upwards
  // all arrays intended to be indexed 1..12
  double[][] rainTable;
  double[] averagetable = new double[13];
  double[] stddevTable  = new double[13];

  void Go() {
    ReadIn();
    ShowResults();
  }
```

```
void ReadIn() {
  StreamReader fin = new StreamReader("rain.dat");
  int yearIndex = 0;   // e.g. 0

  // The actual years are read in and might not be sorted
  // or contiguous. The yearIndex starts at 0 and is
  // used to store the data in an orderly manner.
  startYear = int.Parse(fin.ReadLine());
  endYear = int.Parse(fin.ReadLine());
  int nYears = endYear-startYear+1;
  rainTable  = new double[13][];
  for (int m=1; m<=12; m++)
    rainTable[m] = new double[nYears];

  string line;
  int year;


  while (true) {
      line = fin.ReadLine();
      if (line==null) break;
      string[] elements = line.Split(' ');
      year = int.Parse(elements[0]);
      Console.Write(year+" ");
      int i=1;
      for (int m = 1; m<=12; m++) {
        while (elements[i].CompareTo("")==0)
          i++;
        rainTable[m][yearIndex] = double.Parse(elements[i]);
        Console.Write("{0,6:f1}", rainTable[m][yearIndex]);
        i++;
      }
      Console.WriteLine();
      yearIndex++;
  }
  Console.WriteLine("Data read for "+startYear+" to "+
          endYear+"\n\n");
}

void ShowResults() {
    Console.WriteLine("Rainfall statistics for " +
        startYear + " to " + endYear);
    Console.WriteLine("=====================================\n");
    Console.WriteLine("Month          Mean      Std Deviation");

    for (int m =1; m<=12; m++) {
      averagetable[m] = Stats.mean(rainTable[m]);
      stddevTable[m] = Stats.stddev(rainTable[m], averagetable[m]);
      Console.WriteLine("{0,-10}{1,8:f2}{2,14:f4}",
          new DateTime(2003,m,1).ToString("MMMM"),
          averagetable[m], stddevTable[m]);
    }
}
```

```
      static void Main() {
        new WeatherStats().Go();
      }
   }
```

```
File Stats.cs
```

```
   using system;

   class Stats {

      /* Class with elementary stats functions      N T Bishop 1990
       * ======================================      J M Bishop 1999
       *
       * Provides a mean and standard deviation
       */

      public static double mean(double[] a) {
        double sum = 0;
        for (int i = 1; i<a.Length; i++)
          sum += a[i];
        return sum / a.Length;
      }

      public static double stddev(double[] a, double ave) {
        int n = a.Length;
        double sum = 0;
        for (int i = 1; i<n; i++)
          sum += Math.Pow((ave - a[i]),2);
        return Math.Sqrt(sum/(n-1));
      }
   }
```

Typical output from the program would be:

```
1993   10.0   10.0   10.0    5.0    0.0    0.0    0.0    0.0    0.0   12.0   10.0   15.0
1994   20.0   22.0   17.0   14.0    5.0    0.0    0.0    0.0    7.0   12.0   30.0   20.0
1995   22.0   24.0   19.0   12.0    0.0    0.0    3.0    0.0    8.0   15.0   20.0   25.0
1996   17.0   17.0   17.0   15.0    0.0    0.0    0.0    0.0    6.0   17.0    8.0   20.0
1997   25.0   30.0   25.0   15.0    7.0    0.0    0.0    0.0   20.0   15.0   20.0   30.0
1998   25.0   30.0   25.0   15.0    7.0    0.0    0.0    0.0   20.0   15.0   20.0   30.0
1999   10.0   10.0   10.0    5.0    0.0    0.0    0.0    0.0    0.0   12.0   10.0   15.0
2000   20.0   22.0   17.0   14.0    5.0    0.0    0.0    0.0    7.0   12.0   30.0   20.0
2001   22.0   24.0   19.0   12.0    0.0    0.0    3.0    0.0    8.0   15.0   20.0   25.0
2002   17.0   17.0   17.0   15.0    0.0    0.0    0.0    0.0    6.0   17.0    8.0   20.0
Data read for 1993 to 2002


Rainfall statistics for 1993 to 2002
====================================

Month        Mean      Std Deviation
```

January	17.80	4.8392
February	19.60	6.4312
March	16.60	4.6767
April	11.70	3.3201
May	2.40	3.0667
June	0.00	0.0000
July	0.60	1.2490
August	0.00	0.0000
September	8.20	6.3101
October	13.00	2.3805
November	16.60	8.1434
December	20.50	5.2941

8.4 Sorted lists

In Section 8.2 we considered accessing by name and by number. Now we add some more detail about accessing by name. For those who have used other programming languages, it is worth noting that C#'s approach to accessing by name is very far advanced. The resulting programs are extremely simple to read and write, but are built upon powerful concepts. The simplicity comes from the fact that the designers of the language chose to use the same notation for accessing elements as for arrays, namely square brackets, or indexers.

A *sorted list* keeps a collection of pairs of objects known as the *key* and the *value*. The list is kept in order of the keys, and individual elements can be accessed by the key. Most often, the value is a whole object and the key is one or two fields of that object, repeated for the purposes of the list. C# supplies a class for such a collection, which is defined by the form:

```
SORTEDLIST COLLECTION (ABBREVIATED)

// instance properties
int Count
object this[object key]
ICollection Keys
ICollection Values
// instance methods
void Add(key, value)
bool ContainsKey(object key)
bool ContainsValue(object value)
int  IndexOfKey(object key)
int  IndexOfValue(object value)
void Remove(object key)
void RemoveAt(int index)
void SetByIndex(int index, object value)
```

The methods are fairly self-explanatory. We note that even though there are `Add` and `Remove` methods based on keys, this collection also considers the option of finding and using a numerical index into the collection. The 'contains' methods enable one to search the entire collection. But it is the properties that are interesting, and in particular the use of *this*.

Indexers

The definition of `this` in the class above provides access to elements of the collection via the standard [ ] notation. The `set` method embodied in this property enables us to say:

```
SortedList S;
MyType value1;
S[key1] = value1;
```

Getting a value back out again is a bit more complex, because the type of the elements has to be considered. The `get` part of the indexer supplies an object. Therefore we can transform to the type we expect as follows:

```
Mytype x = (MyType) S[key1];
```

Accessing in this way is almost as good as using arrays indexed by numbers.

As an example, suppose we wish to record class enrolments for various first year courses at university. We might have data such as

```
COS110        350
GEOL210       80
ENG100        600
LAT320        8
```

We would define a class as follows:

```
class Enrolment {
  private string code;
  private int size;

  Enrolment(string c, int s) {
    code = c;
    size = s;
  }
  ... other methods here
}
```

Now we can define a sorted list to keep all the enrolments as follows:

```
SortedList year2003 = new SortedList(100);
```

The fact that we declare the list as having 100 elements is not important – it will grow as needed. Each element of the list has a key and a value. So if we declare a value such as

```
Enrolment e = new Enrolment("PHY215",32);
```

we can put it in the list using the same notation as for arrays as follows:

```
year2003["PHY215"] = e;
```

To get a value out again, there is a slight complication. Because SortedList works for all objects, what is returned from it is an object. It therefore needs to be converted to the expected type explicitly. The appropriate assignment would be:

```
e = (Enrolment) year2003["PHY215"];
```

In our design of the collection, PHY215 will appear twice: as the key and as part of the value object, but that is fine. Referring back to the discussion above, we have the following correspondence:

```
S               year2003
Type            Enrolment
value1          e
key1            PHY215
```

To print out the enrolment for Physics, we could say:

```
Console.WriteLine("PHY215 has " +
   ((Enrolment) year2003["PHY215"]).size + "students");
```

year2003 is the collection (the sorted list), year2003["PHY215"] is an object which is then converted to an Enrolment, and size is a field of that object.

The SortedList class has the property that elements are kept in order of their keys, in this case, alphabetical order. The order will not affect access speed or efficiency, but will show up when such a list is examined element by element, as in printing it out.

Looping through a collection

A major difference between arrays and sorted lists is the way in which we access the structure iteratively. With an array, it is possible to use a for loop based on numerical indices, as in:

```
for (int i=0; i< a.Length; i++)
   // access a[i] in some way
```

Since sorted lists are accessed by a set of keys which have no simple correspondence with counting, we need something more powerful. If we have the list of course enrolments as above and want to print it out so we get (in alphabetical order of key automatically)

```
COS110          350
ENG100          600
GEOL210         80
LAT320          8
PHY215          32
```

we can make use of the `foreach` construct. This loop was introduced in Chapter 4, but we repeat its form here:

FOREACH LOOP FOR A SORTEDLIST

```
foreach (type id in collection.Keys) {
    ... body can refer to id
}
```

The `id` is assigned successive key values from the collection. For each key, the body of the loop is repeated.

Printing the courses and enrolments would be accomplished by this loop:

```
foreach (string course in year2003.Keys) {
   Enrolment e = (Enrolment) year2003[course];
   Console.WriteLine (course + " " + e.size);
}
```

The type of the keys, as we know, is `string`. With a value for the key, we can get the corresponding value of type `Enrolment`. Then we can access fields of the `e` object.

Example 8.4 Public holidays

This example shows how sorted lists can be used to keep track of data and provide a convenient query mechanism. The data in question are various lists of public holidays observed in different countries. A typical list might look like this, for Canada in 2002.

```
1 January New Year's Day
29 March Good Friday
31 March Easter
1 April Easter Monday
20 May Victoria Day
24 June Quebec National Day
1 July Canada Day
5 August Civic or Provincial Holidays
2 September Labour Day
14 October Thanksgiving Day
11 November Remembrance Day
25 December Christmas Day
26 December Boxing Day
```

We would like to store the date opposite the name and then enable users to enquire as to what holiday a specific date is, if any. The declaration of such a collection would be:

```
SortedList H = new SortedList(20);
```

Notice that unlike arrays, the declaration of the list does not reveal what is going into it: both the key and the value are assumed to be of the C# superclass `object`. All classes inherit from `object`, so any objects can be stored in the collection. Once we have read in a date and name, then putting it into the list is a simple:

```
H[date] = name;
```

Checking the list for a date that is supplied by the user could be done by:

```
string text;
if (H.ContainsKey(date)) {
  text = (string) H[date];
} else
  text = "Not a public holiday";
```

To print out the table, we would use the `foreach` construct.

```
foreach (string d in H.Keys) {
  Console.WriteLine(d + " " + H[d});
```

With such an example, the user interface is important, so once again we sketch it out as in Figure 8.9.

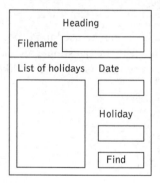

Figure 8.9 Diagram of the Public Holiday GUI

Translated into a specification for Views, it becomes:

```
string spec = @"<Form Text=Holidays>
    <vertical>
      <Label Text='Public Holiday Chooser'
             Font=Bold16 ForeColor=red
             Height=40 halign=center Width=350/>
        <horizontal>
          <Label   Text = 'Read the data from' Width=100/>
```

```
        <TextBox Name = filename text=holidays.dat Width = 80/>
        <Button  Name = 'read in'/>
    </horizontal>
    <horizontal>
      <vertical>
        <Label Text='List of holidays'/>
        <Listbox Name=list/>
      </vertical>
      <vertical>
        <Label Text='Type and Find or Choose and Select'
            Width=100 Height=50/>
        <Label Text='Date'/>
            <TextBox Name=date Text='25 December' Width = 100/>
        <Button  Name=find Text=Find/>
        <space   height=20/>
        <Label    Text='Holiday'/>
        <TextBox Name=holiday Width=150/>
        <Button  Name select Text=Select/>
      </vertical>
    </horizontal>
  </vertical>
</Form>";
```

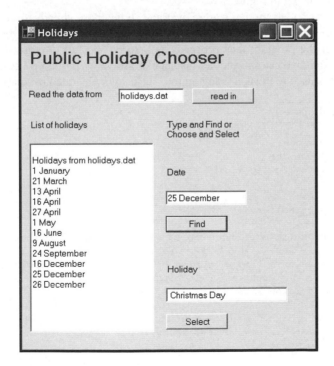

Figure 8.10 Snapshot of the Holidays program

Once the GUI is set up, we provide a handler which will switch on the three buttons shown. This will be:

```
for ( ; ; ) {
  string b = gui.GetControl();
  if (b == null)
    break;
  switch(b) {
    case "read in":
      ReadData(gui.GetText("filename"));
      break;
    case "find":
      HandleSelection(gui.GetText("date"));
      break;
    case "select":
      HandleSelection(gui.GetText("list"));
      break;
  }
}
```

HandleSelection is built from the code above and will take a date as typed in and present back on the GUI the title of the holiday, if it exists. A snapshot of the program while running is shown in Figure 8.10.

In fact, we have added another feature over and above those already discussed, which is the ability to select a date on the list box and press the *Select* rather than the *Find* button; the operation of the program then proceeds as before. The full program follows. In the ReadData section, we can see another instance of arrays when the Split method of the string datatype is used to break a string up into substrings separated by spaces.

```
┌──────────────────────┐
│ File HolidaysGUI.cs  │
└──────────────────────┘
```

```
using System;
using System.IO;
using System.Collections;

using Views;
class PublicHolidays {

  /* The Public Holidays Program        Bishop & Horspool    Feb 2002
   * ===========================
   * Maintains a list of public holiday dates and enables queries on
   * dates. Illustrates collections and string splitters.
   * GUI version with a Date class.
   */

  SortedList H = new SortedList(20);
  Views.Form gui;

  string spec = @"<Form Text = Holidays>
    <vertical>
```

```
              <Label Text='Public Holiday Chooser' Font=sfbf16 ForeColor=red
                  Height=40 halign=center Width=350/>
              <horizontal>
                <Label    Text = 'Read the data from' Width=100/>
                <TextBox Name = filename text=holidays.dat Width = 80/>
                <Button  Name = 'read in'/>
              </horizontal>
              <horizontal>
                <vertical>
                  <Label Text='List of holidays'/>
                  <Listbox Name=list/>
                </vertical>
                <vertical>
                  <Label Text='Type and Find or Choose and Select'
                      Width=100 Height=50/>
                  <Label Text='Date'/>
                      <TextBox Name=date Text='25 December'
                      Width = 100/>
                  <Button  Name=find Text=Find/>
                  <space       height=20/>
                  <Label    Text = 'Holiday'/>
                  <TextBox Name = holiday Width = 150/>
                  <Button  Name = select Text = Select/>
                </vertical>
              </horizontal>
            </vertical>
        </Form>";

void Go() {
  try {
    gui = new Views.Form(spec);
  } catch( Exception e ) {
    Console.WriteLine(e.Message);
    return;
  }
  HandleQueries();
}

void HandleQueries() {
  for ( ; ; ) {
    string b = gui.GetControl();
    if (b == null)
      break;
    switch(b) {
      case "read in":
        ReadData(gui.GetText("filename"));
        break;
      case "find":
        HandleSelection(gui.GetText("date"));
        break;
      case "select":
        HandleSelection(gui.GetText("list"));
        break;
    }
```

```
      }
      gui.CloseGUI();
    }
    bool ReadData(string filename) {
      StreamReader fin = null;
      try {
        fin = File.OpenText(filename);
      }
      catch (FileNotFoundException e) {
        gui.PutText("List", e.Message);
        return false;
      }
      gui.PutText("list","");
      gui.PutText("list","Holidays from "+filename);

      string line;
      string[] elements;
      while ((line = fin.ReadLine()) != null) {
        elements = line.Split(' ');
        string date = elements[0] + " "+ elements[1];
        String name = "";
        // Join the rest of the tokens for
        // the holiday's name
        for (int i = 2; i<elements.Length; i++)
          name += ' '+elements[i];
        gui.PutText("list",date.ToString());
        H[date] = name;
      }
      return true;
    }

    void HandleSelection(string date) {
      String text;
      text = (string) H[date];
      if (text == null)
        text = "Not a public holiday";
      gui.PutText("holiday", text);
      gui.PutText("date", date.ToString());
    }

    static void Main() {
      new PublicHolidays().Go();
    }
  }
```

Other collections

C# provides six collections, of which so far we have only discussed two: `ArrayList` and `SortedList`. The other collections are:

◆   BitArray

- ◆ `HashTable`

- ◆ `Queue`

- ◆ `Stack.`

Each has its own individual properties and methods. A full treatment of these collections is left to a course on data structures.

User-defined collections

Of course, we can also define our own collections. To make them viable, they need to interface correctly with the `foreach` loop and the `CompareTo` function.

Being able to get successive values stored in a collection depends on the type of these objects being *enumerable*. In order to be enumerable, a type must implement the `IEnumerable` interface. It can do so by implementing the `IEnumerator` interface and getting built-in enumerator facilities from the class specified. That is why looping over a `SortedList` is so easy – the enumerable behaviour is already included for `SortedLists`.

In the same way, a collection must be *comparable* if it is to enable its elements to be sorted. This functionality is embodied in the `IComparable` and `IComparator` interfaces. All these interfaces are discussed in Chapter 9, where a new collection is defined.

8.5 Case study 4 – Training schedules

Problem statement

Employees at BlowFish Inc. attend training courses, and a record of each course attended or planned to attend is kept on a file. We wish to discover which employees are signed up for which courses, and which courses overall have been used.

Overall solution structure

The overall structure of the program will be two classes for the employees and courses respectively, and then a driving class which will fill up the course schedules and print them out. We assume that the courses an employee should do are dictated by his/her rank and cannot be a random selection in the data. Thus an example of employee data is:

```
123456 Mr GI Jones 5155 1
```

The first five fields are simple employee data for employee number, title, initials, surname and extension. The last field indicates the rank. What does a rank of 1 mean? In computing and setting up data it is not a good idea to rely on numeric coding of data which does have real meaning. In this case, we may have six different ranks of employees, such as director, manager, researcher, technician, support and trainee. Therefore, we would prefer to say:

```
123456 Mr GI Jones 5155 manager
```

Enumerated types

Talking about ranks with numbers can be both obscure and error-prone. Fortunately, C# does provide a built-in type which enables names to be associated with numbers. These are called enumerated types, and they consist of a list of names in order, which can then be used in the program and printed out. The form appears below.

ENUMERATED TYPE DEFINITION AND USE

`modifiers enum typename {id1, id2, ... idn}`
`or ids can be explicit numbers as in`
`id = value`
`Input via:`
`enumvar = (typename)Enum.Parse(typeof(typename),value);`
`Output via:`
`typename.ToString(enumvar);`

The identifiers as listed are mapped to integers either implicitly or explicitly and form the values of the type. If mapping is implicit, the first number used is zero. For input, a string can be translated to a value in the enum type; an invalid string will cause an exception. For output, an enum variable can be converted to a string.

Using an enumerated type, we can declare in the `Employee` type

```
public enum Ranks = {director, manager, researcher,
                     technician, support, trainee}
```

Internally, `director` will be 0, `manager` 1 and so on. The numbers in the data can be converted to the enumerated type on reading in as in:

```
rank = (Ranks) Enum.Parse(typeof(Ranks),values[5]);
```

Enumerated types can be compared and used in loops, which makes them really worth-while. In general though, in C# (as opposed to C++ or Pascal say), enums are not as necessary to good programming because we can avoid integer coding by using strings instead. The strings can easily be used in hash tables, as case labels of switch statements, and read in via `Parse` methods.

The type defined by an enum, and its values, has a scope within its own type; to use it outside that type, it must be prefixed by the type name, as in `Employee.Ranks`.

Collections

What kind of collections are going to be appropriate? Very often the decision depends on the operations that are to be performed. Consider first a collection for the courses. When the course lists are being set up, we shall perform a set of loops as follows:

```
for each of the courses
   for each of the ranks suggested
      for each employee
         if the employee is that rank, add to the course
```

Since we do not know how many employees there are, and we would like to have the sorted facility, we shall use sorted lists for holding all the objects created of the two collections. Next we examine the types of these objects. Each course has a name, a list of attendees (which the program will create) and the list of suggested ranks. This list can be given a fixed size since we know there are only five ranks. An array seems appropriate. The details are:

```
class Course {
   string name;
   Employee.Ranks[] suggested;
   SortedList attendees;
```

All three fields are going to be used in the main program, so we need to provide properties for them. Is it possible to provide properties for structured values like sorted lists? Certainly it is. An example would be:

```
public SortedList Attendees {
   get {return attendees;}
}
```

The Employee type is a simpler one, as it just contains ints and strings, as in

```
struct Employee {
   public enum Ranks {director, manager, researcher,
                      technician, support, trainee}
   string title;
   string initials;
   string surname;
   int extension;
   Ranks rank;
   int employeeNumber;
```

We made Employee a struct, but Course is a class because it contains other reference items in it.

The control structures to create the attendee lists and print them out are interesting, and are shown in the program.

Test data

There are two data files. The first lists the courses followed by the ranks that they are required for. An example would be:

```
Business_Management director manager
Computer_Literacy director manager support trainee
Advanced_Computer_Skills researcher technician
Accounting_Skills manager support
```

Note that the course names are written with underscores so that they are single strings. This merely simplifies the data input. The other file is the employees file, which has already been described. Here is an example.

```
123456 Mr GI Jones 5555 manager
513094 Miss KL Emm 6464 technician
876632 Dr JM Mullins 3000 director
847646 Mrs B Aye 9119 support
747329 Mr Q Wantiss 3321 researcher
821739 Mr IO Uwing 5435 trainee
```

Program

File StaffTraining.cs

```csharp
using System;
using System.Collections;
using System.IO;

class StaffTraining {

  /// <summary>
  /// The Staff Training Courses Program    Bishop & Horspool Sept 2002
  /// ===================================
  /// Creates lists of employees required to attend courses according
  /// to their rank in the organization.
  /// Illustrates use of collections and enumerated types.
  /// </summary>

  SortedList courses = new SortedList();
  SortedList employees = new SortedList();

  void Go() {
    ReadCourses("course.dat");
    ReadEmployees("employee.dat");
    OrganizeData();
    PrintResults();
  }

  void ReadCourses(string filename) {
    StreamReader fin = null;
```

```
  try {
    fin = new StreamReader(filename);
  } catch (IOException ioe) {
    Console.WriteLine(ioe.Message);
    return;
  }

  string line = fin.ReadLine().Trim();
  while (line != null) {
    if (line == "")
      continue;    // skip any blank lines
    string[] values = line.Split(' ');
    Employee.Ranks[] suggestions =
                  new Employee.Ranks[values.Length - 1];
    for (int i = 1; i < values.Length; i++)
      suggestions[i - 1] = (Employee.Ranks) Enum.Parse(
          typeof(Employee.Ranks),values[i].Trim());
    Course c = new Course(values[0], suggestions);
    courses[c.Name] = c;
    line = fin.ReadLine();
  }
}

void ReadEmployees(string filename) {
  StreamReader fin = null;
  try {
    fin = new StreamReader(filename);
  } catch (IOException ioe) {
    Console.WriteLine(ioe.Message);
    return;
  }

  string line = fin.ReadLine();
  while (line != null) {
    if (line == "")
      continue;
    string[] values = line.Split(' ');
    Employee e = new Employee(values);
    employees[e.EmployeeNumber]=e;
    line = fin.ReadLine();
  }
}

void OrganizeData() {
  foreach(string courseName in courses.Keys) {
    Course c = (Course)courses[courseName];
    foreach(Employee.Ranks i in c.Suggested) {
      foreach(int employeeNumber in employees.Keys) {
        Employee e = (Employee)employees[employeeNumber];
        if (e.Rank == i) c.addAttendant(e);
      }
    }
  }
}
```

```
    void PrintResults() {
      Console.WriteLine("*** Training Schedules ***");
      Console.WriteLine("The course lists");
      Console.WriteLine("=================");
      foreach(string courseName in courses.Keys) {
        Course c = (Course)courses[courseName];
        Console.WriteLine(c.Name);
        if (c.Attendees != null) {
          Console.WriteLine("To be attended by:");
          foreach(int employeeNumber in c.Attendees.Keys) {
            Employee e = (Employee)c.Attendees[employeeNumber];
            Console.WriteLine("\t" + e);
          }
        }
        Console.WriteLine();
      }
      Console.WriteLine("The schedules");
      Console.WriteLine("=============");
      foreach(int employeeNumber in employees.Keys) {
        Employee e = (Employee)employees[employeeNumber];
        Console.WriteLine(e);
        Console.WriteLine("Is to attend:");
        foreach(string courseName in courses.Keys) {
          Course c = (Course)courses[courseName];
          if (c.Attendees !=
                null && c.Attendees.ContainsKey(employeeNumber))
            Console.WriteLine("\t" + courseName);
        }
        Console.WriteLine();
      }
    }

    static void Main(string[] args) {
      new StaffTraining().Go();
    }
  }

class Course {
  string name;
  Employee.Ranks[] suggested;
  SortedList attendees;

  public string Name {
    get {return name;}
    set {name = value;}
  }
  public Employee.Ranks[] Suggested {
    get {return suggested;}
  }
  public SortedList Attendees {
    get {return attendees;}
  }
```

```
    public Course(string n, Employee.Ranks[] s) {
      name = n;
      suggested = s;
      attendees = null;
    }

    public void addAttendant(Employee o) {
      if (attendees == null)
        attendees = new SortedList();
      attendees[o.EmployeeNumber] = o;
    }
}

struct Employee {
  public enum Ranks {director, manager, researcher,
                     technician, support, trainee}
  string title;
  string initials;
  string surname;
  int extension;
  Ranks rank;
  int employeeNumber;

  public Employee(string[] values) {
    title = values[1];
    initials = values[2];
    surname = values[3];
    extension = int.Parse(values[4]);
    rank = (Ranks) Enum.Parse(typeof(Ranks),values[5]);
    employeeNumber = int.Parse(values[0]);
  }

  override public string ToString() {
    return employeeNumber + " " + title + " " + initials +
           " " + surname
      + " (" + rank.ToString()+")";
  }

  public int EmployeeNumber {
    get {return employeeNumber;}
  }

  public Ranks Rank {
    get {return rank;}
  }
}
```

Testing

The program can be tested with the data files as above. Extensions to the program are covered in the exercises.

```
    *** Training Schedules ***
```

```
The course lists
================
Accounting_Skills
To be attended by:
        123456 Mr GI Jones (manager)
        821739 Mr IO Uwing (trainee)


Advanced_Computer_Literacy
To be attended by:
        513094 Miss KL Emm (technician)
        847646 Mrs B Aye (support)


Business_Management
To be attended by:
        123456 Mr GI Jones (manager)
        747329 Mr Q Wantiss (researcher)


Computer_Literacy
To be attended by:
        123456 Mr GI Jones (manager)
        513094 Miss KL Emm (technician)
        747329 Mr Q Wantiss (researcher)
        821739 Mr IO Uwing (trainee)
        847646 Mrs B Aye (support)


The schedules
=============
123456 Mr GI Jones (manager)
Is to attend:
        Accounting_Skills
        Business_Management
        Computer_Literacy


513094 Miss KL Emm (technician)
Is to attend:
        Advanced_Computer_Literacy
        Computer_Literacy


747329 Mr Q Wantiss (researcher)
Is to attend:
        Business_Management
        Computer_Literacy


821739 Mr IO Uwing (trainee)
Is to attend:
        Accounting_Skills
        Computer_Literacy


847646 Mrs B Aye (support)
Is to attend:
        Advanced_Computer_Literacy
        Computer_Literacy


876632 Dr JM Mullins (director)
Is to attend:
```

Concepts in Chapter 8

This chapter covered the following concepts:

classes	collections
references	indexers
sorted lists	inheritance
rectangular and jagged arrays	enumerated types
foreach loop	enum type

and these operators:

[ ]   [ ]

and defined the following forms:

Array class (abbreviated)	ArrayList class (abbreviated)
array declarations – rectangular and jagged	SortedList collection (abbreviated)
foreach loop for a SortedList	enumerated type definition and use

Quiz

Q8.1 The declaration below causes a compilation error because:

```
struct MyType {
    int i;
    double d;
    MyType t;
    string s;
}
```

(a)   a field cannot be declared of the same type as the type it is in

(b)   there are no methods or constructors in the type

(c)   a struct cannot contain a reference to fields of its own type

(d)   a struct cannot contain references

Q8.2   An array type is classified as a

(a)   value type   (b)   reference type

(c)   either value or reference   (d)   neither value nor reference, it is
                                                  in a group of its own

Q8.3   An array that can be used to keep the number of patients an emergency hospital
        sees every hour of the day would be declared as:

(a)   `int[] tally = new int[24];`

(b)   `int[] tally = new int[23];`

(c)   `int[][] tally = new int[24][];`

(d)   `Patients[] tally = new Patients[24];`

Q8.4   We have a list of objects linked by next references, and want to find an object
        with an x field value of 6. Four suggestions have been made:

```
// LOOP 1                         // LOOP 2
n = list;                         n = list;
while (n != null && n.x!=6) {     do {
   n = n.next;                       if (n == null) break;
}                                    n = n.next;
                                  } while (n.x != 6)

// LOOP 3                         // LOOP 4
n = list;                         for (n = list; n != null;
while (n != null) {                               n = n.next) {
   if (n.x == 6) break;              if (n.x == 6) break;
   n = n.next;                    }
}
```

Which of the loops will work?

(a)   loops 2, 3 and 4   (b)   loops 1 and 3

(c)   loops 1, 2 and 3   (d)   loops 1, 3 and 4

Q8.5   Only one of the following statements is false. Which one?

(a)   Arrays are of a fixed size, but ArrayLists can grow indefinitely.

(b)   There is a built-in method to sort arrays but not to sort ArrayLists.

(c)   Indices for arrays must be integers, but for ArrayLists can be anything.

(d)   Arrays can be multi-dimensional but ArrayLists have only one dimen-
       sion.

Q8.6 To declare a jagged array with 4 rows and 1 more column than the row index (i.e. a triangle), we can use:

(a)
```
int a[] [];
for (int i=0; i<4; i++)
    int a[] [i] = new int[4] [i+1];
```

(b)
```
int a[] [] = new int[4] [];
for (int i=0; i<4; i++)
    a[i] = new int[i+1];
```

(c)
```
int a[] [] = new int[4] [Row+1];
```

(d)
```
int a[] [] = new int[4] [];
for (int i=0; i<4; i++)
    a[i] = new int[i];
```

Q8.7 If SL is defined as a sorted list with keys of type `string`, then which loop will print out all the keys?

(a)
```
foreach (string s in SL)
    Console.WriteLine(s.Key);
```

(b)
```
foreach (string s in SL.Keys)
    Console.WriteLine(SL[s]);
```

(c)
```
foreach (string s in SL)
    Console.WriteLine(s);
```

(d)
```
foreach (string s in SL.Keys)
    Console.WriteLine(s);
```

Q8.8 In order to use the `Sort` methods supplied by built-in collection types, the element type must:

(a) be a simple type

(b) define the `Equals` method

(c) define the `CompareTo` method

(d) have reference semantics

Q8.9 If we have declared `SortedList fruits = new SortedList(10)`, and we have inserted some `Fruit` type values into the list where each value consists of a fruit name (the key) and the colour of the fruit (the value), a statement to get a value for a lemon out of the list would be:

(a) `Fruit lemon = SortedList[lemon];`

(b) `Fruit lemon = SortedList["yellow"];`

(c) `Fruit lemon = (Fruit) fruits["lemon"];`

(d) `Fruit lemon = fruits["lemon"];`

Q8.10 A valid declaration for an enumerated type for some planets would be:

> (a)   `type Planets = enum {Mercury, Mars, Venus, Earth};`
>
> (b)   `enum Planets = {Mercury, Mars, Venus, Earth}`
>
> (c)   `enum Planets = {Mercury, Mars, Venus, Earth};`
>
> (d)   `enum Planets {Mercury, Mars, Venus, Earth}`

Exercises

8.1   Pet collection. Starting with the simple Example 8.1 on a Pet list, change it so that it uses one of the built-in collections. Then read in a list of pets of any length and sort it according to name. Define whatever extra methods are needed.

8.2   Computer ids. In the case study on training schedules, we would also like to know which employees need computer user ids, given a list of courses that will be using the computer. Extend the data for courses to include a marker that indicates this is a computer course, and then also print out a list of employees who must get computer ids.

8.3   Training queries. Create a Views interface to the training schedule program that will enable users to make queries such as who is on a course and what courses an employee is signed up for.

8.4   Electrical voltage. The household voltage supplied by a substation is measured at hourly intervals over a 72-hour period, and a report made. Write a program that generates 72 readings and determines:

- the mean voltage measured;
- the hours at which the recorded voltage varies from the mean by more than 10%;
- any adjacent hours when the change from one reading to the next is greater than 15% of the mean value.

The program should print a table of the voltages observed over the 72 hours.

8.5   Sum of squares. Write a typed method which is given two integers as parameters, and returns as its value the sum of the squares of the numbers between and inclusive of the two parameters. Show how to call the method to print the value of i^2 where i runs from 1 to 10. How would the program change if the data were to be read in and stored initially in an array?

8.6 **Standard passes.** The Senate at a university has decreed that at least 75% of students in each course must pass. This means that the pass mark for each course will differ. Write a program that will read in a file of marks and determine the highest pass mark such that the Senate's rule applies.

8.7 **Olympic judges.** In many individual display events such as diving and figure skating, up to eight judges are used, and they each supply a score, usually between 0 and 10. The result for a competitor is then the average of the scores. Write a program which uses arrays to generate or read in eight scores per competitor and determine the scores and the overall winner. Number the judges from 0 to 7. Pay careful attention to class and collection design.

8.8 **Biased judges.** For a special event, it was decided that the scores for the judge giving the lowest and the highest mark would be excluded. Add this functionality to your program.

8.9 **Country judges.** In Exercise 8.7, instead of printing out the judges' numbers, we would like to print out the country from which they come. Use an array to set up a list of country names for the judges on duty, and adapt the program to make the output more explanatory.

8.10 **Population increase.** Since 1980, the penguin population statistics for Antarctica have been stored on a computer file, with each line containing the year followed by the total penguins counted for that year. Write a program that will read this file and find the two consecutive years in which there was the greatest percentage increase in population. The data is not guaranteed to be in strict year order and may need to be sorted first.

8.11 **Bilingual calendars.** Design a program to print out a calendar, one month underneath each other. Then using sorted lists, set up versions for the months and days of the week in another language (say, French, Spanish or German), and let the user select which language the calendar should be printed in.

8.12 **Reversing Public holidays.** As an interesting extension to Example 8.4, enter the data in another table which has the name of the holiday and will provide the date on request.

CHAPTER   9

Polymorphism and inheritance

Modern software development is seldom done by one person, nor in one period of time. Software is intended to evolve and change with the world around it. Object-oriented languages are particularly good at handling such evolution, and C# provides three mechanisms for living in such a changing world – interfaces, inheritance and abstract classes. In providing for polymorphism and extensibility, these mechanisms make use of some subsidiary concepts, namely serialization, operator overloading, class checking and class conversion. We shall study all of these ideas with some ongoing examples.

9.1 Objects in a changing world

The software that we build to model a class of objects will seldom be the last word. There are almost certainly going to be changes and additions as time goes by, if the program is to be of any use at all. We can identify two broad groups of evolutionary needs:

◆ *polymorphism*, where methods and collections can work with a variety of types;

◆   *extensibility*, where additions can be made at a later stage to a type, without altering what already exists.

In C# both of these draw on the three mechanisms – inheritance, interfaces and abstraction.

Polymorphism

Polymorphism can show up in different ways. The first is when we would like to have a collection or array that can have different *types* of objects in it. The types will be related, in that they will have certain fields and methods in common, but they need not be written together, in place or time. So for example, a university may have two completely different filing systems for students and staff, but a register of all computer users could draw on both. The register would then be the polymorphic collection because it has members of different types in it.

The second type of polymorphism refers to *methods* which can act on a variety of types. The classic case is sorting. We have already seen that Array.Sort is a very useful method which does not need to know what type of objects it is sorting. It does need *some* information though, which was possibly not evident while we were sorting built-in types. In order to sort a sequence of objects, there needs to be ordering defined for the type. Sort needs to know at each juncture whether object *a* comes before object *b* in some standard ordering. This functionality is usually encapsulated in a CompareTo method which all sortable types agree to implement. CompareTo is then a polymorphic method. So for example, in the registry of computer users, we would need a method that would know how to compare users, be they staff or students. Presumably, the comparison could work on user ids.

Achieving polymorphism

Polymorphism can be achieved through interfaces or inheritance. The choice depends on how closely the types involved are related. If the types are very independent, written by different organizations or people, and have minimal overlap, then *interfaces* are appropriate. Figure 9.1(a) shows how interfaces work. The central polymorphic collection *A* and the defined polymorphic method *M* both make use of the interface name *I* as their type. *I* sits between the driver method, *D*, of the main class and any number of other classes (three shown here). Each of these implements *M* in its own way.

In Example 9.3 later on in this chapter, we show how access to a list of people allowed to access a building (the list being equivalent to *A*) can be drawn up from staff and student types (equivalent to *C1* and *C2*). Each type would have their own version of the validating method (*M*) to decide whether their access card is valid. *I* would be the interface which would specify that the validating method is what links the polymorphic list *A* with the original types *C1* and *C2*.

Polymorphism can also be achieved through *inheritance*, which we would use if the types are normally more closely coupled than the classes sharing an interface, in the sense that there would be common methods or fields involved. There is a base class, called *C1* in

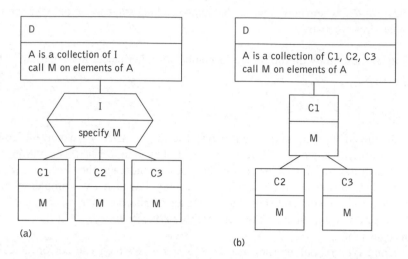

Figure 9.1 The structure of polymorphism

Figure 9.1(b), which is adapted by *C2* and *C3*. The main driver class *D* can declare a collection of type *C1*, but *C2* and *C3* objects can also go in it. All of the classes can implement the *M* method, and there are rules which define which one gets called when.

An example of polymorphism with inheritance would be in the example shown in the last chapter in Figure 8.3. The various performances for a particular event would be stored in some array or other, but some of them would be the plain type, and some would be the extended type, with the special benefit field. There may also be further extensions as time goes by. As mentioned in that section, *M* might be the delete method which would operate differently for ordinary performances (*C1*) and for special ones (*C2*).

The above is a simple introduction to polymorphism. Both inheritance and interfaces have fixed rules about how they can operate and we shall consider these in the next sections.

Extensibility

Extensibility is usually implemented via inheritance, but abstract classes and methods provide an alternative. We start off with a base class, and create derived classes which can

- use base class members unchanged, provided they are accessible;

- override members to provide variety;

- add new members, even with the same names as the old.

Derived classes can be used wherever the base class can be. In this way, the collection *A* can start off with just *C1* type objects, and later on be expanded to include other varieties in *C2* and *C3*. As a concrete example, if the student class postulated above were to be extended later to specially handle postgraduate students then we might add fields for the supervisor and thesis title, which would not be relevant for ordinary students.

With inheritance, the base class is complete in itself, and the derived classes are free to make whatever changes and additions they please. Another option is for the base class, or some methods in it, to be declared as *abstract* which means these methods have no implementations provided. This forces the derived classes to implement those specific members.

In Figure 9.1(b) the difference would be that there would actually be no *C1* objects in *A*, since objects cannot be created from abstract classes. They clearly cannot be created because an abstract class is not fully implemented. *C1* serves chiefly as a definition of what is required later. Continuing the example, in this figure, *C1* could be declared as a `Student` type, but abstract, with certain basic requirements in it. Then *C2* and *C3* could be `Undergrads` and `Postgrads`, and would fill in all the details.

Which mechanism?

It is probably clear by now that interfaces, inheritance and abstract classes provide very much the same facilities, and could most of the time be used interchangeably, with the same effect. The choice between the different mechanisms rests mostly on the overall project design – as we said, the independence of the classes needs to be taken into account – but there are several restrictions that apply to each which would then tilt the balance. Here is a list of the main ones:

1. A type can only inherit from one other type, however it can implement many interfaces.

2. Interfaces may only have methods, properties, indexers and events. They may not include fields and operators, for example, which base classes can.

3. Objects cannot be created from classes with abstract members, but declaring abstract members forces their definition later.

How we make these choices will become clearer as we work through examples. We now look at the mechanisms in detail.

9.2 Interfaces for polymorphism

In Section 9.1 we introduced the idea of methods being able to operate on a variety of types, provided they conformed to certain characteristics. An interface is where these characteristics are defined. An *interface* consists of a useful selection of methods, properties, indexers and events. (Note that this list excludes fields, but of course the provision of properties makes them accessible at the `get` and `set` level.) In other words, interfaces only specify what can be done with objects of conforming types; an interface holds no state or other information itself.

Using an existing interface

We start off our discussion of interfaces by looking at an existing interface in the `System` namespace of C# as shown in this form:

ICOMPARABLE INTERFACE
`public int CompareTo(object obj)`
An implementation of the `CompareTo` method must return a negative result if the current object compares less than `obj` (i.e. comes before it in the desired ordering); zero if they are equal; and a positive result if the current object is greater than `obj`. The meaning of the comparison is defined in the method itself.

`IComparable` is used by the sorting and searching methods already defined for arrays and other collections. It is already implemented for the basic types such as `int` and `string`, and also for all the types defined in the `System` namespace, such as `DateTime`. The important point to note is that the comparison is not a bitwise one, but can be intelligently defined to suit the type.

For a type to implement an interface, it must satisfy two requirements:

1. Declare the interface in its header.

2. Supply bodies for each of the members specified in the interface.

As an example, suppose we have a small class recording the name of staff in an organization and their starting dates of employment. The class might be something like this:

```
public class Staff {
  string name;
  int startDate;

  public Staff(string n) {
    name = n;
    startDate = DateTime.Now.Year;
  }
  public string Name {
    get {return name;}
  }
  public int StartDate {
    get {return startDate;}
  }
  public override string ToString() {
    return "Staff "+name;
  }
}
```

Suppose we now have an array of such staff, with suitable values in it, and want to sort it. The Array.Sort method requires that elements of the array can be compared using the CompareTo method, as defined in the IComparable interface. So we implement the interface for the class. Step 1 gives us:

```
public class Staff : IComparable {
```

For step 2, we have to decide what the CompareTo method must do. If we assume that no two people have exactly the same name (or if they do it doesn't matter how they sort!) then we can define CompareTo like this:

```
public int CompareTo(object o) {
  return (name.CompareTo(((Staff) o).name));
}
```

In other words, we devolve the comparison to the CompareTo method already defined for strings. An important part of this method is the type conversion: CompareTo is specifically defined for objects. All classes inherit from the supertype object, but in order to specifically get at the name field, we have to ensure that the parameter being supplied is indeed of type Staff.

Once Staff is augmented in this way, we can complete the relevant parts of the program as follows:

```
Staff[] staffList = new Staff[100];

// get details for n staff

Array.Sort(staffList,0,n);
```

In this example, Sort is the polymorphic method which would correspond to *M* in Figure 9.1(a); staffList is the collection *A* and Staff could be any of the *C1*, *C2* or *C3* classes.

Alternative comparator methods

It may seem that once we have implemented IComparable in this way, we are bound into using a name comparison only. What if we wanted to sort by the other field, i.e. startDate? There is a way to do this. C# has another interface called IComparer which is in the System.Collections namespace. Its form is:

ICOMPARER INTERFACE
public int Compare(object x, object y)
An implementation of the Compare method returns a negative result if the current object x is less than object y; zero if they are equal; and a positive result if the object x is greater than object y. The meaning of the comparison is defined in the method itself.

We can force the `Sort` method to use a specific `Compare` method by calling it with a fourth parameter as follows:

```
Array.Sort(staffList,0,n,compareByDate);
```

The `compareByDate` object is programmed to have a `Compare` method which does the necessary check between the start dates, i.e.

```
public class StaffByDate : IComparer {
  public int Compare(object x, object y) {
    return (((Staff)x).startDate.
      CompareTo(((Staff) y).startDate));
  }
}
```

Normally, this class would be declared inside the main `Staff` class. Then we can instantiate an object and pass it to the extended version of `Sort` as follows:

```
Array.Sort(staffList,0,count,new Staff.StaffByDate());
```

Using this arrangement, we can extend the number of ways in which objects can be compared indefinitely.

Defining interfaces

The next step is to define our own interfaces. We start by giving a simple example, and itemizing the steps it contains.

Example 9.1 Defining interfaces

The program implements the example which is discussed in Section 9.1 and shown in Figure 9.1(a).

File InterfaceTest.cs

```
using System;

namespace InterfaceTest {

  interface I {
    string M();
  }

  class Driver {

    /// <summary>
```

```
/// Test Interfaces program    Bishop and Horspool   Sept 2002
/// ========================
/// Illustrates the basic structure of polymorphism
/// </summary>

void Go() {
  C1 c1 = new C1();
  C2 c2 = new C2();
  C3 c3 = new C3();
  Poly(c1,c2);
  Poly(c2,c3);
}
void Poly(I i, I j) {
  Console.WriteLine("I am "+i.M()+" you are "+j.M());
}
static void Main() {
 new Driver().Go();
}
}

class C1 : I {
  public string M() {
   return "good old C1";
  }
}

class C2 : I {
  public string M() {
    return "happy C2";
  }
}

class C3 : I {
  public string M() {
    return "beautiful C3";
  }
}
}
```

The steps are:

1. Define the interface I with a method M.

2. For each of the interested classes C1, C2 and C3, declare that they implement I by saying ': I' at the declaration.

3. Provide the body of M in each class.

4. Declare the polymorphic method (called Poly here) with parameters of type I.

5. From within Poly, call M on the parameters supplied.

As a result, the appropriate versions of M will be called and the output from the above driver program will be:

```
I am good old C1 and you are happy C2
I am happy C2 and you are beautiful C3
```

I is a very simple interface, but in fact most interfaces are. For the sake of completeness, here is the form of an interface:

INTERFACE DEFINITION

modifier interface *name* : *base* {
   definitions of methods, properties,
   indexers and events
}

Interfaces can have any of the access modifiers, and can also inherit from other interfaces. They define a set of characteristics which are adhered to by all types implementing the interface.

Class conversions

Polymorphism is going to be used chiefly where we have collections of objects of different types. How then do we ensure that operations are not performed that are inappropriate for a specific type? What we are envisaging is a collection, let's say an array, which is declared on an interface. The array can then be filled with any objects whose classes implement the interface.

Example 9.2 Interfaces for sorting

Using the step-by-step example above, let us first expand two of the classes to include data members n and s respectively, together with their corresponding constructors and properties, as follows. We also alter their *M* methods to report the values of the variables.

```
class C1 : I {
    int n;

    public C1 () {}

    public C1 (int i) {
      n = i;
    }
    public int N {
      get {return n;}
    }

    public string M() {
      return "good old C1 aged "+n;
    }
}
```

```
class C2 : I {
  string s;

  public C2() {}

  public C2 (string t) {
    s = t;
  }
  public string S {
    get {return s;}
  }

  public string M() {
    return "happy C2 "+s;
  }
}
```

If we declare in the driver an array as:

```
I[] A = new I[10];
```

then we can insert into it as follows:

```
A[0] = new C1(23);
A[1] = new C2("today");
```

and so on. According to the principles of interfaces established above, we can still refer to

```
A[0].M();
A[1].M();
```

Then suppose later on in the program we try

```
if (A[0]==A[1]) { ... // etc.
```

Will this be allowed? No, because the two elements of A have been tagged with different types. Can they be made the same? No. They are fundamentally different types. How then can we sort this array, which would perhaps be a nice thing to do? The answer is that we can deal with each element in A by checking its type and perhaps converting it to another type. The three mechanisms we use are shown in the *Type conversions and checks* form, below.

A class may be implicitly *upcast* to a class that it derives from or that it implements, and may be explicitly *downcast* to a class that derives from it. It is this explicit downcast that may fail. For example, if we have

```
C1 c = new C1();
I i;
```

then

```
i = c1;      // upcast    - always works
c1 = (C1)i;  // downcast - may fail
```

To avoid having exceptions raised, we can use the `is` and `as` operators to protect explicit casts. Thus we would say:

```
if (i is C1)
   c1 = (C1)i;
else // ... give an error message
```

This technique is used in the `CompareTo` methods in Example 9.3.

TYPE CONVERSIONS AND CHECKS
objectname is *typename* *objectname* as *typename* (*typename*) *objectname*
The `is` operator returns true if the object is of the given type and false otherwise. The `as` operator converts the object to the given type but if the conversion is not allowed, then it returns null. The third option, known as a *type cast*, converts the object to the given type but if the conversion is not allowed, it raises an `InvalidCastException`.

Example 9.3 Building access control

The Department of Computer Science has much valuable equipment, and has a card entry system to the building for staff and students. At the end of each year, cards can be renewed or nullified. The rules for doing so are built into the 'business logic' of the respective record systems. That is, there is a student record system and a staff record system, built independently and not even housed on the same computer.

In order to run the end of year update, we will assemble from these databases all relevant records and then apply the validate method in each case. This process is our polymorphic method, which requires an interface with a validate method, and two classes, for staff and students, which will implement it. The structure is defined in Figure 9.2.

The program generally follows the pattern of the simple one above, but there are some additional features. First of all, we need to specify the 'business logic' alluded to above. That is, who gets access the following year? We implement the following rules:

1. All staff get access every year.

2. Students who have been employed as tutors for more than one year get access for another year.

3. All other students are denied an update of access: they need to reapply.

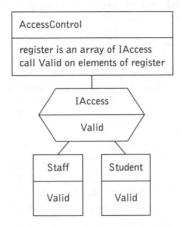

Figure 9.2 Access Control validation via an interface

In the Staff class, therefore, Valid will look like this:

```
public bool Valid() {
   return true;
}
```

and for students it is:

```
public bool Valid() {
   return (tutorYears > 0);
}
```

The interface is of course:

```
interface IAccess {
  bool Valid();
}
```

and both classes implement it.

In order to test the program, we will be entering simple test data through a Views form and storing it in the register, declared as

```
IAccess[] register = new IAccess[100];
```

It would be nice to be able to sort the register before outputting it together with details of who has renewed access. To do so, we must implement IComparable again. The problem is that given a staff member, say, the next element in the register may be a student. How does one compare a staff member and a student when they have completely different fields and were developed independently? We need to make a decision that, say, staff come before anything else, and students come after anything else. Then the `Staff` CompareTo method will be:

```
public int CompareTo(object o) {
  if (o is Staff)
    return (name.CompareTo(((Staff) o).name));
  // o is a Student; Staff always rate before students
  return -1;
}
```

We start by checking whether the second object (the parameter) is a `Staff` object. If so, we can downcast it from `Iaccess` to `Student` and perform the check on names. Otherwise, we return a −1, meaning *less than*. Although the comment refers to students, there is nothing in the code which ties us down at this place to the `Student` class: `Staff` does not know about it at all. Similarly, the `CompareTo` in the `Student` class looks like this (shown without the comment this time):

```
public int CompareTo(object o) {
  if (o is Student)
    return (number.CompareTo(((Student) o).number));
  return 1;
}
```

All that remains is to set up the user interface with Views, the event handlers through `ActionPerformed`, and test the program. Here is the complete program.

File University.cs

```
using System;
using Views;

namespace University {

  /// <summary>
  /// The University Access Control System    Bishop & Horspool   2002
  /// ====================================
  /// Registers details of staff and students then
  /// validates who has access for the next year.
  /// Illustrates defining and using interfaces.
  /// </summary>

  interface IAccess {
    bool Valid();
  }

  class AccessControl {

    Views.Form f;

    void SetUpForm() {
      try {
```

```
        f = new Views.Form(@"<Form>
        <vertical>
        <Label Text='Welcome to Access Control Update'
               Width=350 Font=SansSerifBold14 ForeColor=red/>
        <CheckBox Name=Staff Checked=1/>
        <CheckBox Name=Student/>
        <horizontal>
          <Label Text='Name' />
          <TextBox Name=Name Text='Guest'/>
          <Label Text='for staff'/>
        </horizontal>
        <horizontal>
          <Label Text='Number' />
          <TextBox Name=Number Text='20031111'/>
          <Label Text='for students'/>
        </horizontal>
        <horizontal>
          <Button Name = Enter/>
          <Button Name = Appoint/>
          <Button Name = 'End of Year'/>
        </horizontal>
        <ListBox Name=List Width=350/>
        </vertical>
        </Form>" );
    } catch( Exception e ) {
      Console.WriteLine(
        "Exception caught, message follows:\n{0}", e.Message);
    }
  }

  void Go() {
    SetUpForm();
    string c;
    for (;;) {
      c = f.GetControl();
      if (c==null) break;
      ActionPerformed(c);
    }
    f.Dispose();
  }

  int kind;
  int number;
  string name;
  IAccess[] register = new IAccess[100];
  int count;

  void HandleAppointments() {
    number = int.Parse(f.GetText("Number"));
    bool found = false;
    int i;
    Student s;
```

```
      for (i = 0; i<count; i++) {
        if (register[i] is Student) {
          s = (Student) register[i];
          if (s.Number == number) {
            found = true;
            break;
          }
        }
      }
      if (found) {
        s=(Student) register[i];
        s.Appoint();
        f.PutText("List",s+" appointed: years now "
                 +s.TutorYears);
      } else
        f.PutText("List","No such student\n");
    }

    void EnterPerson() {
      kind = f.GetValue("Student");
      switch (kind) {
        case 1 : {
          number = int.Parse(f.GetText("Number"));
          register[count] = new Student(number);
          break;
        }
        case 0 : {
          name = f.GetText("Name");
          register[count] = new Staff(name);
          break;
        }
      }
      f.PutText("List",register[count].ToString());
      count++;
    }

    void ActionPerformed (string c) {
      switch (c) {
        case "Student" : {
          f.PutValue("Staff",0);
          break;
        }
        case "Staff" : {
          f.PutValue("Student",0);
          break;
        }
        case "Name": case "Number" : {
          break;
        }
        case "Enter" : {
          EnterPerson();
          break;
        }
```

```
      case "Appoint" : {
        HandleAppointments();
        break;
      }
      case "End of Year" : {
        UpdateAccess();
        break;
      }
    } // case c
  } // ActionPerformed

  void UpdateAccess () {
    Array.Sort(register,0,count);
    f.PutText("List", "People granted access for the new year");
    for (int i = 0; i<count; i++) {
      if (register[i].Valid())
        f.PutText("List",register[i]+"          Access Valid\n");
      else
        f.PutText("List",register[i]+"          No Access\n");
    }
  }

  static void Main() {
    new AccessControl().Go();
  }
}

class Student : IAccess, IComparable {
  int number;
  int tutorYears;
  public Student(int n) {
    number = n;
    tutorYears = 0;
  }
  public void Appoint () {
    tutorYears++;
  }
  public int Number {
    get {return number;}
  }
  public int TutorYears {
    get {return tutorYears;}
  }
  public bool Valid() {
    return (tutorYears > 0);
  }
  public override string ToString () {
    if (tutorYears == 0) return "Student "
      +number+"("+tutorYears+")";
    else return "Tutor "+number+"("+tutorYears+")";
  }
  public int CompareTo(object o) {
    if (o is Student)
      return (number.CompareTo(((Student) o).number));
```

```
            else // o is Staff; Staff always rate before students
               return 1;
         }
      }

   public class Staff : IAccess, IComparable {
      string name;
      int startDate;

      public Staff(string n) {
         name = n;
         startDate = DateTime.Now.Year;
      }
      public string Name {
         get {return name;}
      }
      public int StartDate {
         get {return startDate;}
      }
      public bool Valid() {
         return true;
      }
      public override string ToString () {
         return "Staff "+name;
      }
      public int CompareTo(object o) {
         if (o is Staff)
            return (name.CompareTo(((Staff) o).name));
         // o is a Student; Staff always rate before students
         return -1;
      }
   }
}
```

Typical output would be as in Figure 9.3.

Operator overloading

In Example 9.3, we defined CompareTo methods in the Student and Staff classes to
implement the IComparable interface. It was through this interface that Array.Sort
was able to operate. We did not actually call CompareTo in the program itself. If we had
wanted to, it would have been more convenient if we could have used an operator instead.
C# allows us to overload nearly all the standard operators for new types. Note that a few
operators cannot be overloaded, including:

   the constructor keyword new
   method invocation ()
   the conditional boolean operators || and &&
   and the assignment operator = .

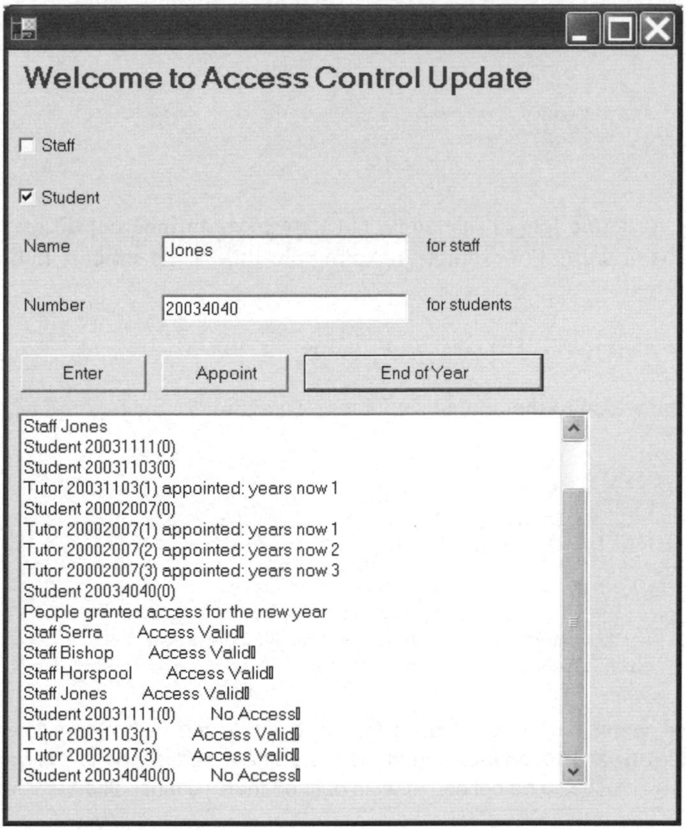

Figure 9.3 Output from the Access Control program

The objective with the `Staff` and `Student` classes is to be able to say:

```
IComparable s1, s2;    // where s1 and s2 are staff or students
// get values into s1 and s2
if (s1<s2) ...
```

and similarly for any other operators we might want to provide. The form for declaring overloaded operators in a class is below. The operators we may wish to overload can be arithmetic ones, so the result will not always be a condition, but could have any type, as shown.

Here is the example of operator overloading for the `Student` class, which uses the body from `CompareTo`:

```
public static bool operator < (Student o1, object o2) {
    if (o2 is Student)
        return ((Student) o1).number < ((Student) o2).number;
```

```
    else // o2 is Staff; Staff always rate before students
      return false;
}

public static bool operator > (Student o1, object o2) {
  return !(o1<o2);
}
```

It is tempting to define lots of operators, but they have an inherent disadvantage in that their meaning is obscure. For example, recalling our little Time struct with hours and minutes, if we defined:

```
public static Time operator + (Time t, int x) {
```

is x going to be added to the hours or minutes? To avoid confusion, it is better to stick to methods.

OPERATOR OVERLOADING

```
public static returnType operator op
             (type1 operand1, type2 operand2) {
  ... statements to determine the value required
  return theResult; // the result has type returnType
}
```

The operator *op* is overloaded for the types in the parameters, giving a return type. These types can all be the same if necessary. If < is defined then > must also be defined. If == is defined then != must also be defined.

9.3 Extensibility with inheritance

As we explained in Section 9.1, both inheritance and interfaces can be used for polymorphism and for extensibility. The title of this section should therefore not be taken to exclude interfaces, but merely to emphasize inheritance.

Inheritance is a mechanism which builds up related classes in a hierarchy. In the simplest case, each class inherits from the one above, and adds some new members, perhaps overriding some of the older ones. More complex hierarchies form trees, but these really are somewhat unusual. Most hierarchies are either a single flat set of classes, all inheriting from the same base class, or a long vertical hierarchy where one class inherits from the one above. In Chapter 10 we shall look at some of the system hierarchies that are richer than this, but here we shall keep it simple.

To be formal, though, the almost complete form for a class with inheritance and interface options is shown below.

Inheritance is a richer mechanism than interfaces for several reasons:

1. *Fields* can be inherited as well as methods.

2. *Overriding* and *hiding* are two options for members within a hierarchy.

3. *Accessibility* modifiers can play a big role in revealing and hiding different members as each new class is developed.

4. *Objects* within such a hierarchy can be assigned across types, not always successfully, depending on a type cast.

5. *Virtual* methods can be implemented in a base class or left as abstract.

This plethora of choices can be studied at a theoretical level. In practice, examples will tend to be simpler.

CLASS DEFINITION

```
modifiers-1 abstract class name : basename, interfaces {
   modifiers-1 modifiers-2 fields
   modifiers-1 modifiers-3 properties
   modifiers-1 modifiers-3 indexers
   modifiers-1 modifiers-3 methods
   modifiers-1 name : base(args) or this (args) {
      statements
   }
   modifiers-1 nested-types
}
```

where *modifiers-1* is any of
   `public    internal    private    protected`
and *modifiers-2* is any of
   `new static`
and *modifiers-3* is any of
   `override    new    virtual    abstract    static`

Other modifiers are also defined under advanced topics.

Each of the elements can appear in any order. For inheritance, the base-name given is that of the base class. In the constructor, the keyword `base` is used to refer to that class. A detailed explanation of this form follows.

Example 9.4 Extending the student class

Given the `Student` class in Example 9.3, suppose we wish to treat postgraduates a little differently. They still have student numbers and tutor years, as well as the `Appoint` and

Valid methods, but we would like to add their supervisor's name to the objects. Thus we create a new class, and inherit from Student. Everything in Student is still available, but PostGrad has more information as follows:

```
class Postgrad : Student {

  string supervisor;

  public Postgrad(int n,string s) : base (n) {
    supervisor = s;
  }
  public string Supervisor {
    get {return supervisor;}
  }
  public override string ToString() {
    return "Postgrad "+base.ToString()+" with "+supervisor;
  }
}
```

Postgrad starts off by inheriting from Student, as stated on the first line. It does not also have to mention the two interfaces (IAccess and IComparable), since it itself does not use them.

It then defines a local field for the supervisor's name, which is private to it, but further on there is a property for accessing its value in the usual way. Then the constructor does two things: it calls its *base* class (Student) to set up the number and tutorYears fields, and it copies in the additional supplied value to the supervisor field. It is good practice to let each class initialize the fields it defines. Accessing the fields directly would require them to be made more accessible, or for their properties to have set parts, which we have so far managed to avoid.

Postgrad has more fields than Student has, so it will have an enhanced ToString method. Once again, it calls the base class to provide that part of the return string which involves the fields defined there.

So, without touching Student, we have extended the program's functionality. Obviously, there will be a few changes elsewhere particularly where the objects are created. We already differentiated between Staff and Student, so it will be simple enough to add a third checkbox to lead us in a third kind of instantiation for PostGrad.

Accessibility and inheritance

Accessibility of fields and methods is important between classes in an inheritance hierarchy, and C# provides extra protection here. There are in fact five access modifiers, in increasing order:

♦   private – access within a type; default for struct and class members;

♦   internal – access within a namespace; default for non-nested types;

♦   protected – access within a class or its derived classes;

◆ `protected internal` – access within a class, its derived classes, or a name-space;

◆ `public` – accessible everywhere; the default for `enums` and interface members.

Many programmers stick to private and public accessibility only, which is what we have done so far. In other words, if a type or member is not private, it must be public. Yet public really opens up the members too much, and can cause problems with one's namespace, since all public members must have unique names. It would be good practice to use internal accessibility to expose members in a class to other classes in the same namespace, and protected internal if inheritance is at work.

For example, consider a skeleton of the `Student` class, with comments inserted about accessibility:

```
class Student : IAccess, IComparable {
    // non-nested types are default internal

  int number;
    // members are default private

  int tutorYears;
    // members are default private

  internal Student(int n) {...}
    // provides exactly the accessibility needed
    // for access within the namespace

  public bool Valid() {...}
    // IAccess interface member is default public
    // so Valid must also be public

  public override string ToString() {...}
    // ToString is public in all base classes
}
```

It may well be good practice now to start putting modifiers on everything. However, the default rules are simple and rational, and there is a case to be made for taking advantage of them.

Data in a hierarchy

How does C# handle the declaration of data in inheritance hierarchies? There are two options:

1. **Unique name**. If we choose a name which is not the same as a data member in the base class, then it will clearly be an original member in the objects created from the derived class. The declaration of `supervisor` in the `Postgrad` class is such an example.

2. **Same name**. If we choose a name that is the same as a data member in the base class, even if we change the type, we are required to declare the member in the derived class as new. The new field then *hides* the base one for the derived objects.

We would have to be careful when declaring a new field with a different type in a derived class, that the base class version is not used explicitly or even via a property, outside the class, otherwise we shall introduce type conflicts in the main program. For example, in the Student class, there is a student number stored as an int type. In the program that processes students and staff, a local copy of the number is stored as an int as well. Therefore, if we were to declare a new type of student number for postgrads as a string, say, the program would no longer compile without errors.

Virtual methods

In C# there are more options for functions than for data. Because the most commonly used ones hinge on the use of the virtual keyword, the language specification refers to the whole area as virtual functions. These are the options:

1. **Unique name**. If we choose a name which is not the same as a function member in the base class, then it will clearly be an original member in the objects created from the derived class.

2. **Overloaded**. We can declare a method more than once, as long as the parameter lists (signatures) are different, so that each can be distinguished from the other. Notice that overloading is also possible within a single class, to provide variations of a method.

3. **Overridden**. The base class can declare a function to be virtual, and then the derived class can supply a function with the identical signature, and override the base class's function. If a virtual function is overridden, then the effect is for that function to be used for all objects of the derived class. The derived class can still gain access to the overridden member by using the base keyword. If the derived class does not override a virtual function, no harm is done: the base function is still available through inheritance.

An example here is ToString. In the object superclass, it is declared as

```
public virtual string ToString();
```

and it does have a body which attempts to display an object as best it can. But every type willingly overrides it, providing a sensible output format specifically for its fields. For example, we have in the Student class

```
public override string ToString() {
  if (tutorYears == 0) return "Student "
    +number+" "+tutorYears+"years";
  else return "Tutor "++number+" "+tutorYears+"years";
}
```

4. **Overridden abstract**. Virtual functions without bodies in abstract classes, or that are specifically declared as abstract, *must* be overridden in each derived class. This mechanism forces the classes to provide whatever behaviour is needed locally, and there is no default behaviour to fall back on.

As an example, suppose we implement IAccess as a class at the top of a hierarchy, instead of as an interface. It would look like this:

```
class Access {
  public abstract bool Valid() {}
}
```

By using the keyword abstract, each subclass is forced to implement Valid.

5. **Hidden**. C# treats each function member as fresh, even if a virtual member of the same name subsequently appears in the base class (which may happen as software evolves). Later on, the derived class can be recompiled with new to make the separation explicit. Once a method is declared as new, it *hides* the virtual method above it in the class hierarchy.

Since hiding can also be done intentionally, when classes are designed, it is an equal option to overriding a virtual class. There is clearly a difference between overriding and hiding, but it really only becomes clear in hierarchies of three or more classes. We shall not be dealing with such complex programs, and the reader is referred to the *ECMA C# Language Specification*, Section 17.5.3, for an excellent example which illustrates all aspects of virtual methods.

When to use inheritance

One of the most common and oft-used examples for explaining inheritance is a system for maintaining records of data, where the data is defined in a hierarchy. The explanatory example of students and postgrads fell into this category. With such examples, it is not so easy to show the power of virtual methods. As we saw above, the derived class, Postgrad, did not override any methods of Student. Of course, we could have overridden Valid, and provided a different way of assessing whether a postgrad could get automatic access for the new year. However, as we already discussed in Section 9.2, if all we want are variations on Valid, then we should use interfaces. Postgrad can also implement IAccess.

The extensible powers of inheritance are less easy to illustrate than the polymorphic ones. What we need is to totally transform an object into a new version of itself based on the derived class. The case study that follows shows this feature well. The key feature is that the derived class overrides method(s) from the base class, thus creating different functionality in the new class, in addition to (possibly) different data.

9.4 Case study 5 – Enhancing the StarLords

Back in Chapter 3, we introduced the idea of starlord characters battling against each other using a simple attack mechanism. We now want to make two enhancements to the program. Firstly, characters should be able to enhance their powers by, say, drinking a magic potion. Secondly, the game should be played out via a GUI, i.e. we want to use Views. Meeting both requirements makes for some interesting programming.

The SuperCharacter class

In Example 3.1, we defined a struct for a starlord. We rework it as a class called `Charac-ter` like this:

```
public class Character {
   string name;
   int points;
   int strength;
   Random r = new Random ();

   public Character(string n, int s) {
      name = n;
      strength = s;
      points = s;
   }

   public string Name {
      get {return name;}
   }

   public int Points {
      get {return points;}
      set {points = value;}
   }

   public int Strength {
      get {return strength; }
      set {strength = value;}
   }

   public void Attack(Character opponent) {
      int damage = r.Next(strength/3+points/2);
      opponent.Points -= damage;
   }

   public override string ToString () {
      return name + " at " + points;
   }
}
```

We now want to build on this a class which has a more advanced `Attack` method. Suppose in determining the damage, the strength is divided by 4, but there is also a risk factor which may or may not cause additional harm. We can write the method like this

```
public override void Attack(Character opponent) {
    // was int damage = r.Next(strength/3+points/2);
    int damage = r.Next(Strength/2+Points/2)-r.Next(1)*4;
    opponent.Points -= damage;
}
```

assuming that there is a random number generator defined. To insert the method in a new class derived from `Character`, we start off with the declaration:

```
public class SuperCharacter : Character {
```

and go on to the constructor. The intention is that a `SuperCharacter` can only be created from a `Character`, so the constructor is passed the original character, and uses its values to set up the new ones via a base constructor. Then the strength is increased slightly.

```
public SuperCharacter(Character c)
                      // start with the same as before
                    : base (c.Name, c.Strength) {
    Strength += r.Next(10);  // enhance strength
}
```

To transform a character into a supercharacter, we simply say:

```
c = new SuperCharacter(c);
```

The old character in the variable c is wiped out by the new enhanced one. The type of c is now `SuperCharacter`, but it can be used interchangeably in the program wherever a `Character` was required.

There are two matters that need attention before we are complete. Firstly, the `Character` class must be updated. This is unfortunate, since one would like inheritance to be transparent to the class that already exist. This cannot be. The `Attack` method has to be declared virtual if it is to be overridden. Then there needs to be an explicit default constructor inserted with no arguments, to satisfy the default one which will exist in `SuperCharacter`.

The second point applies specifically to the logic of this program. Characters are assumed to start with points equal to their strength. Although supercharacters acquire new powers, their points remain the same. Because constructing the base class data is the first operation for a derived class, in the system as it stands, the points will be overridden. Therefore, we need to remember and reinstate them.

```
int rememberPoints = c.Points;
c = new SuperCharacter(c);
c.Points = rememberPoints;
```

Implementing multiple subviews

The form we want to develop will show the details of each of the two warring starlords, some buttons and a box to display the winner. A reasonable display would be that in Figure 9.4. The picture on the left shows Tollkey in normal dress. On the right, Lukesky has been enhanced with armour (presumably because he was losing).

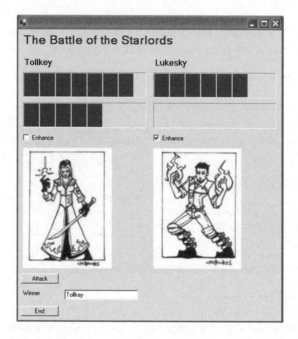

Figure 9.4 Output from the enhanced StarLord program

Setting up most of such a view is straightforward, but we notice one interesting aspect. There is a subview that is repeated across the form. It consists of five controls, all relevant to the character or super character. The Views controls would be specified as in:

```
<vertical>
  <Label Name=A Text=Tollkey Font=ArialBold12 Height=20/>
  <ProgressBar Name=Astrength/>
  <ProgressBar Name=Apoints/>
  <CheckBox Name='Aenhance' Text=Enhance/>
  <PictureBox Name=Aimage Image='starlordA.jpg'/>
</vertical>
```

Repeating the subview in the Views specification is simply a matter of cutting and pasting the lines, changing the names for the five controls:

```
<vertical>
  <Label Name=B Text=Lukesky Font=ArialBold12 Height=20/>
  <ProgressBar Name = Bstrength/>
  <ProgressBar Name = Bpoints/>
  <CheckBox Name='Benhance' Text=Enhance/>
  <PictureBox Name=Bimage Image='starlordB.jpg'/>
</vertical>
```

changing A for B, and changing the names of the characters. Now, we can show that in the program we can write methods that will deal with either subview, depending on a parameter, and we can also access and obtain the name of the character from the view so that the program does not have this level of detail imbedded in it First, consider a method to display the constantly changing data for strength and points. It is:

```
void Display(Character lord, string x) {
    f.PutValue(x+("strength"),lord.Strength);
    f.PutValue(x+("points"),lord.Points);
}
```

and we call it as in

```
Display(A, "A");
```

The `Character` parameter gives access to the values in the object for A; the string parameter is concatenated to the rest of the relevant control names and then will refer correctly to `Astrength` and `Apoints`. If we call

```
Display(B,"B");
```

then we refer to the other character.

Setting up the characters in the first place, and acquiring the names from the views string can be done like this:

```
Label lab = f["A"];
A = new Character (lab.Text, 80);
```

Notice that there was a label defined with the name of the character (say `Tollkey`). An accessible attribute of the `Label` control is `Text`. We then use this in the creation of the character object, storing it away as the field name. When the battle is over, we can retrieve the name for printing, as in:

```
f.PutText("Winner",A.Name);
```

In what follows, the `Enhance` method uses the same techniques to operate on cithcr A or B.

Using a ref parameter

This program illustrates a case of the correct use of a `ref` parameter. We already have an object in the variable A. We want to change it to another object which will be created inside the Enhance method. Thus the variable A itself, which is a reference to an object, is to be changed. The correct call is therefore

```
Enhance(ref A,"A");
```

and the method is declared correspondingly as

```
void Enhance(ref Character c, string x) {
  int rememberPoints = c.Points;
  c = new SuperCharacter(c);
  c.Points = rememberPoints;
  ProgressBar p = f[x+"strength"];
  p.ForeColor = System.Drawing.Color.Red;
  Display(c,x);
}
```

StarLord Two

Putting the program altogether, we have the following.

```
File Character.cs
```

```
using System;

/// <summary>
/// A class of StarLord characters with certain characteristics
/// and the ability to battle against other StarLords
/// </summary>

public class Character {
  string name;
  int points;
  int strength;
  Random r = new Random();

  public Character() {
    // required because of derived class
  }

  public Character(string n, int s) {
    name = n;
    strength = s;
    points = s;
  }

  public string Name {
    get {return name; }
```

```
      }

    public int Points {
      get {return points; }
      set {points = value;}
    }

    public int Strength {
      get {return strength; }
      set {strength = value;}
    }

    public virtual void Attack(Character opponent) {
      int damage = r.Next(strength/3+points/2);
      opponent.Points -= damage;
    }

    public override string ToString () {
      return name + " at " + points;
    }
  }
```

File SuperCharacter.cs

```
using System;

  /// <summary>
  /// A derived class of StarLord characters with
  /// enhanced attacking characteristics
  /// </summary>

public class SuperCharacter : Character {
  Random r = new Random();

  public SuperCharacter (Character c)
        // start with the same as before
        : base (c.Name, c.Strength) {
    // enhance strength
    Strength += r.Next(10);
  }

  // new attacking method
  // more strength (i.e. /2 not 3)
  // but more risky - there is a random +- factor
  public override void Attack (Character opponent) {
    // was int damage = r.Next(strength/3+points/2);
    int damage = r.Next(Strength/2+Points/2)-r.Next(1)*4;
    opponent.Points -= damage;
  }
}
```

File StarLordTwo.cs

```
using System;
using System.Windows.Forms;
using Views;

public class StarLordsTwo {

    /// <summary>
    /// The StarLords Program     Bishop and Horspool Sept 2002
    /// =====================
    /// Simulates a battle, and has two levels of lords
    /// Illustrates inheritance, ref parameters and
    /// extensive use of Views.
    /// </summary>

    Views.Form f;

    void SetUpForm() {
      try {
        f = new Views.Form( @"<Form>
        <vertical>
          <Label Text= 'The Battle of the Starlords'
              ForeColor=Red Font=ArialBold18/>
          <horizontal>
            <vertical>
              <Label Name=A Text=Tollkey Font=ArialBold12 Height=20/>
              <ProgressBar Name=Astrength/>
              <ProgressBar Name=Apoints/>
              <CheckBox Name='Aenhance' Text=Enhance/>
              <PictureBox Name=Aimage Image='starlordA.jpg'/>
            </vertical>
            <vertical>
              <Label Name=B Text=Lukesky Font=ArialBold12 Height=20/>
              <ProgressBar Name = Bstrength/>
              <ProgressBar Name = Bpoints/>
              <CheckBox Name = 'Benhance' Text=Enhance/>
              <PictureBox Name=Bimage Image='starlordB.jpg'/>
            </vertical>
          </horizontal>
          <space Height=5/>
          <Button Name=Attack/>
          <horizontal>
            <Label Text='Winner'/>
            <TextBox Name=Winner/>
          </horizontal>
        </vertical>
      </Form>" );
      } catch( Exception e ) {
        Console.WriteLine(
            "Exception caught, message follows:{0}", e.Message);
      }
    }
```

```
void Go() {
  SetUpForm();
  SetUpCharacters();
  DoBattle();
}

void Display(Character lord, string x) {
  // inserts into the following sub-view
  //<ProgressBar Name = xstrength Text=''/>
  //<ProgressBar Name = xpoints Text=''/>
  f.PutValue(x+("strength"),lord.Strength);
  f.PutValue(x+("points"),lord.Points);
}

Character A;
Character B;

void SetUpCharacters () {
  Label lab = f["A"];
  A = new Character(lab.Text, 80);
  lab = f["B"];
  B = new Character(lab.Text, 74);
  Display(A,"A");
  Display(B,"B");
}

void DoBattle() {
  for ( ; ; ) {
    string c = f.GetControl();
    if (c == null) break;
    if (A.Points > 0 && B.Points > 0) {
      ActionPerformed(c);
    }
    if (A.Points <= 0 || B.Points <= 0) {
      if (A.Points > B.Points)
        f.PutText("Winner",A.Name);
      else
        f.PutText("Winner",B.Name);
    }
  }
  f.CloseGUI();
}

bool AsTurn = true;

void Enhance(ref Character c, string x) {
  int rememberPoints = c.Points;
  c = new SuperCharacter(c);
  c.Points = rememberPoints;
  ProgressBar p = f[x+"strength"];
  p.ForeColor = System.Drawing.Color.Red;
  PictureBox pic = f[x+"image"];
  f.PutImage(x+"image","starlord"+x+"enhanced.jpg");
```

```
        Display(c,x);
      }

   void ActionPerformed(string c) {
     switch (c) {
       case "Attack" : {
         if (AsTurn)
           A.Attack(B);
         else
           B.Attack(A);
         AsTurn=!AsTurn;
         Display(A,"A");
         Display(B,"B");
         break;
       }
       case "Aenhance" : {
         Enhance(ref A,"A");
         break;
       }
       case "Benhance" : {
         Enhance(ref B, "B");
         break;
       }
     }
   }

   static void Main () {
     new StarLordsTwo().Go();
   }
}
```

9.5 Serialization

The last concept in this chapter relates to keeping data between runs of a program. With record keeping programs like the Access Control System in Example 9.3, such persistence is essential. Fortunately, C#, like Java and other modern languages, provides *serialization engines* for saving and restoring data. The word serialization refers to the fact that the data being sent out may be in an arbitrary graph format, connected via object references. The engine must be able to replace the references with values which can then be reinterpreted on a restore and the original structure recreated.

There are two kinds of serialization: binary and XML. The binary serialization is the default and works well with the .NET namespace. To get full text, cross platform serialization, we can use an XML formatter instead of the binary one shown below. This kind of serialization is described in the .NET documentation.

Steps to serialization

Serialization applies to any class of objects, but it is the object collection or structure that is actually serialized. The steps to serialization are:

1. Attribute the classes. For each class that will appear in a collection to be serialized, annotate it with the attribute

    ```
    [Serializable]
    ```

2. Declare that the program uses the three namespaces as follows:

    ```
    using System.IO;
    using System.Runtime.Serialization;
    using System.Runtime.Serialization.Formatters.Binary;
    ```

3. Create Save and Restore methods according to the set patterns below.

4. Call the Save and Restore methods as required.

SERIALIZATION METHOD PATTERNS

```
void Save(object o) {
   Stream databank = new FileStream("file",FileMode.Create);
   IFormatter format = new BinaryFormatter();
   format.Serialize(databank,o);
   databank.Flush();
   databank.Close();
}

object Restore () {
   Stream databank = new FileStream("file",FileMode.Open);
   IFormatter format = new BinaryFormatter();
   object o = format.Deserialize(databank);
   databank.Close();
   return o;
}
```

The Save method has a parameter o, and must also specify a filename. This name can be anything as long as it is the same as is used in the Restore method, and it is not tampered with in between a save and a restore.

The entire object o is placed on the file called "file" by Save. The same object is returned by the Restore method.

The Save and Restore methods are very short and have a set pattern, described in the form above. Then we could, for example, augment the Access Control System, to have two further actions, activated by buttons, as in:

```
case "Save" : {
  Save(register);
  f.PutText("List",count+" records saved");
  break;
}
```

```
case "Restore" : {
  register = (IAccess[]) Restore();
  count = 0;
  while (register[count]!=null)
    count++;
  f.PutText("List",count+" records restored");
  break;
}
```

Note two points about the `Restore` method: the object returned has to be downcast to the type of the array which was originally saved. Then we have to count how many used elements there are in the array. The number may not be the same as the number in the current value of count, if local changes were made, and then we wanted to discard them by restoring the saved version of the array. Serialization is taken up in several of the exercises that follow.

Concepts in Chapter 9

The following concepts were introduced or developed in this chapter:

polymorphism	extensibility
encapsulation	interfaces
inheritance	abstract classes
abstract methods	derived classes
base classes	comparators
class conversions	overriding
hiding	accessibility
hierarchy	virtual methods
overloading	serialization

Keywords and library (API) members introduced or re-examined in this chapter were:

`IComparable`	`CompareTo`
`IComparer`	`is`
`as`	`casting`
`abstract`	`internal`
`private`	`protected`
`IAccess`	`virtual`

```
override                    new
ref                         [Serializable]
BinaryFormatter             IFormatter
Serialize                   DeSerialize
```

Forms covered in this chapter were:

IComparable interface   IComparer interface

interface definition   type conversions and checks

operator overloading   class definition

serialization method patterns

Quiz

Q9.1 For polymorphism, inheritance would be preferred over interfaces when

 (a) The types will have fields and methods

 (b) There is a vertical relationship between the types

 (c) Neither (a) nor (b): the two options are equally applicable

 (d) Both (a) and (b)

Q9.2 The difference between the interfaces IComparable and IComparer is

 (a) IComparable defines a method to be called by Sort directly; IComparer defines a method to be passed to Sort as a parameter and called indirectly

 (b) as in (a), but with the two interfaces interchanged

 (c) IComparable has a default Compare method, but in IComparer it always has to be defined

 (d) nothing – they are two names for the same interface

Q9.3 In Example 9.1, c1 is

 (a) a class   (b) an object

 (c) an interface   (d) a method

Q9.4   In Example 9.2, what would be the output from the following?

```
I[] A = new I[10];
A[0] = new C1(23);
A[1] = new C2("today");
Poly(A[0], A[1]);
```

where `Poly` is defined in Example 9.1.

(a)   `I am good old C1 and you are happy C2`

(b)   `I am good old A[0] aged 23 you are happy A[1] today`

(c)   `I am good old C1 aged 23 you are happy C2 today`

(d)   none of the above

Q9.5   If `IAnything` is an interface, and `Type1` and `Type2` are structs which implement the interface, which statement about the following assignment sequence is correct?

```
IAnything var1;
Type1 var2 = new Type1();
var1 = var2;              // 1
var2 = var1;              // 2
var2 = (Type1) var1;     // 3
```

(a)   The sequence will always execute correctly

(b)   1 will execute correctly; 2 and 3 might fail at runtime

(c)   1 will fail at runtime because var1 has not been instantiated yet; 2 and 3 will execute correctly

(d)   1 will execute correctly; 2 will not compile; 3 might fail at runtime

Q9.6   If `IAnything` is an interface specifying a method `Q`, then a class `C` in the same namespace as `Q` that implements `IAnything` must apply the following accessibility to its version of `Q`

(a)   `internal`

(b)   `private`

(c)   `public`

(d)   `protected internal`

Q9.7   Overloading of methods means that

(a)   They have the same names

(b)   They have the same names but are different classes in a hierarchy

(c)   They have the same names and the same parameter lists

(d)   They have the same names and different parameter lists

Q9.8 If a method is declared as virtual, then any derived class

(a) *may* provide an alternative (overridden) version of it with exactly the same parameters

(b) *must* provide an alternative (overridden) version of it with exactly the same parameters

(c) *may* provide an alternative (overridden) version of it with the same or different parameters

(d) *must* provide an alternative (overridden) version of it with the same or different parameters

Q9.9 A program calls the Save and Restore serialization methods described in Section 9.5 as follows:

```
DateTime[] holidays = new holidays[20];
Save(holidays);
holidays = Restore();
```

There is a compilation error. Why?

(a) DateTime does not have the attribute [Serializable]

(b) The result of Restore needs to be downcast to DateTime[]

(c) The filename has not been specified

(d) holidays does not have any values in it yet.

Q9.10 If B which has a constructor with two fields initialized in its constructor and C derives from this class and has one additional field cField of its own, then which of these C constructors would instantiate a C variable and initialize all three fields?

(a)
```
C(int i, int j, int k) : base(i, j) {
   cField = k;
}
```

(b)
```
C(int i, int j, int k) {
   B(i, j);
   cField = k;
}
```

(c)
```
C(int i, int j, int k) {
   base(i, j)
   cField = k;
}
```

(d)
```
C(int i, int j, int k) {
   super(i, j)
   cField = k;
}
```

Exercises

9.1   **Dates for holidays.** To exercise the `IComparable` interface, redo Example 8.4 as follows. Change the type of the dates from `string` to `Date`, where `Date` is a class that you define and implement. `Date` holds the day and month for a holiday as an `int` and `string`. In order for the `SortedList` to operate properly, it needs to have the `CompareTo` method of `IComparable` implemented. Include it in your implementation of `Date` and check that the program works as before.

9.2   **Serializing pets.** Add serialization to the Pets program of Example 8.1. Use a simple Views interface to enter and display the data and activate save and restore.

9.3   **Sorting pets.** We want to sort the pets in Example 8.1 according to any of the three fields that are stored – name, type and age. Let the Pet class implement `IComparer` and provide three suitable `Compare` methods. Expand on Exercise 9.2 by providing radio buttons on the Views form for selecting the sorting criteria. Then provide a method which copies each element of the list into an array or other collection on which a built-in Sort method can be called.

9.4   **Vaccinated pets.** For newer pets, we have information as to whether they have been vaccinated or not. Change the program so that it uses such a collection from the start, removing the handmade list structure of the example. Then add a new class which inherits from Pets and includes vaccination information. Show that the collection can operate successfully with the two kinds of pets.

9.5   **Contractors.** The university discussed in Example 9.3 employs contractors who come in to maintain the building. Devise a suitable access control policy for contractors and incorporate it into a class which implements the `IAccess` interface. Include contractors on the GUI and check that everything still works correctly.

9.6   **Serializing access data.** Provide serialization for the access register in Example 9.3.

CHAPTER 10

Graphics and networking

The objective of this chapter is to point the reader towards some really interesting and powerful APIs in C#. The first part covers graphics, as well as animation using threads, and the presentation of images. Integrating graphics with the Views system is also shown. Then we move onto networking, giving an introduction to web requests and connecting programs on different computers via sockets.

10.1 Graphics interfaces

Computers really come into their own with the generation of graphical images on the screen. We can identify three aspects of computer graphics: the *specification* in some language of the graphical shapes and images that need to be drawn; the actual drawing of graphics in hardware, known as *rendering*; and the generation of constantly moving graphics, known as *animation*. The sophistication of modern day computer graphics is seen in films, which need very highly specialized graphics languages, hardware and animation techniques. At the other end of the scale, quite pleasing effects can be produced with a common set of drawing methods, ordinary computer hardware and a technique known as *multi-threading*.

We start this chapter by considering the fundamental structures for including graphics in a C# program, and merely list some of the options that are available. The idea is to know how to call graphics methods correctly: once this concept has been grasped, a huge range of drawing tools is available from within a program, but we do not need to cover each one in detail. There is a definite analogy to the drawing modules that one encounters in word processing packages such as Microsoft Word. A range of tools for selecting shapes, colours, sizes, fonts, and so on is available, and the user quickly becomes familiar with how to put these together and to understand how they interact to draw complex figures.

We emphasize that graphics drawing as discussed in this chapter is different from graphical user interfaces as discussed in Chapter 5 with the Views system. The elements of a GUI are controls – buttons, text boxes and labels – most of which are interactive; the elements of a graphical drawing are shapes – circles, rectangles, dots – which are not interactive at all, unless they are overlaid on a GUI.

Graphics interfaces

In most general purpose languages, there will exist a namespace to support drawing and which allows a programmer to create graphics, write text, and manipulate graphical images as objects. On the Windows platform, C# uses a graphics design interface called GDI+. We can use GDI+ to render graphical images on Windows Forms and controls. In this chapter, we introduce the fundamentals of GDI+ programming. Although not intended to be a comprehensive reference, this section includes information on graphics, pen, brush, font and colour types, and explains how to perform tasks such as drawing shapes, drawing text, or displaying images. For more information, see the GDI+ Software Development Kit.

When C# runs on platforms with other operating systems such as Linux and Mac OSX, then GDI+ might be available, but it is not guaranteed. Alternative graphics interfaces would have to be employed, one of the popular ones being Tcl/TK. Given that GDI+ does have very wide coverage, and does exemplify the principles of graphics programming well, we will cover only that package here.

10.2 Simple graphics features

Graphics, like GUIs, are displayed on windows on a computer screen. At the programming level, we know from Chapter 5 that GUIs are created on forms, and the relevant class is `System.Windows.Forms.Form`. To achieve the drawing of graphics on a form, we go through several steps. First, we have the program inherit from the `Form` class. Then in the main program we have a switch in style. Instead of creating a program object using its constructor and calling a method such as `Go`, we use a special C# mechanism to start the program and also display its associated form. This is:

```
Application.Run(new ProgramName);
```

The program name is the constructor name, so control is passed to the constructor at this point. The typical statements that follow adjust the size and title of the form and then it is over to the system to display the contents of the form in a new window. This process is summed up in the first part of the description that follows.

DRAWING PROGRAM PATTERN

```
using System;
using System.Drawing;
using System.Windows.Forms;

class classname : Form {

  classname() {
    this.Width = 450;
    this.Height = 450;
    this.Text = "classname or other heading";
  }

  protected override void OnPaint(PaintEventArgs e) {
    Graphics g = e.Graphics;
    drawing statements based on g
  }

  static void Main() {
    Application.Run(new classname());
  }
}
```

`Application.Run` activates the program and creates its form. The statements in the constructor adjust attributes of the form. Once the constructor is complete, the form is displayed. At this point, the `OnPaint` method is called as one of the events of that form. The appropriate `Graphics` object g is obtained and drawing can commence on it.

As this description explains,[1] an event on the form is caused, which causes the `OnPaint` method to be called by the system. (A word about events below.) From the parameter supplied to `OnPaint`, the program obtains an object of the `Graphics` class. All drawing in

---

1. When it is necessary to avoid confusion between the two meanings of the word *form* (i.e. the syntax box and the Windows abstraction) we replace the first use with the word *description* in this chapter.

the `OnPaint` method will refer to that graphics object. For example, a method to draw a circle is:

```
g.FillEllipse(brush, x, y, 20, 20);
```

The last four parameters indicate where the circle should start in the *x* and *y* direction of the screen, and the size of the circle in pixels. (For information on screen coordinates and pixels consult Section 5.2.) If the two sizes differ, then the shape will not be a circle, but will be an ellipse, as indicated by its name.

The first parameter is necessary in GDI+ although not in many other graphics interfaces. It specifies the kind and colour of the 'paintbrush' that will be used to draw the shape. A simple declaration for a brush would be

```
SolidBrush brush = new SolidBrush(Color.Black);
```

There are other brushes such as `HatchedBrush`, and they all inherit from the `Brush` class, so their objects are all valid as parameters to `FillEllipse`.

Example 10.1 Drawing spots

Consider a very simple example which shows drawing 100 spots on a form. The program is below.

File Spotty.cs

```
using System;
using System.Drawing;
using System.Threading;
using System.Windows.Forms;

public class Spotty : Form {

  ///<summary>
  /// The Spotty Program            Bishop and Horspool    Feb 2003
  /// =====================
  /// Draws spots of different colours.
  /// Illustrates using simple Drawing classes
  ///</summary>

  Spotty() {
    // Adjust the graphics form
    this.Width = 450;
    this.Height = 450;
    this.Text = "Spotty";
  }
```

```
protected override void OnPaint(PaintEventArgs e) {
    Graphics g = e.Graphics;

    // Variables related to the spots and their position
    Random r = new Random();
    SolidBrush brush = new SolidBrush(Color.Red);

    for (int s=0; s<100; s++) {
        // Calculate a new place for a spot
        int x = r.Next(380);
        int y = r.Next(380);
        // Draw the spot
        g.FillEllipse(brush, x, y, 20, 20);
        Thread.Sleep(100);
    }
}

static void Main() {
    Application.Run(new Spotty());
}

}
```

The output of this program is shown in Figure 10.1.

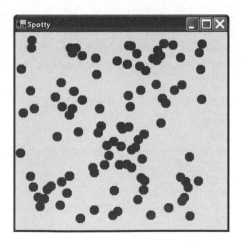

Figure 10.1 Output from the spotty program

Events in graphics

An *event* is a member that enables an object or class to provide notifications. These notifications take the form of calling designated methods, which are known as *handlers*. In the case of a normal program, an event that occurs when a form has to be displayed is that the supplied overridden `OnPaint` method is called. So if we provide all our drawing code in an `OnPaint` method, everything will be displayed. A problem, though, is that a handler runs to completion, and blocks out other events. While the spots are drawing in the above example, we could decide to stop the process and click the close box on the menu bar of the form. The program will not be ready to receive this new event, and may not respond correctly later. However, if we wait till after all the spots are drawn, the window can be closed properly.

Notice that minimizing the window is also an event. If we subsequently maximize the window again, what happens? The spots start drawing from scratch again. This is because the `OnPaint` method is called by the event of maximizing, and drawing 100 spots is what `OnPaint` does.

There is an alternative way of handling events for graphics. Instead of relying on the calling of the default method `OnPaint`, we can specify our own handler with our own name. Suppose this is

```
public void SpottyPaint(Object source, PaintEventArgs e) {
```

The signature of the method must include the additional parameter for a source of the event, but we usually do not need to consult it. Then in the constructor, we register our handler with the required event as follows:

```
this.Paint += new PaintEventHandler(SpottyPaint);
```

Here we are saying that our method, `SpottyPaint`, is going to be supplied as a new handler for paint type events and be connected up (the syntax is rather nice with +=) to the `Paint` event associated with the program (designated by `this`).

The form below sums up the two alternatives for handling paint events.

EVENTS AND HANDLERS FOR GRAPHICS

Option 1: Automatic
Handler signature
```
protected override void OnPaint(PaintEventArgs e) {
```

Option 2: Programmed
In the constructor:
```
this.Paint += new PaintEventHandler(handler);
```
Handler signature:
```
public void handler(Object source, PaintEventArgs e)
```

`OnPaint` is the default method called when a form is to be displayed. It can be substituted by a method with any other name (as in Option 2). This method is registered with the `Paint` event in the constructor.

The reader is encouraged to alter the Spotty program to use Option 2.

Colour

All graphics interfaces provide for colour through a `Color` class which defines various constants with appropriate names. The standard colours are all there, and the remainder of the spectrum is filled in with somewhat curious names, some examples of which are:

```
Color myColor;
myColor = Color.Red;
myColor = Color.Aquamarine;
myColor = Color.LightGoldenrodYellow;
myColor = Color.PapayaWhip;
myColor = Color.Tomato;
```

The `Color` object thus created can be used with brush and pen objects which in turn are used to paint shapes and draw lines.

Shapes, lines and points

There is a fairly standard set of shapes provided by most graphical interfaces. The methods to draw them come in two kinds: the draw methods and the fill methods. Typical shapes are ellipses, rectangles, pies and polygons. Precise details of the parameters required for each are available in the C# API documentation.

Lines (both straight and curved) can also be drawn. A straight line needs `DrawLine` which has two forms, either with x and y coordinates, or using a point structure, which stores the coordinates. Examples of the two methods are:

```
g.DrawLine(myPen, 0, 10, 300, 600);
g.DrawLine(myPen, pointA, pointB);
```

Brushes and pens

In C#, draw methods for shapes need a pen object, and fill methods need a brush object. These objects include information about the colour, thickness of the lines, and so on. Pens are also used when drawing lines. A pen can be created just with a colour, or from the specification of a brush, as in:

```
Brush myBrush = new Brush(Color.Black);
Pen myPen = new Pen(Color.Black);
Pen myFancyPen = new Pen(myBrush);
```

Fonts and text

On a form, text has to be written using the `DrawString` method, which would be called as in:

```
g.DrawString(s, myFont, myBrush, x, y);
```

`DrawString` has three obvious parameters – the position in terms of x and y coordinates and the string to be written – but it also has compulsory parameters for a brush and a font.

The Font class basically allows a font, its size and its style to be selected, as in this example:

```
Font myFont = new Font("Arial", 24, FontStyle.Bold);
```

Summary

This has been a very quick look at the structure of a Graphics class, together with simple event handling. Full details should be available in the API documentation help files. The exercises at the end of the chapter also give some practice in using graphics.

10.3 Images

Any graphics package will make provision for images. In GDI+, image objects can receive data from a file, as in

```
Image pic = Image.FromFile("Jacarandas.jpg");
```

From here, the simplest way to display the image is to rely on the OnPaint method, and to call the DrawImage method on the supplied Graphics object. This would give:

```
protected override void OnPaint(PaintEventArgs e) {
   e.Graphics.DrawImage(pic,30,30);
}
```

DrawImage displays the image object at the position specified by the coordinates for its top left corner. A program displaying an image in this way was shown in Example 2.4. The syntax and semantics for displaying images is:

IMAGE DISPLAYING

```
Image name = Image.FromFile("filename");

protected override void OnPaint(PaintEventArgs e) {
   e.Graphics.DrawImage(name, x, y);
}
```

The image in the specified file is assigned to a new image object. When the form is displayed, the image is drawn. The image will be displayed in the form with its original size, which may mean that some of it may be cut off on the right and bottom. The window containing the form can of course be stretched. Alternatively, the size attributes of the form can be set correctly in the program.

Images in controls

We introduced the concept of a control in Chapter 5 when we discussed the Views.Form class. A control is drawn on a form, and images can be drawn in controls. This means that we can have more than just the image in the window: there could be buttons, lists and labels as well.

The most appropriate control to hold an image is a picture box, because it has built-in facilities for setting the size of the control according to the image. Using a picture box, we can bring the image into the program, and arrange for it to be displayed full size with:

```
PictureBox picture = new PictureBox();
picture.Image = Image.FromFile("Jacarandas.jpg");
picture.SizeMode = PictureBoxSizeMode.AutoSize;
```

To display the picture box, we must in addition add it to the form, as in:

```
this.Controls.Add(picture):
```

These mechanisms are summarized in the form below. A clear advantage of this method of displaying images is the fact that we do not need to ascertain or adjust the size: this can be done automatically. We can, of course, override the size attribute of the picture box, thereby cropping off some of the image or having a border on the right and bottom. The next example shows images combined with drawing

---

IMAGE DISPLAYING IN A CONTROL

```
PictureBox picture = new PictureBox();
picture.Image = Image.FromFile("filename");
picture.SizeMode = PictureBoxSizeMode.AutoSize;
picture.Location = new Point(x, y);

this.Controls.Add(name);
```

The PictureBox object is created and the image from the file assigned to it. Setting the size mode to AutoSize causes the picture box toY3H8cde acquire the size of the image. Other options for SizeMode can be found in the API. The position in the form can also be specified with the Location attribute.

The picture box is added to the program's form. When the form is displayed (e.g. after the constructor is complete), the picture box appears with the image in it.

Example 10.2 Identifying part of an image

Suppose we have an image, and wish to mark a certain part of it with a square. We can always draw in a form, even if there is an image underneath, but in this case, we would like the drawing to be relative to the image itself. The way we do this is to attach the paint handler to the picture box control, rather than to the form. The program follows.

File FetchImageWithBox.cs

```
using System;
using System.Drawing;
using System.Windows.Forms;
using System.Drawing.Imaging;

class FetchImagewithBox : Form {

  ///<summary>
  /// Drawing on an image with a box     Bishop and Horspool March 2003
  /// ===============================
  /// Allows a fixed box to be drawn on an image in a picture box
  /// Shows the paint event handling
  ///</summary>

  public FetchImagewithBox() {
    this.Width=1000;
    this.Height=800;
    this.Text="Fetch Image with Box";

    // Get the image and assign it to a PictureBox
    PictureBox picture = new PictureBox();
    picture.Image = Image.FromFile("Jacarandas.jpg");
    picture.SizeMode = PictureBoxSizeMode.AutoSize;
    picture.Location = new Point(50,50);

    // Add the picture to the controls for this program (object)
    this.Controls.Add(picture);

    // Link the specified method up to the picture's Paint event
    picture.Paint += new PaintEventHandler(FetchImagePaint);
  }

  // When the form associated with program appears, its controls are
  // drawn, including picture, and picture's designated paint event
  // is called
  void FetchImagePaint (Object source, PaintEventArgs e) {
    Graphics g = e.Graphics;
    Pen pen = new Pen(new SolidBrush(Color.Black),10);
    g.DrawRectangle(pen,150,200,100,100);
  }

  static void Main() {
    Application.Run(new FetchImagewithBox());
  }
}
```

Setting up the picture box with the image follows the method above. Then connecting the handler is done as before with:

```
picture.Paint += new PaintEventHandler(FetchImagePaint);
```

The output from the program is shown in Figure 10.2.

Figure 10.2 Output showing drawing on an image

Summary

The discussion in this section focused on the essential mechanisms for drawing images. The GDI+ toolbox provides many more facilities for manipulating the images, and for setting their attributes. All of these can be found in the API descriptions.

10.4 Animation with threads

This section looks at simple animation of graphics. In so doing, it introduces a fundamental concept in programming, the thread. *Threads* are objects which are recognized by the underlying operating system to run as independent units, seemingly simultaneously. They cannot actually run simultaneously on a standard computer, because there is only one processor for all of them to run on. What the system arranges is that each thread gets a slice of time in turn, and the *time-slicing* is done so fast that it seems as if they are all running together. Threads are not confined to being used for animating graphics, and Section 10.5 shows additional uses. However, detailed discussion of threads is left to later computer science courses.

The classes Thread and ThreadStart

Threads are objects but they have a special method connected to them which is designated as the one which will run the thread. By their very nature, threads are intended to run for some time, like mini-programs. They therefore stop in one of two ways:

◆   by reaching a natural end to their computation; or

◆   by some action from outside, like the window closing, or some button being pressed.

To handle the second case, the special run method will be couched in terms of a `while(true)` loop.

There is no set name (such as `Run`) for this method: we can actually choose any name. In order to register the method with the thread maintenance software, we link it up to a delegate of type `ThreadStart`. A *delegate* is an object which accepts registrations of methods and then enables them to be called via the delegate's name.

To create and start a thread, the form is:

```
THREAD CREATION AND START

using System.Threading;

Thread t = new Thread (
    new ThreadStart(object.RunMethodName)).Start;

public void RunMethodName() {
  some loop
    statements
    possibly containing calls to Thread.Sleep(n)
}
```

> The object is either the current one (in which case write `this`) or some other object in which the method is declared. The object's *run* method is registered with a `ThreadStart` delegate. The delegate is passed to the `Thread` class so that the thread class has a standard way of calling run methods. When `Start` is called on the thread, the method linked to the `ThreadStart` delegate of `t` is executed.
>
> *Run* methods often contain an endless loop. If the static method `Thread.Sleep` is called, the thread is put into a waiting state until the number of milliseconds given is over. Then it continues.

The thread does not need to have a name if it is not going to be referenced again, and this case is quite common. The next example illustrates a very simple use of threads before we get onto animation.

Example 10.3 Mixed up numbers

In this example, we show how we can have two threads doing virtually the same thing, but each time we run them, we get different effects, because the threads operate independently. The threads each have a run method which prints 10 numbers. This is the program:

File MixedNumbers.cs

```
using System;
using System.Threading;

class MixedNumbers {

  ///<summary>
  /// The Mixed Up Numbers Program   Bishop and Horspool   March 2003
  /// =============================
  /// Prints 20 numbers through two threads.
  /// Illustrates how threads run independently.
  ///</summary>

  Thread numberThread;

  void Go() {
    new Thread(new ThreadStart(this.LowNums)).Start();
    new Thread(new ThreadStart(this.HighNums)).Start();
  }

  static Random r = new Random();

  void LowNums() {
    for (int i=0; i<10; i++) {
      Console.WriteLine(i + "  ");
      Thread.Sleep(r.Next(100));
    }
  }

  void HighNums() {
    for (int i=1000; i<1010; i++) {
      Console.WriteLine(i + "  ");
      Thread.Sleep(r.Next(100));
    }
  }

  static void Main() {
    new MixedNumbers().Go();
  }
}
```

The two run methods are named LowNums and HighNums. Each is connected to a delegate in a separate thread. Both threads start up, and the first time we run we get the output shown in the Run 1 column of Table 10.1. However, if we run the program again, we might get the output shown in the Run 2 column, which is very interesting, because it shows that the high numbers thread started printing firs.t, even though it starts second in the program.

Run 1	Run 2
0	1000
1000	0
1	1001
1001	1002
2	1
3	2
4	1003
1002	3
1003	4
5	1004
6	1005
7	5
1004	1006
8	6
9	1007
1005	7
1006	1008
1007	8
1008	1009
1009	9

Table 10.1 Output from MixedNumbers program

Animation threads

The essence of a thread at this simple level, therefore, is a method which is linked to a ThreadStart delegate. If we want to perform animation, we work on the basis of drawing a picture, then repeatedly redrawing it very quickly with slight changes, so that it looks like it is moving. We know how to effect the drawing part through paint event handlers. To make this process repeat, we need to put it in a loop. Now we have two steps:

◆ waiting a bit, and
◆ forcing the picture to repaint.

The first is done by a call to Thread.Sleep. The second is handled by setting the Invalidate attribute on the control in the form in which the graphics is being drawn. This process is summed up in the form below.

The subsequent example uses a picture box as the control in which to draw. A picture box is fairly typically associated with drawings because of its resizing capabilities.

```
THREADS FOR ANIMATION

new Thread(new ThreadStart(this.ThreadRunMethod)).Start();

void ThreadRunMethod() {
  while (!ending condition) {
    control.Invalidate();
    Thread.Sleep(n);
  }
}
```

The thread is given the run method to start up. The method repeatedly
invalidates the contents of the specified control, so that it has to be redrawn.

Example 10.4 The ticking clock

We would like to show a clock with three hands (hours, minutes, seconds) that move. This
example is fairly well known as one that illustrates one thread. The emphasis in the way
we present it here is on the structure of the thread's needs versus those of the paint handlers. The connection, as mentioned above, is in the `Invalidate` attribute, which repeatedly triggers the paint handler and causes the hands of the clock to be redrawn. Each time
this happens, of course, we move the number of seconds on. The program is below.

File WorldTime.cs

```
using System;
using System.Windows.Forms;
using System.Threading;
using System.Drawing;

class WorldTime : Form {

  ///<summary>
  /// The Clock Program          Bishop and Horspool    March 2003
  /// ==================
  /// Draws a clock with moving hands
  /// Illustrates a thread for repeated drawing.
  ///</summary>

  PictureBox picture;
  Thread clockThread;

  WorldTime() {
    // Set up a picture box
    picture = new PictureBox();
    picture.Size = new Size(250,250);
    this.Text = "Clock";
```

```
          // add the picture to the form
          this.Controls.Add(picture);

          // add the event
          picture.Paint += new PaintEventHandler(new Clock().ClockPaint);

          // create and start a thread to control the clock
          clockThread = new Thread(new ThreadStart(this.TickClock));
          clockThread.Start();
      }

      bool ended = false;

      void TickClock() {
        while (!ended) {
          picture.Invalidate();
          Thread.Sleep(10);
        }
      }
  }

public class Clock {
    int seconds = 0;
    SolidBrush bluebrush, whitebrush;
    Pen blackpen;
    int start = 100;

    public Clock() {
      blackpen = new Pen(Color.Black);
      bluebrush = new SolidBrush(Color.Blue);
      whitebrush = new SolidBrush(Color.LightGray);
    }

    // The handler redraws the whole clock
    public void ClockPaint(Object source, PaintEventArgs e) {
        Graphics g = e.Graphics;
        g.DrawEllipse(blackpen,start/2,start/2,100,100);
        g.FillEllipse(whitebrush,start/2,start/2,100,100);
        g.FillEllipse(bluebrush,start,start,5,5);

        Hands(g);
        seconds++;
    }

    void Hands(Graphics g) {
        double hourAngle = 2*Math.PI*(seconds - 3*60*60)/(12*60*60);
        double minuteAngle = 2*Math.PI*(seconds - 15*60)/(60*60);
        double secondAngle = 2*Math.PI*(seconds - 15)/60;
        g.DrawLine(blackpen, start, start,
            start + (int)(30*Math.Cos(hourAngle)),
            start + (int)(30*Math.Sin(hourAngle))+5);
        g.DrawLine(blackpen,start, start,
            start + (int)(40*Math.Cos(minuteAngle)),
            start + (int)(40*Math.Sin(minuteAngle)));
```

```
        g.DrawLine(blackpen,start, start,
            start + (int)(45*Math.Cos(secondAngle)),
            start + (int)(45*Math.Sin(secondAngle)));
    }
  }

  static void Main() {
    Application.Run(new WorldTime());
  }
}
```

The output, taken at an instant in time, is shown in Figure 10.3..

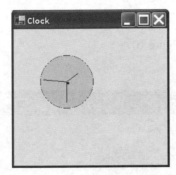

Figure 10.3 The clock output

The first part of the program joins parts of what we did in Section 10.2 on drawing with Section 10.3 on images. In other words, we use a paint handler in a picture box, as in

```
picture.Paint += new PaintEventHandler(new Clock().ClockPaint);
```

Previously, the event to which we added the handler was `this.Paint`, i.e. that of the whole form. The implication of the above handler assignment is that if there were other controls or drawing or writing on the form, they would not be affected by the continuous repainting just of the picture box.

The clock drawing itself works with brushes and pens, ellipses and lines. The lines are drawn based on angles from the main diameter of the clock, using the coordinates at (*r cos a, r sin a*). The mathematics can be studied by those who are interested.

Considering an extension of clock, suppose we would like also to print the time. We can add another control in the constructor as follows:

```
// add a textbox
time = new TextBox();
time.Location = new Point(50,220);
time.BackColor = Color.Pink;
time.TextAlign = HorizontalAlignment.Center;
this.Controls.Add(time);
```

Then in the clock object where the other drawing is done, we can access the time control and alter its value, as in:

```
time.Text = (seconds/3600).ToString() + ":" +
            (seconds/60).ToString() + ":" + (seconds%60).ToString();
```

The only difference between `time` and `picture`, is that `time` will have to be declared as static because it is accessed from within the nested class `Clock`. The picture could have been declared static too, but it is not referred to directly from within the clock: only the graphic associated with it is. To emphasize that we can have a variety of controls, we also include a label at the top of the form with

```
Label title = new Label();
title.Text = "Ticking clock";
```

The new output is given in Figure 10.4.

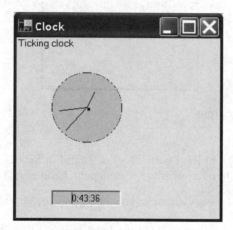

Figure 10.4 A clock with written time

Closing a threaded program

A program like `WorldTime` has two threads: the main program, and the one running the clock. If we click the close box of the window with the clock in it, the window will close, but the clock thread keeps running, as does the main program, and the console window will remain open.

To get both windows to close, we first catch the event of disposing the window, and then close down any 'child' threads – in this case the clock. The form for accepting a dispose event and requesting another thread to close appears below.

This sequence of statements can be inserted into a program such as `WorldTime`.

```
THREAD CLOSE
bool ended = false;

protected override void Dispose(bool disposing) {
   ended = true;
   Console.WriteLine("Wait while we shut down ... ");
   childthread.Join();
   base.Dispose(disposing);
   Application.Exit();
}
```

Dispose is called when the close box of the window is clicked. The ended variable is checked in the loop of the child thread. After the call to Join, ended will be true and the child thread will terminate naturally. Then we dispose the window and exit the program.

Arrays of threads

As with any objects, we can have arrays of threads. These are particularly convenient when we have an object that we wish to have running in several incarnations with slightly different properties.

Example 10.5 Many spots

Suppose we want to display spots of three different sizes and colours at the same time. Example 10.1 is a good beginning, but it relies on a single OnPaint method. What we need is to use a three-step process:

1. Define a class for the objects to be drawn, and instantiate as many objects as needed with their different characteristics.

2. Set up an array of threads and start them all running.

3. In the Dispose method, have a loop which runs over the thread array to join each of the threads back to the main thread once it has successfully ended.

In this program, we do not rely on events. Rather, each thread calls a local Draw method which fetches the graphics reference from the form (stored during instantiation of the object) and draws on it. In this way, all the threads draw in the same window. The program is as follows:

File SpottyThreads.cs

```
using System;
using System.Drawing;
using System.Threading;
```

```
using System.Windows.Forms;

public class SpottyThreads : Form {

  ///<summary>
  /// The Spotty Program with threads   Bishop and Horspool  Feb 2003
  /// ================================
  /// Draws spots of different colours.
  /// Illustrates arrays of simple threads.
  ///</summary>

  static Random r;

  SpottyThreads() {
    //Set up attributes of the graphics form
    this.Width = 450; this.Height = 450;
    this.Text = "Spotty Threads";
    r = new Random();

    // creates three spots objects
    Spots one = new Spots(this, Color.Red,100,20);
    Spots two = new Spots(this, Color.Blue,1000,100);
    Spots three = new Spots(this, Color.Green,10000,200);

    // registers them to threads and starts the threads
    (thread[0] = new Thread(new ThreadStart(one.Run))).Start();
    (thread[1] = new Thread(new ThreadStart(two.Run))).Start();
    (thread[2] = new Thread(new ThreadStart(three.Run))).Start();
  }

  Thread [] thread = new Thread[3]; // Array to hold the threads.
  static bool ended = false;

  protected override void Dispose(bool disposing) {
    ended = true;
    Console.WriteLine("Please wait while we shut down ...");
    for (int i = 0; i < 3; i ++ )
      // Pause running this thread until the other threads terminate
      thread[i].Join();
    base.Dispose(disposing);
  }

  class Spots {
    Form f;
    Color colour;
    int speed;
    int size;
    SolidBrush brush;
    Graphics g;

    public Spots(Form f, Color c, int s, int z) {
      this.f = f;
      g = f.CreateGraphics();
```

```
      colour = c;
      speed = s;
      size = z;
      // Create a brush of the right colour
      brush = new SolidBrush(colour);
    }

    public void Run() {
      while (!ended) {
        Draw();
        Thread.Sleep(speed); // millisecs
      }
    }

    public void Draw() {
      // Calculate a new place for a spot
      int x = r.Next(380); int y = r.Next(380);
      // Fill ellipse on screen.
      g.FillEllipse(brush, x, y, size, size);
    }
  }

  static void Main() {
    Application.Run(new SpottyThreads());
  }
}
```

A typical run of this program is shown in Figure 10.5.

Figure 10.5 Multiple spots

Graphics integrated with Views

As we illustrated in the extension to Example 10.4, animation can carry on while other
controls remain still. The ticking clock program was fairly simple, but it used Windows

Forms controls directly, and doing so eventually becomes verbose and difficult to manage. In particular, we do not cover in this book how to get input from a control. It would therefore be convenient if we could revert to the Views world and include graphics and images there.

In fact, we can do exactly that. In Section 5.7, we discussed how it was possible to access the controls kept by Views directly. Whereas in Example 10.4 we would connect up the picture control as follows:

```
picture.Paint += new PaintEventHandler(new Clock().ClockPaint);
```

in Views, we would use:

```
f["pic"].c.Paint += new PaintEventHandler(new Clock().ClockPaint);
```

Here f is the Views form, which can be indexed by a defined Views control to produce an entry in a table of information about such controls. One of the fields of the entry, c, is the reference to the control itself. From here, we link into the Paint event as before. More or less everything else can stay the same.

In addition to placing controls via the easy manner that Views provides, we can also interact with the controls. It would be interesting to have buttons that would suspend and resume a thread (for example, the clock thread). Suspend and Resume are methods of the Thread class, and we can indeed call them on demand. They are illustrated in the next example.

Example 10.6 The stopwatch with Views

In this example, we make two adaptations of the ticking clock in Example 10.4. Firstly, the user interface is presented in Views, and secondly, there are additional reactive buttons to pause, resume and stop the clock. For that reason, the display resembles more a stopwatch than a clock. Reacting to the buttons follows the usual Views patterns. The program omits the Clock class, which is exactly the same as that in Example 10.4. One additional change is that the main program structure reverts to calling the Go method, since Application.Run is called within Views itself.

File StopWatchWithViews.cs

```
using System;
using System.Drawing;
using System.Drawing.Imaging;
using System.Windows.Forms;
using System.Threading;
using Views;

public class StopWatchwithViews {
```

```
///<summary>
/// The Stop Watch with Views    Bishop and Horspool    March 2003
/// =========================
/// Implements a stopwatch
/// Shows the integration of animation with Views.
///</summary>

Views.Form f;
Thread clockThread;

void SetUp() {
  f = new Views.Form(
    @"<Form Text='Stop Watch'>
      <vertical>
        <horizontal>
          <Button Name=Pause/>
          <Button Name=Resume/>
        </horizontal>
        <Picturebox Name=pic Height=150 Width=150/>
        <horizontal>
          <Button Name=Start/>
          <Button Name=End/>
        </horizontal>
      </vertical>
    </Form>");
  // c is the reference to the actual control variable
  // whose name is listed as f["pic"] in Views
  // add the event
  f["pic"].c.Paint +=
          new PaintEventHandler(new Clock().ClockPaint);

  // create and start a thread to control the clock
  clockThread = new Thread(new ThreadStart(this.TickClock));
  clockThread.Start();
}

bool done = false;

void Go() {

  SetUp();
  while (!done) {
    string c = f.GetControl();
    if (c == null) break;
    ActionPerformed(c);
  }
  f.CloseGUI();
}

void ActionPerformed(string c) {
  switch (c) {
    case "Start" :
      clockThread.Start();
      break;
```

```
          case "Resume" :
            clockThread.Resume();
            break;
          case "Pause" :
            clockThread.Suspend();
            break;
          case "End" :
            clockThread.Suspend();
            done = true;
            break;
          default :
            break;
        }
      }

    void TickClock() {
      while (true) {
        f["pic"].c.Invalidate();
        Thread.Sleep(10);
      }
    }

... insert Clock class here

  static void Main() {
    new StopWatchwithViews().Go();
  }
}
```

The program can be easily understood at this stage. The output is given in Figure 10.6.

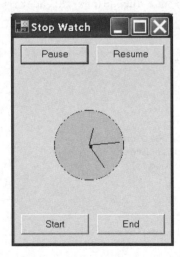

Figure 10.6 The stopwatch output

10.5 Networking

C# was designed in the late 1990s, when the internet was definitely part of daily life, and Java had shown the way for easy interoperability between files and programs over the network. C# similarly exhibits excellent facilities for networking, but we are going to illustrate only two here. These are *web requests* and *sockets*. C# also has APIs for database connectivity and remote object handling (known as *remoting*), but these are beyond the scope of this book at this stage.

Web requests

We can make a request across the internet to link to a file at a given URL. The file could contain an image, or text. C# supports three popular protocols – 'http://', 'https://' and 'file://' – for fetching the data. All of them are accessed via the abstract class WebRequest, which ascertains the type of the file, and returns a WebResponse of the appropriate type. From the web response, we can set up a Stream, and from the stream, we can get the actual data required.

The step-by-step process is summarized in Figure 10.7.

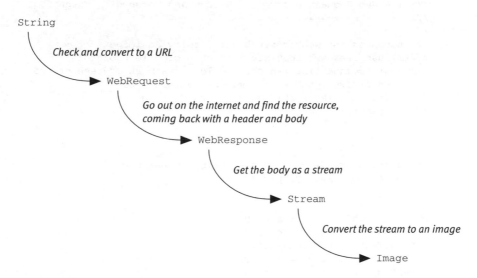

Figure 10.7 Steps to fetching an image on the internet

The entire object is fetched in the second step. The object can also be obtained in stages, using the different methods BeginGetResponse and EndGetResponse.

Example 10.7 Fetching an image on the internet

Suppose we have an image on the internet somewhere that we would like displayed as part of a program. We can use the steps described here to start with an ordinary URL and get to an `Image` object which can then be drawn in the usual way with `DrawImage`. The additional advantage of the C# `WebRequest` type is that it will adapt to protocols other than 'http://'. In particular, it can accept 'file://' as well. Thus in the program below, we can run it from the command line with a name of a resource which is either far away or local.

File FetchImageFromWeb.cs

```
using System;
using System.Drawing;
using System.Windows.Forms;
using System.IO;
using System.Net;

public class FetchImageWeb : Form {

  /// <summary>
  /// The Web Request program    Bishop and Horspool   March 2003
  /// =========================
  ///
  /// Accesses the web to fetch and display an image
  /// Illustrates web requests with http or file protocols.
  /// Your command line request should contain an address of the form
  ///    http://www.google.com/images/logo.gif   or
  ///    file://c:/My Work/images/Jacarandas.jpg
  /// </summary>

  Image pic;

  protected override void OnPaint(PaintEventArgs e) {
    e.Graphics.DrawImage(pic,30,30);
  }

  public FetchImageWeb(String url){
    this.Size = new Size(400,400);
    this.Text = "Web request";
    WebRequest request = WebRequest.Create(url);
    WebResponse response = request.GetResponse();
    Stream stream = response.GetResponseStream();
    pic = Image.FromStream(stream);
  }

  static void Main(string[] args) {
    Application.Run(new FetchImageWeb(args[0]));
  }
}
```

We can run it with

```
FetchImageWeb "http://www.google.com/images/logo.gif"
FetchImageWeb "file://c:/MyWork/images/Jacarandas.jpg"
```

and the appropriate image will be displayed in a window for each of the two runs.

Ports and sockets

All modern general-purpose languages provide a means for programs to communicate by sending messages to each other. The messages can be in any agreed format, and they are transported over the underlying TCP/IP transport layer of the network. Here we have a lower level protocol than 'http://', but one which gives us more direct control over the interaction.

TCP/IP relies on hardware *ports*, of which every computer has several, but also has a way of sharing them over many programs, provided they are given different numbers. So, if two C# programs are to communicate, they first agree that they will do so via a port with a particular number, such as 8190. Generally speaking, the higher numbered ports are not used by the computer system, and are available to users.

Next, the programs adopt a paradigm known as *client–server*. In other words, one program is generally considered to be in control, and have access to data or computational power which the others need. It is called the *server*. Then we define a *client* type, and we can have many clients instantiated, all of which will access the server through the specified port. The server starts up first, gets its data ready, and then starts listening for clients. It does this with a software object known as a *socket*. The C# type for these sockets is a `TcpListener`. Once a client comes in on the port and is directed to the `TcpListener`, the server will create a `Socket` object based on the initial communication (which will capture the address of the distant computer), start up a new thread for that client, and then go back to listening for more clients.

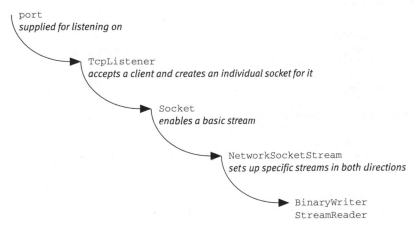

Figure 10.8 Steps for socket communication

Within the client handling thread, there are three more classes which complete the handling of the socket. These are `NetworkSocketStream`, `BinaryWriter` and `StreamReader`. (In fact, other versions of the readers and writers could be used, but these two work well for simple programs such as the one below.) A `NetworkSocketStream` object is set up to communicate directly between each client and the server. The communication is two-way, so we need a reader and a writer. Figure 10.8 outlines the progress from an integer port number to two streams for input and output between computers.

10.6 Case study 6 – An ATM client–server system

To illustrate socket communication, we shall use the example of a simple ATM (automatic teller machine) system. The bank is the server, and clients are customers who approach different ATMs to do bank transactions. In this scenario there can be multiple clients at once, and we will handle them by means of threads.

We start off by defining the server. It will have a simple Views window which waits for clients. When a client starts up on the same port, the server is automatically activated (at its `TcpListener`) and will set up a socket and then create a new thread for the client (called a handler). The handler continues with setting up all the communication necessary with the client, as in Figure 10.8. Then it will ask for a PIN number and the client dispatches this on its `BinaryWriter`. The server reads it on its `StreamReader`. Some checking and further interaction can take place, and then the customer should be able to start making bank transactions. However, in this example we are just interested in one set of communicating streams, and therefore stop the simulation at this point. Figure 10.9 shows a typical interaction with a server and two clients.

The programs are fairly long, but they include all the points raised above. We start with the server.

File ATMServer.cs

```
using System;
using System.ComponentModel;
using System.Threading;
using System.Net.Sockets;
using System.IO;

public class ATMServer {

    /// <summary>
    /// The ATMServer program          Bishop and Horspool    Feb 2003
    /// =====================
    /// Simulates the beginning of an ATM protocol.
    /// Allows successive connections.
    /// Illustrates sockets and networking.
    /// </summary>
```

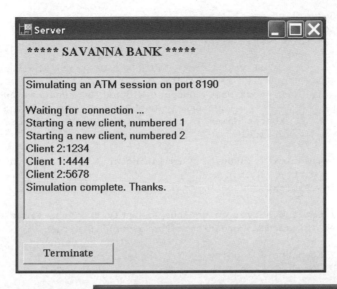

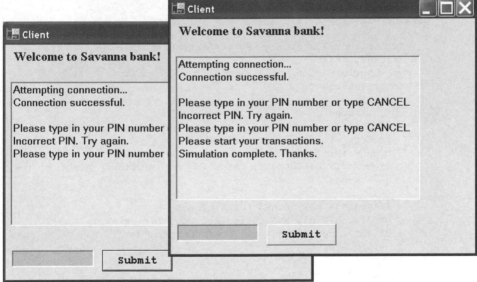

Figure 10.9 The ATM client–server system

```
Socket socket;
Thread client;
static string magicPIN = "5678";
static int port = 8190;
static bool done = false;

Views.Form view;
```

```
ATMServer(int port) {
  view = new Views.Form(
    @"<Form Text='Server'>
        <vertical>
          <Label Text='***** SAVANNA BANK *****' halign=center
                 Font=bold12 />
          <Listbox Name='Output' Width='300' Height='200'
                 Font=sans10 BackColor=BlanchedAlmond/>
          <Button Name='Terminate' Width='110' Font=bold10/>
        </vertical>
      </Form>");
  view.PutText("Output", "Simulating an ATM session on port " +
    port);
  view.PutText("Output", "");

  // Set the server going independently from the Views GUI
  new Thread(new ThreadStart(RunServer)).Start();

  // Keep the GUI going
  GUICommunication();
}

public void RunServer() {
  try {
    TcpListener listener = new TcpListener(port);
    listener.Start();
    view.PutText("Output", "Waiting for connection ...");
    int counter = 0;

    while (!done) {
      // This is where the server sits and waits for clients
      socket = listener.AcceptSocket();
      counter++;
      view.PutText("Output", "Starting a new client, numbered " +
        counter);

      // Start a new thread for a client
      Handler h = new Handler(socket, counter, view);
      client = new Thread(new ThreadStart(h.Run));
      client.Start();
    }
  } catch(Exception) {
    Console.WriteLine("Port " + port +
      " may be busy. Try another.");
  }
}

void GUICommunication() {
  while (view != null) {
    string b = view.GetControl();
    // Must be terminate
    done = true;
```

```
    if (socket != null) {
      socket.Close();
      client.Join();
    }
    view.PutText("Output", "Server terminated.");
    view.CloseGUI();
  }
}

public class Handler {
  Socket socket;
  NetworkStream socketStream;
  BinaryWriter writer;
  StreamReader reader;
  Views.Form view;
  int id;

  public Handler(Socket s, int i, Views.Form f) {
    socket = s;
    id = i;
    view = f;
  }

  public void Run() {
    try {
      // establish the communication streams
      socketStream = new NetworkStream(socket);
      writer = new BinaryWriter(socketStream);
      reader = new StreamReader(socketStream);

      writer.Write("Connection successful.");
      writer.Write("");

      bool okay = false;
      for (int tries = 0; tries < 3 && !okay; tries++) {
        writer.Write("Please type in your PIN number " +
          "or type CANCEL");
        string message = reader.ReadLine();
        message = message.Substring(1,message.Length-1);
        view.PutText("Output", "Client " + id + ":" + message);
        okay = true;
        switch (message) {
          case "SHUTDOWN" :
            writer.Write("Shutting down. Goodbye.");
            done = true;
            break;
          case "CANCEL" :
            writer.Write("Transaction halted. Goodbye.");
            break;
          default :
            if (message.Equals(magicPIN)) {
              writer.Write("Please start your transactions.");
              break;
```

```
                            } else {
                              writer.Write("Incorrect PIN. Try again.");
                              okay = false;
                            }
                            break;
                    }
                  }
                  writer.Write("Simulation complete. Thanks.");
                  view.PutText("Output", "Simulation complete. Thanks.");
            } catch(Exception error) {
                  Console.WriteLine(error.ToString());
            }
          }
      }

      static void Main(string[] args) {
        if (args.Length > 0)
          port = int.Parse(args[0]);
        new ATMServer(port);
      }
}
```

Notice that the handler threads are passed their socket reference, an id number that the server will know them by, and a reference to their Views form. Is there more than one Views form? Yes, there is one in each running version of the client. Thus the commands to set up the system from the console would be:

```
@rem open a cmd window
ATMServer
@rem open another cmd window
ATMClient
@rem open a third window
ATMClient
```

With these commands, the default port 8190 will be used. Now for the client program:

```
File ATMClient.cs
```

```
using System;
using System.ComponentModel;
using System.Threading;
using System.Net.Sockets;
using System.Windows.Forms;
using System.IO;

public class ATMClient {

  ///<summary>
  /// The ATMClient Program          Bishop and Horspool   Feb 2003
  /// =====================
  /// Allows communication by connecting to an ATM Server.
  /// Illustrates network communication.
  ///</summary>
```

```
private NetworkStream output;
private BinaryWriter writer;
private BinaryReader reader;
private string message = "";
private Thread readThread;
Views.Form view;
static int port = 8190;

ATMClient() {
  try {
    view = new Views.Form(@"<Form Text = 'Client'>
      <vertical>
        <Label Text='Welcome to Savanna bank!' halign=center
                 Font=bold12/>
        <ListBox Name='Out' Width='300' Height='200' Font=sans10
                 BackColor=BlanchedAlmond/>
        <horizontal>
          <TextBox Name='In' Text='' Width='100' Font=Courier10
                 BackColor=LightBlue/>
          <Button Name=Submit Width=85 Font=monospacebold/>
        </horizontal>
      </vertical>
    </form>");

    readThread = new Thread(new ThreadStart(Connect));
    readThread.Start();
    GUICommunication();
  } catch(Exception e) {
    Console.WriteLine(e.Message);
  }
}

void Connect() {
  TcpClient client;
  view.PutText("Out", "Attempting connection...");
  client = new TcpClient();
  client.Connect("localhost", port);
  output = client.GetStream();
  writer = new BinaryWriter(output);
  reader = new BinaryReader(output);
  do {
    try {
      message = reader.ReadString();
      view.PutText("Out", message);
    }  catch(Exception error)        {
      Console.WriteLine(error.ToString());
    }
  } while (message != "Simulation complete. Thanks.");
  reader.Close();
  writer.Close();
  output.Close();
}
```

```
        void GUICommunication() {
          while(view != null) {
            string b = view.GetControl();
            switch(b) {
              case "Submit":
                writer.Write(view.GetText("In") + "\n");
                view.PutText("In", "");
                break;
            }
          }
          view.CloseGUI();
        }

        static void Main(string[] args) {
          if (args.Length > 0)
            port = int.Parse(args[0]);
          new ATMClient();
        }
      }
```

Concepts in Chapter 10

This chapter covered the following concepts:

graphics interfaces	multi-threading
animation	events
handlers	colour
shapes, lines and points	text and fonts
images as objects	

API classes and methods specifically addressed here were:

`System.Windows.Forms.Form`	`Application.Run`
`FillEllipse`	`SolidBrush`
`System.Drawing`	`System.Threading`
`OnPaint`	`PaintEventArgs`
`PaintEventHandler`	`Color`
`DrawLine`	`Pen`
`DrawString`	`Font`
`Image`	`FromFile`
`DrawImage`	`SizeMode`

Forms were provided in this chapter for:

drawing program pattern	events and handlers for graphics
image displaying	image displaying in a control
thread creation and start	threads for animation
thread close	

Quiz

Q10.1 OnPaint is

    (a)   an event   (b)   a method

    (c)   a graphics object   (d)   a form

Q10.2 To enable a method called DrawMe to be called whenever a form needs to be painted, we use:

    (a)   `this.Controls.Add(DrawMe)`

    (b)   `this.Paint += OnPaint(DrawMe);`

    (c)   `this.Paint += new PaintEventHandler(DrawMe)`

    (d)   `DrawMe.PaintEventHandler.Add()`

Q10.3 FromFile is

    (a)   a static method of Image   (b)   an instance method of Image

    (c)   a GDI+ command   (d)   a graphics event

Q10.4 Threads are

    (a)   instance methods   (b)   static methods

    (c)   events   (d)   objects

Q10.5 ThreadStart is

    (a)   a method which loops till some condition is met to end the thread

    (b)   a delegate which keeps a register of a thread's run method

    (c)   an object which starts a thread running by entering its run method

    (d)   an event which activates the start of a thread

Q10.6   A statement to force a drawing in a picture box, p, to be redrawn is:

(a)   `p.Invalidate();`   (b)   `p.Validate();`

(c)   `OnPaint(p);`   (d)   `p.ReDraw();`

Q10.7   When we do a web request, the result is

(a)   a resource accessed by the `http://` protocol

(b)   a web response accessed by the `http://` protocol

(c)   a web response accessed by any one of several protocols

(d)   a URL

Q10.8   The protocol used for communicating between sockets is:

(a)   socket protocol   (b)   https://

(c)   stream   (d)   TCP/IP

Q10.9   The statement in a client server that enables the server to wait for clients to contact it is:

(a)   `Thread.Sleep(100);`

(b)   `listener.AcceptSocket();`

(c)   `listener.Start();`

(d)   `client.Start();`

Q10.10   If we have the ATM system with three clients, how many threads in total are running?

(a)   one   (b)   three

(c)   four   (d)   impossible to say

Exercises

10.1   Coloured spots. Adapt the Spotty program so that it prints out spots of four different colours chosen at random.

10.2   Sized spots. Have the Spotty program interact with the user through the console window to decide on a size for the spots before it starts drawing.

10.3 **Spots with Views.** Redo the Spotty program with a Views interface and offer choice boxes for several colours and sizes of spots. (Hint: draw the spots in a picture box.)

10.4 **Moving the identifying box.** Put Example 10.2 in a Views interface and use controls such as track bars to resize the rectangle, and to move it around the image. Also output the position of the rectangle using text boxes.

APPENDIX A

List of forms

This appendix is intended to provide a convenient reference tool for looking up brief descriptions of C# constructs and classes in the C# namespaces.

Keywords and operators

Further information about the keywords and operators may be found in the C# language specification. Not all of them have been covered in this book.

B.1 Keywords

The keywords for C# are given here in five groups to make them easier to spot. In some cases, a keyword could belong to more than one group: we have chosen the more commonly used one.

Simple types

bool	byte	char	const
decimal	double	enum	false
fixed	float	int	lock
sbyte	short	true	uint
ulong	ushort		

Structured types

abstract	base	class	delegate
event	interface	namespaces	null
object	readonly	sealed	string
struct	using	volatile	

Expressions

as	base	checked	is
new	sizeof	stackalloc	this
typeof	unchecked	unsafe	

Control structures

break	case	catch	continue
default	do	else	finally
for	foreach	goto	if
in	switch	throw	try
while			

Methods

explicit	extern	internal	operate
out	override	params	private
protected	public	ref	return
static	virtual	void	

Special words

In some places, specific identifiers have special meaning, but are not keywords. For example, within a property declaration, the get, set and value identifiers are used with special meanings.

B.2 Operators and punctuators

There are several kinds of operators and punctuators. Operators are used in expressions to describe operations involving one or more operands. Punctuators are for grouping and separating.

Punctuation

{ }	( )	.	,
:	;		

Assignment

=	+=	-=	*=
/=	%=	&=	|=
^=	<<=	>>=	

Expressions

+	-	*	/
%	&	|	^
!	~	[ ]	<
>	? :	++	--
&&	||	<<	>>
==	!=	<=	>=
->			

APPENDIX C

Formatters

This appendix expands on the discussion of Section 3.6, revealing more of the formatting options available in C#.

C.1 Format specification

The specification for formatters given in Section 3.6 is repeated below.

FORMAT SPECIFICATION
$\{N,M:s\}$
N is the position of the item in the list of values after the format string passed to the Write call; position numbers start from 0. M is the width of the region to contain the formatted value. If M is absent or negative, then the value will be left-justified, otherwise it will be right-justified. s is an optional string of formatting codes which can be used to control formatting of numbers, date-times, currencies, and so on.

N and *M* are programmer specific. What we need to do is list the options for *s*. *s* is known as a format specifier. There are three standard types of format specifiers in the .NET framework, for numbers, date and time objects and enumerations.

C.2 Number format specifiers

There are six standard specifiers for numbers and it can be quite confusing as to which to choose. Table C.1 shows the options, with an example of output for the number 1234.5 if decimal places are allowed and 1234 if not The value used with the P format is 89 and with the X format is 89AX3. An underscore indicates a space.

Specifier	Letter	Applies to	Example	String
General	G	all (adaptable)	`8:G`	`__1234.5`
			`8:G`	`____1234`
Fixed point	F	all	`8:F2`	`_1234.50`
Round trip	R	all	`8:R2`	`1234.5`
Number	N	all	`8:N1`	`1,2345.6`
Exponential	E	all	`14:E6`	`_1.234500E+003`
Decimal	D	integers only	`8:D`	`00001234`
Currency	C	all	`10:C`	`_$1,234.50`
Percentage	P	all	`0:P`	`89.00%`
Hexadecimal	X	integers only	`8X`	`0089AX3`

Table C.1 Examples of number format specifiers

For numbers, the G specifier is designed to be the most flexible. It adapts to the type of the value it receives and takes no notice of precision specifiers. It is a good specifier if one is writing numbers in text. It is not as good for tables. In order to line up numbers and points, one should rather use F or even R. R will produce output similar to F or E, but has the added advantage that numbers will be translated back exactly on input, so is good for serialization. N is useful for large numbers in that it breaks the digits up in groups of three, but in many parts of the world, the comma needs to be replaced by a space (see below). E is used for large numbers, and D would be used for serial numbers e.g. bank accounts, where the number of digits is always constant.

The currency specifier is useful, but may need to be customized (see below). The P specifier can be confusing because it multiplies the value by 100 first. The X specifier is specialized for hexadecimal numbers and would often be used with a fixed field, causing leading zeros to appear.

Specifiers are embedded in format strings. A format string can appear as the first parameter of a `WriteLine` call, with the necessary items following it, for example:

```
Console.WriteLine("{0:G} + {1:G} = {2:G}",
                  63, 7.005, 63+7.005);
```

```
63 + 7.005 = 70.005
```

C.3 Customizing number formatters

The above nine specifiers are built in. We can create variations using special symbols indicating the position of leading zeros, decimal separators, and so on. These symbols are familiar from other programs such as MS Word and Excel, and older computer languages like COBOL. Some of the available symbols are '0', '#', '.' and ','. A 0 symbol indicates that a zero must appear in that position if there is no digit, whereas # will leave a space. A full stop indicates the position of the decimal point, comma(s) indicate the position(s) of group separators. Notice, though, that when using these symbols we cannot change what the point and separator look like: for this we must alter information elsewhere. So they are of rather limited usefulness on their own. An example might be a variation on the F format where trailing zeros are replaced by spaces. We would construct such a specifier and example as:

```
8:"####0.0#"         _1234.5_           __12345.0
```

The zeros on either side of the point will force a well-formed number, even if it is an integer, as shown. Using such a string in a `WriteLine` statement might be:

```
Console.WriteLine("{0,8:"####0.0#"}",1234.5);
```

```
_1234.5_
```

The information we are seeking is stored in the `NumberFormatInfo` class, mentioned in Section 3.6 in connection with currencies. A list of useful attributes for the N and C specifiers is:

```
CurrencyGroupSeparator         NumberGroupSeparator

CurrencyDecimalDigits          NumberDecimalDigits

CurrencyDecimalSeparator       NumberDecimalSeparator

CurrencySymbol
```

With these we can create output that matches that of countries other than the default which is the US on most machines. If the region on your computer is set differently, it could be that these values will be fetched from there. In addition, C# has a large selection of preset countries in the `System.Globalization` namespace, which can be selected programmatically.

Whereas format specifiers can be used directly in format strings in `WriteLine` and `ToString` calls, linking up to a formatter object – called a format provider – requires an extra conversion. There exists a `Format` method in the `String` class which formats a string and items according to such an object. For example,

```
NumberFormatInfo f = new NumberFormatInfo();
f.CurrencyDecimalSeparator = ",";
f.CurrencyGroupSeparator = " ";
f.CurrencySymbol = "R";
double salary = 10000;

Console.WriteLine(
    String.Format(f,"Your new salary is {0:C}",salary*1.04));
```

which will print

```
Your new salary is R10 400,00
```

C.4 DateTime formatters

Format specifiers are written as strings. The methods they are passed to then interpret the contents of the string according to defined rules. The rules for numbers have been built in to the functioning of the `WriteLine` method in the `Console` class, and are described above.

The `DateTime` type also has a selection of single letter format specifiers to choose from, and these are interpreted by its `ToString` method. If `myDate` is a `DateTime` object and `"D"` is such a specifier, then we would have:

```
Console.WriteLine(myDate.ToString("D"));
```

Tables C.2 and C.3 show most of the specifiers that `DateTime` accepts, together with two examples, to illustrate the effect of locale on the output. In this case, we just reset the region on the computer to get the necessary effects. Notice that the U format records universal time, and so used a time two hours earlier for South Africa and six hours earlier for French Canada.

Format	Code	English (South African)
Year-month	Y	October 2003
Month-day	M	07 October
Long date	D	07 October 2003
Short date	d	2003/10/07
Long time	T	15:02:27
Short time	t	03:02 PM
Full date long time	F	07 October 2003 15:02:27
Full date short time	f	07 October 2003 03:02 PM
General date long time	G	2003/10/07 15:02:27
General date short time	g	2003/10/07 03:02 PM
Universal sortable time	U	07 October 2003 13:02:27

Table C.2 DateTime formats for English (South Africa) locale

Format	Code	French (Canadian)
Year-month	Y	octobre, 2003
Month-day	M	7 octobre
Long date	D	7 octobre, 2003
Short date	d	2003-10-07
Long time	T	15:02:27
Short time	t	15:02
Full date long time	F	7 octobre, 2003 15:02:27
Full date short time	f	7 octobre, 2003 15:02
General date long time	G	2003-10-07 15:02:27
General date short time	g	2003-10-07 15:02
Universal sortable time	U	7 octobre, 2003 09:02:27

Table C.3 DateTime formats for French (Canadian) locale

APPENDIX D

Unicode

Unicode is a standard for international character specifications. This appendix builds on Section 4.5 and gives some tables of commonly used characters. The full details for Unicode can be found at http://www.unicode.org.

D.1 Inputting Unicode characters

We address the issue of character sets from the point of view of programming. Most often we want to use Unicode to extend the characters available on a keyboard. We will not be writing long sequences of Unicode, rather we'll have a few such characters in strings, usually in `WriteLine` calls.

First we have to enter the character into the program in some way. The program we are using might have extensions that recognize an extended range of key combinations, using *alt*, *shift* and *ctrl*. Microsoft Word is such a program. If we type *alt-ctrl-c*, it is shown as ©. However, the same combination will not work in Visual Studio, and it won't work in Adobe Framemaker (which we used to produce this book). Microsoft Word also has a standard Unicode inputting scheme which applies to all keyboards: type the Unicode then *ctrl-X*.

The upshot is that in most programming development environments, one cannot enter special characters from the keyboard so that they are visible. One must use Unicode. Referring then to Table D.2, we see that the Unicode value for the copyright symbol, ©, is 00A9. Therefore to include © in a `WriteLine`, we say:

```
Console.WriteLine("\u00A9 2003");
```

which will display the line:

© 2003

D.2 Selected characters

Not all keyboards have currency symbols in addition to the $ character. The Unicode values are therefore very useful. The keystrokes accepted by Microsoft Word are often augmented for particular keyboards, for example in many European countries, the keyboard has an *ALT-GR* key (standing for *alternate graphic*) and *alt-gr-e* is typically where one finds the euro symbol. We can see that € is a newer symbol than the others, because it has a higher Unicode, and would have been added later. The $ symbol, however, is found in the straight Latin table.

Symbol	Unicode	Word keystroke
¢	00A2	*unicode* alt-X
€	02AC	*unicode* alt-X
£	00A3	*unicode* alt-X
¥	00A5	*unicode* alt-X
$	0024	shift-4

Table D.1 Currency symbols

In the Latin-Supplement table, we find many punctuation marks, some of which are shown in Table D.2.

Symbol	Unicode	Word keystroke
°	00B0	*unicode* alt-X
¿	00BF	alt+ctrl+shift+?
©	00A9	alt-ctrl-c
2	00B2	*unicode* alt-X
½	00BD	*unicode* alt-X

Table D.2 Special punctuation

Finally, there is a full range of international characters with accents of one sort or another. Table D.3 lists only some of the possibilities. The others can be interpolated from what is shown, or looked up on the Unicode pages. In this table, the keystroke sequence accepted by Microsoft Word for an accented character such as *à* is the ctrl+` combination followed by the letter *a*. Instead of the letter *a*, other letters in either upper or lower-case may be substituted. For example, ctrl+` followed by *E* gives *È*.

Symbol	Unicode	Word Keystroke
ß	00DF	ctrl+shift+&, s
à	00E0	ctrl+`, *the letter*
á	00E1	ctrl+´, *the letter*
â	00E2	ctrl+shift+^, *the letter*
ä	00E4	ctrl+shift+:, *the letter*
å	00E5	ctrl+shift+@, *the letter*
ç	00E7	ctrl+, , c
è	00E8	ctrl+`, *the letter*
é	00E9	ctrl+´, *the letter*
ë	00EB	ctrl+shift+:, *the letter*
ñ	00F1	ctrl+shift+~, *the letter*
ö	00F6	ctrl+shift+:, *the letter*
û	00FB	ctrl+shift+^, *the letter*
ü	00FC	ctrl+shift+:, *the letter*
ø	00F8	ctrl+/, o

Table D.3 International characters

APPENDIX E

Useful namespaces

This appendix presents a summary of the C# namespaces used in this book, showing the hierarchy of types that each has. Only a selection of types is shown in each case, as full details can be found in the Help files of Visual Studio, or in other reference works devoted to .NET. In the first section of the appendix, we consider the namespaces one by one. In the second section we group them according to how they would be used in a typical program.

E.1 The .NET framework class library

The .NET framework class library is the guts of any non-trivial C# program. It provides support for anything from input–output to dates and times, from remote networking to sorting and searching. In this section, we look at the namespaces and how they are structured. Although it is referred to as a 'class' library, it is more correctly a type library, since it includes structured types such as structs which are not classes.

How to read these lists

The .NET library is divided into many namespaces. One of these is called System, and most of the others are called System.*something*. This is slightly confusing (especially for those used to, say, Java). For example, System.IO is not a sub-namespace of System. It is a separate namespace in its own right.

The lists that we are giving here are not lists of types defined in the namespaces, but of the types as they are in an inheritance hierarchy applicable to that namespace. So, for example, the last three lines of the `System.Collections` namespace are shown as

```
System.Collections.Stack
System.ValueType
    System.Collections.DictionaryEntry
```

`System.ValueType` is not defined in this namespace, but is used as a base type for the struct listed below it. You can detect those types that are defined in the namespace because they start with exactly the same prefix. So lines one and three above are defined in `System.Collections`, and line two refers to a type defined in the `System` namespace.

Finally, do remember that most of the lists below are selections of what is available. Please consult the full APIs for the complete lists of types.

System namespace

The `System` namespace contains 135 types, grouped into hierarchies. At the top level, there are 29 types most of which contain inherited subtypes. Of these, some are mentioned in this book. Together with their subtypes, the ones we mentioned are:

```
System namespace (selection)
  System.Object
    System.Array
    System.Console
    System.Math
    System.Random
    System.String
    System.TimeZone
    System.ValueType
        System.ArgIterator
        System.Boolean
        System.Byte
        System.Char
        System.DateTime
        System.Decimal
        System.Double
        System.Enum
        System.Int16
        System.Int32
        System.Int64
        System.IntPtr
        System.SByte
        System.Single
        System.TimeSpan
        System.UInt16
        System.UInt32
        System.UInt64
        System.UIntPtr
        System.Void
```

Not all the types under `System.ValueType` are recognizable, but the ones above it are all very well known. Also in the `System` namespace is a hierarchy of classes related to exceptions. A selection of these is:

```
System.Exception (selection)
    System.SystemException
        System.ArgumentException
            System.ArgumentNullException
            System.ArgumentOutOfRangeException
            System.DuplicateWaitObjectException
        System.ArithmeticException
            System.DivideByZeroException
            System.NotFiniteNumberException
            System.OverflowException
        System.ArrayTypeMismatchException
        System.BadImageFormatException
        System.FormatException
            System.UriFormatException
        System.IndexOutOfRangeException
        System.InvalidCastException
        System.InvalidOperationException
        System.MemberAccessException
            System.FieldAccessException
            System.MethodAccessException
            System.MissingMemberException
                System.MissingFieldException
                System.MissingMethodException
        System.NullReferenceException
        System.OutOfMemoryException
        System.RankException
        System.StackOverflowException
        System.TypeInitializationException
        System.TypeLoadException
            System.DllNotFoundException
            System.EntryPointNotFoundException
        System.TypeUnloadedException
        System.UnauthorizedAccessException
```

System.Collections namespace

The `System.Collections` namespace contains many well-known and useful types for handling multiple objects, including `ArrayList`, `Comparer` and `SortedList`. The full list of types is:

```
System.Collections (full)
    System.Collections.ArrayList
    System.Collections.BitArray
    System.Collections.CaseInsensitiveComparer
    System.Collections.CaseInsensitiveHashCodeProvider
    System.Collections.CollectionBase
    System.Collections.Comparer
    System.Collections.DictionaryBase
```

```
System.Collections.Hashtable
System.Collections.Queue
System.Collections.ReadOnlyCollectionBase
System.Collections.SortedList
System.Collections.Stack
System.ValueType
    System.Collections.DictionaryEntry
```

System.Diagnostics namespace

This namespace contains many types for diagnosing problems in a program, but we have confined our discussions to just one:

```
System.Diagnostics (selection)
    System.Diagnostics.Debug
```

System.Drawing namespace

Some of the Drawing types were discussed briefly in Chapter 10. System.Drawing contains many, many types, but a small subset is:

```
System.Drawing (selection)
    System.Drawing.Brushes
    System.Drawing.ColorTranslator
    System.Drawing.ImageAnimator
    System.Drawing.Pens
    System.Drawing.Font
        System.Drawing.FontFamily
        System.Drawing.Graphics
        System.Drawing.Icon
        System.Drawing.Image
            System.Drawing.Bitmap
        System.Drawing.Pen
        System.Drawing.Region
        System.Drawing.StringFormat
    System.ValueType
        System.Drawing.CharacterRange
        System.Drawing.Color
        System.Drawing.Point
        System.Drawing.PointF
        System.Drawing.Rectangle
        System.Drawing.RectangleF
        System.Drawing.Size
        System.Drawing.SizeF
        System.Enum
```

System.Globalization namespace

Although this namespace was not explicitly discussed in the book, one or two of its types (e.g. NumberFormatInfo) were used, and it is interesting to see what is available. For that reason it is listed in full here.

```
System.Globalization (full)
System.Object
    System.Globalization.Calendar
        System.Globalization.GregorianCalendar
        System.Globalization.HebrewCalendar
        System.Globalization.HijriCalendar
        System.Globalization.JapaneseCalendar
        System.Globalization.JulianCalendar
        System.Globalization.KoreanCalendar
        System.Globalization.TaiwanCalendar
        System.Globalization.ThaiBuddhistCalendar
    System.Globalization.CompareInfo
    System.Globalization.CultureInfo
    System.Globalization.DateTimeFormatInfo
    System.Globalization.DaylightTime
    System.Globalization.NumberFormatInfo
    System.Globalization.RegionInfo
    System.Globalization.SortKey
    System.Globalization.StringInfo
    System.Globalization.TextElementEnumerator
    System.Globalization.TextInfo
    System.ValueType
        System.Enum
            System.Globalization.CalendarWeekRule
            System.Globalization.CompareOptions
            System.Globalization.CultureTypes
            System.Globalization.DateTimeStyles
            System.Globalization.GregorianCalendarTypes
            System.Globalization.NumberStyles
            System.Globalization.UnicodeCategory
```

System.IO namespace

`System.IO` is a well-known namespace. Notice that it has several exceptions listed. Also, the main classes inherit from two other classes – `System.MarshalByRefObject` and `System.ComponentModel.Component` which enable them to be used in remoting, which is rather beyond the scope of this book.

```
System.IO (selection)
System.Exception
    System.SystemException
        System.IO.InternalBufferOverflowException
        System.IO.IOException
            System.IO.DirectoryNotFoundException
            System.IO.EndOfStreamException
            System.IO.FileLoadException
            System.IO.FileNotFoundException
            System.IO.PathTooLongException
System.IO.BinaryReader
System.IO.BinaryWriter
System.IO.Directory
System.IO.File
```

```
System.IO.Path
System.MarshalByRefObject
    System.ComponentModel.Component
        System.IO.FileSystemWatcher
    System.IO.FileSystemInfo
        System.IO.DirectoryInfo
        System.IO.FileInfo
    System.IO.Stream
        System.IO.BufferedStream
        System.IO.FileStream
        System.IO.MemoryStream
    System.IO.TextReader
        System.IO.StreamReader
        System.IO.StringReader
    System.IO.TextWriter
        System.IO.StreamWriter
        System.IO.StringWriter
```

System.Net namespace

The System.Net namespace provides many classes for linking to other computers via a variety of protocols. Once again the main classes are under MarshalByRefObject and ComponentModel.

```
System.Net (selection)
    System.Exception
        System.SystemException
            System.FormatException
                System.Net.CookieException
            System.InvalidOperationException
                System.Net.ProtocolViolationException
                System.Net.WebException
    System.MarshalByRefObject
        System.ComponentModel.Component
            System.Net.WebClient
        System.Net.WebRequest
            System.Net.FileWebRequest
            System.Net.HttpWebRequest
        System.Net.WebResponse
            System.Net.FileWebResponse
            System.Net.HttpWebResponse
    System.Net.SocketAddress
    System.Net.WebProxy
```

System.Net.Sockets namespace

Working together with System.Net, this namespace provides specific classes for the implementation of sockets.

```
System.Net.Sockets (selection)
    System.Exception
        System.SystemException
```

```
            System.Runtime.InteropServices.ExternalException
                System.ComponentModel.Win32Exception
                    System.Net.Sockets.SocketException
        System.MarshalByRefObject
            System.IO.Stream
                System.Net.Sockets.NetworkStream
        System.Net.Sockets.LingerOption
        System.Net.Sockets.MulticastOption
        System.Net.Sockets.Socket
        System.Net.Sockets.TcpClient
        System.Net.Sockets.TcpListener
        System.Net.Sockets.UdpClient
```

System.Runtime.Serialization namespace

There is a variety of serialization formatters available in different namespaces. The one we used has only the one class.

```
    System.Runtime.Serialization.Formatters.Binary
        System.Runtime.Serialization.Formatters.Binary.BinaryFormatter
```

System.Text namespace

This is a small namespace concerned with coding and decoding characters. But it also includes one class that we covered in the book:

```
    System.text (selection)
        System.Text.StringBuilder
```

System.Threading namespace

There are many types in System.Threading, some of them related to synchronization, which we haven't covered. Here is a selection of the others.

```
    System.Threading (selection)
    System.Object
        System.EventArgs
            System.Threading.ThreadExceptionEventArgs
        System.Exception
            System.SystemException
                System.Threading.ThreadAbortException
                System.Threading.ThreadInterruptedException
                System.Threading.ThreadStateException
        System.Threading.Thread
        System.Threading.ThreadPool
        System.Threading.Timeout
        System.ValueType
            System.Enum
                System.Threading.ApartmentState
                System.Threading.ThreadPriority
                System.Threading.ThreadState
```

System.Windows.Forms namespace

This is one of the biggest namespaces, and encompasses types for every kind of control available to be drawn and manipulated. Here is a just a typical selection.

```
System.Windows.Forms (selection)
  System.Delegate
    System.MulticastDelegate
      System.Windows.Forms.ContentsResizedEventHandler
      System.Windows.Forms.ControlEventHandler
      System.Windows.Forms.DrawItemEventHandler
      System.Windows.Forms.InvalidateEventHandler
      System.Windows.Forms.ItemChangedEventHandler
      System.Windows.Forms.ItemCheckEventHandler
      System.Windows.Forms.KeyEventHandler
      System.Windows.Forms.KeyPressEventHandler
      System.Windows.Forms.LabelEditEventHandler
      System.Windows.Forms.MouseEventHandler
      System.Windows.Forms.PaintEventHandler
      System.Windows.Forms.ScrollEventHandler
    System.Windows.Forms.InvalidateEventArgs
    System.Windows.Forms.ItemChangedEventArgs
    System.Windows.Forms.ItemCheckEventArgs
    System.Windows.Forms.ItemDragEventArgs
    System.Windows.Forms.KeyEventArgs
    System.Windows.Forms.KeyPressEventArgs
    System.Windows.Forms.MouseEventArgs
    System.Windows.Forms.PaintEventArgs
    System.Windows.Forms.ScrollEventArgs
  System.MarshalByRefObject
    System.ComponentModel.Component
      System.Windows.Forms.ColumnHeader
        System.Windows.Forms.CommonDialog
        System.Windows.Forms.ColorDialog
        System.Windows.Forms.FileDialog
          System.Windows.Forms.OpenFileDialog
          System.Windows.Forms.SaveFileDialog
        System.Windows.Forms.FontDialog
        System.Windows.Forms.PageSetupDialog
        System.Windows.Forms.PrintDialog
      System.Windows.Forms.Control
        System.Windows.Forms.Button
          System.Windows.Forms.CheckBox
          System.Windows.Forms.RadioButton
        System.Windows.Forms.GroupBox
        System.Windows.Forms.Label
        System.Windows.Forms.ListControl
          System.Windows.Forms.ComboBox
          System.Windows.Forms.ListBox
            System.Windows.Forms.CheckedListBox
        System.Windows.Forms.ListView
        System.Windows.Forms.PictureBox
        System.Windows.Forms.ProgressBar
```

```
System.Windows.Forms.ScrollableControl
System.Windows.Forms.Panel
System.Windows.Forms.ScrollBar
    System.Windows.Forms.HScrollBar
    System.Windows.Forms.VScrollBar
System.Windows.Forms.TextBoxBase
        System.Windows.Forms.TextBox
System.Windows.Forms.ToolBar
System.Windows.Forms.TrackBar
System.Windows.Forms.Application
```

E.2 Usage of the namespaces

Another way of looking at the namespaces is to identify functionality that is extraneous to the C# language itself, and must be carried by the namespaces, and then to order by functionality. Here we list the main requirements covered in this book. To access any of these namespaces, one must put an appropriate a `using` at the start of the program.

Numbers

The definition of structs for numbers is covered in the `System` namespace. Input and output, as provided by the `Console` class, are also in `System`. Input and output to files would use types in the `System.IO` namespace. For detailed formatting of numbers, there are types in `System.Globalization`, particularly for customizing input and output according to different languages and regions.

Dates and times

These follow the same path as numbers, making use of the `System`, `System.IO` and `System.Globalization` namespaces, where the `DateTimeFormatInfo` class is to be found. `System.Globalization` has a particularly rich set of types for handling dates in different languages. Note the interesting distinction in the extract of the `System` namespace shown in Section E.1 where `DateTime` is a struct under `ValueType` and `TimeZone` is a class directly under object.

Strings and characters

Strings and characters are covered by `System` and `System.IO`. Some useful information can be found in `System.Globalization`, and the `StringBuilder` class is defined in `System.Text`.

Mathematical functions and random numbers

Full facilities for mathematical functions and random number generators are to be found in the `System` namespace, in the `Math` and `Random` classes respectively.

Arrays

Arrays can exist without the support of a namespace but, as discussed in Chapter 8, C# does provide very helpful extensions and methods in the `Array` class which is provided in the `System` namespace. There are also the `ArrayList` and `BitArray` classes in the `System.Collections` namespace. It is likely that the `IComparable` or `IComparer` interfaces will be needed when sorting.

Files

File handling is covered by the `System.IO` namespace. Files can also be accessed over the network, in which case we would make use of the classes in `System.Net`. To save data onto serialized files, we use one of the serialization namespaces. In this book we covered `System.Runtime.Serialization`. There is also XML serialization with its own namespace.

Data structures

Data structures in addition to arrays and files are found in the `System.Collections` namespace.

Networked access

Accessing across the network is supported by `System.Net`, and also by the classes for socket handling in `System.Net.Sockets`. Serialisation, as mentioned above, is also relevant here.

Graphics and GUIs

Graphics and GUIs (graphical user interfaces) are really two different areas of concern. Graphics – drawing shapes and writing in fonts – is supported by the `System.Drawing` namespace; GUIs are covered by the well-known `System.Windows.Forms` namespace. Both of these are large namespaces with many types. In addition, both graphical drawings and GUIs can benefit from animation through multi-processing, in which case, the `System.Threading` namespace will be used.

APPENDIX F

The Views.Form class

The Views.Form class provides an alternative to the Visual Studio design tool for developing graphical user interfaces. This appendix provides a specification for the XML notation used by the class constructor to lay out the elements of a form and describes the properties and methods exported by the class.

F.1 Creating Forms with Views

The Form class in the Views namespace provides a simple way to create sophisticated graphical user interfaces (GUIs). On Windows systems, it is possible to create GUIs by using classes in the System.Windows.Forms namespace. Writing the code to use these classes is possible but tedious and error-prone. Professional programmers would normally use the Microsoft Visual Studio development environment to generate much of the code automatically.

Views offers an alternative approach which is designed to be easy to use. The GUIs created with Views support only a subset (albeit a rich subset) of the full repertoire of controls possible with Windows forms. Interaction between the calling program and the controls used on a Windows form is normally implemented using events. The interface provided by the `Views.Form` class is simplified so that programs cannot achieve the same effects as a full Windows program. If the calling program needs more sophisticated interaction with the control, it is possible but only by implementing its own event handlers and abjuring the simplified methods for interaction provided by the `Views.Form` class.

Views is intended to be easy to use, to require a small memory footprint on the computer, and is being ported to different platforms. Views is available for download in both compiled and source code versions from the official website. Its URL is

```
http://www.cs.up.ac.za/csharp
```

On Windows systems where you type a command into a command window (or MS-DOS window) to invoke the C# compiler, you need to use one of the following commands to compile a program that uses Views:

```
csc file1.cs file2.cs ...
```

or

```
csc /r:Views.dll file1.cs file2.cs ...
```

where your C# source code files are named `file1.cs`, `file2.cs`, etc.

The first, and simpler, command will work if the Views namespace has been installed and registered by the system administrator. The second version must be used otherwise. It requires that a copy of the file `Views.dll` be located in the same folder as your source code files. (It is a relatively small file and therefore you are unlikely to run out of disk space if you keep several copies of the file, one for each of the programs you are working on.)

F.2   Syntax of specifications for Views.Form

The `Views.Form` class constructor checks the argument string to verify that it is a valid specification for laying out the controls on a Windows form. The verification includes checking that the tags are nested appropriately, that the tags are provided with all the necessary attributes, that the tags are only provided with attributes supported by Views, and that attribute values are reasonable.

The tags may be nested according to the rules shown in Table F.1. The first two rules say that a form may be constructed in two ways.

form:	`<Form>` *controlGroup* `</Form>`
	| `<Form>` *positionList* `</Form>`
controlGroup:	`<vertical>` *controlList* `</vertical>`
	| `<horizontal>` *controlList* `</horizontal>`
	| `<Panel>` *positionList* `</Panel>`
controlList:	{ *control* }
positionList:	{ *positionedControl* }
positionedControl:	`<position>` *control* `</position>`
textItemList:	{ `<item>` *text* `</item>` }
control:	*controlGroup*
	| `<Button/>`
	| `<CheckBox/>`
	| `<CheckedListBox>` *textItemList* `</CheckedListBox>`
	| `<DomainUpDown>` *textItemList* `</DomainUpDown>`
	| `<GroupBox>` *radioButtonList* `</GroupBox>`
	| `<Label/>`
	| `<ListBox/>`
	| `<OpenFileDialog/>`
	| `<PictureBox/>`
	| `<ProgressBar/>`
	| `<SaveFileDialog/>`
	| `<TextBox/>`
	| `<TrackBar/>`
radioButtonList:	{ `<RadioButton/>` }

Table F.1 Syntax of the Views XML Specification

1. The first way is by writing the tag `<Form>` followed by a *controlGroup* followed by the closing tag `</Form>`.

2. The second way is by writing the tag `<Form>` followed by a *positionList* followed by `</Form>`.

In turn, a *controlGroup* is defined by the three rules which come later in the table, and a *positionList* by another rule later in the table.

If we look at the rule for *positionList* we see that it is defined as { *positionedControl* }. The curly braces are used to indicate that the material within the braces may be repeated indefinitely often. That is, a *positionList* consists of zero or more *positionedControl* constructions, one after the other.

Note that the rule which says that a *control* can be a *controlGroup* is a rule that permits nesting of `<vertical>...</vertical>` groups inside `<vertical>...</vertical>` groups, and so on.

The attributes which can be provided for each tag are detailed in the following sections of this appendix where the tags are listed with some explanations.

Note that capitalization of the tag names in Table F.1, such as `RadioButton`, matches that of the name of the corresponding class in the `System.Windows.Forms` namespace. The full name of the `RadioButton` class is therefore

```
System.Windows.Forms.RadioButton
```

and exactly this capitalization must be used in a C# program that refers to the class.

For your convenience, the `Views.Form` class accepts any capitalization of the tag names and the attribute names. However, it would be good practice for you to adopt the same capitalization as the Windows class names because you will be less likely to make mistakes when you subsequently use those classes.

F.3   Grouping tags

The tags listed in Table F.2 are those which enclose groups of other tags. The `<vertical>`, `<horizontal>` and `<Panel>` tags are used for generic control groups (called *controlGroup* in Table F.1) whereas the `<Form>` and `<GroupBox>` are used in more restricted circumstances.

An asterisk alongside an attribute (usually the `Name` attribute) indicates that the attribute must be specified. Explanations of the code letters used for the attribute values in the table appear in Section F.5.

Grouping construct	Attributes	Description

`<Form>`
`...`
`</Form>`
	`Text=S`
	`ForeColor=C`
	`BackColor=C`
		The outermost pair of tags needed to begin and end a complete specification. The enclosed contents must be a vertical list, or a horizontal list, or a panel, or a single control, or a list of `<position>` ... `</position>` controls

`<vertical>`
`...`
`</vertical>`
	`Width=M`
	`Height=M`
	`ForeColor=C`
	`BackColor=C`
		Display the enclosed constructs in a vertical list

`<horizontal>`
`...`
`</horizontal>`
	`Width=M`
	`Height=M`
	`ForeColor=C`
	`BackColor=C`
		Display the enclosed constructs in a horizontal list

`<Panel>`
`...`
`</Panel>`
	`*Name=S`
	`Width=M`
	`Height=M`
	`ForeColor=C`
	`BackColor=C`
		The enclosed contents must be a list of `<position>` ... `</position>` controls, each of which places a control at a precise location

`<GroupBox>`
`...`
`</GroupBox>`
	`*Name=S`
	`Text=S`
	`Width=M`
	`Height=M`
	`ForeColor=C`
	`BackColor=C`
		The enclosed contents must be `<RadioButton>` controls

Table F.2 Views.Form grouping constructs

F.4 Control tags

Table F.3 lists all the basic controls supported by the Views.Form class. The table lists all the attributes appropriate for each control *except* for `halign` and `valign`. The `halign` attribute may be used with any open tag which is immediately nested inside a `<vertical>` ... `</vertical>` group, while a `valign` tag may be used with an open tag immediately nested inside a `<horizontal>` ... `</horizontal>` group.

An asterisk alongside an attribute (usually the `Name` attribute) indicates that the attribute *must* be specified. Explanations of the code letters used for the attribute values in the table appear in Section F.5.

Views.Form control	Attributes	Description

`<Button/>`	`*Name=S`
	`Text=S`
	`Image=F`
	`Width=M`
	`Height=M`
	`ForeColor=C`
	`BackColor=C`
	`Font=FNT`
		Creates a push button.
		The button can be labelled with a string (taken from the `Text` attribute) or with a picture (where the name of the file containing the picture is taken from the `Image` attribute) or both.
		The size of the button defaults to something large enough to hold the label, either text or an image.
		Clicking the button causes `GetControl` to return with the name of the control

`<CheckBox/>`	`*Name=S`
	`Text=S`
	`Width=M`
	`Height=M`
	`ForeColor=C`
	`BackColor=C`
	`Font=FNT`
		Creates a small square which the user can click to add or remove a check mark.
		The `GetValue` method can be used to retrieve the status of a check box

`<CheckedListBox>`
`...`
`</CheckedListBox>`
	`*Name=S`
	`Text=S`
	`Width=M`
	`Height=M`
	`ForeColor=C`
	`BackColor=C`
	`Font=FNT`
		Creates a pull-down list of check boxes.
		The `GetValue` method can be used to retrieve the status of each check box in the list

`<DomainUpDown>`
`...`
`</DomainUpDown>`
	`*Name=S`
	`Text=S`
	`Width=M`
	`Height=M`
	`ForeColor=C`
	`BackColor=C`
	`Font=FNT`
		Creates a pull-down list from which a single item in the list can be selected as the current value.
		The `GetValue` method can be used to retrieve the index of the currently selected item in the list

`<GroupBox>`
`...`
`</GroupBox>`
	`*Name=S`
	`Text=S`
	`Width=M`
	`Height=M`
	`ForeColor=C`
	`BackColor=C`
	`Font=FNT`
		Displays a rectangular box used to hold a group of radio buttons. Only one radio button at a time can be selected – if the user clicks on one, it is enabled and another one becomes disabled.
		The `GetText` method can be used to retrieve the label of which radio button in the group is currently selected

`<Label/>`	`Name=S`
	`Text=S`
	`Width=M`
	`Height=M`
	`ForeColor=C`
	`BackColor=C`
	`Font=FNT`
		Displays a string

Table F.3 Views.Form controls

Views.Form control	Attributes	Description

`<ListBox/>`	`*Name=S`
	`Text=S`
	`Width=M`
	`Height=M`
	`ForeColor=C`
	`BackColor=C`
	`Font=FNT`
		Creates a rectangular box which can be used for input or output of many lines of text.
		Currently selected text in a `ListBox` can be retrieved by the `GetText` method; the `PutText` method appends new text to the `ListBox` contents

`<OpenFileDialog/>`	`*Name=S`
	`Text=S`
	`Width=M`
	`Height=M`
	`ForeColor=C`
	`BackColor=C`
	`Font=FNT`
		Creates a button which, if pressed, causes a new window to open where an existing file can be selected by navigating through the file system.
		Clicking the button and selecting a file causes `GetControl` to return with the name of the control; the name of the selected file can be retrieved by the `GetText` method

`<Panel>`
`...`
`</Panel>`
	`Name=S`
	`Text=S`
	`*Width=M`
	`*Height=M`
	`ForeColor=C`
	`BackColor=C`
	`Font=FNT`
		Creates a rectangular region, called a panel, within which controls may be individually placed. The panel may be scrollable horizontally or vertically, as neeeded to view all the controls.
		The controls inside the panel are placed at specific coordinates using `<position>` ... `</position>` tags

`<PictureBox/>`	`Name=S`
	`Image=F`
	`Width=M`
	`Height=M`
		Displays a graphics image.
		If the `Image` attribute is left undefined, a grey rectangle will be displayed. If `Width` and `Height` are omitted, they default to the size of the image held in the file

`<ProgressBar/>`	`*Name=S`
	`Value=D`
	`Minimum=D`
	`Maximum=D`
	`Width=M`
	`Height=M`
	`ForeColor=C`
	`BackColor=C`
		Creates a horizontal bar where the shaded part on the left is used to indicate how much of a task has been completed.
		Note: Views provides a default value for `Minimum` of 0 and a default for `Maximum` of 100.
		The amount of progress displayed by the control can be changed by calling the `SetValue` method

`<RadioButton/>`	`*Name=S`
	`Text=S`
	`Checked=D`
	`Width=M`
	`Height=M`
	`ForeColor=C`
	`BackColor=C`
	`Font=FNT`
		Creates a round button which becomes checked when clicked. A list of radio buttons is enclosed by `GroupBox` tags.
		The checked state of the button can be determined by calling the `GetValue` method. Alternatively, the name of which button in the group is checked can be obtained by calling the `GetText` method on the `GroupBox` control

Table F.3 Views.Form controls (continued)

Views.Form control	Attributes	Description

`<SaveFileDialog/>`	`*Name=S`
	`Text=S`
	`Width=M`
	`Height=M`
	`ForeColor=C`
	`BackColor=C`
	`Font=FNT`
		Creates a button which if pressed causes a new window to open where either an existing file to be overwritten can be selected by navigating the file system or a new filename can be entered. Clicking the button and selecting a file causes `GetControl` to return with the name of the control; the name of the selected file can be retrieved by the `GetText` method

`<TextBox/>`	`*Name=S`
	`Text=S`
	`Width=M`
	`Height=M`
	`ForeColor=C`
	`BackColor=C`
	`Font=FNT`
		Creates a rectangular text box which can be used for input or output of a short text item. The current text in a text box can be retrieved by the `GetText` method and can be changed by the `PutText` method

`<TrackBar/>`	`*Name=S`
	`Value=D`
	`Minimum=D`
	`Maximum=D`
	`Width=M`
	`Height=M`
	`ForeColor=C`
	`BackColor=C`
		Creates a slider control where the user can drag a marker backwards or forwards with the mouse. Note: Views provides a default value for `Minimum` of 0 and a default for `Maximum` of 100. Moving the slider causes `GetControl` to return with the name of the control, and the new value represented by the slider can be read by the `GetValue` method

Table F.3 Views.Form controls (continued)

F.5   Attribute values

The nature of each attribute value is indicated in Tables F.2 and F.3 by a code letter. The meanings of the letters are as follows:

A	an alignment (see below)
S	a text string written enclosed in single quotes or double quotes or as an unbroken sequence of letters, digits, hyphens and periods (full stops)
M	a size measure (see below)
C	the name of a colour
F	the name of a file (actually a path to a file)
D	a decimal value
FNT	a font specification (see below)

Font specification. The font for the text displayed in a control can be selected using the Font attribute. Views provides a simple notation for specifying fonts. The specification is composed of four parts: the name of the font family, the weight of the font, the slant of the font and the size of the font. The abbreviations for the first three components that are accepted by Views are follows:

Family			
`sansserif` `sans` `sf`	*SansSerif*	`roman` `rm`	*Roman*
`monospace` `courier` `tt` `teletype`	*Monospaced*		
Weight			
`medium` `md`	*Medium*	`bold` `bf`	*Bold Face*
Style			
`upright` `up`	*Upright*	`italic` `it` `emphasis` `em`	*Italic*

The name *Roman* (and its synonym *rm*) refers to a generic serif font, usually Times Roman; *SansSerif* (and its synonyms *sans* and *sf*) usually refers to Arial or Helvetica; *Monospace* (and its synonyms *Courier*, *tt* or *teletype*) refers to a generic monospaced font such as *Courier*.

The name *Bold* (and its synonym *bf*) gives a bold font; a regular unemboldened font may be obtained by using the name *Medium* (or its synonym *md*).

The name *Italic* (or its synonyms *it*, *Emphasis* or *em*) gives a slanted font style; a normal upright font style may be obtained by using the name *Upright* (or its synonym *up*).

The size of the font may be obtained by writing the size in points as a decimal number; that number may optionally contain a fractional part.

The descriptors may be combined in any order. Some examples are shown in the following table:

Font description	Sample
`Bold24`	**Hello there**
`ItalicSans16`	*Hello there*
`Courier9.5`	`Hello there`

Size measures. The height or width of a control can be expressed as simply a decimal number, in which case the unit of size defaults to points. If desired, a different unit of measurement may be supplied immediately following the number. The recognized units are listed in Table F.4.

Name	Meaning
in	Inches
cm	Centimetres
mm	Millimetres
pt	Points (the default)
pc	Picas

Table F.4 Measurement units

There are 72 points per inch. Views assumes that the screen resolution is one pixel per point, i.e. 72 pixels per inch.

Some examples of attribute settings are:

```
Width=64
Height=2.5cm
Image='C:\Temp\MyPhotos\picture1.jpg'
Name=Start
Text='Select the input file'
```

Alignment settings. The `valign` and `halign` attributes may be assigned the following values:.

```
valign:     Top (the default), Middle, Bottom
halign:     Left (the default), Centre (or Center), Right
```

F.6 Views.Form methods

The methods supported by the `Views.Form` class are listed in Table F.5.

Note that because the Windows implementation of `Views.Form` inherits from the `System.Windows.Forms.Form` class, you may also call any public method of that parent class when you compile your C# program on a Windows system.

Views.Form method	Description

`Form(`
`  string spec,`
`  ...)`
	It is the constructor: a Windows Form with the controls defined by the XML specification is created and displayed. The first argument may be either the XML specification, provided as a string constant, or it may be the name of a file which contains the specification.
	The specification may contain {0}, {1} ... patterns, and these refer either to optional arguments which follow the XML specification, or to elements of an optional second argument which is an array of objects. If the $\{i\}$ pattern is used, the `ToString` method of the *i*-th optional argument is invoked and the resulting string is substituted for the $\{i\}$ pattern in the specification string

`void` `CloseGUI()`	Terminates the execution thread which waits for the user to click on the form and releases other system resources. It is important that this method be invoked when the form no longer needs to be displayed
`string` `GetControl()`	Waits for the user to perform an action on the form (e.g. clicking a button) and then returns the name of the control that was clicked

`string`
`GetText(`
`  string name )`
	Returns a text value that is associated with the control whose name is given. If the control is a `TextBox` or `ListBox`, that text has been entered by the user. If the control is a `OpenFileDialog` or `SaveFileDialog`, the text is the name of a file

`int`
`GetValue(`
`  string name )`
	Returns an integer value associated with the control whose name is given. For a `TrackBar` or `ProgressBar` control, this integer denotes the current position of the marker. For a `CheckBox` control, a zero or one result indicates whether the box is currently unchecked or checked, respectively. For a `DomainUpDown` control, the result is the index of the currently selected item in the list (the first item is numbered 0)

`int`
`GetValue(`
`  string name,`
`  int index)`
	For a `CheckedListBox` control, the result is the status of the check box at position *index* in the list, where 1 means checked and 0 means unchecked.
	For other controls, the result is the same as would be returned by `GetValue(name)`

`void`
`PutText(`
`  string name,`
`  string cval )`
	Sets the `Text` attribute of the control whose name is specified. It can be used to display text in a `TextBox` or `ListBox` control

`void`
`PutValue(`
`  string name,`
`  int v )`
	Sets an integer value associated with the control whose name is specified. This method is used to adjust the state of a `ProgressBar` or to set the state of a `CheckBox` control

Table F.5 Views.Form methods

Views.Form method	Description
void PutImage(string name, string f);	Replaces the image displayed in a control which has an Image attribute with a new image obtained from the file whose name is supplied as f
void PutImage(string name, Image im);	The same as above except that the image to be used is an instance of the Image class
(instance of Views.Form) [string name]	This is an indexer operation which returns the control whose name is provided. For the Windows implementation of Views, the control is an instance of a class in the System.Windows.Forms namespace

Table F.5 Views.Form methods (continued)

F.7 Recommended coding style

To maintain reasonable resemblance to the code used with Windows forms created with Microsoft Visual Studio, the following basic code pattern is recommended.

```
string f = @"<Form> ... </Form>";

try {
  Views.Form form = new Views.Form(f);
  for (;;) {
    string name = form.GetControl();
    if (name == null) break;
    ActionPerformed(name);
  }
  form.CloseGUI();
} catch( Exception e ) {
  Console.WriteLine("Error while using Views.Form:\n\n{0}",
    e.Message);
}
```

The try statement will intercept all errors from the statement where the form is created through to the statement where the form is closed.

The ActionPerformed method could have a structure like the following, though simplifications for especially simple forms and some special cases may be appropriate:

```
void ActionPerformed( string name ) {
  switch(name) {
  case "name1":
    ...
    break;
  case "name2":
    ...
    break;
  case ...          // as many cases as needed
  }
}
```

F.8 Use of the indexer operation

If an instance of the `Views.Form` class is created, for example like this

```
Views.Form f = new Views.Form( @"<Form>
      <vertical>
          <Label Name=Label1 Text='Enter Your Name: '/>
          <TextBox Name=Box1 Width=150/>
      </vertical>
    </Form>";
```

then the displayed form contains instances of controls. Access to an individual control may be obtained by using the indexer operation, and that access may be used to achieve run-time effects.

For example, assuming the above example of a form, the program that created the form instance may execute these statements

```
System.Windows.Forms.TextBox tb = f["Box1"];
System.Windows.Forms.Label lab = f["Label1"];
lab.BackColor = Color.Red;
lab.ForeColor = Color.Yellow;
f.Invalidate();  // force form to be redrawn with new colours
```

to change the font used for the `TextBox` control and the colours on the `Label` control.

Notes:

◆ The colour names are also defined in the `System.Drawing` namespace.

◆ The `Invalidate` method is inherited by `Views.Form` from its parent class, `System.Windows.Form`.

APPENDIX G

Debugging with Windows

This appendix reviews the tools available on Windows systems for debugging C# programs.

G.1 Introduction

Compiling the program

It is important to compile the C# program with the debug flag in effect. Without that flag, few of the techniques described in this appendix can be used.

An example command line that performs a compilation and provides the debug flag is as follows:

```
csc /debug:full myprogram.csc
```

Assuming that there are no errors that prevent the compilation from completing successfully, two files will be created. They will be named myprogram.exe and myprogram.pdb. The former is the executable file, as usual. The latter is a program database file which contains information about the program for use by the debugger and by the stack trace mechanism of exceptions.

If Visual Studio is being used to edit and compile the files, then it is essential to use the *Debug* configuration for the project. The following steps can be followed to force use of the Debug configuration.

1. In the Solution Explorer subwindow, select the name of the project.

2. In the pull-down menu named *Project* on the taskbar for Visual Studio, select *Properties*.

3. In the *Property Pages* menu which appeared as a result of step 2, select *Configuration Properties* in the left pane.

4. Make sure that the box alongside the label *Configuration* says either *Debug* or *Active(Debug)*. If not, click on that box and select Debug.

Command-line debugger and GUI debugger tools

A full .NET installation, including Visual Studio, on Windows should make three different debugging tools available. They are listed below.

1. The Just-In-Time debugger used to analyze an executing program which has encountered an error (i.e. an unhandled exception). The correct name for the tool is the DbgCLR debugger. It uses a GUI to interact with the user.

2. The cordbg command-line debugger, which uses commands typed into a command window to cause a program to be executed and be monitored during its execution.

3. The Visual Studio .NET debugger. It can be used either for analyzing a program which encountered an error or for tracing the execution of a program. It too uses a GUI, one very similar to that provided by the DbgCLR debugger.

G.2 The cordbg debugger

Cordbg commands

A selected list of the commands appears in Table G.1. A complete list can be obtained by starting the debugger and typing the command help.

In this table, a notation like b[reak] means that the full name of the command is break but it can be shortened to just the letter b (i.e. the letters enclosed in square brackets are optional). Several commands have synonyms; for example, break and stop work identically. Synonyms are listed in the table.

Help information for debugger commands	
`h[elp]` `?`	Display descriptions of the debugger commands

Starting and stopping the debugger and the program	
`r[un]`	Start a process for debugging
`ex[it]` `q[uit]`	Kill the current process and exit the debugger
`k[ill]`	Kill the current process
control-C	Interrupt the current process

Accessing variables and program state	
`p[rint]`	Print variables (locals, args, statics, etc.)
`sh[ow]`	Display source code lines
`w[here]`	Display a stack trace for the current thread
`d[own]`	Navigate down from the current stack frame pointer
`u[p]`	Navigate up from the current stack frame pointer
`set`	Modify the value of a variable (locals, statics, etc.)

Breakpoint handling	
`b[reak]` `stop`	Set a new breakpoint, or display list of current breakpoints
`del[ete]` `rem[ove]`	Remove one or more breakpoints

Single-step execution	

`i[n]`
`si`
`s[tep]`
	Step into the next source line

`n[ext]` `so`	Step over the next source line
`o[ut]`	Step out of the current function
`cont` `g[o]`	Continue the current process

Table G.1 Selected cordbg commands

Starting the cordbg debugger

The cordbg debugger is invoked from the command line. Therefore the first step is to open a command window. Once that window has been created, `cd` commands should be typed into that window to navigate to the folder where the executable file of the program to debug resides. An example session using `cd` (change directory) commands might look like the one below.

```
Microsoft Windows XP [Version 5.1.2600]
(C) Copyright 1985-2001 Microsoft Corp.

C:\Documents and Settings\nigelh>d:

D:\>cd "Csharp Programs\Debugging
```

First, 'd:' was typed to switch to the filesystem volume with the code letter D. If the destination folder had been on the C drive, this initial command would have been unnecessary. Second the `cd` command was entered to switch to the folder with the path 'D:\Csharp Programs\Debugging'. The double quotes had to be typed at the beginning of the argument to `cd` because the path contained space characters.

Second, the command to start the debugger should be entered. It should be as typing the name of the program: `cordbg` (or `cordbg.exe` if one is pedantic). However, it is quite likely that the PATH environment variable on the Windows system does not contain the name of the folder where the `cordbg.exe` file resides. The response

```
'cordbg' is not recognized as an internal or external command,
operable program or batch file.
```

is the response if the PATH variable is not set appropriately. If that is the case, it is first necessary to find where the `cordbg` program has been installed. Some exploration of the filesystem or use of the Search feature (on the Start menu) may be necessary. The default installation location is

```
C:\Program Files\Microsoft Visual Studio NET\FrameworkSDK\Bin
```

Once located, here are three possible ways to proceed:

- ◆ Use the system control panels to change the PATH variable setting to include the location of `cordbg`, and try over again.

- ◆ Enter the full path name, enclosed in a pair of double quote characters, as the command name in the command window.

- ◆ Use a text editor (e.g. the notepad program) to create a batch file in the current folder named, say, `RunCordbg.bat` which contains the single line of text

```
"C:\Program Files\Microsoft Visual Studio NET\FrameworkSDK\Bin\cordbg
.exe"
```

(The line should be changed in the obvious way if `cordbg.exe` is located in a different folder from the one named there.)

Then type the command `RunCordbg` in the command window.

A successful invocation of `cordbg` using the third method, above, should look similar to the following. (Note the second line is too long to fit and is split across two lines.)

```
D:\>cd "Csharp Programs\Debugging> runcordbg
D:\CSharp Programs\Debugging>"C:\Program Files\Microsoft Visual Stud
io .NET\FrameworkSDK\Bin\cordbg.exe"
Microsoft (R) Common Language Runtime Test Debugger Shell Version
1.0.3705.0
Copyright (C) Microsoft Corporation 1998-2001. All rights reserved.

(cordbg)
```

The `(cordbg)` string is a prompt for input. The user can now type `cordbg` commands, many of which are listed in Table G.1.

Note that the help command is one of the most useful. Typing just *help* (or its synonym, a question mark) will produce a list of all the commands with one-line summaries. If further information about any command is desired, typing *help* followed by the name of the command will provide it. For example, typing

```
help run
```

will display information about how the `run` command is used.

Starting the program to be debugged

The run *command.* If the program to be debugged is named `myprogram.exe`, then type

```
run myprogram.exe
```

after starting the debugger. The two files `myprogram.exe` and `myprogram.pdb` must both be located in the same folder as where the `cordbg` program was started. (Recall that the `/debug:full` option causes a file with the '`.pdb`' extension to be generated.)

The program is loaded with control stopped at the first line in the `Main` method.

The go *command.* Using the command `go` (or its synonym `cont`) will cause the program to execute until control reaches a breakpoint or until an error is trapped or until the program exits, whichever occurs first. If the program gets caught in an infinite loop, it can be stopped by hitting the *control-C* key combination on the keyboard, causing the debugger to take over and accept more commands.

Using breakpoints

The break *command.* A new breakpoint is set with a command similar to one of these

```
break 47
break myfile.cs:47
break FooClass::BarMethod
```

The first version of the command sets the breakpoint at the statement in line 47 of the source code file currently being debugged. The second version sets it at line 47 of the file named 'myfile.cs'. The third version sets it at the first line of the method named BarMethod in the class named FooClass.

A list of the breakpoints which are in effect can be displayed with the command

```
break
```

i.e., without any arguments. The list gives a number alongside each breakpoint.

The remove *command.* The breakpoint number can be used in the remove command to remove a breakpoint from the program. For example,

```
remove 3
```

removes the breakpoint that has number 3.

Single-step execution

When the program is in a stopped state (either at the first statement in the program after using the run command or because execution reached a breakpoint), one statement can be executed and the program stopped again, at the following statement. This is called *single-step execution.*

The next *command.* (Or its synonym so for *step over*) causes a complete simple statement to be executed, even if the statement contains calls to other methods within the program.

The step *command.* (Or its synonyms in or si for *step into*) causes one simple statement to be executed. However, if that statement contains a call to a method, then the program stops again at the start of that method.

The next and step commands can be followed by numbers which are repetition counts. For example,

```
next 10
```

is equivalent to typing the next command 10 times.

The out *command.* If a method has been entered (perhaps with the step command), execution can be continued until control returns from that method by using the out command.

Accessing variables and program state

The where *command.* When the program is stopped at a statement in the program, the sequence of active methods (methods which have been entered but not yet exited) can be viewed with the where command.

The show *command.* Typing the command show causes a sequence of source code lines surrounding the current statement to be displayed. By default, five lines before and five lines after the current statement are included in the sequence.

The print *command.* When the program is stopped at a statement in the program, the value of any variable visible at that point in the program can be displayed using the print command. For example,

```
print a[10].count
```

causes the value of the count field of the object stored in element number 10 of the array a to be displayed.

The up *and* down *commands.* The where command shows a list of active methods; each method has local variables which may not be visible at the current statement in the program. These methods may belong to other classes which contain member fields which are also not visible at the current statement. To obtain access to such variables and fields, the up command may be used one or more times. Typing the up command has the effect of making the current statement be the statement which called the current method. That is, the debugger is moved up the chain of the called methods towards the initial Main method.

The down command is the opposite of the up command, causing the debugger to move one level down the chain, away from Main and towards the last active method in the chain.

The set *command.* Sometimes it is desirable for debugging purposes to force a variable to hold a different value from the one that it currently holds. Perhaps the best use of this command is when a variable has, through a bug, been assigned the wrong value and it would be nice to see if setting the variable to the correct value causes the program to complete its execution normally.

G.3 The Just-In-Time debugger

If the execution of a program ends because of an unhandled exception, Windows displays a window like the one shown in Figure G.1.

The first choice in the list shown in the window, Microsoft CLR debugger, refers to a program named DbgCLR which would normally be installed on a Windows system as part of the .NET Software Development Kit (SDK). The second choice shown, Microsoft Development Environment (MDE), would normally be installed with Visual Studio and is the Visual Studio debugger.

Selecting one of these choices and clicking the Yes button will start the selected debugger (just in time to debug the program). The debugger will allow the location of the unhandled exception in the program to be found and the values of variables at the time of the error to be inspected. Both debuggers are visual tools and provide similar means of inspecting the program. The Visual Studio debugger is covered in the next section.

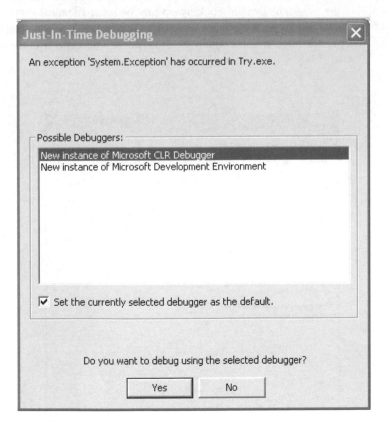

Figure G.1 Just-In-Time debugger

G.4 The Visual Studio debugger

The Visual Studio interactive development environment provides interactive editing of source code and an interactive debugger. Each program is developed as a project; the name of that project would normally match the name of the folder in which all the source code files for the program reside.

To use all the features of the debugger, it is important to set the configuration of the to be Debug. Instructions are provided at the beginning of this appendix.

Suppose that we have reached the stage where a program has been developed, and it compiles without any error messages. However, it does not work correctly. The program may be executed under the control of the Visual Studio debugger, with us halting the program at breakpoints and inspecting the values of variables.

Setting breakpoints

Note that the Solution Explorer subwindow lists the names of all the source code files which comprise the program. Double clicking on any of these filenames will cause the source code file to be displayed in the main Visual Studio window. It will be convenient to display the source code files which contain the statements where we want to set breakpoints.

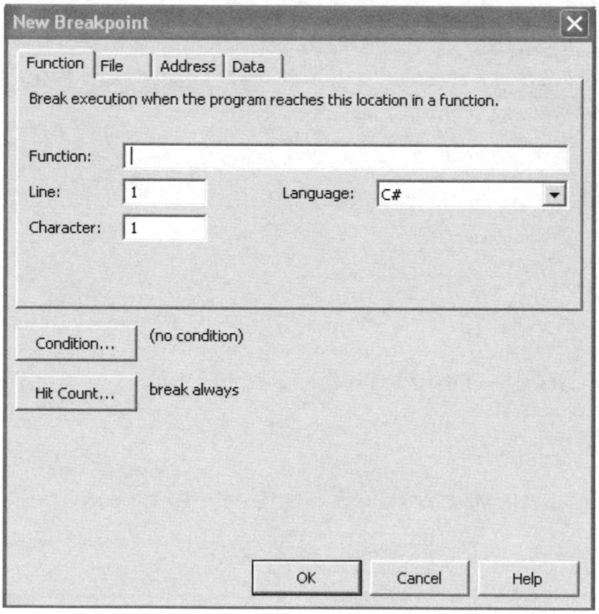

Figure G.2 Visual Studio breakpoint window

Statement breakpoints. To set a breakpoint at some statement in the program, open the file where the breakpoint is to be located and click on the start of the line for that statement. Now choose *New Breakpoint...* in the *Debug* pull-down menu on the taskbar. That will cause a window to open which looks like the one in Figure G.2.

With this window, you can select where to set the breakpoint. The window allows the breakpoint to be set at some position in a function (i.e. a method) or at some line in the file. The latter possibility is likely to be more convenient. Clicking on the *File* tab at the top of the window causes the appearance to change to be similar to that shown in Figure G.3. The filename, line number and column number within the line are filled in automatically with the location of the cursor in the source code window.

When the breakpoint has been placed, a large orange circle should appear at the left of the source code line.

An alternative way to set the breakpoint is to select the statement in the source code window, perform a right-click with the mouse, and then select *Insert Breakpoint* from the menu of options which appears.

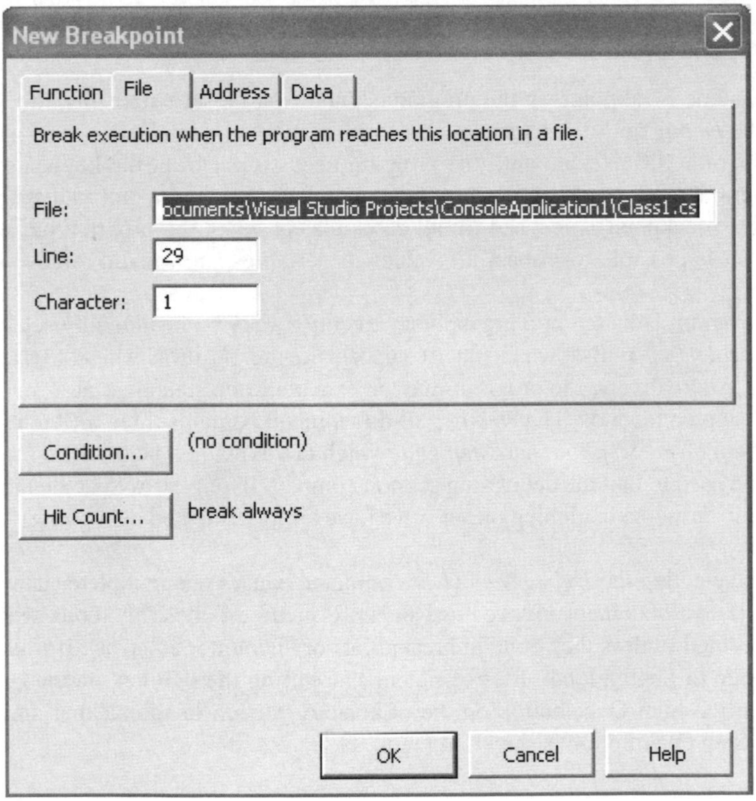

New Breakpoint

| Function | File | Address | Data |

Break execution when the program reaches this location in a file.

File: `ocuments\Visual Studio Projects\ConsoleApplication1\Class1.cs`

Line: `29`

Character: `1`

Condition... (no condition)

Hit Count... break always

OK   Cancel   Help

Figure G.3 Setting a breakpoint at a line in the file

Data breakpoints. Some of the most perplexing bugs involve variables that mysteriously take on wrong values. Some debuggers allow a breakpoint to be attached to a variable; whenever the program performs an assignment to that variable, the program is halted. Unfortunately, this feature is not supported by the current C# compiler.

Deleting breakpoints. All breakpoints may be removed by using the *Clear All Breakpoints* command in the *Debug* pull-down menu. To remove just a single breakpoint, it is easiest to open the source code window and select the statement which has an attached breakpoint. A right-click action with the mouse brings up a menu which contains the option *Remove breakpoint*.

Disabling breakpoints. Sometimes it is convenient to remove one or more breakpoints temporarily. The *Disable all breakpoints* command in the *Debug* pull-down menu provides the first possibility. Right-clicking on a statement in the source code window brings up a menu which contains the *Disable breakpoint* option. Subsequently, the *Enable all breakpoints* command in the *Debug* pull-down menu allows all these disabled breakpoints to be reactivated.

Executing the program

If needed, some breakpoints in the program should first be set. After this, the *Start* command in the *Debug* pull-down menu on the taskbar should be selected.

The program will execute until the program needs input from the keyboard (or some other program or device), or the program completes execution normally, or an error occurs, or a breakpoint is reached. In all cases except when the program has terminated execution, it is possible to inspect the values of variables and to add, remove or disable breakpoints.

If the program is halted at a breakpoint, execution may be resumed by selecting *Continue* in the *Debug* pull-down menu (it appears in the position where *Start* originally appeared). Alternatively, the program may be executed one statement at a time by using the single-step commands. The *Debug* pull-down menu contains three different step commands – *Step Over*, *Step Into* and *Step Out*, which are explained below. The *Debug* menu may also be used to halt the debugging session completely (e.g., if we decide that we want to start again from the beginning or when we have simply finished debugging).

Step Over. Selecting the *Debug/Step Over* command causes one complete statement to be executed. If that statement invokes one or more methods, those methods will be completely executed (unless they contain breakpoints or encounter an error). If it is necessary to single-step through a long series of statements, hitting the F10 key on the keyboard or clicking on the Step Over button on the taskbar. A portion of the taskbar and where to locate the Step Over button is shown in Figure G.4.

Step Into. Selecting the *Debug/Step Into* command also causes one statement to be executed. However, if the statement contains a call to a method elsewhere in the program, then execution is stopped at the first statement of that method. The *Step Into* command is useful if one wants to watch every single statement executed by the program. The *Step Over* command is useful if some methods are known to be correct and need not be observed. Other ways of executing the *Step Into* command are to hit the F11 key or to click the *Step Into* button on the taskbar (see Figure G.4).

Step Out. If it is desirable to resume normal execution of the program up to the point where the current method has completed execution and control is about to return to the caller, then the *Debug/Step Out* command has that effect. It is useful when the *Step Into* command was used accidentally or when enough of the current method has been traced to be confident that it works. Other ways of executing *Step Out* are to use Shift-F11 (i.e. hit the F11 key with the shift key held down) or to click on the Step Out button on the taskbar (see Figure G.4).

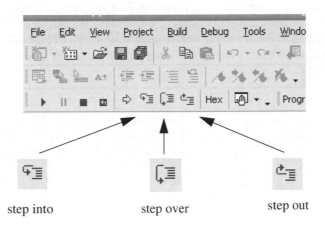

step into   step over   step out

Figure G.4 Single-step buttons on the taskbar

Inspecting program state

Program location. The statement that is about to be executed appears, highlighted in yellow, in the source code window. The *Call Stack* subwindow in the Visual Studio debugger shows a list of all the active methods in the program, along with the values of the method arguments. Clicking on different items in that call stack window causes the source code window to change, highlighting the line where the method was invoked.

Values of variables. While there is an active program being executed under the control of the debugger, the values of variables can be inspected.

The easiest way to view the value of a simple variable is to run the mouse over an occurrence of the variable in the source code window. A little box appears which shows the current value of that variable.

While there is an active program, the debugger makes two subwindows available. One is titled *Autos* and the other is titled *Locals*. To make these subwindows appear, it may be necessary to click on *Windows...* in the *Window* pull-down menu on the taskbar. Selecting *Autos* or *Locals* in the menu which appears will activate the selected window. The Autos window displays the values of all variables used in the current statement and the preceding statement. (It is called *Autos* because it is automatically updated as statements are single-step executed.) The *Locals* window shows the values of variables visible at the current point in the program.

Selecting *Debug/Windows/Watch/Watch1* (i.e. the *Windows* option in the pull-down menu for *Debug* on the taskbar yields a submenu containing *Watch* and that leads to a final submenu containing *Watch1* as a choice) causes a subwindow titled *Watch1* to be displayed. In that window, the names of variables can be entered in the left-hand column, and their values and datatypes will appear in the middle and right-hand columns respectively. While the program executes, the contents of the window are updated dynamically. There are four watch windows, named *Watch1* through *Watch4*. They can be used to watch different groups of variables. The tabs on these watch windows can be used to select which one is currently displayed. A sample watch window is shown in Figure G.5. Note that by double-clicking in the Value column and typing a constant, it is possible to store a new value in a variable.

Watch 1			📌 ✖
Name	Value		Type
num	0		int
plural	null		string

🖳 Watch 1 | 🔍 Search Results for Autos

Figure G.5 A watch window for variables

A *QuickWatch* window can be created using the *QuickWatch...* command in the *Debug* menu. It is convenient for inspecting the value of an expression, such as `myArray[i*2]`. The window must be closed, however, before execution of the program can continue.

Index